West New Guinea

The Dispute And Its Settlement

WEST NEW GUINEA

THE DISPUTE AND ITS SETTLEMENT

BY

William Henderson

1973

PUBLISHED FOR THE
AMERICAN-ASIAN EDUCATIONAL EXCHANGE
SETON HALL UNIVERSITY PRESS

The American-Asian Educational Exchange was founded in October 1957, having as its major purpose "... the exchange of information, literature and personnel for the purpose of creating a broader understanding between the peoples of the United States and the independent nations of Asia."

Since that time, the Exchange has maintained an effective international educational program with two basic categories: publication, circulation and translation of printed material on the subject of concern in the United States and Asia; the maintenance of liaison and cooperation between the Exchange and similar organizations and academic groups in Asia and the United States.

To M.B.H.

With Gratitude and Love

Acknowledgements

Most of this study was written between Summer 1968 and Summer 1969, during which period I held an appointment as Research Associate of the American Geographical Society. I am grateful to Dr. Shannon McCune, former Director of the Society, for this opportunity. The study was completed during the Spring of 1972.

I wish to express my thanks to Professor W. Howard Wriggins of Columbia University for his helpfulness throughout this project. Without his interest and friendly prodding, the study would never have been completed. Professors Leland M. Goodrich and Roger Hilsman also gave me valuable advice at various stages. Mr. Arnold C. Brackman very kindly read the entire manuscript before publication, and Professors Thomas P. Peardon and Frank N. Trager parts of it, and their comments have saved me from many errors.

I owe a special debt to Mr. Donald Wasson, Librarian, Miss Janet Rigney, Assistant Librarian, and their colleagues on the staff of the Council on Foreign Relations Library, New York City. The resources of that splendid collection were made available to me on the most generous terms, and the unfailing helpfulness of my friends there greatly simplified my research problems.

A great many persons were consulted in the preparation of this study, including many United Nations, United States, and other government officials. I am grateful to all of them for their candor in discussing various aspects of the West New Guinea problem with me, even though the canons of confidence preclude mentioning them by name. In any event, as I have stated elsewhere in this volume, I have not used information derived from such sources except where I could verify it from data in the public domain.

Finally, I freely acknowledge my indebtedness to the many scholars who have already written on the West New Guinea dispute, and whose books and articles I have used extensively—as reference to the footnotes will indicate—in the preparation of this study.

The published work is dedicated to my wife, Maxine B. Henderson, with gratitude and love.

William Henderson

Contents

Acknowledgements   **vii**

Chapter 1.   Introduction   **1**
           The Political Context—Framework and Focus

Chapter 2.   Origins   **8**
           Early Historical Background—Genesis of the Dispute, 1945-49—The Hague Round Table Conference and the 1949 Settlement—The Failure of Bilateral Negotations

Chapter 3.   Dynamics of the Dispute   **26**
           The Sources of Indonesian Policy—Bases of the Dutch Position—Arguments Pro and Con—The Question of Self-Determination

Chapter 4.   West New Guinea as an International Issue   **48**
           West New Guinea Before the United Nations— Rising Tensions, 1953-57

Chapter 5.   Confrontation   **59**
           The Diplomacy of Confrontation—The Australian Position—Malaya Attempts to Mediate—"A Contest in All Fields"

Chapter 6.   Reappraisal at The Hague   **81**
           The Evolution of Dutch Policy—A Decade of Modest Achievement—A New Program for the Development of West New Guinea

Chapter 7.   A Serious International Crisis   **100**
           The Luns Plans—"All Means at Our Disposal"

Chapter 8.   The Evolution of United States Policy   **114**
           Studied Neutrality—Enter Kennedy

Chapter 9.   The Decision to Intervene   128
             The Problem of Indonesia—The Relevance of
             West New Guinea—Prelude to Intervention—The
             United States as Mediator

Chapter 10. The Role of the United Nations   150
             The Hammarksjold Approach—The Secretary-
             General as Mediator—United Nations Peace-
             keeping and United States Policy—The Rationale
             of a Joint Approach

Chapter 11. Toward Negotiations   162
             First Steps—New Alarums—The Dutch and
             Indonesian Positions Summarized—Preliminary
             Talks Arranged

Chapter 12. Negotiations Under United Nations Auspices   180
             First Round—The Bunker Plan—A Test of Wills
             —The Role of the Mediator

Chapter 13. Settlement   200
             Last Flurry—Alone—A Settlement at Last

Chapter 14. Epilogue   213
             The U.N.T.E.A. Phase—Indonesian Rule—In-
             donesia and the "Act of Free Choice"—"Self-
             Determination" for the Papuans

Chapter 15. Conclusions   241
             The Great Powers as Third-Party Intermediaries
             —The Great Powers and United Nations Peace-
             keeping—The United Nations as an Instrument
             of United States Policy—Evolving Concepts of
             Self-Determination

Appendix   253

Bibliographical Note   263

Index   273

Chapter One

Introduction

The era of decolonization, as it has been called, is one of the watersheds of contemporary history. Within the short space of 20 years after World War II, the great colonial empires of the nineteenth and early twentieth centuries were almost entirely dismantled. Dozens of succession states emerged onto the stage of world politics, especially in Asia and Africa, enriching but complicating the international environment, and confronting the more established actors with a multiplicity of new and baffling dilemmas.

For the most part, the decolonization process was carried out with remarkably little violence. The imperial powers may have been reluctant to let their empires go; but relinquish them they did, with what grace and good will they could muster in face of the irresistible force of postwar nationalist sentiment in the colonies. Where the metropoles attempted to stay the course of history, the result was war of the most bitter and bloody sort. These independence struggles—in Indonesia, Algeria, Vietnam, and elsewhere—produced some of the more difficult crises of the postwar period.

But whether peacefully or violently, independence came to the colonies. It has proved not to be the Eden that the more romantic nationalists often seemed to expect. The range of problems confronting the newly independent countries — political instability, economic stagnation, social unrest — has been staggering, to say nothing of the task of defining their international orientation in a chaotic world torn by Cold War and the threat of nuclear catastrophe. These problems have been much written about; the literature of economic development, for example, already overwhelms the most diligent student.

Another kind of problem inherent in the liquidation of colonialism has been less frequently examined. This concerns the residual dilemmas between a newly independent state and its former colonial overlord left in the wake of decolonization. For the process of decolonization was often messy, especially when the nationalists had to fight for freedom, and where subsequent relations were embittered by memories of the independence struggle. This study deals with one such problem — the long and seemingly intractable dispute between Indonesia and the Netherlands as to the future of West New Guinea.

The Political Context

The Hague Round Table Conference of 1949, at which the Dutch agreed to the terms and modalities of Indonesian independence after four years of intermittent conflict, left unsettled the question of West New Guinea's political future. The Dutch were resolved to hold onto this remote, inhospitable territory for an indefinite period, at least until such time as the indigenous Papuan population could intelligently exercise its presumed right of political self-determination. The Indonesians, on the other hand, insisted that West New Guinea, as a constituent part of the former Netherlands Indies empire, should properly be incorporated *ab initio* within the boundaries of the new republic. For more than a decade, the dispute over the territory was a critical irritant in Dutch-Indonesian relations, and compromised whatever prospect may have existed after 1949 for the development of a cooperative and fruitful relationship between the two countries.

Until late 1957, Indonesia sought to deal with the issue through bilateral negotiations with the Netherlands, and by appeals to the United Nations General Assembly. While these efforts were uniformly unproductive, in general the repercussions of the conflict on the international system during this period were minimal. Thereafter, Indonesia resorted increasingly to more forceful measures in an openly proclaimed "contest of power" with the Dutch.[1] Dutch property in Indonesia was sequestered (and eventually nationalized), and most Dutch citizens expelled from the country. Diplomatic relations were severed in 1960. The threat of force became a prominent theme of Indonesian policy statements on West New Guinea. The military services were progressively strengthened, and a spectacular arms deal negotiated with the Soviet Union. Guerrilla units were infiltrated into the territory, and clashes occurred with increasing

---

[1]The term was employed in a statement by Indonesian Foreign Minister Subandrio in July 1959. See *Antara Daily Newsbulletin*, August 4, 1959.

frequency. By 1961, the situation appeared to be deteriorating rapidly into a serious international crisis.[2]

Throughout the 1950s, Dutch policy remained frozen in its determination to retain control over West New Guinea, largely because of the exigencies of domestic politics. By 1961, however, the Dutch were gradually coming to understand the strength and fanaticism of Indonesia's ambition to recover West New Guinea, and to realize that they might have to fight a major war to maintain their position — a war which would be difficult to win, which was in any case hardly worth winning, and in which the Netherlands could probably count on little if any assistance from its traditional friends and allies. Only then did the Dutch reluctantly accept that the game simply was not worth the candle, and that they would have to relinquish control over the territory earlier rather than late, as evidenced by their proposals in the United Nations General Assembly that Fall to establish an international trusteeship for West New Guinea. Thereafter, the problem was to find a solution acceptable to both sides, in an atmosphere of great bitterness clouded by the threat of war.

The dispute posed difficult policy choices for the United States. We were bound to the Netherlands by ancient ties of sentiment and history, and by the more practical bonds of the North Atlantic Treaty Alliance signed in 1949. The indigenous peoples of West New Guinea were palpably unprepared for the responsibilities of self-government. While the Dutch record there was decidedly mixed, their claims to the territory and to the thankless privilege of discharging the white man's burden (as they saw it) were not wholly without merit. In view of the political turmoil and economic stagnation that often seemed to characterize Indonesia since independence, it was difficult to argue that the Papuans would be better off, or better equipped for their inevitable emergence into the modern world, if ruled from Jakarta rather than The Hague.

Indonesia, on the other hand, was the fifth most populous nation on earth, and potentially at least the dominant regional power of Southeast Asia. For the United States, deeply engaged in the affairs of Asia and caught up in a worldwide confrontation of power with the Communist countries, the future development of Indonesia along lines not antithetical

---

[2]For a suggestive discussion of the nature and characteristics of international crises, see Oran R. Young, *The Intermediaries, Third Parties in International Crises* (Princeton: Princeton University Press, 1967), pp. 9-25. He defines an international crisis as "a set of rapidly unfolding events which raises the impact of destabilizing forces in the general international system or any of its subsystems substantially above 'normal' (i. e., average) levels and increases the likelihood of violence occurring in the system." *Ibid.*, p. 10. The West New Guinea dispute clearly reached this stage in 1961-62.

to the larger American position in Asia and the world was a major national interest. Indonesia, too, had a defensible case with respect to West New Guinea as the presumed heir to *all* of Netherlands India. Its preoccupation with the dispute, which by 1961 had become a national obsession,[3] could plausibly account for the neglect of more pressing but prosaic concerns such as economic development and the nurture of stable political institutions. And the Indonesian cause had captured the magic aura of anticolonialism, which meant that most of the Afro-Asian countries, plus the Communist world, would in the long run stand with Indonesia against the Dutch.

For more than a decade, the United States simply straddled the issue. Washington declined to take sides publicly on the merits of the dispute, and systematically abstained on substantive votes in the United Nations. Predictably, the Indonesians interpreted our neutrality as support for the status quo, and thus for the Dutch position. The latter were realistic enough to recognize that American noninvolvement did, on balance, work to their advantage. But The Hague nevertheless complained from time to time about American indifference to the special interests of old friends and trusted allies. The steady deterioration of the situation in 1961 [4] finally led the United States to modify its posture late that year and to underake a much more decisive role in the search for a peaceful settlement.

The thrust of Washington's intervention reflected an appreciation on the part of the new Kennedy administration that the United States had to come to terms with the forces of Asian nationalism if we hoped to develop a viable and mutually satisfactory relationship with these countries in the future. More concretely, there was a growing apprehension that large-scale hostilities over West New Guinea might have important and adverse consequences on Indonesia's domestic political situation, by strengthening the position of the Indonesian Communist Party in the internal struggle for power, and on Jakarta's international orientation, by driving the country still further toward alignment with the Communist

[3]Grant states: "The years 1961 and 1962 saw Indonesian policy preoccupied, indeed obsessed, with West Irian. As the military campaign against the rebels in Sumatra and Sulawesi ended, the nation's leadership turned toward the other major item of unfinished business," that is, the recovery of West New Guinea from the Dutch. Bruce Grant, *Indonesia* (London and New York: Cambridge University Press, 1964), p. 140.

[4]A significant milestone was the mission of the Indonesian Army Chief of Staff, General Abdul Haris Nasution, to Moscow in December 1960-January 1961, which resulted in the arms deal mentioned in the text. See Guy J. Pauker, "General Nasution's Mission to Moscow," *Asian Survey*, vol. 1, no. 1 (March 1961), pp. 13-22.

bloc, especially the Soviet Union, in its search for support and material assistance in the struggle with the Dutch. The analysis was that, if Indonesia were ever to begin the formidable task of setting its chaotic house in order, such diversionary preoccupations as the dispute over West New Guinea first had to be removed from the agenda, and largely on Indonesia's terms.

At about the same time, the Acting Secretary-General of the United Nations, U Thant, also undertook to intervene actively in the dispute, and to lend the prestige and potentialities of his office in a sustained effort to find a peaceful solution. Thereafter, the Acting Secretary-General's office was almost constantly seized of the problem; and the United Nations played a highly important part in what became, with the United States, a cooperative search for peace. The settlement achieved in August 1962 was largely the product of these parallel but closely coordinated initiatives, which were dramatically symbolized in the key mediatory role of retired United States Ambassador Ellsworth Bunker as the representative of the Acting Secretary-General in the climactic negotiations between Indonesia and the Netherlands.

Framework and Focus

This study focuses on the later stages of the West New Guinea dispute, and on the search for settlement under the joint auspices of the United States and the United Nations. We begin with three introductory chapters on the origins of the dispute; it internal dynamics; and its emergence as an international issue during the 1950s, including early consideration by the General Assembly. These chapters are designed primarily as background for the subsequent analysis, and recapitulate in part the considerable scholarship already published on the subject. Subsequent chapters treat in detail with Indonesia's dramatic "confrontation" policy against the Netherlands; changing Dutch perspectives on West New Guinea; the dispute as a serious international crisis; the evolution of United States policy; Washington's decision to intervene; the role of the Acting Secretary-General; negotiations under United Nations auspices; and the achievement of a settlement in 1962. A supplementary chapter summarizes the brief interlude of international administration under the United Nations Temporary Executive Authority; developments in West New Guinea after 1963 under Indonesian control; and the implementation of the socalled "act of free choice" (provided for in the 1962 agreement) during the course of 1969.

Apart from its intrinsic interest as a case study in recent diplomatic history, the West New Guinea experience throws light on four more general problems of contemporary international relations. With respect to the conditions for effective third-party intervention in serious international crises, for example, it is often assumed that a major aligned power would have difficulty in effectively mediating a dispute occurring in the Third World, or arising out of the liquidation of colonialism. This is because such a great power would presumably lack certain necessary qualifications for the role, such as perceived impartiality as between the antagonists. Nevertheless, the United States did play an effective role as a third-party intermediary in the West New Guinea case, and it is a purpose of this study to clarify the circumstances and policies that made this possible. Generalizing from these circumstances, the West New Guinea experience would appear to support a broadened definition of the possible range of effective interventions by major aligned states, including the United States, in certain kinds of disputes and under certain types of power relationships.

Second, United Nations intervention in the West New Guinea controversy served to isolate and localize a dispute that might easily have been drawn into the vortex of the Cold War, and ultimately contributed importantly to a peaceful settlement. While the Hammarskjold concept of United Nations peacekeeping has usually presupposed that the superpowers would voluntarily stand aside from the procedures of settlement in such cases, the United States in fact played a major role in the West New Guinea negotiations, and exerted a decisive influence on both sides to accept the settlement. We shall examine the conditions that permitted a successful collaboration in this case. The West New Guinea episode illustrated the potentialities of the Hammarskjold concept of United Nations peacekeeping, and also appeared to broaden it with respect to the possibilities of fruitful great power involvement in the immediate processes of settlement in some circumstances. (Although the subject is outside the scope of this inquiry, the West New Guinea case also contributed importantly to the repertoire of United Nations peacekeeping techniques and procedures, in that it demonstrated the feasibility of internationally administered trusteeships as a possible means of dealing with territorial disputes and with the problems of transition from one political authority to another, and also afforded useful practical experience in the operation of a United Nations executive authority for this purpose.)

Third, the Kennedy administration was reluctant for a variety of reasons to promote a peaceful settlement of the controversy through open and unilateral mediation. In the circumstances, however, the United States was prepared actively to encourage and assist the Acting Secretary-General's initiative to intervene, and to support the United Nations effort behind the scenes with timely pressure on both sides. We shall analyze the reasons why the Washington government considered it both necessary and possible to give the formal lead to the United Nations in this instance. The outcome was highly favorable from the official American point of view, and undoubtedly underscored the utility of the United Nations as an instrumentality for promoting United States objectives in certain circumstances.

Fourth and finally, the West New Guinea settlement served to clarify international practice with respect to the socalled "right" of self-determination. The principle of self-determination has been an important doctrinal support for justifying the claim of colonial territories to be liberated from their imperial overlords. But once a colony has achieved independence, is that right still available to distinctive ethnic minorities, such as the Papuans, who inhabit fixed territories within the claimed boundaries of the former colony? We shall explore the lessons to be drawn from the West New Guinea case as to the "people" in whom the right of self-determination is presumed to vest, and as to how that right is considered to have been properly exercised.

While primary attention in this study will be given to an exposition of the historical record within the framework outlined above, the analysis is also designed to relate the West New Guinea experience to these broader themes. Each of them is discussed at some length at appropriate stages of the text; and the concluding chapter summarizes the significance of the West New Guinea episode for our understanding of these four perspectives on world politics.

Chapter Two

Origins

The territory once popularly known as West or Western New Guinea, more properly as Netherlands New Guinea, and now under Indonesian rule as West Irian or Irian Barat, comprises that half of the island of New Guinea lying west of the 141st meridian of east longitude. The world's second largest island (after Greenland), New Guinea is located just south of the equator and directly north of Australia, and lies on the eastern extremity of what is now the Indonesian archipelago. With adjoining islands, its area is approximately 344,000 square miles, of which 161,000 square miles or 47 percent make up West New Guinea, and the balance Australian New Guinea (which is divided into Papua and the Trust Territory of New Guinea, both administered by Australia). If the island were laid upon a map of the United States, with the eastern end at New York City, its western tip would stretch into the middle of Nebraska.

West New Guinea includes some of the most inhospitable country on earth. Swampy, malarial lowlands, especially along the southern coasts, contrast with the wild, rugged mountains of the interior. There are few rivers navigable by large vessels. The climate in the lowlying regions is very warm and humid, and the generally abundant rainfall tends to increase with altitude. Tropical rain forest covers most of the island, but the stands are heterogeneous in character and much of the timber has little commercial value. West New Guinea has not been adequately explored. So far as is known, soils in the upland areas are for the most part unsuitable for farming, except in the valleys and a few plateaus; coastal soils are more fertile, but here the swampy nature of the terrain is a complicating factor. Known mineral resources are not extensive, although West New Guinea has some oil, and the recent exploitation of a rich copper deposit suggests that more extensive geological surveys could modify the resource outlook substantially. Even so, difficulties of terrain will greatly complicate the task of resource development.[1]

---

[1]For an excellent brief physical description of West New Guinea, see M. Halim Khan and Alice Taylor, "Western New Guinea," *Focus*, vol. 12, no. 5 (January 1962), pp. 1-5.

In the polemics of the Dutch-Indonesian dispute over West New Guinea, the correct political interpretation to be placed on the natural history of the territory was debated interminably. The island of New Guinea lies along the northern edge of the Sahul Shelf, which "is best considered as a northern extension of the Australian continental mass, partially inundated by the shallow Arafura Sea." [2] Geologically it is quite distinct from the rest of the Indonesian archipelago, the main islands and island groups of which are subsumed in other geological formations.[3] But the possible political significance of this is reduced by the fact that peninsular Southeast Asia and the main Indonesian islands form "a discontinuous bridge between Asia and Australasia, roughly paralleled to the east by a subsidiary and more broken line of stepping stones running through Formosa, the Philippines, and New Guinea." [4] This whole region should properly be viewed as a vast transitional area between the Asian and Australasian-Pacific worlds. Thus the flora and fauna of each have tended to spread to the other, and in these respects New Guinea cannot be described as uniquely Australasian. Exactly where the dividing line should be drawn has been much discussed. In the standard Dutch reference work on New Guinea, the authors conclude that the island's fauna are primarily Australian in type, while its flora show close affinities to Indonesia.[5]

The dominant racial stock is Papuan.[6] A sharp distinction can be made between the Papuans and the peoples indigenous to the other main islands of present-day Indonesia. The Papuans are a Negroid race who arrived in

[2]E. H. G. Dobby, *Southeast Asia,* 7th edition (London: University of London Press, 1960), p. 20.

[3]See, for example, the classification in R. W. van Bemmelen, *The Geology of Indonesia,* vol. 1A, *General Geology of Indonesia and Adjacent Archipelagos* (The Hague: Government Printing Office, 1949), pp. 14-16. Van Bemmelen's study is probably the most comprehensive work in English on the geology of the Indonesian archipelago.

[4]Charles A. Fisher, "Southeast Asia," in W. Gordon East and O. H. K. Spate, eds., *The Changing Map of Asia,* 3rd edition (London: Methuen, 1958), p. 196. See also the map in *From the Stone Age to the 20th Century,* an unpaginated pamphlet obviously published by the Netherlands government to support its claim to West Guinea, but with no indication of authorship or other publication data.

[5]H. Boschma and C. G. G. J. van Steenis, cited in Arend Lijphart, *The Trauma of Decolonization* (New Haven: Yale University Press, 1966), p. 25. Pelzer states simply: "The fauna and flora of the islands closest to Australia showing strong affinities to that continent, while those of western Indonesia resemble the life on the Malay Peninsula." Karl J. Pelzer, "Physical and Human Resource Patterns," in Ruth T. McVey, ed., *Indonesia* (New Haven: Human Relations Area Files, 1963), p. 8.

[6]See J. P. Kleiweg de Zwaan, "The Papuans of Dutch New Guinea: A Physico-Anthropological Survey," *Antiquity and Survival,* vol. 1 (1955), pp. 321-342.

New Guinea as the result of very early migration. While not racially homogeneous — there appear to be three main types [7] — they are fundamentally different from the rest of the Indonesians, who are mainly Mongoloid. A similar division holds as between Papuan and Indonesian languages and culture, which are almost totally different from each other. But the geographical line of division is somewhat less clear. There is undoubtedly a substantial admixture of Papuan blood in some of the islands of East Indonesia closest to New Guinea, while conversely an Indonesian ethnic imprint is clearly discernible along the western coasts of the latter.[8] This is, of course, consistent with the abovestated view of New Guinea and the other Indonesian islands as parts of a geographical transitional area.

With respect to cultural development, all observers agree as to the backwardness of the Papuans. Writing in 1952, the Dutch economist Stratenus stated:[9]

> The Papuan people of New Guinea belong to the most primitive in the world. Their development stands in some respects . . . behind the culture of the Neolithic period, the new stone age, which in Europe must be dated at about 2000 years before the beginning of our era.

> For centuries New Guinea remained isolated from all contact with the outside world . . . the majority of the Papuans still live in their old state of virtually complete isolation . . . New Guinea is inhabited by a greater number of peoples and races than Europe, differing from each other in stature, language, religion, intellectual development and ways of life. The Papuan (usually) lives in . . . a very small social unit, which is not only economically self-sufficient, but also, in all other respects, is enclosed within itself . . . Sometimes, separated by not more than several kilometers from each other, there are groups with languages as little related as Dutch and Russian.

[7] ". . . those who are dark, short, and longheaded; those with broad faces and thick lips, resembling the Melanesians; and those who are almost as short as pygmies, and have round heads, broad faces, and broad noses." Khan and Taylor, *op. cit.*, p. 2.

[8] "It is in the western coastal areas of New Guinea, particularly along the shores of the Bogelkop and the Bomberai Peninsula . . . that an admixture of Indonesian elements has taken place within historic times." Robert C. Bone, Jr., *The Dynamics of the Western New Guinea (Irian Barat) Problem* (Ithaca: Modern Indonesia Project, Cornell University, 1958), p. 4. Bone's study is the best and most comprehensive treatment of the West New Guinea dispute from its beginnings down to 1958.

[9] R. J. Stratenus, quoted in *ibid*, p. 5. But the blanket characterization of a race as primitive is not always helpful. See, for example, Leopold Pospisil, *The Kapauku Papuans of West New Guinea* (New York: Holt, Rinehart and Winston, 1965), in which the author describes a Papuan society that has developed a fairly complex capitalist economy based on money, credit, trade, and competitive free enterprise.

Acculturation is proceeding fairly rapidly along the coasts, especially in the north; and even in more remote areas of the interior, the reach of administration and the activities of missionaries are accelerating the rate of cultural change. By and large, however, the Papuan peoples still remain among "the most primitive in the world."

The island is thinly populated. For New Guinea as a whole, an estimate for 1969 of approximately three million (including the comparatively few Europeans and Asians) would seem reasonable.[10] Less than a third of these, or perhaps 800,000, live in West New Guinea. The main centers of population in West New Guinea are Jayapura (formerly Hollandia), the capital; Biak and Japen islands, along the northern coast at the entrance to Geelvink Bay; Manokwari, Sorong, and the Vogelkop Peninsula in general; Fakfak in the west; and Merauke on the southern coast near the border with East New Guinea.

Early Historical Background

Little is known of New Guinea's early history. In support of Indonesia's claim to West New Guinea as against the Dutch, contemporary Indonesian statesmen including Sukarno embraced the theory that the island was included within the Indonesian political orbit as early as Majapahit, the great Indonesian kingdom founded c. 1293.[11] Until fairly recently, most

[10]Figures for the Australian and Indonesian censuses of 1961 showed a population in Papua and the Trust Territory of New Guinea of approximately 1,970,000; and in West New Guinea, of approximately 758,000. See Judy Tudor, ed., *Handbook of Papua and New Guinea*, 4th edition (Sydney: Pacific Publications, 1964), p. 31; and McVey, *op. cit.*, p. 15. The Dutch government estimated the population of West New Guinea in 1960 at just over 700,000. See Lijphart, *The Trauma of Decolonization*, p. 53.

[11]Before independence, some nationalist leaders held grandiose views as to the appropriate territorial boundaries of an independent Indonesia. At a meeting of the socalled Investigating Committee for Preparation of Indonesia's Independence, set up under Japanese auspices late in World War II to facilitate the transfer of authority which the Japanese had decided upon, Muhammad Yamin appealed to the history of the Majapahit period in defending his stand that an independent Indonesia should include not only the former Netherlands East Indies, but also Portuguese Timor, North Borneo, Malaya, and "Papua," which territories, he argued, had "since the beginning of history . . . been inhabited by the people of Indonesia." Quoted in *The Territory of the Indonesian State: Discussions in the Meeting of the Investigating Committee for Preparation of Indonesia's Independence*, extracted and translated from the book *Naskah Persiapan Undang-Undang Dasar 1945*, vol. 1 (Kuala Lumpur: Federal Department of Information, 1964), pp. 2, 6. The original volume was edited by Yamin and published in 1959; it is the most complete source available on the deliberations of the Investigating Committee.

Sukarno ringingly endorsed Yamin's claim. "I have never said that Indonesia com-

historians of the region accepted the view that at the height of its power
the Majapahit kingdom spread over much of present-day Indonesia, perhaps including New Guinea, and over parts of the Southeast Asian mainland as well. This view is now disputed. Berg, for example, "suggests that
possibly only East Java, Madura, and Bali were under Majapahit's direct
control;" [12] and van der Kroef concludes that "certainly (Majapahit) did

prises only those areas that were ruled by the Dutch. In fact, I have on one occasion
in my life dreamt of a Pan-Indonesia, which will include not only Malaya and
Papua but also the Philippines . . . But the Philippines is already independent, and
we must respect the sovereignty of the Philippine nation . . . I shall support . . .
those who advocate that independent Indonesia should extend to Malaya and
Papua." Quoted in *ibid.,* pp. 20-22. Mohammad Hatta took a much more modest
position. "I am inclined to say that I do not need Papua and that it should be left to
the Papuan people themselves. I recognize that the Papuans have the right to be an
independent nation and that the Indonesians for the time being — i. e., for decades
to come — will not be prepared nor have they the capacity to educate and bring up
the Papuans until they can become an independent people . . . As regards Malaya,
let us leave it to the people of Malaya." Quoted in *ibid.,* pp. 17-19.

On this subject, see also Benedict R. O'G. Anderson, *Some Aspects of Indonesian
Politics Under the Japanese Occupation: 1944-1945* (Ithaca: Cornell University
Modern Indonesia Project, 1961); Garth N. Jones, "Soekarno's Early Views
Upon the Territorial Boundaries of Indonesia," *Australian Outlook,* vol. 18, no. 1
(April 1964), pp. 30-39; and, for a good example of how the Dutch later made dev-
astating polemical use of the revelations contained in the Yamin volume, see the
address by C. W. A. Schurmann, the Permanent Representative of the Netherlands at
the United Nations, before the sixteenth session of the General Assembly, and reproduced in General Assembly, *Official Records* (hereafter cited as *GAOR),* Sixteenth Session (1961), A/PV. 1055.

In January 1950, Yamin asserted that "the whole of New Guinea is Indonesian. If
the Netherlands and Australia were permitted to maintain sovereignty there it would
mean a continuation of colonial rule in the Indonesian archipelago . . . we cannot
allow one piece of colonial territory within our archipelago." Quoted in J. A. C.
Mackie, "Australia and Indonesia 1945-60," in Gordon Greenwood and Norman
Harper, eds., *Australia in World Affairs 1956-1960* (Melbourne: Cheshire, 1963), p.
286. Several months later, Sukarno declared that "Since the Modjopahit era, — that
ancient Indonesian Kingdom which flourished before the Dutch occupation of Indonesia in the 16th century — the Irians of New Guinea have been considered Indonesians in both the political and racial sense of the word." *Report on Indonesia,*
vol. 1, no. 45 (June 2, 1950), p. 2.

[12]Robert Van Niel, "The Course of Indonesian History," in McVey, *op. cit.,* p.
275, citing the Dutch historian C. C. Berg. See also Bernard H. M. Vlekke,
Nusantara, A History of Indonesia, revised edition (The Hague and Bandung: W.
van Hoeve, 1960), pp. 68-73; W. F. Wertheim, *Indonesian Society in Transition*
(The Hague and Bandung: W. van Hoeve, 1956), pp. 51-52; and, for a somewhat
different view, D. G. E. Hall, *A History of South-East Asia* (New York: St. Martin's
Press, 1955), pp. 37-84.

not encompass Western New Guinea." [13] On the other hand, the inhabitants of various islands of East Indonesia had intermittent contact with parts of West New Guinea and its offshore islands from early times. The great island was long on the outer fringe of the Indonesian nexus of trade.[14] When European explorers first set foot upon its coasts and offshore islands in the sixteenth century, petty Indonesian rulers in the Moluccan archipelago were asserting claims to various parts of West New Guinea.[15]

By 1660, the Dutch had established themselves as the dominant power in the Moluccas, the fabled Spice Islands. In December of that year, they sought to delimit by treaty the territories of three Moluccan sultanates, Ternate, Tidore, and Batjan, which for all practical purposes were now vassal states of the Dutch East India Company. By the terms of this settlement, "the Papuan islands in general" [16] were assigned to Tidore, although at the time the Dutch knew little about "the Papuan islands" or about the extent or validity of Tidore's claims, which derived from occasional trade and slaving contacts. Almost three centuries later, this treaty was to acquire unusual significance as the ultimate legal basis for the Dutch assertion of sovereignty over West New Guinea as successor to the rights of Tidore.

With the passage of time, Dutch knowledge of West New Guinea increased. The wild, desolate, primitive, and altogether unpromising character of the country offered little inducement for attempts at development, or even for the establishment of a nominal administration. But the Dutch did recognize its strategic importance as a barrier against other European intrusion into the Moluccas and the rest of the Indies, and it came to be settled policy that West New Guinea should not be allowed to fall into alien hands. Given the evolving Dutch preference for indirect rule throughout the Indies, this could most conveniently be accomplished by maintain-

[13]Justus M. van der Kroef, *The West New Guinea Dispute* (New York: Institute of Pacific Relations, 1958), p. 9. While less comprehensive than Bone's study, this is a useful analysis of the subject down to 1958, written from a moderately pro-Dutch point of view.

[14]". . . the Javanese have traded for ages on the Molucca Islands and Banda . . . They fetched Papuan slaves there and the scented bark called *masoi* and used as *jamu* (a medicine) — both of which commodities were imported from New Guinea." B. Schrieke, *Indonesian Sociological Studies,* Part One (The Hague and Bandung: W. van Hoeve, 1955), p. 227.

[15]Bone, *op. cit.,* p. 9. This brief account of the early history of West New Guinea relies heavily on Bone's study.

[16]Quoted in *ibid.,* p. 11, from an eighteenth century Dutch report on the treaty.

ing the fiction of Tidore's sovereignty over the area.[17] Hence the terms of
the 1660 settlement with Tidore as it affected West New Guinea were
confirmed and redefined at frequent intervals thereafter by the East India
Company and later by the Dutch government. An agreement in 1779
declared "that the state of Tidore is no more in alliance, but now is a
vassal in relation to the Netherlands Company;"[18] and a subsequent
agreement in 1824 recognized the "supremacy and sovereignty of the
Netherlands government," which had by now succeeded to the rights of
the East India Company, over Tidore.[19] In 1814, Tidore's rule was defined
by treaty as extending over "the whole of the Papoa (*sic*) Islands, and
four districts of Mansarij, Karendefur, Ambarpura and Umbarpun."[20]
This was apparently the first time that reference was made to presumably
mainland districts as being under the jurisdiction of Tidore. Following an
expedition in 1828, the Dutch laid direct claim to extended portions of
West New Guinea, especially in the northwest, "except for the rights
which the Sultan of Tidore may have" in the four mainland districts just
mentioned.[21] Finally, a secret proclamation in 1848 in effect declared the
whole of West New Guinea from the 141st meridian to be within the
territorial limits of Tidore. This boundary was recognized by Great Britain
and Germany in 1885, in an exchange of notes between these two powers
delimiting their respective territorial claims in East New Guinea.[22] A
Dutch treaty with Tidore in 1894 defined the latter as including "the
entire area of Western New Guinea;" and a further agreement in 1909
recognized "the right of the Netherlands-Indies Government to incorporate
(annex) the sultanate of Tidore (or any of its territories) at any time as
a directly governed territory."[23]

---

[17]". . . while Company officials . . . were frank in indicating their scepticism as
to the validity of Tidorese claims they were equally ready to accept them at face
value, and sometimes more, when it served the purpose of hindering other European
penetration into the Moluccas. *Ibid.*, pp. 14-15.

[18]Quoted in *ibid.*, p. 15.

[19]Quoted in *ibid.*, p. 17.

[20]Quoted in Paul W. van der Veur, "New Guinea Annexations and the Origin of
the Irian Boundary," *Australian Outlook*, vol. 18, no. 3 (December 1964), p. 317.

[21]Quoted in *ibid.*, p. 318.

[22]See *ibid.*, pp. 322-327. Minor rectifications of the border have subsequently been
agreed upon. See *ibid.*, pp. 327-339; and, by the same author, "The Irian Boundary
Slumber, 1905-1962," *Australian Outlook*, vol. 19, no. 1 (April 1965), pp. 73-96.

[23]Quoted in Bone, *op. cit.*, pp. 20, 21. Material in parentheses added; on these
interpretations, see *ibid.*, p. 55.

Until the end of the nineteenth century, the actual Dutch presence in West New Guinea was largely confined to occasional exploratory expeditions, casual visits, and a few abortive attempts to establish permanent posts. But the activities of the British and Germans in the eastern half of the island made imperative a more substantial effort on the part of the Dutch if their claims to West New Guinea were not to attenuate. In any case, the eventual development and exploitation of the territory was not possible without effective occupation and at least a rudimentary administrative framework. The first permanent Dutch settlements were implanted in 1898 at Manokwari in the north and Fakfak in the southwest, and others followed shortly thereafter. But down to World War II, relatively little progress was made in opening up the country. It was still "an almost forgotten land . . . Administrative control was haphazard and limited to a few scattered posts along the fringes." [24] The only significant investment in large-scale resource development were the oilfields of the Vogelkop Peninsula.

Genesis of the Dispute, 1945-49.

There is no doubt that when the Indonesian nationalist leadership headed by Sukarno and Mohammad Hatta proclaimed the independence of the Indonesian Republic on August 17, 1945, they intended to assert the authority of their new regime over all the territories historically incorporated within the boundaries of Netherlands India, the Netherlands East Indies. This certainly included West New Guinea as then delimited, which had been considered a part of the Netherlands East Indies at least since the secret decree of 1848, and over which Dutch sovereignty had long been accepted by the international community.[25] The dispute over the future of West New Guinea arose as a function of the much larger conflict that quickly developed between the Dutch and the Indonesian nationalists. The Dutch realized that the status quo ante in the East Indies could not be precisely restored after World War II, and that extensive changes would have to be accepted. The idea of transforming the whole

[24]Paul W. van der Veur, "Political Awakening in West New Guinea," *Pacific Affairs*, vol. 36, no. 1 (Spring 1963), p. 54.

[25] At the July 11, 1945, meeting of the Investigating Committee for Preparation of Indonesia's Independence, the 66 delegates voted on proposals relating to the territory to be included within an independent Indonesia. A clear majority of 39 supported a grandiose scheme for Pan-Indonesia, while only six voted for a plan excluding New Guinea. See p. 27, fn. 3, below. Circumstances soon obliged the Indonesian nationalists to limit their ambitions to the former territory of the Netherlands East Indies only.

Dutch empire into a kind of commonwealth of nations in which, however, the Dutch would continue to have a predominant voice, had long been discussed. With the emergence immediately after the war of the Republic of Indonesia, and the incompatibility of Republican demands with Dutch objectives, the idea quickly took shape of separating out various segments of the former Netherlands East Indies, including West New Guinea, from the territories to be conceded to the Indonesian Republic (which was centered on Java and Sumatra), and creating a special relationship for them with the Netherlands. The effect of this policy, if successful, would have been not only to diminish the authority of the Republic, but also to preserve a large measure of Dutch influence in the remaining areas.[26]

A series of conferences was held during 1946 to discuss the future of the archipelago. At Malino (South Celebes) in July, the Dutch met with Indonesian leaders from outside the territory of the Republic. Here the notion of a federal Indonesia was discussed concretely for the first time, but there was no suggestion that West New Guinea might be excluded from the proposed federation.[27] The Pangkalpinang (Bangka) conference in October, which was called to consult the views of Indonesia's principal minority groups, heard a strong plea that West New Guinea be given a special status as a new homeland for the Eurasian community and for Dutch settlers as well.[28] With obvious reference to West New Guinea, a resolution adopted at the conference recommended that various territories of Indonesia have the option of developing a special status within the Kingdom of the Netherlands, rather than with an independent Indonesia;

[26]For a comprehensive treatment of Indonesia's struggle for independence, see George McTurnan Kahin, *Nationalism and Revolution in Indonesia* (Ithaca: Cornell University Press, 1952). Useful studies of the early years of the conflict may be found in David Wehl, *The Birth of Indonesia* (London: Allen and Unwin, 1948); and Charles Wolf, Jr., *The Indonesian Story* (New York: Day, 1948). An exhaustive analysis of the United Nations role in the conflict may be found in Alastair M. Taylor, *Indonesian Independence and the United Nations* (Ithaca: Cornell University Press, 1960). Much briefer accounts of the same subject are J. Foster Collins, *The United Nations and Indonesia*, International Conciliation Series no. 459 (March 1950); and William Henderson, *Pacific Settlement of Disputes, The Indonesian Question 1946-1949* (New York: Woodrow Wilson Foundation, 1954).

[27]"The name 'Irian' for New Guinea was introduced by Frans Kaisiepo during this conference. Kaisiepo came from the island of Biak, where Irian is the name of the mainland of New Guinea." Lijphart, *The Trauma of Decolonization*, p. 11, fn. 2. Kaisiepo represented West New Guinea at the conference.

[28]Such proposals had some currency even before World War II. See Bone, *op. cit.*, p. 22. The notion of West New Guinea as a Eurasian homeland took on added strength after the war as this minority, which had enjoyed a somewhat protected position under the Dutch, became fearful of its prospects in an independent Indonesia and cast about for some way to safeguard the future.

and another motion (not adopted by the whole conference) urged that a "separate political status within the Kingdom should be awarded to New Guinea, separated from Indonesia." [29] But the Dutch government was non-committal at this time.

During negotiations with Republican representatives at Jakarta and Linggadjati (near Cheribon, Java) in October-November, a comprehensive effort was made to settle the Dutch-Indonesian conflict. West New Guinea was apparently not discussed during these sessions.[30] But the terms of the agreement finally reached, commonly known as the Linggadjati Agreement, were important for the emerging dispute over the future of the island. Article 3 and the first sentence of Article 4 provided:[31]

Article 3. The United States of Indonesia shall comprise the entire territory of the Netherlands Indies with the provision, however, that in case the population of any territory, after due consultation with the other territories, should decide by democratic process that they are not, or not yet, willing to join in the United States of Indonesia, they can establish a special relationship for such a territory to the United States of Indonesia and to the Kingdom of the Netherlands.

Article 4. The component parts of the United States of Indonesia shall be the Republic of Indonesia (that is, Java and Sumatra), Borneo, and the Great East (that is, the territories of East Indonesia including West New Guinea) without prejudice to the right of the population of any territory to decide by democratic process that its position in the United States of Indonesia shall be arranged otherwise . . .

By now, the Netherlands had decide upon a federal solution for the Indonesian problem; and at Linggadjati, it was agreed that a territory could "by democratic process" opt out of the proposed United States of Indonesia and enter into a special relationship with it and with the Netherlands. The question was whether and how all this applied to West New Guinea. On instructions from The Hague, the Dutch negotiators subsequently issued a carefully worded "explanation" of the agreement which alluded to the "difficulties" which could arise from the application of these clauses to West New Guinea (in view of the manifest impossibility that the primitive Papuan population of the island could, or that means could be found to enable them to, decide any question so complicated as their corporate political future "by democratic process"). It might be necessary, therefore,

[29]Quoted in *ibid.,* p. 30.
[30]See Lijphart, *The Trauma of Decolonization,* p. 12.
[31]The full text of the Linggadjati Agreement may be found in Taylor, *op. cit.,* pp. 464-467. Material in parentheses added.

to hold "further discussions on the possibility of offering New Guinea a special status on another basis." [32] In parliament in December, the Dutch government went further in declaring that *"in the spirit"* of these articles, West New Guinea *"must* be able to obtain its own status;" and reference was also made to the desirability of keeping open the possibility of large-scale Dutch and especially Eurasian settlement there.[33] These steps indicated that Dutch policy on West New Guinea was solidifying rapidly. When the Linggadjati Agreement was finally signed in March 1947, the Indonesians disavowed the unilateral Dutch interpretations relating to West New Guinea.

Meanwhile at Denpasar (Bali) in December, representatives from the Great East met with a Dutch delegation to organize that region into a constituent element of the future United States of Indonesia. Here the Dutch were highly ambiguous about the long-term future of West New Guinea, and pressed for its exclusion from the territory of the new state of East Indonesia, at least for the time being.[34] This policy gravely disturbed the Federalists (as representatives of the non-Republican territories came to be called). They reluctantly accepted a draft provision on the boundaries of the new state which declared that "a decision will be made later concerning the status of the territory of the present residency of New Guinea," but only after having succeeded in adding the phrase "and its relationship to the State (of) East Indonesia and the future United States of Indonesia" to the offending provision.[35] Federalist sentiment on the issue was reflected in a strongly worded resolution, approved overwhelmingly by the conference, which argued that West New Guinea had hitherto been part of the Great East, and that it was bound to Indonesia by traditional ties; that it had great strategic and economic significance for all of

[32]Quoted in *ibid.,* p. 30.

[33]Quoted in *ibid.,* p. 33. Italics added.

[34]See, for example, statements made to the conference by Lieutenant Governor-General Hubertus J. van Mook, the head of the Netherlands Indies government (the Dutch did not appoint a full Governor-General after the war), quoted in van der Kroef, *The West New Guinea Dispute,* p. 4, and Bone, *op. cit.,* pp. 36-37. Much later, in July 1949, van Mook explicitly advised the Dutch Ministry of Foreign Affairs not to exclude West New Guinea from Indonesia. See Lijphart, *The Trauma of Decolonization,* p. 14, fn. 10.

Unlike the conference at Malino, West New Guinea was not represented at Denpasar.

[35]Quoted in Lijphart, *The Trauma of Decolonization,* p. 13.

Indonesia; and that, therefore, the question of its inclusion in East Indonesia should be investigated promptly.[36]

The future of West New Guinea was now in open dispute. While Dutch intentions were still vague at the time of the Denpasar conference, doubtless because they were not yet precisely formulated, the general tendency of Dutch policy was unmistakable. It was also clear that almost all responsible Indonesian spokesmen, whether Republican or Federalist, would strongly oppose the sacrifice of West New Guinea as the price of independence.

During the next three years, the issue was often submerged in the larger conflict between the Dutch and the Indonesian Republicans. Following the first Dutch "police action" against the Republic in Summer 1947, another truce agreement was negotiated under the auspices of the newly created United Nations Committee of Good Offices on the Indonesian Question.[37] Its terms did not modify the parameters of the West New Guinea dispute in any significant respect. Accepted by both sides in January 1948, the political principles included in the socalled Renville Agreement provided,[38] *inter alia,* that "Sovereignty throughout the Netherlands Indies is and shall remain with the Kingdom of the Netherlands until, after a stated interval, the Kingdom of the Netherlands transfers its sovereignty to the United States of Indonesia;" and further, that "Should any state decide not to ratify the constitution and desire, in accordance with the principles of Articles 3 and 4 of the Linggadjati Agreement, to negotiate a special relationship with the United States of Indonesia and the Kingdom of the Netherlands, neither party will object." The first of these clauses could be construed to support the Indonesian claim with respect to West New Guinea, inasmuch as it stipulated an eventual transfer of sovereignty "throughout the Netherlands Indies;" while the second, by

[36]See Bone, *op. cit.,* pp. 37-38.
In practice, the Dutch carefully excluded West New Guinea from the federal structure they laboriously built up over the next three years. "New Guinea remained outside the federal-state organization. This was a factor which enabled the determination of the status of New Guinea to be postponed when the sovereignty of the rest of Indonesia was transferred in December, 1949." A. Arthur Schiller, *The Formation of Federal Indonesia, 1945-1945* (The Hague and Bandung: W. van Hoeve, 1955), pp. 206-207.

[37]The membership of the Good Offices Committee (and later of the United Nations Commission for Indonesia, which succeeded it) consisted of Australia, chosen by the Indonesians to represent their interests; Belgium, designated by the Netherlands; and the United States, coopted by Australia and Belgium to serve as impartial third party.

[38]The full text of the political principles incorporated in the Renville Agreement may be found in Taylor, *op. cit.,* pp. 468-470.

confirming the indicated articles of Linggadjati, buttressed the Dutch contention that territories of the Netherlands Indies could choose to remain-
outside of the future United States of Indonesia in favor of establishing a
special relationship with it and with the Netherlands. During 1948, the
Dutch constitution was amended to allow for such a special relationship
with "any part of Indonesia." [39]

Throughout this period, the Indonesian Federalists tried hard to reverse
the tide with respect to West New Guinea. A Federalist conference at
Bandung in July 1948, for example, declared that the future United States
of Indonesia "shall comprise the entire territory of the Netherlands Indies,
undiminished by the stipulation in Article 3 of the Linggadjati Agreement." [40] But to no avail. Following the failure of their second "police
action" launched in December 1948, and just prior to the opening of The
Hague Round Table Conference, the Dutch in July 1949 exercised their
legal rights under the treaty of 1909 with Tidore and brought West New
Guinea under the direct administration of the colonial government. The
stage was now set for the definitive separation of West New Guinea from
the territory of the new Indonesian state that was soon to be brought into
existence.

The Hague Round Table Conference and the 1949 Settlement

Chastened by the failure of their second "police action" against the
Republicans to impose a military solution in Java and Sumatra, and by the
sharply adverse international reaction to this thrust as mainfested in the
United Nations and bilaterally by the United States and other interested
powers, as well as by the heavy criticism which even the Indonesian
Federalists — hitherto staunch allies of the Dutch in most important
matters — now levelled against them, the Dutch at last came to realize the
necessity for farreaching concessions to Indonesian nationalism. During
Spring 1949, preliminary negotiations were conducted under the aegis of
the United Nations Commission for Indonesia (into which the Committee
of Good Offices had been transformed in January), first between the Dutch
and Indonesian Republicans, and then with a Federalist delegation also
taking part, and a cessation of hostilities arranged. In August-November,
a Round Table Conference met at The Hague, also with the assistance of
the United Nations Commission for Indonesia (although technically sponsored by the Dutch), to draw up the terms of a final settlement and transfer of sovereignty.

[39]Quoted in Bone, *op. cit.*, p. 44.
[40]Quoted in *ibid.*, p. 46.

Not unexpectedly, West New Guinea became a major issue at the conference. The virtual irreconcilability of Dutch and Indonesian views as to the future of the territory had long since become apparent. In the preliminary negotiations earlier that year, the Dutch had made clear that inclusion of the question on the agenda of the forthcoming Round Table Conference did not prejudice their claim to hold onto West New Guinea, while the Republican and Federalist spokesmen insisted that the territory should be included in the future United States of Indonesia.[41] At The Hague, the Federalist delegation championed the Indonesian claim with special tenacity.[42] When the conference met, formal consideration of the West New Guinea question was deliberately postponed in order not to impede progress on other major issues. Eventually, however, the anticipated impasse developed; and in desperation the three negotiating parties (Dutch, Republican, Federalist) turned to the United Nations Commission for assistance in dealing with it. The Commission had already given thought to some form of international trusteeship as a possible solution, but discarded this in favor of a simple formula for postponing the issue. With modifications, this proposal was accepted by the three negotiating parties.[43] The conference thereupon concluded successfully with the adoption of a Draft Charter of Transfer of Sovereignty (as well as of other instruments), which was subsequently ratified by all parties, and formally signed and put into effect on December 27, 1949.

The relevant portions of Articles 1 and 2 of the Charter of Transfer of Sovereignty affecting the status of West New Guinea provided: [44]

Article 1. The Kingdom of the Netherlands unconditionally and irrevocably transfers complete sovereignty over Indonesia to the Re-

[41]See Taylor, *op. cit.,* p. 222.

[42]This was partly because West New Guinea would be incorporated into East Indonesia, a Federalist state. (At the Denpasar conference, December 1946, a Balinese had remarked plaintively that "The Great East without New Guinea must properly be considered the Small East!" Quoted in Bone, *op. cit.,* p. 36.) But the Federalists were also determined to demonstrate their zeal as good Indonesian nationalists, a quality that had hitherto been in some doubt. A victory over the Dutch on this issue would also strengthen their hand in relation to the Republicans in the future United States of Indonesia.

[43]For the role of the United Nations Commission with respect to the West New Guinea issue, see Taylor, *op. cit.,* pp. 235-239. The author served on the Secretariat of the Commission.

[44]The full text of the Draft Charter of Transfer of Sovereignty, as well as of other agreements reached, may be found in *Round Table Conference Results as Accepted in the Second Plenary Meeting Held on 2 November 1949 in the "Ridderzaal" at The Hague* (The Hague: Secretariat-General of the Round Table Conference, 1949). The clauses quoted in the text are on p. 9.

public of the United States of Indonesia and thereby recognizes said
Republic of the United States of Indonesia as an independent and
sovereign State.

Article 2. With regard to the residency of New Guinea it is decided:

a. in view of the fact that it has not yet been possible to reconcile the views of the parties on New Guinea, which remain, therefore,
in dispute . . .

that the status quo of the residency of New Guinea shall be maintained with the stipulation that within a year from the date of transfer
of sovereignty to the Republic of the United States of Indonesia the
question of the political status of New Guinea be determined through
negotiations between the Republic of the United States of Indonesia
and the Kingdom of the Netherlands.

In a simultaneous exchange of letters between the chairman of the Dutch
delegation and the chairmen of the Republican and Federalist delegations,
it was further stipulated that the "clause in Article 2 of the Draft Charter
of Transfer of Sovereignty reading: 'the status quo of the residency of
New Guinea shall be maintained' means: 'through continuing under the
Government of the Netherlands.' " [45] A clear statement as to where sovereignty over West New Guinea resided in the interim was deliberately
and necessarily avoided.

The Failure of Bilateral Negotiations

From 1946 on, the essence of Dutch policy with respect to West New
Guinea was to devise a special political status for the territory such that,
whatever its legal relationship to an independent Indonesia, the reality of
Dutch control would be preserved. During the years 1946-49, however,
the Dutch never enunciated clearly and unequivocably their long-term
constitutional objectives for West New Guinea, nor did they ever force the
issue in various negotiations with the Indonesians. This was in part because
the Dutch recognized that their policy offended both Republicans and
Federalists alike. But it was also because the Dutch did not know themselves precisely what they intended, or the circumstances in which their
policy would have to be implemented. They could not, and they certainly
did not, control the course of events which ultimately led to Indonesian
independence in an atmosphere of much bitterness after four years of sharp
conflict. By the time of The Hague Round Table Conference, it was
reasonably clear what the Dutch were up to in West New Guinea. But
there remained the possibility that the dispute could still be resolved in the
bilateral negotiations called for in the Charter of Transfer of Sovereignty.

[45]*Ibid.*, pp. 79-80.

Unfortunately the prospects for meaningful negotiations were seriously compromised only two days after Indonesian independence formally took effect, when on December 29, 1949, the Dutch government issued a decree establishing a permanent colonial administration for West New Guinea under a governor designated by and responsible solely to the Dutch crown.[46] The terms and timing of this decree could only be interpreted as underscoring the Dutch determination to retain effective control over the territory for a long time.

Meanwhile, the Indonesian attitude was also hardening. Before the Round Table Conference, West New Guinea had been only one, and by no means the most important, of many intractable problems to be resolved between the Dutch and Indonesians. During 1950, it became *the* issue in their mutual relations. President Sukarno stated the case forcefully in his Independence Day address on August 17: [47]

This is not a trifling question; this is a major issue. I fear that the Netherlands does not yet understand that the Irian question is a major issue to us . . . (It) is a question of colonialism or independence. Part of our country is still colonized by the Dutch . . . and we do not accept this . . . according to our Constitution, Irian is also *Indonesian territory,* territory of the Republic of Indonesia—not tomorrow, not the day after tomorrow, but *now,* at this very moment. The Dutch *de facto* authority over Irian is recognized *for this year only.* If a settlement by negotiation cannot be arrived at within this year, a major conflict will arise over the issue of who will be in power in that island from then onward.

The future of West New Guinea was considered at the first ministerial conference of the Netherlands-Indonesian Union,[48] at Jakarta in March 1950, but without significant result. The conference communique noted that a solution to the problem "still could not be found;" [49] and a mixed Dutch-Indonesian commission was set up to study the whole subject in

[46]For the terms of this decree, see Bone, *op. cit.,* pp. 69-72.

[47]Quoted in George McT. Kahin, "Indonesian Politics and Nationalism," in William L. Holland, ed., *Asian Nationalism and the West* (New York: Macmillan, 1953), p. 165. Italics in original.

[48]The Netherlands-Indonesian Union, which was set up at The Hague Round Table Conference in 1949, represented an effort to formalize links between the two states on the basis of sovereign equality between the two partners. Its model was the British Commonwealth of Nations, but the spirit necessary to vitalize it was almost entirely lacking, especially on the Indonesian side. See Kahin, *Nationalism and Revolution in Indonesia,* pp. 433-434. The full text of the Union Statute may be found in *Round Table Conference Results as Accepted in the Second Plenary Meeting Held on 2 November 1949 in the "Ridderzaal" at The Hague.*

[49]Quoted in Bone, *op. cit.,* p. 76.

preparation for a second ministerial conference to deal specially with West New Guinea. The commission duly visited the territory, and held extensive consultations in Jakarta and The Hague, but could reach no agreement on substantive policy recommendations.[50] In December, the special ministerial conference convened at The Hague. By this time, Dutch-Indonesian relations — never too promising — had already sharply deteriorated, in part because of the failure to settle the West New Guinea question, but also because of various developments within Indonesia, including the outbreak of a number of localized rebellions in which Dutch nationals were implicated, and because of the abrogation of the federal political system (which the Dutch had painfully fostered as a device for preserving a residue of influence within an independent Indonesia) in favor of a unitary state dominated by the Republicans. To Indonesian demands that West New Guinea be turned over to them, subject to suitable guarantees for Dutch interests in the territory, the maximum Dutch concessions were rather meaningless proposals to create a joint New Guinea Council whose main function would be to receive reports on Dutch administration of the territory; or alternatively to vest sovereignty over West New Guinea in the already moribund Netherlands-Indonesian Union, but with actual control remaining firmly in Dutch hands. The conference ended in complete deadlock on December 27, the last day of the year provided in the Chapter of Transfer of Sovereignty for negotiating a settlement to the dispute.[51]

In Summer 1951, informal discussions were resumed in preparation for another conference at The Hague called to revise the Round Table Conference agreements. Dutch and Indonesian delegations met December 1951-February 1952 in an atmosphere clouded by simultaneous parliamentary action to amend the Dutch constitution so as to include West New Guinea specifically within the territory of the kingdom, and by Indonesia's retaliatory seizure of arms found on two Dutch ships in Jakarta harbor bound for West New Guinea. No progress was made toward resolving the dispute. A Dutch proposal that the question of sovereignty be submitted to international adjudication was rejected by Indonesia on the ground that the dispute was essentially a political, not a legal, question; and an Indonesian suggestion that, pending settlement of the sovereignty issue through further negotiations, a joint Dutch-Indonesian "responsibility" for the administration of the territory be established, was not taken up by the

[50]See *ibid.*, pp. 76-83; and J. A. C. Mackie, "The West New Guinea Argument," *Australian Outlook*, vol. 16, no. 1 (April 1962), pp. 33-34.

[51]See Bone, *op. cit.*, pp. 89-97; Mackie, "The West New Guinea Argument," *loc. cit.*, pp. 34-36; and van der Kroef, *The West New Guinea Dispute*, pp. 6, 18.

Netherlands government.[52] In July 1953, the Dutch government "summarily rebuffed" an Indonesian suggestion that it be consulted with respect to Dutch-Australian plans for closer cooperation in the administration of their respective New Guinea territories;[53] and a year later, The Hague declined to include the West New Guinea question on the agenda of another bilateral conference, convened primarily to negotiate the dissolution of the Netherlands-Indonesian Union, on the ground that there was no further point in discussing the issue. A final effort to resolve accumulated Dutch-Indonesian differences was made in discussions at The Hague and Geneva, December 1955-February 1956, but without success. Shortly thereafter, Indonesia announced its withdrawal from the Netherlands-Indonesian Union, and unilaterally abrogated most of the remaining Round Table Conference agreements.[54] This marked the termination of serious bilateral efforts to resolve the West New Guinea dispute.

[52]See Bone, *op. cit.*, pp. 112-116; Mackie, "The West New Guinea Argument," *loc. cit.*, pp. 36-37; and van der Kroef, *The West New Guinea Dispute*, pp. 7, 19.

[53]Bone, *op. cit.*, p. 122, fn. 5.

[54]See *ibid.*, p. 143; and van der Kroef, *The West New Guinea Dispute*, p. 20.
In the Summer 1954 negotiations, agreement had already been reached on the dissolution of the Netherlands-Indonesian Union, and on the modification of other Round Table Conference agreements; but the Indonesian parliament subsequently failed to ratify this revised settlement. See van der Kroef, *The West New Guinea Dispute*, p. 19.

Chapter Three

Dynamics of the Dispute

In the analysis of any political controversy it is important to distinguish, in so far as such a distinction is valid or relevant, between the real motivations of the parties to the dispute, and the reasons or justifications which they themselves ascribe to their positions in the surrounding polemics. In the West New Guinea case, the distinction is significant, and helps to explain why the dispute aroused such passions, especially on the Indonesian side, and ultimately approached the brink of war. Lijphart summarizes the point in the following terms:[1]

> In their dispute, the Dutch and Indonesians resorted to a mass of historical, geographical, ethnological, legal, and ethical arguments to justify their policies . . . One should keep in mind that these propaganda arguments were not the mainsprings of either the Dutch or the Indonesian policies. The real motives of both countries revolved around a set of highly subjective and psychological factors . . . Most of the opposing arguments canceled each other out or were invalid or irrelevant.

This chapter analyzes briefly the underlying motivations of Dutch and Indonesian policy, and then recapitulates the formal arguments advanced by both sides in defense of the positions taken. It is difficult to escape the conclusion that, while the formal Dutch case was reasonably sound and even persuasive, Indonesia's posture was much stronger in the increasingly anticolonialist environment of postwar international politics.

The Sources of Indonesian Policy

Indonesian attitudes with respect to West New Guinea were shaped in part by the content of Indonesian nationalism, rather than by any special attachment of sentiment or material interest to the territory itself. Even before World War II, the claim of the nationalist movement, which was based largely on Java and Sumatra, was to succeed to Dutch rule over

[1]Lijphart, *The Trauma of Decolonization*, p. 22.

26

the *whole* of Netherlands India.[2] But the validity of this claim was open to serious challenge. While the centuries of colonial experience had contributed to some sense of common identity throughout the archipelago, the nationalist leadership was well aware of Indonesia's ethnic and linguistic diversity, and the strong centrifugal tendencies inherent in the country's geography. The nationalist slogan, "one people, one country, one language," often seemed to express aspirations that defied the objective facts. But there was one crucial respect in which the nationalist claim could be defended. However fanciful the appeals of Sukarno and others to the presumed extent of the Majapahit kingdom, Netherlands India was an undoubted historical reality, with settled boundaries and a common political structure. In the circumstances, this reality took on immense significance. It both defined and, failing other arguments, justified the aspirations of the nationalists. In Lijphart's words, there was "no clear criterion for the single national whole other than the common history of Dutch colonial rule." This meant that the national territory had to be preserved intact. "If West Irian were to be regarded as not essential to this national whole, the definition of national unity would cease to operate." [3] Dutch policy to retain control over West New Guinea meant not only the loss of a substantial territory. It compromised the organizing principle of the state.

[2]On this point, see L. Metzemaekers, "The Western New Guinea Problem," *Pacific Affairs,* vol. 24, no. 2 (June 1951), pp. 135-136.

[3]Arend Lijphart, "The Indonesian Image of West Irian," *Asian Survey,* vol. 1, no. 5 (July 1961), p. 11. This brief article presents an excellent analysis of certain aspects of the problem, including the point summarized in this paragraph of the text.

Following the sentences quoted in the text, Lijphart adds in a footnote: "For the same reason, it is highly unlikely that the Indonesians would lay claim to Eastern New Guinea. Such an action would be contrary to the character of Indonesian nationalism." (P. 15, fn. 2.) This perhaps carries the point too far. At one time, Indonesian nationalist leaders were able to contemplate an independent Indonesia embracing territories not included in the Dutch East Indies, or alternatively excluding certain territories. At the July 11, 1945, meeting of the Japanese-sponsored Investigating Committee for Preparation of Indonesia's Independence, to which Lijphart also calls attention in his article (p. 13), the delegates voted on various proposals relating to the territorial extent of an independent Indonesia. Of the 66 votes cast, only 19 were for a territorial definition coterminous with the historical Dutch East Indies, while 39 were for a Pan-Indonesia embracing, in addition, the territories of North Borneo, Brunei, Sarawak, Portuguese Timor, and Malaya. With the advantage of hindsight, one might add that the record of Indonesia's abortive "confrontation" policy against Malaysia (1963-65) suggests the possibility, at least, of continuing expansionist tendencies.

The possibility could not be admitted that the surrounding geographical, ethnic, and historical circumstances were such as to constitute West New Guinea as a special case. Distrust of the Dutch was simply too strong. The Indonesians could not forget the bitter struggle for independence and Dutch efforts to fragment the country through the imposition of a loose federal system before the transfer of sovereignty, nor could they forgive alleged Dutch involvement in various separatist movements during the decade of the 1950s. In their suspicious eyes, the Dutch position in West New Guinea could only be construed as a base from which to undermine the independence and integrity of the nation.

Like the preponderant position which the Dutch retained in Indonesian economic life even after The Hague Round Table Conference, West New Guinea was, moreover, a standing affront to the sensitive nationalism of a proud and newly independent people, a remnant of colonialism that could not be tolerated indefinitely. While the Dutch held onto West New Guinea, the Indonesian revolution remained incomplete. It is perhaps open to question whether the Indonesian masses, caught up in an increasingly precarious struggle for existence amid chronically deteriorating political and economic conditions, would have developed much interest in the "liberation" of the territory if their political leaders had not harangued them so unceasingly about it. But surely the point is that, from a variety of motives, public figures did deliberately whip up popular passions over West New Guinea, and eventually the people responded. In time, the national claim came to arouse quite genuine sentiment throughout the archipelago.[4]

[4]The extent to which the West New Guinea dispute aroused genuine popular sentiment in Indonesia has been much discussed. Compare, for example, the views of Angus Maude, formerly a British Conservative member of parliament, and Denis Warner, an Australian journalist, on this point.

Maude states: "There can be no doubt that to the mass of Indonesians the future of West Irian was a matter of more or less complete indifference until the end of the 1950s, if not to this day. For years it remained no more than a subject for passionate speeches by demagogues." Angus Maude, *South Asia* (London: Bodley Head, 1966), p. 167.

Warner takes the opposite view. Writing in the *Melbourne Herald* of November 26, 1957, he declared:

It is generally assumed in Australia that the Indonesian Government has turned on its Dutch New Guinea campaign like a tap to divert attention from its own appalling internal problems.

Of all the current misunderstandings about Dutch New Guinea, none is more misleading or dangerous. It's a nice plausible explanation but it just doesn't happen to be true. From the very first day of Indonesian independence in December, 1949, Indonesia has been shouting for Irian as Dutch New Guinea is known there . . .

To be sure, the issue caused a "sharp ambivalence" among the more sophisticated, largely Dutch-trained elite, who were "much more vulnerable to conflicting arguments and feelings." [5] They could see the other side of the coin: that the Indonesian case was not nearly so sound as the propagandists alleged; that in terms of its apparent material potential, the territory was not worth much; that there was little danger of a serious Dutch effort to reassert control over the archipelago, using West New Guinea as a base; and that Indonesia had much more serious problems to contend with. But even the most moderate statesmen had to recognize the strength of national sentiment to "recover" the lost territory, and go along with the political tide. Thus Mohammad Hatta, whose private views on the subject were certainly less militant, wrote in 1959 that:[6]

The claim to West Irian is a national claim backed by every Indonesian party without exception . . . In Indonesian eyes continued Dutch occupation of West Irian is both a remnant of colonialism and illegal seizure of a portion of Indonesian territory.

And again in 1961, he stated:[7]

Indonesia's claim to West Irian represents a continuation of her struggle against colonialism, a struggle to complete her national independence. In this effort to achieve the highest ideal there is no place for compromise, as history in all periods has demonstrated. In

Maybe the issue has snowballed a little in size, but it was serious three years ago and it is serious today—not just a political expedient . . .

We may bitterly disapprove of what Indonesia is doing. We may doubt the legality of her claim.

But we're kidding no one but ourselves if we persist in the argument that it's all merely a matter of crying wolf abroad to cover up the fact that the fox is eating the chickens at home.

Quoted in Bone, op. cit., pp. 154-155.

My view is that "the common history of Dutch colonial rule" as the "criterion for the single national whole" was important primarily in the sense of justifying the concept of a single Indonesian nation rather than several, and in giving meaningful territorial definition to Indonesian nationalist aspirations primarily—such is the frailty of human nature—in the sense of setting minimum limits.

[5]Lijphart, "The Indonesian Image of West Irian," loc cit., p. 13.

[6]Mohammad Hatta, "Indonesia Between the Power Blocs," Foreign Affairs, vol. 36, no. 3 (April 1958), p. 487.

At the previously noted meeting of July 11, 1945, of the Investigating Committee for Preparation of Indonesia's Independence, Hatta had expressed misgivings as to the wisdom of incorporating New Guinea within the boundaries of an independent Indonesia. See p. 12, fn. 11, above.

[7]Mohammad Hatta, "Colonialism and the Danger of War," Asian Survey, vol. 1, no. 9 (November 1961), p. 13.

the course of the accompanying excitement, armed conflict can hardly be avoided.

It should be recognized, too, that such sentiments were closely related to the central place of revolutionary struggle in the Indonesian nationalist mystique. The concept of struggle was intellectually congenial to the political leadership as the historically validated means by which Indonesia had won its independence. It was also utilitarian in sustaining patriotic enthusiasm among a population with little else to cheer about. Sukarno's approach to Indonesian politics was the supreme example of both these strands. As Feith states:[8]

(His) view of Indonesia's problems centers on national unity and national spirit. He insists that nothing is more important than the maintenance of revolutionary *élan,* the creation and recreation of a mystique and sense of momentum which will tie the people, or some important segments of them, to the government.

In this context, the quest for West New Guinea was an almost perfect issue. It is perhaps too simplistic to assert that the political leadership played upon this theme simply to divert the population from massive political and economic problems at home which the leadership itself seemed imcapable of coming to grips with. The demand for West New Guinea came to be a much more genuine popular emotion that was also shared in varying degrees by the political elites, despite their more realistic grasp of the underlying complexities of the issue. But the leadership must also have been aware that, however sincere and patriotic their motives in pressing the Indonesian claim, their policy also served to stimulate sentiments of national unity in a divided country, and to contain pressures for change from the increasingly restive masses.[9]

From another perspective, the West New Guinea issue was inextricably involved in the dynamics of internal Indonesian politics. During its heyday, the political partnership of Sukarno and the Army "share(d) an emphasis on the importance of the revolution as a source of legitimate authority; each of them ha(d) an interest in maintaining the argument

[8]Herbert Feith, "Dynamics of Guided Democracy," in McVey, *op. cit.,* p. 331.

[9]With respect to national unity, van der Kroef observes, for example, that party strife "created an atmosphere of such violent ideological dissension and political disunity that few Indonesian leaders (particularly those who continued to hitch their fortunes to Sukarno's star) could fail to realize the importance of the issue as a rallying point, and hence deliberately lent themselves to an intensified, anti-Dutch campaign (Indonesia's 'confrontation policy') precisely at a time when secessionist elements were readying their plans to proclaim a new government in Sumatra." Justus M. van der Kroef, "Indonesia and the Dutch," *Pacific Affairs,* vol. 36, no. 3 (Fall 1963), pp. 290-291.

that those who led the struggle for independence ha(d) a moral right to govern." [10] If the controversy over West New Guinea could be presented as a continuation of the revolutionary struggle for independence, this would serve to undergird the claims of Sukarno and the Army to continuing authority. Commenting on the period up to 1963, Feith remarks:[11]

> For if indeed this is a period of revolution, if its tasks are essentially the same ones which were faced in the days of the guerrilla struggle against the Dutch, then it follows that the national leaders needed today are men who can rally and inspire the people to fight against the enemy and men who can organize the actual shooting; Indonesia therefore needs the leadership of specialists in symbols and military activity, not of specialists in economics or administration. Thus the doctrine serves to justify the great power now wielded by President Sukarno and the army; and it helps to explain why little influence lies in the hands of men like Hatta, whose claim to power lies in their skills in running a modern state.

West New Guinea was, in short, a symbol of immense importance to Sukarno and the Army in maintaining their respective positions in Indonesian government and politics. Perhaps more than any other issue, it nourished their image as the vanguard of the continuing revolutionary struggle; and for the Army (and the other services), it also had the practical utility of justifying an enormous buildup of the Indonesian armed forces.[12]

In somewhat similar fashion, West New Guinea also had a role in party conflict. While all parties across the political spectrum felt obliged to support the national claim, the more extremist of them, especially the Nationalist Party (P.N.I.) and the Communist Party (P.K.I.) did so with special vigor, no doubt in order to capitalize on popular sentiment in this respect. This was an aspect of the West New Guinea problem that especially troubled Hatta:[13]

> . . . to permit West Irian to continue indefinitely as a bone of contention between Indonesia and the Netherlands is to afford Communism an opportunity to spread in Indonesia . . . By putting itself in the vanguard of those demanding realization of this national ideal, and because it agitates about West Irian as a national claim — in line with President Sukarno's standpoint — and because it backs this up by good organizational work, the Communist Party of Indo-

[10]Feith, *op. cit.*, p. 327.

[11]*Ibid.*, p. 386.

[12]*Ibid.*, p. 353.

[13]Hatta, "Indonesia Between the Power Blocs," *loc. cit.*, pp. 486-487.

nesia is able to capture the imagination of an ever-growing section of the population . . . so long as West Irian is in Dutch hands, that long will the Communist Party of Indonesia be able to carry on a violent agitation, using nationalism as an excuse, to oppose colonialism and thereby touch the soul of the newly-emancipated Indonesian people whose memories are still fresh with the struggle for freedom against colonialism.

On the other hand, West New Guinea also served to bind together the disparate elements that made up the Indonesian power structure. By the early 1960s, the relationship between Sukarno, backed by a varied constituency including preeminently the P.K.I. and to a lesser extent the P.N.I., and the Indonesian military (especially the Army) comprised a delicate balance of power already in danger of exploding into violent internecine struggle. Sukarno was well aware that dispute over the island territory was the kind of national issue that — temporarily, at least — could unite these antagonistic forces in common cause, thereby preserving his position at the pinnacle of the equipoise, and indefinitely postponing the perhaps inevitable night of the long knives.

Palmier advances the thesis that the significance of the West New Guinea issue in internal Indonesian politics should be appraised largely in the light of the historic conflict between Javanese and non-Javanese ethnic groups in Indonesia, a rivalry which he (among other historians) considers to be a principal key to understanding contemporary Indonesian politics.[14] Since independence, government had been largely in the hands of three Java-based political parties, the P.N.I. and its allies, the P.K.I.,[15] and the Nahdatul Ulama (the socalled Muslim Scholars), which "though professing very different ideologies, have been able to work together." [16] Palmier goes on to say:[17]

The division between Javanese and non-Javanese expresses itself in the attitudes to government priorities. Whilst all Indonesian parties are opposed to the foreigner, relatively speaking the non-Javanese

[14]See Leslie H. Palmier, *Indonesia and the Dutch* (London: Oxford University Press, 1962), especially pp. 153-159, 168-170.

[15]The question whether the P.K.I. should be considered a "Javanese" party has been much discussed. Van der Kroef supports Palmier's position: "Granted that the Indonesian Communist Party's following in the areas beyond Java has significantly grown in the past five years, the fact remains that its principal strength is overwhelmingly located in Java, and its national ideological appeal as well as its political strategy is oriented toward the mystiques of Sukarno's modern Javanism." Van der Kroef, "Indonesia and the Dutch," *loc. cit.*, p. 291.

[16]Palmier, *op. cit.*, p. 153. It should be noted that Palmier's book was published in 1962, several years before the attempted Communist coup of October 1965.

[17]*Ibid.*, pp. 154-155.

parties would place their emphasis on economic development; the Javanese would give the greatest urgency to ousting foreign enterprise and influence, and emphasize the need to retain the national culture, language and religion . . . These differences of political opinion are based on fundamental differences in culture . . . (which, in turn,) have been animated by a fundamental economic imbalance between the two groups.

In this context, the West New Guinea issue emerges as an important political weapon in the struggle between the Javanese and non-Javanese for control of the Indonesian inheritance. During the struggle for independence, it was the (non-Javanese) Federalists who fought hardest to save the territory, in part because its inclusion within the federal state would increase their moral and political stature *vis-à-vis* the (predominantly Javanese) Republicans. The latter were at first not inclined to be adamant on this issue, even at The Hague Round Table Conference, because of their anxiety to achieve independence before the Federalists were strong enough to challenge them for political control of an independent Indonesia. But after independence and the formation of a unitary state, the situation changed radically. As a minority within the state, the Javanese now had to justify their claim to continued political dominance. And one such means was:[18]

> . . . to emphasize the fact that it was their intransigence alone which had brought results, and therefore they alone who had the right to rule so long as the same circumstances prevailed. Of these, the most important was the presence of colonialism; and the fact put forward as evidence of it (was) Dutch control of Western New Guinea.

What emerges from this brief discussion is the conclusion that, for a variety of reasons, West New Guinea became a vital issue in Indonesian political life. Whether it should have, whether the territory was "worth it," were really irrelevant considerations, as was also the fabric of historical, ethnic, legal, and other arguments with which the Indonesians buttressed their claim as against the Dutch. The future of West New Guinea aroused strong, deepseated emotions among the Indonesian people at large, and to some extent the political elites shared, or were engulfed by, these sentiments. Perhaps more important, the dispute came to be a bread-and-butter issue with diverse utilities in the internal political struggle, and the more extremist factions were not likely to forego attempts to exploit the issue even for the most persuasive reasons of larger national interest.

[18]*Ibid.*, pp. 169-170.

Bases of the Dutch Position

Postwar Dutch policy to retain a preponderant position in Netherlands
India for the indefinite future, albeit under the guise of a new structure of
imperial "partnership," [19] was entirely comprehensible, even if it ultimately
proved historically unwise and politically untenable: an outcome which
the Dutch themselves reluctantly accepted by 1949. By contrast, the decision to hold onto West New Guinea thereafter, which the Dutch persisted in with such tenacity for more than a decade, and at such heavy cost
to their economic interests and political relations with the independent
Republic of Indonesia, seems more difficult to understand in terms of a
rational calculus of national interest. The explanation for the course chosen
must rather be sought in the psychological reaction of the Dutch to the
loss of their empire in the Indies.

An economic interpretation of Dutch policy cannot be sustained.[20] The
Dutch did not establish permanent settlements in West New Guinea until
the twentieth century; and, partly because of the extreme difficulties of
terrain, their efforts to open up the country were severely limited down to
the 1950s. As late as 1951, the entire territory was "served by only
160 miles of automobile roads, five airfields and one good harbor." [21]
Despite the more optimistic appraisals of occasional commentators,[22]
official estimates as to West New Guinea's economic potential were uniformly discouraging. So far as was then known, West New Guinea did not
have the mineral, agricultural, or human resources to sustain large-scale
economic development; and, in fact, relatively little Dutch capital was
invested in resource development, with the exception of the oilfields in
the Vogelkop Peninsula.[23] It is true that a few Dutch companies had
significant interests in the territory; but in almost every case, these companies also operated in Indonesia, where their interests were usually much
larger. There is apparently little evidence that such firms constituted a
pressure group to support Dutch retention of West New Guinea. With

[19]For a brief discussion, see Henderson, *op. cit.,* pp. 6-8; and Taylor, *op. cit.,* p.
271.

[20]An excellent analysis of the economic "value" of West New Guinea to the Dutch
may be found in Lijphart, *The Trauma of Decolonization,* pp. 39-61.

[21]Metzemaekers, *op. cit.,* p. 132.

[22]For some examples, see Lijphart, *The Trauma of Decolonization,* pp. 39-41.

[23]The Vogelkop oilfields eventually proved to be a great disappointment. Reserves
were much lower than originally forecast. Production, which never amounted to
more than an insignificant fraction of world totals, reached a peak in 1954 and
thereafter declined sharply. See *Statistical Yearbook 1960* (New York: United Nations, 1960), p. 140.

respect to government revenues and expenditures, Lijphart observes that:[24]

> During the period of Dutch sovereignty over West New Guinea, the budgets for the colony showed constant deficits, which were made up by direct grants by the Netherlands . . . Especially during the later years, Holland had to contribute about two thirds of the actual cost of running New Guinea.

Over the years, the balance of trade was also heavily unfavorable. This was not, moreover, the consequence of large imports of capital goods, which might have indicated a substantial measure of economic development; indeed, the most important import item was foodstuffs.[25]

The concept of West New Guinea as a potential outlet for Dutch overpopulation, and especially as an area for resettlement by the Eurasians of Indonesia, clearly had some impact on the formulation of official policy. Such proposals gained a limited currency during the interwar period, and were revived after World War II by a number of pressure groups, both in the Netherlands and Indonesia. In practice, however, the territory was never a magnet for Dutch colonization. While the Netherlands has felt the stress of rapid population growth in recent decades, and has experienced large-scale emigration which has been actively encouraged by the government, by and large Dutchmen simply did not go to West New Guinea as settlers.[26] Hence it is difficult to accept that the romantic notion of the territory as a tropical Holland, which was so vigorously espoused by the various Dutch colonization societies, could have had much formative influence on policy. The case of the Eurasians was somewhat more complicated. Their historical position in the socioeconomic structure of Netherlands India was always precarious, despite a degree of protection afforded by the Dutch; and their long-term prospects deteriorated sharply when Indonesian independence became inevitable.[27] In such circumstances, the development of West New Guinea as a Eurasian fatherland seemed a plausible solution to the problem of their future, despite the dismal failure of sporadic efforts at Eurasian settlement in the territory during the inter-

[24]Lijphart, *The Trauma of Decolonization*, pp. 41-42.

[25]*Ibid.*, p. 48.

[26]See John W. Dykstra, "The Population Problem of the Netherlands," *American Journal of Economics and Sociology,* vol. 17 (1958), pp. 290-294.

[27]For analyses of the Eurasian problem, see W. F. Wertheim, "The Indo-European Problem in Indonesia," *Pacific Affairs,* vol. 20, no. 3 (September 1947), pp. 290-298; Justus M. van der Kroef, "The Eurasian Minority in Indonesia," *American Sociological Review,* vol. 18 (1953), pp. 484-493; and Paul W. van der Veur, "The Eurasians of Indonesia: Castaways of Colonialism," *Pacific Affairs,* vol. 27, no. 2 (June 1954), pp. 124-137.

war period. It may be recalled that a proposal to this effect was formally tabled by Eurasian representatives as early as the Pangkalpinang conference in October 1946; and it remained a constant theme in the propaganda of Eurasian pressure groups. There is no doubt that they and their Dutch supporters exerted a considerable influence on the decision to hold onto West New Guinea.[28] But in the long term, the outcome was ironic. Except for a brief influx immediately before and after Indonesian independence, relatively few Eurasians actually chose to go there; and even fewer stayed.[29] After 1952, the Dutch government no longer cited the potential for Dutch and Eurasian settlement as a justification for its West New Guinea policy.

The extent to which strategic considerations helped to shape that policy is unclear. Historically, the Dutch looked on West New Guinea primarily as a "shield of protection against foreign intrusion on the eastern flank of the Dutch colonial empire." [30] With the loss of that empire, this perspective could no longer have had much meaning for Dutch policy. But on the larger stage of world politics, New Guinea as a whole was generally regarded during World War II as having great strategic significance, both as a buffer for Australia and as a gateway to the Indonesian and Philippine archipelagos. While strategic concepts have changed enormously in the

[28]Lijphart concludes: "(The Eurasians) were responsible for first raising the question of a special political status for West New Guinea after the Second World War. Their activities were supported by the large majority of the Eurasians and were well organized and well coordinated. They also had representatives and organizations close to the center of the Dutch government in The Hague, and had members in key administrative positions in the East Indies government. Finally, they effectively cooperated with the principal nationalistic pressure groups in the Netherlands. (On the other hand,) one cannot conclude that the Eurasian groups were the only or even the most important factor responsible for the exclusion of West New Guinea from Indonesia. After all, the Eurasians constituted only a very small group compared with the white population of Holland: not more than 2 or 3 per cent." Lijphart, *The Trauma of Decolonization,* pp. 104-105.

Metzemaekers states the case more strongly: "The idea of separating New Guinea from the rest of Indonesia probably began with the desire of many members of the Indo-European (Eurasian) community immediately after the outbreak of the Netherlands-Indonesian conflict to migrate to that island. Advocating the designation of New Guinea as a territory for Indo-European settlement, they urged that it be excluded from all negotiations on the future of Indonesia. Many Dutch politicians—particularly those opposed to any transfer of sovereignty to Indonesia—were won over by this argument and finally compelled the Netherlands government to reserve the New Guinea question for separate negotiation with Indonesia." Metzemaekers, *op. cit.,* p. 134.

[29]See van der Kroef, *The West New Guinea Dispute,* pp. 14-15; and Lijphart, *The Trauma of Decolonization,* pp. 55-56.

[30]Lijphart, *The Trauma of Decolonization,* p. 63.

postwar period, Dutch policy on West New Guinea was formulated in the late 1940s, before the full impact of nuclear weapons and postwar political alignments on military strategy had been assessed. This was also the period when the N.A.T.O. alliance was organized; and the Netherlands, as a member of N.A.T.O., properly considered itself a partner in the emerging free world coalition against the threat of Soviet expansion. There is some evidence that at the time of the 1949 Hague Round Table Conference, the United States favored Dutch retention of West New Guinea, presumably on strategic grounds.[31] Certainly Australia supported this position from 1950 onward; the Australian Minister for External Affairs, Percy (later Sir Percy) Spender, declared in March 1950 that New Guinea was "an absolutely essential link in the chain of Australian defence;" and he reiterated in June "that, for security and strategic reasons, Australia had a vital interest in the question of the future status of Dutch New Guinea." [32] More narrowly, retention of the colony would provide the

[31]For a discussion of the strategic significance of New Guinea by a leading American military analyst, see Hanson W. Baldwin, "Vital New Guinea," *The New York Times,* November 28, 1954.

The United States, represented by the veteran diplomat H. Merle Cochran, was the "disinterested" third-party member of the United Nations Commission for Indonesia at The Hague Round Table Conference. (The other two members were Australia and Belgium, designated by Indonesia and the Netherlands, respectively.) Bone comments about Cochran that "Aided by the tremendous power of the United States and his own diplomatic adroitness coupled with the great prestige he had acquired with all parties concerned, he was, to say the least, *primus inter pares* among the members of the (Commission) and a highly influential factor in the developments of the Conference." Bone, *op. cit.,* p. 48. The temporary compromise on West New Guinea reached at the Round Table Conference, which left the territory under Dutch control, originated with the Commission, and certainly had the support of the United States.

[32]Quoted in Alan Watt, *The Evolution of Australian Foreign Policy, 1938-1965* (Cambridge: Cambridge University Press, 1967), p. 252. The Australian Labor government was replaced in December 1949 by a Liberal-Country Party coalition that was much more friendly to the Dutch, and less so to the Indonesians, than its predecessor. Spender spoke for the new government. Taylor points out, however, that "Even prior to the elections (which brought in the Liberal-Country Party coalition), this writer had gained the distinct impression that the Australian Government was far from anxious for a change in the existing *status quo* in Western New Guinea." Taylor, *op. cit.,* p. 442, fn. 9. Taylor served on the staff of the United Nations Commission for Indonesia. By the time of Spender's statement in June 1950, which was made in the Australian House of Representatives, the position of the Labor Party had changed completely. Following Spender's statement, Herbert V. Evatt, on behalf of the Labor opposition, expressed his "complete agreement" with Spender's analysis of Australia's interest in the island. *London Times,* June 9, 1950.

A few years later, Spender's successor as Minister for External Affairs, Richard G. (later Lord) Casey wrote: "Its importance has been clearly demonstrated in two

Netherlands with a territorial *locus standi* in the Far East, both to influence (so it was then hoped) the course of developments in Indonesia, and to assure a Dutch voice in the affairs of Asia and the Pacific generally. But while such strategic considerations may have had some weight in the formulation of Dutch policy, it is difficult to accept that they could have been decisive.

Scholarly opinion is virtually unanimous that the critical factor has to be sought in the psychological reaction of the Dutch to the loss of the Indies. The point may be summarized briefly. Possession of the archipelago transformed the Netherlands from a small, insignificant state on the gloomy shores of the North Sea into a power with global responsibilities. Holland with Indonesia was the world's third largest colonial empire, and The Hague's voice counted for something in the counsels of the mighty. Dutchmen cherished their ancient ties with the Indies. Whether rightly or wrongly, they took pride in their supposed record as "the world's best colonial rulers;" and there was still much work to be done. They felt a strong sense of moral obligation toward the Indonesian peoples, and perceived it a positive duty to exercise a benevolent tutelage over them until some indefinite time in the future. The sentimental attachment ran especially deep: "(The Dutch) believed they had loved the Indonesians and were loved in return with a child-like devotion." [33] In economic terms, it would be difficult to exaggerate the importance of the archipelago for the Netherlands. The two economies were closely linked, and perhaps one fifth of Holland's national income was derived from the Indies. This was the last frontier, reserved for them alone, where Dutchmen could still go (or, at least, dream of going) in search of fortune and personal fulfilment.

The loss of all this was almost too much to bear, the more so for being so entirely unexpected. Dutch opinion conspicuously failed to gauge the strength of Indonesian nationalism after World War II, and for a long time could not reconcile itself to the prospect of Indonesian independence. For many it was all a wicked plot, fomented by a ragtag band of "traitors" and "Communists" who should have been crushed with ruthless decision.[34] The ensuing struggle, with its cruelties and calumnies, inflicted deep and

world wars, especially when the Japanese gravely threatened Australia by their landings in New Guinea. It is on our doorstep, and we cannot be indifferent to what becomes of it." R. G. Casey, *Friends and Neighbors, Australia and the World* (Melbourne: Cheshire, 1954), p. 102.

For a brief discussion of some Australian views on the strategic importance of New Guinea, see Mackie, "Australia and Indonesia, 1945-60," *loc. cit.,* 314-315.

[33]Mackie, "The West New Guinea Argument," *loc. cit.,* p. 29.

[34]See, for example, the volume by the rightist political leader and wartime Prime Minister P. S. Gerbrandy, *Indonesia* (London: Hutchinson, 1950).

lasting scars. Its outcome left the Dutch shocked, outraged, and frustrated. This was the psychological climate in which Dutch policy to exclude West New Guinea from Indonesia was formulated. Retention of the territory afforded both a measure of revenge against the Indonesian nationalists, and the opportunity to retrieve a fragment of vanished glory, "this last emerald from the girdle of emeralds." [35] Lijphart summarizes his exhaustive analysis of the origins of Dutch policy in these terms: [36]

> The real motives behind Holland's reluctance to decolonize were entirely subjective and psychological: the search for national self-esteem, feelings of moral superiority, egocentric altruism, and deep resentment against Indonesia. The common denominator was the sense of frustrated nationalism. To the Dutch, New Guinea became the symbol of Holland's continued national grandeur, power, and moral worth. The attachment to New Guinea was definitely pathological: it was a symptom of a serious and protracted inferiority complex, which healed only very slowly. The symbolic value of New Guinea overshadowed all other considerations.

This perhaps goes too far in discounting the sincerity and determinative influence of security motives, for example, or of Dutch concern for the fate of the Eurasians and for the political future of the Papuans of West New Guinea. On the other hand, it seems clear that such considerations would not have carried decisive weight in a realistic assessment of Dutch national interests and responsibilities in 1949 and the years thereafter. In the context of the time, these factors served more than anything else as useful pretexts or justifications for a course basically determined on other grounds.

The conclusion is surely correct that Dutch policy with respect to West New Guinea was primarily the consequence of an irrational psychological reaction to a painful and resented loss. Whatever the possible misgivings of individual statesmen in office, the Dutch government was responsive to this emotion for more than a decade. When the Round Table Conference agreements came up for ratification in the Dutch parliament late in 1949, the government had great difficulty in mustering the necessary two-thirds majority in both houses. The requisite votes were ultimately found; but this majority could never have been obtained except on the absolute precondition that West New Guinea was excluded from the transfer of

[35]Quoted in Mackie, "The West New Guinea Argument," *loc. cit.*, p. 29.
[36]Lijphart, *The Trauma of Decolonization*, p. 288.

sovereignty.[37] Precisely because the motivations were profoundly psychological, the Dutch pursued their West New Guinea policy thereafter with great tenacity and despite costs wholly incommensurate with the supposed interests at stake. Throughout the 1950s, Dutch determination to hold onto the territory was more than a match for Indonesian zeal to recover it. Here were the ingredients of intractable political conflict.

Arguments Pro and Con

In light of the foregoing analysis, the more formal geographical, ethnic, historical, legal, and other arguments advanced over the years by Indonesia and the Netherlands seem less significant, although they received a great deal of attention in the public polemics. By and large, they simply did not reflect the basic determinants of policy on either side. On balance, the Dutch had a logically more persuasive case, while the Indonesian position was rooted much more firmly in the realities of contemporary world politics.

The objective facts of physical and ethnic geography tended to support the Dutch view that West New Guinea should properly be dealt with separately from the rest of Indonesia. But the validity of the assumption underlying this position, namely, that markedly distinct ethnic groups should necessarily be organized into separate polities, is somewhat more debatable, even if one knows reasonably well where to draw the ethnic line.[38] During the course of the conflict over West New Guinea, the Indonesians sometimes argued that "racially, culturally and economically the people of West Irian are closely related to the neighboring island groups of East Indonesia;" [39] but they more often insisted that such considerations were irrelevant:[40]

[37]See *ibid.*, pp. 114-124; and Bone, *op. cit.*, pp. 50-55.
Van der Kroef comments that "by the time that the Round Table Conference met in August 1949 salvaging something of Holland's Far Eastern Empire had become something of an obsession with many Dutch politicians." Van der Kroef, *The West New Guinea Dispute*, p, 6. Kahin states: ". . . the Dutch cabinet, evidently with good reason, was convinced that if New Guinea was not retained it might be impossible to muster the necessary two-thirds vote (requisite to change the Netherlands Constitution) in both houses of Parliament to get the Hague Agreement ratified." Kahin, *Nationalism and Revolution in Indonesia*, p. 444.
[38]The principle of self-determination and its relationship to the West New Guinea dispute will be dealt with at later stages of the text.
[39]*Some Facts About West Irian* (New York: Permanent Mission of the Republic of Indonesia to the United Nations, 1957), p. 1.
[40]*Some Questions and Answers Concerning the Dispute over West Irian* (New York: Permanent Mission of the Republic of Indonesia to the United Nations, 1957), p. 8.

Even if West Irian were racially and culturally different from other parts of Indonesia, this is not a valid reason for continuing Dutch colonial rule in West Irian. As a matter of fact the population of Indonesia is composed of several ethnic groups, with varying degrees of cultural and social development.

From the Indonesian standpoint, this was undoubtedly a sounder position to take, especially in view of the country's patently diverse ethnic composition, even without West New Guinea.

Modern historical scholarship has not sustained Indonesian claims to West New Guinea based on the presumed extent of the precolonial Majapahit empire. Nor were the original pretensions of the Moluccan sultanate of Tidore to suzerainty over parts of the territory much less shadowy. For reasons of high policy, the Dutch chose to foster the aspirations of Tidore from as early as 1660, and eventually the sultanate came to be vested with a theoretical sovereignty over all of modern West New Guinea. This evolution might have provided a stronger historical basis for Indonesian claims, since Tidore was undoubtedly part of the Indonesian world, and there was never any suggestion that it be excluded from the territories of the Indonesian state. But unfortunately the sultanate never exercised effective control over West New Guinea, and everyone recognized that the formality of Tidorese sovereignty was, and always had been, a complete fiction. In any case, the Dutch had meticulously laid the basis, in various treaties with Tidore, for separating the territory from the sultanate if this should ever become desirable; and their action in July 1949 to exercise this right and bring West New Guinea under direct colonial administration was entirely proper from a constitutional point of view. The best historical argument available to the Indonesian nationalists was simply that the territory was always considered to be an integral part of Netherlands India, even by the Dutch, although it is also true that West New Guinea was often the subject of special administrative treatment during the colonial period.[41]

The main legal argument revolved around the question whether Indonesia succeeded to Dutch sovereignty over the whole of the Indies, or whether the Netherlands retained sovereignty over West New Guinea after The Hague Round Table Conference agreements came into effect. During the course of the independence struggle, the nationalist leadership tried to maintain that Dutch sovereignty had lapsed with the Japanese occupation, and that thereafter the Indonesians had achieved independence

[41]See *Western New Guinea and The Netherlands* (The Hague: Government Printing Office, 1954), pp. 12-13.

by their own efforts, and not at the hands of the Dutch.[42] The legal basis of the Round Table Conference agreements, however, was that the Dutch were thereby transferring sovereignty to Indonesia, as the title of the principal document (the Charter of Transfer of Sovereignty) indicates; and the implication was, of course, that until the effective date of the agreements, sovereignty vested in the Netherlands.[43] Accepting this much, the question was whether sovereignty over West New Guinea was included in the transfer. This, in turn, hinged on the proper interpretation to be given to Articles 1 and 2 of the Charter of Transfer of Sovereignty and to the accompanying interpretive letters. But precisely because these documents reflected a temporary compromise on an issue in grave dispute, no single interpretation of their ambiguities could hope to gain the acquiescence of both sides.

There is little point in detailing the debate. Interminable appeals were made by both sides to such landmark agreements as Linggadjati and Renville, whose terms were unhappily also open to conflicting interpretations, and to the statements of Dutch and Indonesian spokesmen over the years which presumably afforded historical support for the respective legal positions.[44] The outcome of the discussion was predictably inconclusive. But a possible indication as to which side may have had the stronger

[42]The thesis is summarized in a *Memorandum to the United Nations Committee of Good Offices,* dated January 20, 1949, in the following terms:

The historical facts are . . . that the Republic of Indonesia was not born as a result of a rebellion against the Dutch, but that it came into existence after the Dutch had completely surrendered Indonesia to the Japanese, without any shadow of a proper attempt to defend it . . .

No honest person can deny the historical truth that Indonesia paid a very high price when thousands of her sons fell in their efforts to wrest power and arms from the Japanese to enable Indonesia to achieve the independence that was proclaimed on August 17, 1945. For that independence we have paid with blood. We have not received it from the hands of the Dutch.

We cannot agree with the Dutch claims that they have a historic right to Indonesia. Their *alleged* historic right lapsed at the moment when they proved unable to discharge their responsibility towards Indonesia.

Quoted in Taylor, *op. cit.,* p. 346, fn. 39. Italics in original.

[43]For a discussion of the sovereignty question, see *ibid.,* pp. 344-355, 444-446; and van der Kroef, *The West New Guinea Dispute,* pp. 1-8.

[44]A few examples may be helpful. As early as the December 1946 conference at Denpasar, Lieutenant Governor-General Hubertus J. van Mook, declared that "it is decidedly not the intention of the Government to exclude New Guinea from Indonesia." This seemingly unequivocal statement gave much comfort to the Indonesian nationalists. But van Mook also said at that conference: "Time will be necessary to determine the wishes of the population, and furthermore, it appears—generally speaking—that it would be better not to hitch such a territory, in essence non-Indonesian, to an Indonesian State, but rather to make it into a special territory, which,

legal case is the undoubted fact that Indonesia declined to accept a Dutch proposal, made during a conference at The Hague, December 1951-February 1952, that the issue be submitted to the International Court of Justice for adjudication, on the ground that the issue was essentially political. After some initial uncertainty as to what position to take, Indonesia maintained consistently for several years that the December 1949 transfer of sovereignty applied to the whole of Netherlands India, including West New Guinea, and that the Dutch merely retained *de facto* control over the latter territory.[45] With the abrogation of the Round Table Conference agreements in April 1956, the Jakarta government reverted to the view that its sovereignty over the entire archipelago dated from August 17, 1945, the date of the original proclamation of independence.[46]

Leaving aside for the moment the relevance of the principle of self-determination to Dutch and Indonesian claims, the plain fact was that whichever country actually exercised authority over West New Guinea, the resulting relationship with the indigenous population was bound to be quasi-colonial in nature for an indefinite period into the future, because of the extreme backwardness of the Papuans. Under whose rule would the Papuans prosper more? In one respect, Indonesia had much better credentials for the task; as Mackie puts it:[47]

. . . the Indonesians are closer to the people of West New Guinea than the Dutch are in any geographical, cultural, economic or ethnographic sense—closer too in the all-pervasive factor of skin colour,

as the case may be can be united with the United States of Indonesia, the Netherlands-Indonesian Union or the Netherlands." Quoted in van der Kroef, *The West New Guinea Dispute*, pp. 2, 4.

Similar ambiguities could be found on the Indonesian side. In his Independence Day speech of August 17, 1950, only a few months after the Round Table Conference, Sukarno took the position that "Irian is also *Indonesian territory,* territory of the Republic of Indonesia—not tomorrow, not the day after tomorrow, but *now,* at this very moment. The Dutch *de facto* authority over Irian is recognized *for this year only,*" Quoted in Kahin, "Indonesian Politics and Nationalism," *loc. cit.,* p. 165. Italics in original. (This portion of Sukarno's speech was quoted in a somewhat different context on p. 23, above.) But in a statement to the Indonesian parliament on January 3, 1951, Prime Minister Mohammad Natsir stated that "any negotiations in the future can only be held on the basis of the transfer of sovereignty over Irian to Indonesia . . . and negotiation which does not result in sovereignty over Irian being transferred to Indonesia will result in the Indonesian-Dutch relations becoming more strained and tense." Quoted in Bone, *op. cit.,* p. 98.

[45]This was Sukarno's position. It was officially set forth in a memorandum to the Dutch government dated November 10, 1951. See Lijphart, *The Trauma of Decolonization,* pp. 27-28.

[46]See *ibid.,* p. 28.

[47]Mackie, "The West New Guinea Argument," *loc. cit.,* p. 41.

which in situations of political dependence has so often bedevilled the noblest intentions of the rulers.

But in practice, the Indonesians were not conspicuously successful after the 1949 transfer of sovereignty in carrying on the routine business of government within the territories of the Republic. Internal politics became increasingly chaotic, and the economy deteriorated steadily over the years. Relatively little progress was made in fostering the development of primitive peoples elsewhere in the archipelago, for example, in central Borneo.[48] Nor has the Indonesian record in West New Guinea since 1963 vindicated their claim to rule on moral grounds. On the Dutch side, their stewardship of the island down to 1949 was characterized mainly by indifference and official neglect. Thereafter a substantial effort was made to open up the country, and to foster its economic and social development. Government subsidies for these purposes were doubtless much greater than the Indonesians would have provided. In 1960, an extensive program of political development was also instituted in order to prepare the Papuan population to exercise intelligently its presumed right of self-determination in the finite future; and in the remaining few years of Dutch rule, this belated effort achieved considerable success.[49]

---

[48]See *ibid.*, p. 44; and Lijphart, *The Trauma of Decolonization*, p. 33.

[49]With respect to the moral issue, a judgment in favor of the Dutch assumes, of course, that forced modernization is a positive contribution to the long-term welfare of primitive peoples, or at least, a necessary evil in the modern world. But the case is not entirely clear. As Mackie notes:

. . . (especially if a development program cannot be sustained), the benefits to the Papuans may be outweighed by the social dislocation and uprooting of communities which had at least established some sort of harmony with their environment.

In broad terms, the entire welfare judgment hinges around one's assessment of this contrast — according to one's preference for the static security of primitive tribal societies or the expanding freedoms, insecurities and birthrates of communities in transformation. Indonesia would probably approach the problem of modernisation in the same manner as she has in Central Borneo. There she makes little effort to penetrate into the Dayak hinterland beyond the up-river towns on the fringe of the developed regions, but the administration encourages Dayaks to come down to the towns, experience the benefits of education and health services, begin to understand the ways of the wider world and then return to their villages to tell their own people and send others down. It is a slower process, but we need to consider whether that makes it substantially less beneficial than the Papuans may expect to experience under other circumstances.

Mackie, "The West New Guinea Argument," *loc. cit.*, pp. 43-44.

The Question of Self-Determination

In the later stages of the West New Guinea dispute, the relevance (if any) of the principle of self-determination, as asserted in Article 1 of the United Nations Charter and as developed in international practice, became central to the formal debate. The Dutch position was that the Papuans were a separate and distinct people, and that they had an ultimate right to determine their own political future, including the option of remaining outside the Republic of Indonesia. Dutch administration of West New Guinea was to preserve this right until such time as the autochthonous population could intelligently exercise it. This posture was consistent with Dutch policy during the years 1946-49 when, as part of their overall strategy to fragment the Indonesian nationalist movement, the Dutch fostered the concept that the various peoples of the archipelago should have the right to decide for themselves the nature of their relationship to the proposed federal Indonesian state and to the Netherlands. Such a principle was, for example, written into Articles 3 and 4 of the Linggadjati Agreement, although at the time the Dutch stated that there might be "difficulties" in applying it to West New Guinea because of the backwardness of the Papuans. At the Round Table Conference, the Dutch position was that the territory "would be administered in accordance with the United Nations Charter and advance progressively to autonomous status through education of its population and development of its economy." [50] Thereafter the Dutch came to realize that the principle of self-determination afforded the best ground on which to defend continued Dutch rule. In the increasingly anticolonial atmosphere of world politics, the assertion of this principle at least had the ring of high moral purpose. At the special ministerial conference convened at The Hague in December 1950, the Dutch maintained that they would continue to exercise sovereignty "until the right of self-determination is utilized by the population of New Guinea." [51] Following Indonesia's submission of the West New Guinea question to the United Nations General Assembly in 1954, this became the oft-reiterated core of the Dutch position.

The Indonesians rejected the view that the Papuans of West New Guinea were a separate people in a separate country. There was only one Indonesian people and nation, and the Papuans were an intrinsic part thereof. In any case, ethnic differences were not especially relevant to the question of political boundaries; the countries of Europe exhibit many examples where ethnic frontiers have been disregarded.[52] Hence the ques-

[50]Taylor, op. cit., p. 236.
[51]Quoted in ibid., p. 441.
[52]See Metzemaekers, op. cit., p. 135.

tion of self-determination for the Papuans simply did not arise. As an official publication put it:[53]

The question of self-determination is NOT an issue in the dispute over West Irian since the whole Indonesian nation, including naturally West Irian, already exercised the right of self-determination on 17 August 1945 when it threw off the chains of colonialism and proclaimed Indonesia free and independent.

Implicit in the Indonesian position was the contention that the Indonesian state had succeeded to sovereignty over all of the Dutch East Indies, either at the time of the transfer of sovereignty in 1949, or by the autonomous proclamation of independence in 1945; that both of these events necessarily embraced West New Guinea; and that the Papuans had, therefore, already given a valid expression of the right of self-determination.

The Indonesians acknowledged that the special character of West New Guinea had to be taken into account. They gave assurances at the Round Table Conference that Indonesia would administer the territory in accordance with the objectives of the United Nations Charter, and prepare it for eventual autonomy.[54] This remained a standard theme in the Indonesian argument. A much later statement, for example, declared that ". . . under the terms of the Indonesian Constitution, West Irian, like all other parts of Indonesia, will be granted broad regional autonomy." [55] But beyond this the Indonesians obviously could not go. In 1953, the Jakarta government stated flatly that it was not willing "to consult the population of West Irian as to whether it is really prepared to accept association with Indonesia." [56]

The issue was not so much whether international law recognized an abstract "right" of self-determination, to which the Papuans might have recourse. To be sure, Article 1 of the United Nations Charter speaks only of the "principle of equal rights and self-determination of peoples." But various United Nations resolutions over the years seemed to indicate, as Higgins concludes, that:[57]

. . . the great majority of states in the United Nations believe that a legal right of self-determination exists and that neither Article 2(7), nor indeed domestic constitutional issues in general, can impede the

---

[53]*Some Questions and Answers Concerning the Dispute over West Irian*, p. 5. Capitals in original.

[54]See Taylor, *op. cit.*, p. 236.

[55]*The Question of West Irian* (Jakarta: Ministry of Foreign Affairs, n. d.), p. 25.

[56]Quoted by the Dutch Foreign Minister, J. M. A. H. Luns, in a speech before the United Nations General Assembly, September 20, 1957.

[57]Rosalyn Higgins, *The Development of International Law through the Political Organs of the United Nations* (London: Oxford University Press, 1963), p. 103.

implementation of that right and United Nations jurisdiction for that purpose . . . It therefore seems inescapable that self-determination has developed into an international right.

The real question was, in whom did that right properly vest? Emerson puts the problem in these terms:[58]

> The inescapable heart of the matter is the necessity of establishing what "self" it is to which the right attaches; and it may be said at once that it is no meaningful answer to say that it is the "nation" which constitutes the self, since the make-up of the nation is likely to be precisely the point most bitterly in dispute. With whom does the prerogative rest to delimit the relevant "self," and, once this determination has been made, who within the designated community has the authority to speak for it, binding the whole?

The outcome of the West New Guinea dispute was to contribute significantly to a concept of accepted international practice in this respect.

As to what course the Papuans themselves might have chosen at the time of the Round Table Conference settlement in 1949, the evidence is unclear.[59] For most of the indigenous population, still living in or close to a Stone Age culture, the expression of meaningful political choice on an issue so complicated as self-determination would have been entirely out of the question. But a small, modernized Papuan elite had come into existence during the first postwar years, and there were also a few thousand non-Papuan Indonesians living in the territory. The Indonesian nationalist revolution had an impact on both groups, and there is no doubt that a few important members of the new Papuan elite supported the Indonesian cause.[60] It would appear, however, that pro-nationalist sentiment in this early period was largely confined to the local Indonesian population, and never became widespread among the Papuans. In any case, such manifestations were soon suppressed by the Dutch; and after 1949, articulate Papuan opinion was almost entirely pro-Dutch. But in the circumstances, the spontaneity of this orientation, and the extent to which it reflected widespread popular sentiment, were obviously suspect.

[58]Rupert Emerson, *Self-Determination Revisited in the Era of Decolonization* (Cambridge: Center for International Affairs, Harvard University, 1964), p. 27.

[59]On this subject, see Bone, *op. cit.*, pp. 40-41; van der Kroef, *The West New Guinea Dispute*, pp. 17-18; Lijphart, *The Trauma of Decolonization*, pp. 30-33; van der Veur, "Political Awakening in West New Guinea," *loc. cit.*, pp. 58-59; and Charles A. Fisher, "West New Guinea in its Regional Setting," in George W. Keeton and Georg Schwarzenberger, eds., *The Year Book of World Affairs, 1952* (London: Stevens, 1952), pp. 200-201.

[60]One of the pro-Indonesian groups, the Indonesian Independence Party Irian, had a Papuan leader, Silas Papare, although this group worked mainly among the local Indonesians.

Chapter Four

West New Guinea
As An International Issue

Ever since the struggle for independence, Indonesia has figured prominently if intermittently in the concerns of the United Nations.[1] As early as January 21, 1946, only four days after the inaugural meeting of the Security Council, the Ukrainian S.S.R. forwarded a complaint to that body alleging that British military forces in Indonesia were undertaking operations "directed against the local population," and that the resulting situation "constitute(d) a threat to the maintenance of international peace and security."[2] The Ukrainian complaint was less a reflection of genuine concern for the already embattled Indonesian nationalist movement than a tactic in the developing world struggle between the U.S.S.R. and the Western powers, which were simultaneously pressing the Soviet Union to withdraw its occupation forces from Iran. After several days of inconclusive debate, the Security Council failed to take any action in the case, although one result of the Ukrainian submission was to focus world attention on the deepening Dutch-Indonesian conflict.

Following breakdown of the Linggadjati Agreement and the first Dutch "police action" in Summer 1947, the conflict was again brought to the attention of the Security Council, which thereafter remained more or less constantly seized of the problem until after The Hague Round Table Conference and the transfer of sovereignty. Discussion in the Security Council during August 1947 led first to creation of a Consular Commission at Batavia (Jakarta), whose mission was to observe and report on developments; and later to establishment of the socalled Committee of Good Offices on the Indonesian Question, as an arm of the Security Coun-

[1]The most comprehensive analysis of United Nations involvement through 1950 is Taylor, *op. cit.* Briefer accounts may be found in Collins, *op. cit.,* and Henderson, *op. cit.* For a fairly detailed study of Indonesian submissions of the West New Guinea question to the General Assembly during the years 1954-57, see Bone, *op. cit.,* pp. 120-170.

[2]For the full text of the complaint, see Security Council, *Official Records,* First Year: First Series (1946), Supplement No. 1, Annex 4, p. 76.

cil to extend the latter's good offices in facilitating a peaceful settlement of the dispute. Negotiations under the auspices of the Good Offices Committee resulted in January 1948 in the Renville Agreement, which represented a second comprehensive effort (after Linggadjati) to find a satisfactory political basis for resolving the Dutch-Indonesian conflict. But prolonged efforts thereafter to negotiate the details necessary for implementing the Renville Agreement ultimately ended in failure.

Breakdown of the Renville truce and the second Dutch "police action" in December 1948, which together marked a major turning point in the Indonesian independence struggle, in effect constituted a repudiation by the Dutch of an agreement negotiated under United Nations auspices which the Security Council itself had approved by resolution of February 28, 1948.[3] Subsequent Security Council interventions in the dispute took on an increasingly anti-Dutch flavor, and were a decisive factor in forcing the Dutch to reverse the course of their policy in the Indies and reluctantly to accept the inevitability of Indonesian independence. In January 1949, the Security Council adopted an omnibus resolution calling for the cessation of hostilities, renewed negotiations on the basis of the Linggadjati and Renville agreements, and replacement of the Good Offices Committee by a United Nations Commission for Indonesia as "the representative of the Security Council in Indonesia" with greatly enlarged powers, including the right to initiate recommendations of its own.[4] Over the next several months, the Commission, sustained by the Security Council and supported by strong diplomatic pressures exerted unilaterally by the United States and other powers on the Netherlands, played a key role in working out a final settlement of the Dutch-Indonesian conflict, first during informal negotiations at Batavia, April-June, and then at The Hague Round Table Conference, August-November. The Commission was responsible for suggesting the temporary compromise relating to West New Guinea adopted by the parties at the Round Table Conference. In December, the General Assembly adopted a resolution commending all parties on the achievement of a settlement and welcoming the forthcoming establishment of an independent Indonesian state; while in the Security Council, the Soviet Union vetoed a draft resolution to the same effect.

Thereafter, the United Nations Commission for Indonesia continued to function, primarily to assist with the implementation of The Hague agreements, until it adjourned *sine die* in April 1951. At the special ministerial

[3]Security Council, *Documents,* Third Year (1948), S/678.

[4]Security Council, *Documents,* Fourth Year (1949), S/1234.

conference in December 1950, the Dutch proposed that negotiations on the West New Guinea question continue under the auspices of the Commission, but Indonesia rejected the offer.

West New Guinea before the United Nations

In August 1953, the moderate Wilopo government was replaced by the first cabinet of Ali Sastroamidjojo, under whose leadership Indonesia adopted a much more dynamic and assertive foreign policy. With respect to West New Guinea, repeated efforts to resolve the dispute through bilateral negotiations with the Netherlands had already ended in failure. And a year later, in mid-1954, the Dutch declined even to include the subject on the agenda of a conference called to discuss the dissolution of the Netherlands-Indonesian Union. The first Ali Sastroamidjojo government took the decision to broaden the West New Guinea dispute, which had hitherto been confined within the framework of bilateral negotiations, into a more general problem of world politics, and to seek the support of the international community, especially the Asian and African nations, for Indonesia's claim to the territory. At the same time, a variety of steps was taken to mobilize popular sentiment in support of the national campaign to recover West New Guinea.

A major element in this strategy was to bring the dispute formally to the attention of the United Nations. On August 17, 1954, Indonesia requested for the first time that the question of West New Guinea be inscribed on the agenda of the forthcoming ninth session of the General Assembly, as a "latent threat to the peace" which "should be of vital concern . . . to the world as a whole and certainly to the United Nations." [5] When the General Assembly convened that fall, the debate in the First Committee set the tone of subsequent United Nations discussions on the issue. Both sides reviewed at length the historical, ethnic, legal, and other bases of their respective claims to West New Guinea. The Indonesian representative insisted that there could be no peace in the area while this remnant of Dutch colonialism persisted; while his Dutch counterpart emphasized that the primary purpose of Dutch policy in the territory was to prepare the indigenous population for eventual self-determination, and stated also that the possibilities for further bilateral negotiations on the subject had been exhausted. Opposition to colonialism in all its forms became the main theme of delegations supporting the Indonesian position, while safeguarding the right to self-determination for the Papuans was the principal argument of those on the Dutch side.[6]

[5]GAOR, Ninth Session (1954), Annexes, A/2694.
[6]For the debate, see GAOR, Ninth Session (1954), A/C. 1/SR. 726-736.

The Indonesian delegation introduced a draft resolution calling for the resumption of bilateral negotiations, and also inviting the Secretary-General to appoint a person to render his good offices to the parties;[7] but this draft was not pressed to a vote. Instead the Committee adopted a milder draft, submitted jointly by eight member states led by India and acceptable to Indonesia, which provided, *inter alia,* that:[8]

> *The General Assembly, . . .*
>
> 1. *Expresses the hope* that the Governments of Indonesia and the Netherlands will pursue their endeavors in respect of the dispute that now exists between them to find a solution in conformity with the principles of the Charter of the United Nations;
> 2. *Requests* the parties to report progress to the General Assembly at its tenth session.

But on December 10, this draft resolution, which the Dutch construed as critical of their own position and favorable to Indonesia, failed of adoption in the General Assembly itself. The vote on the key first operative paragraph was 34 in favor, 23 against, and three abstentions, less than the two-thirds majority required. With the exception of Nationalist China, the Asian and African countries supported Indonesia, as did the Soviet bloc; while the Western countries, excepting Greece, voted against the resolution; and the Latin Americans split. The United States abstained, which reflected its determination at the time to stay aloof from an intramural quarrel between two friendly states. But the probable effect of its abstention was to sustain the status quo, since presumably a number of Latin American and other states might have voted differently if the United States had supported the resolution. For Indonesia, there was the satisfaction of having focussed world attention on the West New Guinea issue, and of having obtained a clear majority of the votes cast. But this hardly compensated for the frustration and bitterness of not securing a formal recommendation from the General Assembly for concrete steps to resolve the dispute.

The question was again on the agenda of the General Assembly at its tenth session in Fall 1955. But at this time, the moderate government of Burhanuddin Harahap, which had succeeded the first Ali Sastroamidjojo cabinet in August, was preparing for a final effort at comprehensive bilateral negotiations with the Dutch. There was a predisposition on all sides not to press the West New Guinea issue simultaneously at the United Nations, in order not to prejudice prospects for the negotiations by

[7] *GAOR,* Ninth Session (1954), Annexes, A/C. 1/L. 109.
[8] *GAOR,* Ninth Session (1954), Annexes, A/C. 1/L. 110.

a repetition of the acrimonious debate that had marked consideration of the question at the preceding session. In consequence, the First Committee was satisfied to adopt without formal vote an innocuous draft resolution expressing the hope that the negotiations would "be fruitful." [9] This draft was subsequently approved by the General Assembly on December 16, also without objection. But all to no avail; the Dutch-Indonesian negotiations ended in complete deadlock in February 1956. Shortly thereafter the Harahap cabinet fell, to be replaced by the second Ali Sastroamidjojo government, while Indonesia announced its withdrawal from the Netherlands-Indonesian Union and repudiated the principal agreements of The Hague Round Table Conference.

That fall, at the eleventh session of the General Assembly, the question appeared on the Assembly agenda for the third time. The debate in the First Committee followed a predictable course, although its tone was a good deal more embittered than two years previously.[10] A 13-member draft resolution called for more decisive action to resolve the dispute. It requested:[11]

1.   the President of the General Assembly to appoint a Good Offices Commission consisting of three members, with a view to assisting in negotiations between the Governments of Indonesia and the Netherlands in order that a just and peaceful solution of the question may be achieved, in conformity with the principles and purposes of the Charter.

2.   the Good Offices Commission to report to the General Assembly at its next regular session.

Delegations opposed to the resolution argued correctly that it implied support for the Indonesian position, which sought to transfer West New Guinea to Indonesian control without consulting the Papuan population as to their political future. The draft resolution was adopted by the First Committee, but failed in the General Assembly on February 28, 1957, by a vote of 40 to 25, with 13 abstentions, short of the necessary two-thirds majority. The Soviet bloc and the Afro-Asian countries (excepting Nationalist China, opposed, and Laos and Cambodia, abstaining) supported the resolution; the Western countries (excepting Greece) opposed it; and the Latin Americans again split. Once more the United States abstained. The vote actually represented a slight erosion of overall support for the Indonesian position. In 1954, the affirmative vote represented almost 57

[9]*GAOR*, Tenth Session (1955), Annexes, A/C. 1/L. 155.

[10]For the debate, see *GAOR*, Eleventh Session (1956-57), A/C. 1/SR. 857-863.

[11]*GAOR*, Eleventh Session (1956-57), Annexes, A/C. 1/L. 173.

percent of the votes cast, as against only 51 percent of the votes cast by a considerably enlarged membership in 1957.

The impact of this defeat at the United Nations was temporarily obscured in Indonesia by a domestic political crisis which saw the fall of the second Ali government shortly after the General Assembly vote, and the advent to power of the "extraparliamentary" cabinet of Djuanda Kartawidjaja, under which Sukarno's experiment in "guided democracy" was launched. But the Djuanda government returned promptly to the charge. On August 16, 1957, 20 other Afro-Asian countries joined Indonesia in requesting that the New Guinea question again be placed on the agenda of the General Assembly at its forthcoming twelfth session.[12] Tension over the dispute increased steadily all during 1957; and the hardening mood of the Jakarta regime was reflected in the warning issued on October 3rd by Indonesian Foreign Minister Subandrio during the General Assembly's opening debate: [13]

The only question is whether the United Nations is the place where (a) solution may be worked out, or whether we must embark upon another course, even at the risk of aggravating conditions in South-East Asia and perhaps inviting "cold war" tensions to muddy further the waters of peace in that region of the world.

Discussion in the First Committee [14] centered around a 19-power draft resolution which, reverting to the general concept proposed by Indonesia at the ninth session of the General Assembly in 1954, called upon the parties to continue their efforts to find a solution to the dispute, but also requested the Secretary-General to assist in this process as he thought appropriate and to report back to the next regular session of the General Assembly. This draft was approved by the First Committee, but fell short of the necessary two-thirds majority in the General Assembly on November 29, where the vote was 41 to 29, with 11 abstentions. A breakdown of the ballot reveals some loss of Latin American support for the Indonesian position, and a further microscopic erosion of the overall pro-Indonesian vote to just over 50 percent of the total. The United States again abstained.

Following the vote in the General Assembly, Subandrio gave an indication of his government's reaction to this latest rebuff:[15]

Up to now we have done our utmost to conduct our policy in such a way as to discourage any action which might lead to disturbances in the territory under dispute, West Irian, and its surroundings; but

[12]*GAOR*, Twelfth Session (1957), Annexes, A/3644.
[13]*GAOR*, Twelfth Session (1957), A/PV. 700.
[14]For the debate, see *GAOR,* Twelfth Session (1957), A/C. 1/SR. 905-912.
[15]*GAOR*, Twelfth Session (1957), A/PV. 724.

to maintain this policy would be an almost impossible task for any Indonesian Government now.

. . . no international problem and certainly not such a grave dispute as that between Indonesia and the Netherlands, can be isolated. In one way or another, this dispute is likely to become an issue in the over-all struggle of international power politics.

His comments seemed to hint at the use of force, and to suggest that Indonesia would now turn increasingly to the Communist countries for support in resolving the dispute. Shortly thereafter, Subandrio announced that Indonesia had brought the West New Guinea question to the United Nations for the last time.[16]

Rising Tensions, 1953-57.

Indonesian policy at the United Nations was a major element in a broad strategy to focus international attention on the West New Guinea dispute, and to mobilize domestic and foreign support for the national cause. On the home front, a steady stream of government propaganda and vituperative press commentary kept the issue alive from day to day. Great public rallies and inflammatory speeches dramatized Indonesia's demand for the lost territory. In December 1953, an Irian Bureau was established in the Prime Minister's office, "the first of a series of organizations which would be established during the next few years as the Irian campaign was increasingly accentuated." [17] The structure of an autonomous province of West Irian was created by the Indonesian parliament in August 1956; and a month later, the Sultan of Tidore was installed as its first Governor. On the international scene, President Sukarno's well-publicized visits to foreign capitals, where the West New Guinea issue was almost unfailingly raised in official statements and doubtless dwelt upon in private discussions, were another important aspect of the campaign. The conference of Asian and African countries at Bandung, April 1955, was made to serve a similar purpose.

The concept of an Asian-African conference was first advanced by Ali Sastroamidjojo at the April 1954 meeting of the socalled Colombo powers (Burma, Ceylon, India, Indonesia, Pakistan). The idea was eventually taken up by the other governments, and final plans agreed to at Bogor (Indonesia) in December of that year. The Bogor communique of the Colombo powers gave an indication of their views on several issues to be discussed at the conference, including West New Guinea: "In the context

[16]*Antara Daily Newsbulletin*, December 10, 1957.
[17]Bone, *op. cit.*, p. 122.

of their well-known attitude towards colonialism," they "supported the position of Indonesia in this matter," and "expressed the earnest hope that the Netherlands Government would reopen negotiations to implement their obligations under the solemn agreements concluded by them with Indonesia." [18] In due course, the dispute was considered at Bandung, and the position outlined at Bogor given a firm endorsement. The final communique of the conference read, in part:[19]

The Asian-African Conference, in the context of its expressed attitude on the abolition of colonialism, supported the position of Indonesia in the case of West Irian based on the relevant agreements between Indonesia and the Netherlands.

The Asian-African Conference urged the Netherlands Government to reopen negotiations as soon as possible, to implement their obligations under the above-mentioned agreements and expressed the earnest hope that the United Nations would assist the parties concerned in finding a peaceful solution to the dispute.

Such Indonesian initiatives yielded important results in mobilizing explicit diplomatic support for the national claim to West New Guinea, especially among the Asian and African nations and, independently of Bogor and Bandung, among the European Communist countries as well. While this support was not sufficient to precipitate United Nations action in the dispute at this stage, it did serve to polarize international sentiment and to dramatize West New Guinea as a major anticolonial issue with incipient Cold War overtones.

During 1957, Dutch-Indonesian tensions reached a breaking point. One of the five main points in the program of the emergency Djuanda cabinet, which took office in April, was the "return of West Irian to the jurisdiction of the Republic of Indonesia;" [20] and a West Irian Liberation Committee was promptly set up to mobilize and intensify domestic sentiment on the issue.[21] Before long, the country was swept by demands for drastic action, and a sense of impending crisis enveloped the nation. Prominent public

[18]Quoted in George McTurnan Kahin, *The Asian-African Conference* (Ithaca: Cornell University Press, 1956), p. 4.

[19]The full text of the final communique of the Asian-African Conference may be found in *ibid.,* pp. 76-85. The quoted sentences are on p. 82.

[20]Quoted in Grant, *op. cit.,* p. 157.

[21]"This Committee in particular made a name for itself with its 'protest waves' against the Dutch community in October and November 1957. The Committee was later charged by former Vice-President Hatta of having contributed to the general disruption of the Indonesian economy, and its task was subsequently taken over by the Indonesian Security Council. But there can be no doubt that such efforts amplified the militant spirit of the whole Indonesian community in regard to the Irian problem." Van der Kroef, *The West New Guinea Dispute,* p. 24.

figures called on the government to adopt a "non-peaceful" course if the dispute could not be settled amicably, and to "proceed with the confiscation of all Dutch possessions in Indonesia." [22] In October, the West Irian Liberation Committee engineered a four-day boycott of Dutch business enterprises. A key question appeared to be whether Indonesia would obtain some measure of satisfaction at the United Nations that Fall. Sukarno declared that if the current appeal to the General Assembly failed, Indonesia would "resort to methods which will startle the world." [23] At a mass rally in November, which both he and former Vice President Hatta addressed in a rare display of public unity by Indonesia's two foremost revolutionary heroes, a resolution called for the "consolidation" of national energies in support of the Indonesian delegation's efforts at the United Nations;[24] and proposals were again heard for the nationalization of Dutch properties and the expulsion of all Dutch citizens who did not contribute significantly to national reconstruction.

When it became known that Indonesia's fourth appeal to the General Assembly had, in fact, failed in the balloting on November 29, the reaction within the country was sharp and immediate. An attempt to assassinate Sukarno the following day added to the prevailing tension. On December 1, the Indonesian government announced a general strike against Dutch enterprises. This quickly set in motion a nationwide movement for the seizure of Dutch estates, plantations, banks, factories, trading concerns, shipping lines, and other businesses by Indonesian workers, often egged on by Communist militants. A few days later, the Minister of Justice announced that most of the approximately 50,000 Dutch nationals still in the country would be required to leave; and ultimately the great majority of them were forced to go. Dutch consulates throughout the country were ordered closed, although the embassy in Jakarta was not affected by this step. Beginning in mid-December, the government, in a series of sweeping decrees, itself asserted control over seized Dutch properties valued at upwards of $2 billion (although the process of formal nationalization was delayed for more than a year), and in the following months moved systematically to sever almost every remaining economic tie with the Netherlands.[25]

[22]Quoted in *ibid.,* p. 24.

[23]Quoted in *The New York Times,* November 8, 1957. Foreign Minister Subandrio issued a similar warning at the United Nations.

[24]Quoted in van der Kroef, *The West New Guinea Dispute,* p. 26. Hatta resigned as Vice President on December 1, 1956.

[25]For accounts of the takeover of Dutch properties and the expulsion of Dutch nationals, see Palmier, *op. cit.,* pp. 102-110; and Justus M. van der Kroef, "Disunited Indonesia," *Far Eastern Survey,* vol. 27, no. 4 (April 1958), pp. 49-63; and "Decolonization in Indonesia," *United Asia* (February 1958), pp. 13-17.

It should be pointed out that, while the seizure of Dutch possessions was touched off in December 1957 by the failure of the United Nations General Assembly to act in the West New Guinea dispute, there were other causative factors at work. In general, the privileged economic position of the Dutch in Indonesia after the 1949 Hague Round Table Conference settlement was an anachronism that could not survive indefinitely in the increasingly nationalistic and anticolonial atmosphere of postindependence Indonesia. The real questions were when and how the inevitable adjustments would be made. From another point of view, the Jakarta government, anticipating the outbreak of a regionalist civil war,[26] probably instigated the measures against the Dutch in part, at least, to assure the backing of the more nationalistic segments of the Indonesian population, and also of the armed forces (which were assigned responsibility for managing most of the sequestered properties), in the coming crisis.[27]

The immediate result of these measures was economic chaos, which Sukarno justified on the ground that the campaign for West New Guinea "had to be fought in Indonesia" and not elsewhere.[28] Perhaps for the first time, the outside world had some measure of the extremes to which Indonesia might go in its determination to recover the lost territory. The Dutch were appalled by the severity and violence of what happened. A first reaction was to appeal to a forthcoming N.A.T.O. Heads of Government meeting for support in the crisis;[29] and in due course, the Netherlands' allies registered their "concern" over these developments.[30] Later in December, The Hague directed a letter to the Secretary-General of the United Nations, Dag Hammarskjold, protesting the Indonesian measures.[31] In its response to this protest, delivered to the United Nations in mid-January 1958, the Jakarta government vigorously defended the steps taken.[32] The Dutch Prime Minister, Willem Drees, was reported to favor the reactivization of the United Nations Commission for Indonesia, which

---

[26]See pp. 59-60, below.

[27]On the latter point, see Palmier, *op. cit.*, p. 164; and Feith, *op. cit.*, p. 321.

[28]Quoted in Palmier, *op. cit.*, p. 106.

[29]See *The New York Times*, December 7, 1957.

[30]The Declaration and Communique issued December 19, 1957, stated: "In the course of our review of the international situation we gave consideration to recent serious events in Indonesia. We view them with concern." *Department of State Bulletin*, vol. 38, no. 967 (January 6, 1958), p. 13.

[31]See *The New York Times*, December 24, 1957.

[32]See *ibid.*, January 14, 1958. The full text of the Indonesian reply may be found in *Letter Addressed to the Secretary-General of the United Nations from H. E. Dr. Ali Sastroamidjojo, Permanent Representative of Indonesia to the United Nations, January 13, 1958* (New York: Permanent Mission of the Republic of Indonesia to the United Nations, 1958).

was still technically in existence, to deal with the situation; but the Indonesian Foreign Ministry opposed this on the ground that the membership of the Commission (Australia, Belgium, and the United States) was now weighted in favor of the Netherlands.[33] As it turned out, the Secretary-General took no substantive action in the matter.

In time, the sense of crisis subsided. If the Indonesians anticipated that measures of economic retaliation would induce The Hague to modify its West New Guinea policy at this stage, they were sorely disappointed. The Dutch government stood firm, even though Jakarta made clear that the question of possible compensation hinged on a policy shift.[34] As if to underline their determination despite the huge economic losses sustained, the Dutch dispatched two destroyers to West New Guinea to reinforce their military dispositions in the territory.[35]

[33]See The New York Times, January 10, 1958.

[34]See London Times, January 9, 1958, reporting a statement by the Indonesian Ambassador to Australia, Dr. Helmi, in Canberra to the effect that Indonesia "would not consider compensating Dutch businesses whose assets had been appropriated until the Netherlands Government agreed to discuss the sovereignty of West New Guinea." This was reiterated a year later in a Foreign Ministry declaration that (according to The New York Times) "Indonesia will pay compensation for nationalized Dutch-owned enterprises only after she and the Netherlands settle all their outstanding problems, including the controversy over Netherlands New Guinea." See ibid., February 18, 1959.

[35]See The New York Times, December 8, 1957; and Palmier, op. cit., p. 105.

Chapter Five

Confrontation

The events of late 1957 marked a major turning point in the Indonesian struggle for West New Guinea. As an instrument for facilitating recovery of the lost territory by peaceful means, the United Nations had been tried and found wanting. Henceforth Indonesia would rely increasingly upon its own strength and resources to impose a solution on the Dutch. There was no thought of abandoning the quest. "We will continue fighting," declared Sukarno in his New Year's Day speech of January 1, 1958, until West New Guinea was taken.[1] The drastic economic reprisals initiated in December were an earnest of things to come.

For a season, the campaign for West New Guinea had to give way to overwhelming problems of domestic politics. In February 1958, the smoldering discontent of regional leaders (especially military commanders) in Sumatra and Celebes with the policies of the Jakarta regime erupted into a series of rebellions and the proclamation of a Revolutionary Government of the Republic of Indonesia at Padang (Sumatra). The disastrous economic consequences of the seizure of Dutch possessions were an important factor in aggravating the regionalist dissidence. To the surprise of many observers, the central government proved equal to this challenge. The bulk of the armed forces remained loyal to Jakarta, and moved with dispatch to suppress these revolts. Padang was captured in April, almost without a fight. Bukittinggi, the last rebel stronghold in Sumatra, fell a few weeks later. Much harder fighting took place in North Celebes during June and July, but ultimately the regionalists were driven from every major town. By the end of 1958, the back of the rebellions had been broken. Although guerrilla activity continued in both Sumatra and Celebes for three more years, it never again constituted a serious threat to the central government.[2] Throughout this period, a major preoccupation of Indonesian diplomacy was to counter the efforts of rebel agents to generate

[1]Quoted in *The New York Times,* January 2, 1958.
[2]For brief accounts of these rebellions, see Feith, *op. cit.,* pp. 318-322, 344-347; and Palmier, *op. cit.,* pp. 160-167.

political support overseas and to obtain military supplies for their cause.[3]

Even during this period, the West New Guinea issue remained a symbol of unity that transcended the civil conflict. Thus the revolutionary council of Central Sumatra placed the recovery of the lost territory at the head of its list of political demands. The Jakarta government made adroit use of the issue against the regionalists in asserting that national unity and a strong central government were essential if the national claim were to be successfully prosecuted.[4] In both cases, such tactics were significant as indicating the extent to which West New Guinea had become a subject which aroused, or was thought to arouse, the passions of the political public despite the preoccupations of a tumultuous internal political crisis.

In its struggle with the regionalists, the policy of the central government was to "create a 'momentum' of national power" against the rebels.[5] In part, this involved the further undermining of parliamentary democracy, which had long been under attack as unsuited to Indonesia's political requirements, and the emergence of an authoritarian regime (with power shared by Sukarno and his supporters, and the Army) under the style of "guided democracy," which presumably could mobilize the power and resources of the state more effectively in the campaign against the dissidents. By the end of 1958, with victory over the regionalists assured, "Constitutional democracy was clearly a thing of the past;"[6] and a capstone was placed on this evolution in July 1959, when Sukarno dissolved the constituent assembly elected in 1955 and decreed the restoration of Indonesia's 1945 constitution (which provided for a strong President not responsible to parliament). Thereafter the "momentum of national power" was turned increasingly against the Dutch. Foreign Minister Subandrio reiterated that Indonesia would not again take its case to the General Assembly, but instead would prosecute a relentless "contest of power" with the Netherlands, "as was the case during the struggle between 1945 and 1950." [7] The Dutch would be challenged by a "confrontation" of power "in all fields;" and Subandrio forecast that "a time will come that the Dutch, whether they like it or not, will cede West Irian to us." [8]

As it evolved with respect to West New Guinea, confrontation was essentially a protracted war of nerves to undermine the determination of the Dutch. Every available instrument of political and economic pressure

[3]See Feith, *op. cit.*, p. 351.

[4]See *Manchester Guardian Weekly,* February 13, 1958.

[5]Justus M. van der Kroef, "The West New Guinea Settlement," *Orbis,* vol. 7, no. 1 (Spring 1963), p. 125.

[6]Feith, *op. cit.*, p. 322.

[7]*Antara Daily Newsbulletin,* August 4, 1959.

[8]Quoted in van der Kroef, "The West New Guinea Settlement," *loc. cit.*, p. 125.

was brought to bear in this campaign, which the Indonesians conducted with great skill and pertinacity. Apart from harassing the Dutch, a primary objective was to generate a sense of crisis and impending conflict, and thereby to transform the controversy into a major international problem. Sufficient international support might be mustered over the years to compel the Dutch to negotiations and an eventual capitulation to Indonesia's claim. In the early stages, there was apparently no detailed strategic plan for the implementation of confrontation, and still less a rigorous timetable. The conception was rather to exert pressure "in all fields" as opportunity afforded, and then to wait upon events. In time, the Indonesians carried out a comprehensive buildup of their armed forces, largely with Soviet assistance, and the threat of military invasion became a principal psychological weapon against the Dutch. But except for small harrying operations having more symbolic than practical military significance, confrontation always relied primarily on nonviolent techniques of political conflict. One can only speculate as to whether Indonesia would ultimately have launched an all-out attack against West New Guinea. As it turned out, the Dutch gave way and yielded control of the territory before the situation got completely out of hand. But until the final capitulation, there was always the danger that miscalculation or recklessness might have precipitated a major conflict.

The Diplomacy of Confrontation

This was a period of intense diplomatic activity, as Jakarta sought to move the West New Guinea dispute to the forefront of world attention, to isolate the Dutch diplomatically, and to consolidate international support for the Indonesian case, especially among the Afro-Asian and Communist countries.[9] Sukarno, Subandrio, and other leading government figures roamed the world, expounding Indonesia's position in the controversy, and soliciting military and economic assistance from all sides. In a notable speech before the fifteenth session of the United Nations General Assembly in Fall 1960, which was attended by so many of the world's political leaders, including Khrushchev, Nasser, and Nehru, the Indonesian President dramatically appealed for a peaceful settlement of the dispute, but warned that if the Dutch "fail correctly to estimate the current of history,

---

[9]". . . probably the biggest single focus of diplomatic activity in the post-1958 period, and particularly since early 1960, has been the struggle for West Irian." Feith, *op. cit.*, p.. 351.

we are not to blame." [10] And he returned to this theme again at the Belgrade Conference of Non-Aligned Countries in September 1961, where he played a leading role. The final declaration of the conference demanded "the immediate termination of all colonial occupation . . . in Asia and Africa," although there was no specific reference to West New Guinea.[11]

Innumerable visitors, including chiefs of state and heads of government, were invited to Jakarta, and wherever possible a ringing declaration in support of the national claim made public. In January 1960, for example, the Prime Minister of Singapore, Lee Kuan Yew, subscribed to a joint statement with Djuanda which asserted that Singapore "fully supports the Indonesian struggle for the return of West New Guinea into the territorial jurisdiction of the Republic of Indonesia." [12] Following the highly publicized visit of Nikita Khrushchev a month later, the inevitable joint communique declared that "the Government of the U.S.S.R. fully supports the right and claim of the Republic of Indonesia with regard to West Irian." [13] And on April 1, 1961, the Foreign Minister of Communist China signed a friendship agreement in Jakarta backing the Indonesian position.[14]

Diplomatic relations between Indonesia and the Netherlands were a major casualty of confrontation policy. Despite the drastic economic measures taken by the Jakarta government in December 1957, and the enforced closing of Dutch consulates throughout the country, official contacts were nevertheless maintained at embassy level for more than two years thereafter. The end finally came in 1960. During the Spring of that year, The Hague made public a bold new program to speed the political development of West New Guinea, and also announced a series of measures to strengthen the defenses of the territory, including the assignment of jet fighters and dispatch of the aircraft carrier *Karel Doorman,* with escort vessels, on a mission to "show the flag" in eastern waters. These steps caused a furor in Indonesia. A spokesman for the Front for the Liberation

[10]*GAOR,* Fifteenth Session (1960), A/PV. 880. In December 1960, the Indonesian Foreign Ministry addressed a letter to the Secretary-General of the United Nations warning that Dutch intransigence over West New Guinea constituted a threat to world peace, and that Indonesia would be obliged to adopt "more energetic measures to cope with the situation." Quoted in Howard Palfrey Jones, *Indonesia: The Possible Dream* (New York: Harcourt Brace Jovanovich, 1971), p. 191.

[11]The full text of the final declaration of the Belgrade Conference of Non-Aligned Countries may be found in *Documents on International Affairs, 1961* (London: Oxford University Press, 1965), pp. 621-629.

[12]Quoted in *London Times,* February 2, 1960. At the time, Singapore was not yet independent. The British government was much embarrassed by the episode, and felt it necessary specifically to disavow Lee's statement. See *ibid.*

[13]Quoted in *Information on Indonesia,* March 10, 1960.

[14]See Jones, *op. cit.,* p. 193.

of West Irian (one of many organizations set up over the years to mobilize popular sentiment on the issue), for example, denounced the decision to send the *Karel Doorman* as an "act of war;" [15] and the Indonesian Army called on the North Atlantic Treaty Organization to restrain the Netherlands from implementing its military plans for West New Guinea.[16] Early in May, Jakarta warned the Dutch that they were "playing with fire" if they carried out this "projected military challenge;" [17] and a few days later, hundreds of Indonesian students stormed the Dutch embassy compound, causing considerable damage before the authorities intervened.

In August, during his annual Independence Day speech, Sukarno announced the severance of formal diplomatic relations with the Netherlands. He excoriated the Dutch for becoming "increasingly stubborn," and promised that Indonesia "will intensify her policy of formation of power and the use of power" against the Dutch to "liberate West Irian." [18] For some months thereafter, the British embassy represented Dutch interests in Indonesia, and the United Arab Republic performed a similar role on behalf of Indonesian interests in the Netherlands. But even this tenuous tie was broken in March 1961, when Jakarta requested both governments to terminate this representational function immediately. "Indonesia wants no more dealings with the Dutch," a spokesman for the Foreign Ministry explained.[19]

The Australian Position

An important objective of Indonesian policy during this period was to soften Australia's posture with respect to the disputed territory, as part of a general strategy for isolating the Netherlands in the international arena. A brief examination of this record may serve to illustrate the purposes and tactics of confrontation diplomacy.[20]

[15]Quoted in *London Times*, April 28, 1960.
[16]See *The New York Times*, April 29, 1960.
[17]Quoted in *ibid.*, May 7, 1960.
[18]Quoted in *ibid.*, August 17, 1960.
[19]Quoted in *ibid.*, March 11, 1961.
[20]For discussions of Australian policy with respect to West New Guinea, see Mackie, "Australia and Indonesia, 1945-60," *loc. cit.*, pp. 272-273, 302-319; Gordon Greenwood, "Australian Foreign Policy in Action," in Gordon Greenwood and Norman Harper, eds., *Australia in World Affairs 1961-1965* (Melbourne: Cheshire, 1968), pp. 86-94; T. B. Millar, "Australian Defence, 1945-1965," in *ibid.*, pp. 278-283; Norman Harper, "Australia and the United States (with special reference to South-East Asia)," in *ibid.*, pp. 319-328, 333-337; Watt, *op. cit.*, pp. 248-264; Henry S. Albinski, "Australia and the Dutch New Guinea Dispute," *International Journal*, vol. 16, no. 4 (Autumn 1961), pp. 358-382; and Amry and Mary Belle Vandenbosch, *Australia Faces Southeast Asia* (Lexington: University of Kentucky Press, 1967), pp. 40-77.

After taking office in December 1949, the Liberal-Country Party coalition of Prime Minister Robert G. Menzies significantly modified the pro-Indonesian policy of its Labor predecessor. While naturally desirous of maintaining friendly relations with Australia's closest neighbor in the "Near North," the Menzies government was strongly opposed to the transfer of West New Guinea to Indonesian control. Grant summarizes the rationale of this posture in the following terms:[21]

> The government's view, which had the official support of the Labor party, was put by Mr. Spender on several occasions throughout 1950. These reasons, in varying emphasis, were to dominate Australian thinking on this issue during the next decade. First was the fear that if Indonesia were given West New Guinea 'it would be but a matter of time . . . when the claim will be pushed farther so as to include the Trust Territory of Australian New Guinea and its people'. Second was the determination to keep communism, which was believed to be rising in Asia as shown by the war in Korea, from gaining a foothold among the New Guinea people. Third was the belief that New Guinea was 'an absolutely essential link in the chain of Australian defence'. Self-determination, which became a frequently used argument later, was not popular at this stage.

In his statement of June 1950 (to which reference has already been made), Percy Spender, who was the Minister for External Affairs, also staked out a claim to be consulted on any proposed arrangement which would alter the status of the territory. "In the future of Western New Guinea," he said, "Australia has direct and vital interests, and feels strongly that those interests are entitled to be considered." [22]

This policy line, which undoubtedly had the overwhelming endorsement of the Australian public, was rigidly adhered to by Spender's successor, Richard G. Casey. Speaking in February 1952, Casey declared that "Australia recognizes Dutch sovereignty over Dutch New Guinea and agrees with the Dutch that their sovereignty should be continued . . . Indonesia has no real claim to the territory." [23] Two years later, the leader of the opposition Labor Party, Herbert V. Evatt, stated that he "agree(d) with (Mr. Casey) that sovereignty over Dutch New Guinea without doubt resides in the Netherlands. Nothing has taken that sovereignty away . . . The defense of New Guinea . . . is integral with the defense of Aus-

[21]Grant, op. cit., p. 156.

[22]Quoted in Watt, op. cit., p. 252.

[23]Quoted in Norman Harper and David Sissons, Australia and the United Nations (New York: Manhattan Publishing Company, 1959), p. 314.

tralia." [24] While Casey would have preferred to put the question in diplomatic "cold storage," [25] Indonesian policy made this impossible. Throughout the 1950s, Australia struggled to carry water on both shoulders; but when necessary, Canberra gave strong public and diplomatic support to Dutch position, especially in debates at the United Nations.

To some extent, the two powers also cooperated informally in the administration of the island. In November 1957, just prior to consideration of the West New Guinea question at the twelfth session of the General Assembly, Canberra and The Hague issued a joint statement which looked to the development of progressively closer bonds among the various New Guinea territories until such time as the inhabitants could intelligently exercise the right of self-determination;[26] and thereafter, several conferences were held to consider problems of administrative cooperation. A possible long-term outcome of such cooperation was the evolution of a self-governing Papua uniting East and West New Guinea, and perhaps other adjacent territories as well; the concept of an eventual Melanesian union independent of Indonesia had a considerable currency at this time.[27] But as it turned out, little came of all this beyond regular exchanges of information. Writing in late 1959, an Australian observer commented that the two countries were "getting nowhere together, because Australia remains anxiously sitting on the fence . . . (Canberra) talks vaguely about

[24]Quoted in *ibid.*, p. 314.

[25]See Watt, *op. cit.*, pp. 252-253.

[26]The statement read, in part, as follows:

The Territories of Netherlands New Guinea, the Australian Trust Territory of New Guinea, and Papua are geographically and ethnologically related and the future development of their respective populations must benefit from co-operation in policy and administration.

The Australian and Netherlands Governments are therefore pursuing, and will continue to pursue, policies directed toward the political, economic, social and educational advancement of the peoples of their territories in a manner which recognizes this ethnological and geographical affinity.

At the same time, the two Governments will continue, and strengthen, the co-operation at present existing between their respective administrations in the Territories.

In doing so the two Governments are determined to promote an uninterrupted development of this process until such time as the inhabitants of the Territories concerned will be in a position to determine their own future.

Quoted in Palmier, *op. cit.*, pp. 99-100.

[27]On this concept, see John Andrews, "New Guinea and Nauru," in Greenwood and Harper, eds., *op. cit.*, pp. 275-377; Palmier, *op. cit.*, p. 126; Justus M. van der Kroef, "West New Guinea in the Crucible," *Political Science Quarterly*, vol. 75, no. 4 (December 1960), p. 520; and, for comments in the Dutch parliament in April 1960 by T. H. Bot, the Secretary of State responsible for West New Guinea affairs, *The New York Times*, April 6, 1960.

'cooperation,' 'mutual understanding,' and 'good will,' but that is all." [28] By the closing years of the decade, it was clearly an objective of Dutch policy to coordinate the political development of West New Guinea with the Australian half of the island. But an increasing Dutch emphasis on accelerating the process, and the crash program announced in April 1960,[29] gave rise to serious misgivings in Canberra, which contemplated a much slower tempo of development for the Australian territories.[30] A desire to avoid antagonizing Indonesia through too close cooperation with the Dutch may also have been a factor in Australia's hesitancy to push this line of policy.[31]

The November 1957 statement deeply offended the Indonesians. It was condemned as an attempt to prejudice world opinion just prior to General Assembly consideration of the West New Guinea question, and there was speculation in Jakarta as to whether this step foreshadowed a military alliance between Australia and the Netherlands for the defense of their respective territories.[32] Subandrio warned in the United Nations that if his government "were to conclude that such an alliance did in fact exist and threatened its national security, it would have to adjust itself to the exigencies of the new situation." [33] When the General Assembly failed to take action on the dispute at this session, Subandrio inveighed against "the incomprehensible attitude of the Australian Government on the problem of West Irian," and pointed out that "Either in terms of defence or economics, Indonesia as a whole is far more important for Australia than the territory of West Irian alone." [34]

Australian relations with Indonesia reached a low point during 1958. After proclamation of the Revolutionary Government of the Republic of Indonesia at Padang in February, Canberra adopted an official policy of nonintervention in the rebellions, but made little effort to disguise its sympathy for the rebel cause. Its failure left the Australians in an awkward position, and also gave rise to lively fears that Jakarta would next proceed to an invasion of West New Guinea. Indonesian spokesmen were already alternating threats of military action to "recover" the territory with pledges to abstain from the use of force, in a pattern that continued

[28]Stuart Inder, quoted in van der Kroef, "West New Guinea in the Crucible," *loc. cit.*, p. 532, fn. 25.

[29]See pp. 94 ff., below.

[30]See Mackie, "Australia and Indonesia, 1945-60." *loc. cit.*, pp. 309-310.

[31]See Palmier, *op. cit.*, p. 126.

[32]See Vandenbosch, *op. cit.*, pp. 49-50.

[33]*GAOR,* Twelfth Session (1957), First Committee, A/C. 1/SR. 905.

[34]*GAOR,* Twelfth Session (1957), A/PV. 724.

until final settlement of the dispute in 1962.[35] There was an urgent need to mend fences, and a real effort was made in this respect during the course of 1959.

In February 1959, the Indonesian Foreign Minister, Subandrio, visited Canberra at the invitation of the Australian government. During the course of discussions, he traded assurances against the use of force in West New Guinea for an apparent concession from the Australian side which seemed to suggest some slight movement away from Canberra's previous position that the territory remain under Dutch control. This understanding was couched in the following phrases of a joint communique:[36]

> There was a full explanation of the considerations which have led each country to a different view over west New Guinea (West Irian), with Australia recognizing Netherlands sovereignty and recognizing the principle of self-determination. This difference remains, but the position was clarified by an explanation from Australian Ministers that it followed from their position of respect for agreements on the rights of sovereignty that if any agreement were reached between the Netherlands and Indonesia as parties principal, arrived at by peaceful processes and in accordance with internationally accepted principles, Australia would not oppose such an agreement.

> The Ministers indicated that they believed the issue between the Netherlands and Indonesia over Western New Guinea (West Irian) was one to be resolved by peaceful means, and that they were in accord with the view that force should not be used by the parties concerned in the settlement of territorial differences.

Apart from Canberra's explicit acknowledgement that it would accept a settlement arrived at by peaceful processes, the statement also reflected the increased emphasis that the Australians were now placing on the argument of self-determination for the Papuans (as were the Dutch). Nor was any mention made of Australia's earlier insistence that it be consulted on any proposal to change the status of the territory.

Probably Canberra reasoned that since negotiations between Indonesia and the Netherlands were unlikely to be successful, if indeed they took place at all, relatively little had been given away. Nevertheless the statement caused a storm in Australia as an unwarranted shift in policy and even as a sellout of the Papuans, which indicated the depth of public sentiment on the West New Guinea issue. Menzies emphatically denied

[35]See Mackie, "Australia and Indonesia, 1945-60," *loc. cit.*, p. 303.
[36]Quoted in *ibid.*, p. 305.

that any change was implied, or that Canberra now intended to urge negotiations on the Dutch. He added:[37]

> . . . for us to urge the Dutch to negotiate would be to take up a
> position that we desire to see the sovereignty changed. This would
> be a clear reversal of our position and we will not do it. We will
> therefore not advocate a negotiation.

Whatever Canberra's real intention, public reaction to the statement apparently shook the government and stifled any further initiative to modify
Australian policy on West New Guinea,[38] and thus to bring about a
rapprochement with the Indonesians. In August, Menzies commented
publicly that he looked forward to self-government for the whole of New
Guinea. To this, Subandrio retorted sharply that "we expect Australia to
conduct a 'hands off' policy" with respect to the territory.[39] When the
Australian Prime Minister visited Jakarta in December, little was accomplished beyond a reaffirmation of known positions, although Menzies extracted from Sukarno a renewed assurance that "Indonesia had no intention of settling the West New Guinea dispute by force but by peaceful
means." [40]

For more than a year thereafter, relations between Canberra and
Jakarta remained relatively tranquil, while the tempo of Indonesia's confrontation policy against the Dutch quickened to menacing proportions,
and the prospect of large-scale hostilities became increasingly real.[41] In
April 1961, General Nasution, now Indonesian Minister of Defense as
well as Army Chief of Staff, visited Canberra to press for a more precise
definition, and if possible a modification, of Australia's position in the
controversy. Indian and Pakistani officials had recently advised the Indonesian government that "the hard core of Commonwealth resistance" to
Indonesian aims with respect to West New Guinea came from Australia.[42]
Jakarta's assessment apparently was that Canberra's support was a major
factor in sustaining Dutch determination to resist a settlement acceptable
to the Indonesians; and that if Australia could be persuaded to adopt a
more neutral posture similar to that of the United States, the Dutch would
have to yield.[43] Nasution gave assurances that Indonesia would not be the

---

[37]Quoted in *ibid.*, p. 307.
[38]See Watt, *op. cit.*, p. 254.
[39]Quoted in *London Times,* August 5, 1959.
[40]Quoted in *ibid.*, December 7, 1959.
[41]See pp. 109 ff., below.
[42]Grant, *op. cit.*, p. 160. President Ayub Khan visited Indonesia in December
1960, and General Nasution was in New Delhi a month later.
[43]See Vandenbosch, *op. cit.*, pp. 63-64.

first to use force in the territory,[44] but warned that armed incidents were likely to occur as a result of increased patrolling activity.[45] He urged that Australia "should be strictly neutral in the dispute and the discussions between Indonesia and Holland and should not encourage and support the Dutch generally or in the United Nations." [46]

Menzies stood firm, but with a significant change of emphasis. The Australian Prime Minister reiterated that his country recognized Dutch sovereignty over West New Guinea, and approved of the policy of ultimate self-determination for the Papuans; and he cautioned against the consequences of armed conflict in the area. But while Canberra would not exert pressure on The Hague to accept a settlement that did not safeguard the right of self-determination for the local population, Australia would respect any settlement freely reached between Indonesia and the Netherlands, including a decision of the International Court of Justice.[47] Menzies also emphasized that although Australia was an obviously interested neighbor, it was "neither a party principal nor a self-appointed arbitrator;" [48] and he gave categorical assurances that Australia had no military arrangement with the Dutch affecting West New Guinea.[49] From all this, it was clear that Australia still strongly supported the Dutch position, and the principle of self-determination as the basis of an ultimate solution. But Canberra must have realized that it lacked the power to impose its policy without the backing of powerful friends including the United States; and the Australians were apparently beginning to reconcile themselves to the possibility of a settlement contrary to the declared objectives of their diplomacy.

From the Indonesian point of view, this was something; but it was not neutrality, and it could scarcely have satisfied Jakarta. In mid-1961, Indonesian officials were reportedly criticizing Australia for having become "tougher" than the Dutch.[50] In fact, Canberra did not alter its basic objective of keeping West New Guinea out of Indonesian hands until the pressures of confrontation, shifts in Dutch policy, and the joint intervention of the United States and the United Nations made settlement along these lines inevitable.

[44]See *London Times,* April 27, 1961.
[45]See Palmier, *op. cit.,* p. 132; and Mackie, "Australia and Indonesia, 1945-60," *loc. cit.,* p. 312.
[46]Vandenbosch, *op. cit.,* p. 62.
[47]See Harper, "Australia and the United States (with special reference to South-East Asia)," *loc. cit.,* pp. 320-321.
[48]Quoted in Greenwood, "Australian Foreign Policy in Action," *loc. cit.,* p. 89.
[49]See *ibid.,* p. 89.
[50]See Grant, *op. cit.,* pp. 160-161.

Malaya Attempts to Mediate

In the closing months of 1960, the Prime Minister of Malaya, Tengku Abdul Rahman, attempted to mediate between Indonesia and the Netherlands in an effort to revive negotiations between the two antagonists in the steadily worsening dispute over West New Guinea.[51] Basing his initiative on conversations with the Dutch earlier that year, which he interpreted as indicating that The Hague might now be prepared to transfer authority over the territory to a United Nations trusteeship, Rahman sought to take advantage of this apparent shift in Dutch policy to devise an approach to settlement that might prove acceptable to both sides.

The essence of his plan was "to transfer West Irian to the United Nations as a trust territory with the purpose of an eventual transfer of the territory directly to the Republic of Indonesia" after a specified period of time.[52] Rahman recognized that the Dutch would not agree to hand over West New Guinea directly to the Indonesians. But he reasoned that, once the territory were placed under United Nations control, the Netherlands would thereafter be disinclined to argue about, or unable to prevent, its subsequent transfer to Indonesia. The initial transfer from Dutch to United Nations control would, in any case, be on the understanding that West New Guinea was to be turned over to Indonesia in due course. While in trusteeship status, the territory would be administered directly by the world organization, or alternatively by a consortium of several powers designated by the United Nations.[53] Rahman apparently thought that the Dutch would now accept a plan that did little more than save face in providing for a staged transfer of West New Guinea to Indonesian control.

His plan was submitted formally to the Jakarta government in mid-September, and accepted by Djuanda later that month in his capacity as Acting President (in the absence of Sukarno, who was out of the country), subject to the conditions that the sole purpose of the trusteeship was to prepare for the transfer of West New Guinea to Indonesian control, that the period of trusteeship would not exceed one year, and that thereafter the territory would be turned over to Indonesia unconditionally. In Octo-

[51]For the official Malayan account of Rahman's mediation, see *Malaya/Indonesia Relations, 31st August, 1957 to 15th September, 1963* (Kuala Lumpur: Government Printing Office, 1963), pp. 7-11; Appendix VII, "Prime Minister's Offer to Mediate in West Irian Issue," pp. 53-55; Appendix VIII, "Indonesia's Acceptance of Prime Minister's Offer to Mediate in West Irian Issue," pp. 56-58; Appendix IX, "Prime Minister's Report on his Efforts at Mediating in West Irian Dispute," pp. 59-62; and Appendix X, "President Sukarno's Reply to Prime Minister's Report," pp. 39-41. The appendices are in Malay. (Hereafter cited as *Malaya/Indonesia Relations.*)
[52]*Ibid.,* p. 8.
[53]See *ibid.,* pp. 53-54.

ber, General Nasution visited Kuala Lumpur at Rahman's invitation. Shortly thereafter, Nasution "publicly welcomed the Tengku's offer to mediate, provided it met Indonesia's conditions for a settlement;" [54] while Rahman described their discussion as "very encouraging," and added "It is obvious from (Nasution's) attitude that the Indonesians want to seek a peaceful settlement of this very vexing problem." [55]

The Australians were consulted at an early stage, and Canberra reiterated its standard view that "the future of the territory should be determined by the freely expressed will of the inhabitants and that any decisions that might be made between Indonesia and the Netherlands should not be influenced by fear of threats." [56] Presumably this response implied at least tacit support for the objectives of Rahman's undertaking, if not for the substance of his proposal.[57]

Immediately following his discussions with Nasution, the Malayan Prime Minister left on official visits to Canada and the United States. In Washington he solicited the "moral support" of the United States for his proposal, and received a promise from the outgoing Eisenhower administration that it would be studied; but press reports at the time noted that "the United States has preferred to say out of the dispute, taking a role described by one State Department official as 'benevolent neutrality.' " [58] Rahman also met with Dag Hammarskjold, the Secretary-General of the United Nations, early in November. Hammarskjold expressed reservations as to whether a trusteeship agreement which provided for automatic transfer of West New Guinea to Indonesia, after a fixed interval and without consulting the wishes of the local population, would be consistent with the terms of the Charter;[59] but at the same time, he gave his support to Rahman's effort at mediation.[60]

The Malayan Prime Minister next visited London before arriving at The Hague. Following talks with the Dutch government in late November, a joint communique stated that the Netherlands was prepared to submit its policies affecting West New Guinea to the "scrutiny and judgment" of the United Nations.[61] Unfortunately Rahman and the Dutch immediately

[54]Mackie, "Australia and Indonesia, 1945-60," loc. cit., p. 311, citing Indonesian press reports.

[55]Christian Science Monitor, October 14, 1960.

[56]Vandenbosch, op. cit., pp. 60-61, citing a later statement by Prime Minister Menzies in the Australian parliament.

[57]See ibid., p. 60; and Mackie, "Australia and Indonesia, 1945-60," loc. cit., p. 311.

[58]The New York Times, October 27, 1960.

[59]See Malaya/Indonesia Relations, pp. 59-60.

[60]See ibid., p. 9.

[61]Ibid., p. 60.

disagreed as to what this undertaking implied. The Tengku stated at a press conference his understanding that, following an investigation by a United Nations commission, the General Assembly would be empowered to decide on the future of the territory based on the findings of the commission; and he had to admit that he did not yet have Indonesia's agreement to this procedure.[62] The Dutch Foreign Minister, J. M. A. H. Luns, on the other hand, immediately thereafter informed Rahman privately that Dutch readiness to submit its policies to the "scrutiny and judgment" of the United Nations did not imply a basic change in Dutch policy, or that the matter of Netherlands sovereignty over West New Guinea would be subject to the judgment of the world organization.[63] Rahman then felt it necessary, in view of his above statements to the press, to make public this misunderstanding at a second press conference which he held at the airport prior to his departure from The Hague.[64]

Rahman's attempt at mediation, which up to this point seemed to be making progress, now suddenly collapsed. At first, Indonesian press comment on the enterprise had been more favorable than the Dutch reaction.[65] But after The Hague communique and Rahman's press conferences, the Indonesian attitude changed completely. Rahman was bitterly attacked in the press, and his mission publicly repudiated by Subandrio, who insisted that "any solution must be based on the ultimate transfer of the territory to Indonesia, whether straight or through the United Nations." [66] The tenor of press criticism was that "there would be no point in the UN organization sending a mission to the territory or otherwise interesting itself in the controversy;" that "the only possible settlement of the West New Guinea question (was) unconditional cession to Indonesia;" that Rahman was "wasting his time and energy;" and that there was "no use expecting justice from the UN in its present form." [67] Early in December, Rahman informed the Malayan parliament that he was discontinuing his mediation, largely because of Indonesian reactions to his efforts, especially as reflected in the press. He said that he had not realized that the Jakarta government would be unwilling to have the dispute considered by the United Nations. While the Dutch now agreed to this, there was no further point in pursuing the matter with the Indonesians in view of their vehement

[62]See ibid., pp. 60-61; The Economist, May 6, 1961, p. 526; and Christian Science Monitor, December 7, 1960.
[63]See Mackie, "Australia and Indonesia, 1945-60," loc. cit., p. 311; and Malaya/Indonesia Relations, p. 61.
[64]See Malaya/Indonesia Relations, p. 61.
[65]See Mackie, "Australia and Indonesia, 1945-60," loc. cit., p. 311.
[66]The Economist, May 6, 1961, p. 526.
[67]Christian Science Monitor, December 7, 1960.

rejection of the idea.[68] Subsequently, General Nasution spoke more considerately of Rahman's mission; and the latter indicated that he was willing to resume his mediatory role;[69] but nothing came of this.

From the evidence available, it would appear that Rahman's mission failed primarily because the two parties were still too far apart on the terms of a possible settlement. The Dutch were moving toward the concept of international trusteeship as a solution for the West New Guinea problem, but they were not yet prepared to see the territory automatically turned over to the Indonesians. One also has the impression that the Malayan Prime Minister fumbled The Hague discussions in this respect. He read much more into the terms of his understanding with the Dutch concerning United Nations consideration of the dispute than the Dutch were then willing to concede; and what he actually got from the Dutch fell far short of what he had originally proposed to the Indonesians. Sentiment in Indonesia, on the other hand, was hardening under the persistent hypnosis of confrontation; and the only point that Jakarta was now prepared to negotiate concerned the modalities of transfer. Bitter experience had engendered profound distrust of the United Nations. An estimate that the world organization might conceivably endorse a solution not compatible with Indonesian objectives may have led the Jakarta government to reject at this time any approach to settlement that involved a United Nations framework, except on the basis of an unconditional transfer of West New Guinea to Indonesian control.[70]

"A Contest in All Fields"

The seizure of Dutch properties and enterprises in December 1957 exhausted Indonesia's principal sanction against the Dutch without, however, forcing The Hague to modify its West New Guinea policy. Thereafter, relatively little could be done in the economic field to bring pressure on the Dutch, although the Indonesians kept trying. During 1958, various Dutch interests not taken over in the first wave of seizures were systemati-

[68]See *ibid.*, December 7, 1960.
[69]See *ibid.*, December 7, 1960.
[70]In the background of this whole episode was a history of uneasy relations between Jakarta and Kuala Lumpur. The regionalist rebellions, in particular, gave rise to much ill feeling. Kahin states: "The conviction among Indonesian leaders, Soekarno especially, that the Malayan Prime Minister, Tunku Abdul Rahman, favored the rebel cause and that the rebels on Sumatra were able to arrange for supplies in Malaya has strongly affected the Indonesian government's attitude toward that country." George McTurnan Kahin, "Indonesia," in George McTurnan Kahin, ed., *Major Governments of Asia,* 2nd edition (Ithaca: Cornell University Press, 1963), p. 684.

cally sequestered; and eventually all seized properties and enterprises were formally nationalized. The remaining immovable assets of Dutch citizens who had left the country were also confiscated. A major effort was launched to find new markets for Indonesian exports away from the Netherlands. In April 1960, the government banned all Dutch shipping from participation in Indonesian commerce, asserting that this step was "a further consequence of the Indonesian campaign for the liberation of West Irian from Dutch colonial domination." [71]

From time to time, Jakarta also threatened to nationalize Dutch holdings in mixed capital enterprises operating in Indonesia, the largest of which was the local subsidiary of Royal Dutch Shell. Thus Sukarno warned in his 1959 Independence Day speech that "if in the question of West Irian the Dutch remain stubborn, if in the question of our national claim they remain headstrong, then all the Dutch capital, including that in mixed enterprises, will bring its story to a close on Indonesian soil." [72] A year later, the Indonesian parliament again urged that all remaining Dutch investment in Indonesia be confiscated.[73] But this step was never taken, both because it would have disrupted the vital oil industry, and because of the complications that would have resulted with third countries.

A major aspect of confrontation policy was the enormous effort expended by the regime to arouse and sustain popular enthusiasm for the "liberation" of West New Guinea. The Indonesian people were subjected to an incessant drumfire of rallies, speeches, pronouncements, and "commands" relating to the dispute, which served also to intensify the atmosphere of crisis surrounding the issue. An ugly dimension of this campaign involved allegations of unexampled brutality on the part of the Dutch in their administration of the territory, and reports of widespread unrest among the Papuans. The Dutch were accused of committing "acts of terror" against the indigenous population in the implementation of an "increasingly ruthless" policy of suppression.[74] Another account insisted that "Prisons are full and there are reports of torture and execution without trials." [75] In one alleged incident, "thousands of West Irians struggling for freedom from Dutch oppression" were said to have been "massacred" by the colonial authorities.[76] According to Lieutenant-Colonel Murtono, Acting Secretary of the National Front for the Liberation of West Irian,

[71]Quoted in *The New York Times,* April 15, 1960.
[72]Quoted in *ibid.,* August 18, 1959.
[73]See *ibid.,* September 1, 1960.
[74]Quoted in van der Kroef, "The West New Guinea Settlement," *loc. cit.,* p. 126.
[75]Quoted in *Christian Science Monitor,* November 26, 1960.
[76]Quoted in Justus M. van der Kroef, "Recent Developments in West New Guinea," *Pacific Affairs,* vol. 34, no. 3 (Fall 1961), p. 283.

the "natives" have "started to wake up and show their real desire for freedom without thinking of the consequences, because they no longer are able to stand colonialism." [77] Early in 1961, the Indonesians claimed that rebellion was "flaring up in almost every section" of West New Guinea, and asserted that "thousands of Papuans daily seek refuge in Indonesian territory." [78] The Western press carried no substantiation of these reports; and the Dutch vigorously denied their authenticity, although they did admit that there had been some pro-Indonesian subversive activity.[79]

Organizations to mobilize national strength for recovery of the lost territory proliferated; perhaps the best known of these was the National Front for the Liberation of West Irian. Apart from their sometimes important role in intramural political maneuvering, however, such structures were usually little more than facades for further propagandizing the Indonesian people. Except in the military field, few concrete steps were actually taken to consolidate the power of the state. Problems of economic reconstruction and development, for example, were almost entirely ignored, and the alarming deterioration of the economy allowed to proceed virtually unchecked. Indeed, the consequences of such neglect were often justified in terms of "sacrifices" demanded by the West New Guinea campaign.

Final liquidation of the regionalist rebellions did mark a significant step toward the achievement of national unity. The revolts had been reduced to guerrilla proportions by the end of 1958; and although a good deal of fighting remained, the Army leadership thereafter tended to favor a negotiated settlement with the dissidents. Feith notes that the conflict "had, in fact, been characterized throughout by an extraordinary absence of ruthlessness on either side, resulting in part from feelings of affinity between the two officer groups involved." [80] Negotiations with various regionalist forces began as early as 1958; and, although hampered by opposition from Sukarno and the Communists, were ultimately brought to fruition during 1961, when almost all the dissidents "returned to the fold of the Republic." [81] In the process, two much older Islamic rebellions, in

[77]Quoted in *Christian Science Monitor*, November 26, 1960.

[78]Quoted in van der Kroef, "The West New Guinea Settlement," *loc. cit.*, p. 126.

[79]See *ibid.*, p. 126; Justus M. van der Kroef, "Nasution, Sukarno and the West New Guinea Dispute," *Asian Survey*, vol. 1, no. 6 (August 1961), p. 21; and, by the same author, "Recent Developments in West New Guinea," *loc. cit.*, p. 285, for some details of the subversive activity.

[80]Feith, *op. cit.*, p. 344.

[81]Variations of this revealing euphemism are cited in *ibid.*, p. 346; and van der Kroef, "The West New Guinea Settlement," *loc. cit.*, p. 126. See also Herbert Feith and Daniel S. Lev, "The End of the Indonesian Rebellion," *Pacific Affairs*, vol. 36, no. 1 (Spring 1963), pp. 32-46.

Atjeh (northwestern Sumatra) and South Celebes, which had entered into alliance with the regionalists, were also terminated. Except for some areas of West Java still controlled by the Darul Islam movement, security was thus restored throughout most of Indonesia; and the Army could safely redeploy substantial forces to the islands facing West New Guinea. The successful campaign against the rebels had enormously enhanced the prestige and self-confidence of the armed forces, and also suggested the feasibility of a military solution to the vexed problem of recovering the lost territory.

Quite apart from considerations of patriotic sentiment, moreover, the armed forces had a parochial interest in pressing the national claim, both to perpetuate the prominent position already achieved by the military in government and administration, and also to justify the huge arms buildup that began in 1958. The previous year, Jakarta had sought a $600 million line of credit from the United States in order to initiate a farreaching rearmament program. The request was turned down, although Washington did agree in 1958 to reequip 20 infantry battalions.[82] The Indonesians thereupon turned to the Communist bloc for military aid, and received prompt assistance, "probably in the neighborhood of $200 million," [83] including submarines and jet aircraft. This was followed (after Washington, in 1960, again rebuffed an Indonesian request for sophisticated weaponry) by a much more spectacular arms deal negotiated by General Nasution with the Soviet Union in 1961, and "conservatively estimated as amounting to $400 million." [84] The result of these and subsequent transactions was undoubtedly to modernize and strengthen the Indonesian armed forces significantly, although many observers still questioned their fighting potential and especially their logistical capabilities.[85]

[82]See Arnold C. Brackman, *Southeast Asia's Second Front* (New York: Praeger, 1966), pp. 97-98.

[83]Pauker, "General Nasution's Mission to Moscow," *loc. cit.*, p. 13.

[84]*Ibid.*, p. 13. This aid was apparently first offered during Khrushchev's visit to Indonesia in February 1960 as part of an even larger military and economic assistance package. The Indonesian armed forces were reluctant, however, to accept arms from the Soviet Union on such a massive scale; and the implementing agreements were not signed by Nasution until January 1961. See Guy J. Pauker, "The Soviet Challenge in Indonesia," *Foreign Affairs,* vol. 40, no. 4 (July 1960), p. 614. In this article, Pauker suggests that the first installment of Communist bloc military assistance mentioned in the text amounted to $250 million, and that the military credits offered by Khrushchev in February 1960 came to between $450 and $550 million. See *ibid.*, p. 614.

[85]"As it developed, (Nasution's January 1961 deal with the Soviet Union) was only the first installment on a long-term, massive military build-up which, by 1965, exceeded $1.4 billion, the largest Soviet military-aid program in the Afro-Asian world. Although the quality of its armed forces is open to serious doubt, Indonesia

Indonesian spokesmen made no effort to disguise the purpose of the arms buildup, and threats of military action against the Dutch became an increasingly prominent feature of confrontation policy from 1960 onward. In February of that year, Nasution informed the Indonesian parliament of plans for the "liberation" of West New Guinea, and warned that "Indonesians should be prepared to face all consequences of the struggle to regain West Irian, including territorial war;" [86] and in August, he declared that "it is on West Irian soil itself that the fight to claim that territory is decisive." [87] Following Nasution's mission to Moscow in January 1961, a joint Soviet-Indonesian communique stated that: [88]

> The mission had been sent to the Soviet Union by the Government of Indonesia in accordance with measures taken to build up the armed forces of the Republic of Indonesia, mainly in connection with the special situation which has arisen as a result of the tension increasing of late on the question of West Irian.

Sukarno himself admitted that the Russian arms were necessary to deal with the Dutch in West New Guinea.[89] In January, a leading military commander asserted that the Indonesian Army was "only waiting for the order to liberate Irian;" [90] and a month later, Nasution was reported to have assured Sukarno that the armed forces would require less than a

now possessed impressive defensive and offensive capabilities — on paper: a 330,000-man army, a 40,000-man navy, 10,000 marines, a 30,000-man air force. The Soviet program has concentrated on developing Indonesia's naval and air arm. Naval equipment includes 26 submarines, a 19,000-ton cruiser, a dozen destroyers, and scores of other warships ranging from torpedo boats to helicopters and submarine tenders. The air force has more than 500 modern aircraft, including 26 TU-16 long-range bombers, 25 IL-20 medium-range turbo-prop bombers, 27 MIG-16's, 50 MIG-17's, 13 MIG-19's, and 17 MIG-21's. Djakarta's sea-lift capability ranges between 8,000 and 10,000 troops, with 725,000 lbs. of cargo. In October 1964, on the eve of Khrushchev's ouster, Sukarno personally extracted new promises of military assistance. Among other items, he requested parachute equipment for two Indonesian divisions of his "crush Malaysia" campaign. Brezhnev later honored this commitment, and in 1965, new shipments of Soviet weapons arrived in Djakarta, including MIG-23's.

"In addition, Indonesia's paramilitary forces included 10,000 municipal police, 110,000 mobile brigade troops, 500,000 reservists, and 21 million "volunteers" who are subject to mobilization."
Brackman, *op. cit.*, pp. 98-99.

[86]Quoted in van der Kroef, "West New Guinea in the Crucible," *loc. cit.*, p. 521.

[87]Quoted in van der Kroef, "Recent Developments in West New Guinea," *loc. cit.*, p. 286.

[88]Quoted in Pauker, "General Nasution's Mission to Moscow," *loc. cit.*, p. 16.

[89]See Palmier, *op. cit.*, p. 130.

[90]Quoted in van der Kroef, "Nasution, Sukarno and the West New Guinea Dispute," *loc. cit.*, p. 20.

month to take the territory.[91] While accompanying Sukarno on a visit to Washington in April, Foreign Minister Subandrio alleged that a military invasion was a distinct possibility.[92]

Such statements must, of course, be set against others — often by the same individuals — to the effect that Indonesia had no intention of resorting to force in order to settle the controversy. Jakarta's diplomacy toward Australia, for example, was liberally sprinkled with assurances of peaceful intent. What the more belligerent utterances reflected was not so much a fixed determination to press on to a military solution, as a calculated campaign to undermine Dutch resolve and to engage the attention of the world through the deliberate evocation of a crisis atmosphere.

On numerous occasions, the Indonesians undertook to infiltrate armed bands into West New Guinea. One such attempt was made as early as October 1954, when 48 armed Indonesians "under the auspices of the Indonesian army" [93] were landed in the Etna Bay area along the southern coast, and quickly rounded up by the Dutch authorities. Similar forays were occasionally reported over the years, and the tempo of such activity palpably increased after 1959. In May 1960, the Dutch Minister of Defense, S. H. Visser, informed the Dutch parliament that four landings had been carried out in the vicinity of Fakfak (in the far west) during the previous six months.[94] A Dutch note of protest addressed to Indonesia in February 1961 referred to another landing in the Etna Bay area in November 1960, and to the interception that month of an Indonesian vessel carrying men and equipment from the nearby Aru Islands north to West New Guinea.[95] At first, the Indonesians disclaimed responsibility for such activities; but in February 1961, Subandrio asserted that "infiltrations from both sides have been intensified lately," and he added that it was "a question mark whether West Irian can be settled in a peaceful way." [96] Attempts at infiltration continued intermittently throughout 1961 and the first half of 1962. By August 1962, when the West New Guinea dispute

[91]See van der Kroef, "The West New Guinea Settlement," *loc. cit.*, p. 128.

[92]See Palmier, *op. cit.*, pp 130-131.

[93]Van der Kroef, "The West New Guinea Settlement," *loc. cit.*, p. 123.

[94]See *ibid.*, p. 127.

[95]The text of the note may be found in "Indonesians Refuse Dutch Note of Protest," news release of the Netherlands Information Service, New York (n. d.). Diplomatic relations between Indonesia and the Netherlands having been severed in August 1960, the attempt to deliver the protest was made by the British Ambassador in Jakarta, who had the responsibility for looking after Dutch interests in the country, but the Indonesians refused to accept it. Shortly thereafter, the Jakarta government requested the British embassy to cease representing Dutch interests in Indonesia.

[96]Quoted in *The New York Times,* February 12, 1961.

was finally settled, the Dutch reportedly held 400 Indonesian troops as prisoners, and hundreds of others who had infiltrated into the territory were still unaccounted for.[97] Van der Kroef has analyzed the significance of this activity in the following terms:[98]

> Certain aspects of these invasion attempts are noteworthy. First, they assumed over time a more and more overt military character. Earlier infiltration groups, though all trained by the army, had usually worn civilian clothing and were only lightly armed; the November 1960 group (and its successors) generally wore army uniforms, was heavily armed, and, according to one of its members, had been addressed by Army Chief of Staff Nasution himself prior to its departure. Second, although the government-controlled Indonesian news media claimed at various times that the infiltrators had captured whole towns, were "encircling" others and "liberating" large territories, and were operating in "90 per cent of Irian" and even threatening the territorial capital of Hollandia itself, the fact is that at no time did they constitute a serious military threat to the Dutch. In most instances the Papuan population quickly reported the presence of the invaders — although in the Fak-Fak and Manokwari areas the intruders found some support among the local Indonesian inhabitants — and the effective Dutch military countermeasures, the lack of supplies, and the difficulties of the terrain rendered the infiltrators ineffective. Third, it soon became clear that the real significance of the infiltrations lay in their cumulative psychological effect, both on the West New Guinea inhabitants and in world capitals. The presence of guerrillas and saboteurs lurking in the jungle might prove in the long run to be rather demoralizing. At the same time, . . . it became clear that such a gradually accelerating infiltration — a kind of invasion on the installment plan — could eventually escalate the scattered, military operations in the territory into a more serious conflict.

This was a real danger. After 1959, the Dutch slowly built up their military forces in West New Guinea, which had hitherto consisted of about 1,000 marines, several hundred artillerymen, and a few small naval vessels.[99] In Spring 1960, The Hague made public plans to send the aircraft carried *Karel Doorman* to the Far East, and also to assign jet aircraft to the disputed territory. Late in November came the dramatic announcement that an additional 28 million guilders was being allocated for the defense of West New Guinea, primarily for the purchase of Neptune patrol

[97]See *ibid.*, August 26, 1962.
[98]Van der Kroef, "The West New Guinea Settlement," *loc. cit.*, pp. 127-128.
[99]See *London Times*, April 28, 1960.

bombers.[100] Steps were also taken to organize and train a Papuan militia of about 3,000 men for internal police duties.[101] Predictably, the Indonesians heatedly denounced these measures as presaging a Dutch attack on their country. In December, Foreign Minister Subandrio commented that "What the Dutch are doing seems to mean they are planning an over-all aggression against Indonesia;" [102] and later that month, Jakarta protested to the United Nations Secretary-General that the Netherlands was preparing "an all-out aggression." [103] The Hague promptly denied this accusation in a letter to Hammarskjold early in January 1961, and invited the United Nations to conduct an investigation on the spot.[104] But Indonesia opposed this step, and nothing came of the proposal.[105]

The scale of the Dutch buildup should not be exaggerated. T. H. Bot, the State Secretary for West New Guinea Affairs, was reported in 1961 to have said that the Dutch could deal with an invasion force of 1,000 men;[106] this did not suggest an unduly augmented defense capability. But there is little doubt that the Dutch would have resisted much larger Indonesian incursions that any actually attempted before settlement of the dispute in August 1962.

[100]See Mackie, "Australia and Indonesia, 1945-60," loc. cit., p. 312.

[101]See Christian Science Monitor, March 29, 1961.

[102]Quoted in ibid., December 7, 1960.

[103]Quoted in "Indonesians Refuse Dutch Note of Protest," loc. cit., p. 1.

[104]See The New York Times, January 5, 1961.

[105]See The Economist, May 6, 1961, p. 526.

[106]See van der Kroef, "Recent Developments in West New Guinea," loc. cit., p. 285.

Chapter Six

Reappraisal at The Hague

For a decade following The Hague Round Table Conference settlement in 1949, the determination of the Dutch government to hold onto West New Guinea remained unshaken. Early bilateral negotiations with Indonesia made no progress toward resolving the issue. Dutch proposals to set up a joint New Guinea Council to receive reports on the territory, or alternatively to transfer formal sovereignty to the Netherlands-Indonesian Union, but with the Netherlands continuing to conduct the actual administration and also retaining a veto over the decisions of both ostensible supervisory bodies, were rejected by Indonesia as unacceptable subterfuges. Jakarta's minimum terms were the unconditional transfer of both sovereignty and effective control to Indonesia, and nothing less, although initially the Indonesians were prepared in return to offer farreaching guarantees for Dutch material interests in the territory. Between the respective positions taken, there was little room for compromise; and the Dutch were candid, if not wise, when they stated flatly in 1954 that they did not wish to negotiate further on the question of West New Guinea,[1] although a final effort was actually made in this respect in late 1955 and early 1956. Debates at successive sessions of the United Nations General Assembly from 1954 to 1957 served only to envenom an already embittered atmosphere, and contributed little to the search for settlement.

The Evolution of Dutch Policy

Dutch policy toward West New Guinea derived primarily from the adverse psychological reactions of the Dutch to the unexpected, painful, and deeply resented loss of their East Indian empire after World War II. Retention of West New Guinea was both a kind of consolation for the Dutch, and also a means of retribution against the Indonesians for the injuries they were thought to have inflicted on their erstwhile colonial masters. A succession of events during the 1950s served only to harden

[1]See Justus M. van der Kroef, "Dutch Opinion on the West New Guinea Problem," *Australian Outlook*, vol. 14, no. 3 (December 1960), p. 277.

Dutch resolve that control over the territory should be retained in their hands for the indefinite future.

One such development was the speedy disappearance during 1950 of Indonesia's federal system, which the Dutch had tried so carefully to nurture before conceding independence to Indonesia, and its replacement by a unitary state dominated by the largely Java-based Republicans. The Dutch looked upon this as a betrayal. Their interest in the federal structure was occasioned in part, no doubt, by a desire to weaken the position of the Republicans in postindependence Indonesia and to preserve as much as possible of their own influence in the non-Republican territories. But it reflected also a genuine concern for the political future of the diverse "peoples" of the outer islands, who for the most part had remained loyal to the Netherlands during the civil war. The centralizing policies of the Republicans in the months immediately following independence were a major factor provoking the outbreak of a serious rebellion in the Moluccas, centering on Ambon, which the Republican-dominated Jakarta government eventually suppressed by force after thousands of Ambonnese had fled to the Netherlands. This tragic episode deeply moved the Dutch, not least because it gave them a guilty conscience. Lijphart states:[2]

> The Ambonnese revolt had an immediate and profound impact on Dutch feelings about New Guinea. The frustration caused by the Indonesian crisis was magnified, because the Ambonnese rebellion unmistakably showed that the Dutch had betrayed the minorities by reaching an agreement with the Republicans. The conviction grew that Holland should never allow a similar development in New Guinea, which should be kept firmly under Dutch control.

Such events also affected the arguments by which the Dutch justified their West New Guinea policy. The colonization thesis lost its currency when it became apparent in the early 1950s that the Eurasians of Indonesia, to say nothing of Dutchmen from Holland, were simply not attracted in any significant numbers to settlement in the territory. Economic expectations were also belied by the apparent reality that West New Guinea was not a Golconda of natural wealth, and relatively little Dutch capital flowed into the colony. But the principle of self-determination remained to make it all seem right, and the Dutch increasingly came to rationalize their role in the territory in terms of a sacred mission to preserve the presumed right of the Papuans to determine their own political future until such time as the autochthonous population could exercise it intelligently. This argument took on added prominence after 1954, when the Dutch were obliged

---

[2]Lijphart, *The Trauma of Decolonization*, p. 127. This analysis of the evolution of Dutch policy toward West New Guinea relies heavily on Lijphart's study.

to defend their policy publicly before the international forum of the United Nations, and found in the principle of self-determination a persuasive platform on which to build their case.

In more general terms, the whole pattern of Dutch relations with Indonesia after 1949 tended to reinforce the conviction that the Dutch should remain in West New Guinea: the multiplying frictions of stillborn partnership; Dutch outrage over accusations (some of which were well-founded) of complicity in various rebel movements, and other calumnies laid against them in Indonesian polemics over the years; the ill-treatment and petty harassment to which Dutchmen still living and working in Indonesia were increasingly subject; the frustration of repeated failures to resolve the West New Guinea dispute through bilateral negotiations; the ultimate breakdown of the whole Round Table Conference settlement, culminating in Indonesia's unilateral abrogation of the principal agreements in 1956 and its withdrawal from the Netherlands-Indonesian Union; the years of acrimonious and sterile debate in the General Assembly, leading directly to the calamitous seizure of Dutch properties in December 1957 and the expulsion of most Dutch nationals from Indonesia; later on, confrontation and the final rupture of diplomatic relations in 1960. Throughout the decade, the Dutch could not contemplate rewarding such long-continued injustice and contumely (as they saw it) by turning West New Guinea over to Indonesia.

The apparent inability of the Indonesians to put their domestic house in order buttressed the determination of the Dutch. Opinion in the Netherlands was genuinely shocked by the disorder of political life in Indonesia, the decay of its parliamentary institutions, the stagnation and mismanagement of the economy, and the perceived irresponsibility of political leadership. Surely the Papuans deserved better masters than these. Moreover, the assumed excellence and high moral purpose of Dutch rule in West New Guinea contrasted sharply with the morass of postindependence Indonesia, and thereby served to restore Dutch *amour propre,* which had been badly shaken by the civil war and its outcome, and the prewar Dutch estimate of themselves as "the world's best colonial rulers." Finally, the strategic argument was seen to make a good deal of sense in view of developments in Indonesia. As the years went by, the emergence of President Sukarno (who was especially unpopular in the Netherlands [3] as a wartime collab-

---

[3]"In a public opinion survey conducted in 1961, 54 per cent of the respondents expressed a favorable opinion of the Indonesian people and 18 per cent had an unfavorable opinion. But President Sukarno did not share in the generally favorable opinion Dutch respondents had about his people. Only 12 per cent were favorably inclined toward him, and no less than 64 per cent expressed disapproval." *Ibid.,* pp. 129-130, fn. 3.

orationist with the Japanese and now the archvillain of Indonesian nationalism, and who was largely blamed for stirring up the West New Guinea
issue) as Indonesia's strong man, with virtually unchallenged leadership
in the field of foreign policy; the rebirth of the Indonesian Communist
Party (P.K.I.) after the disaster of the Madiun rebellion, and its spectacular rise to a position of great prominence on the political stage as one
of Sukarno's principal sources of support; Jakarta's neutralist and increasingly anti-Western posture in world affairs, culminating in a prolonged
flirtation with the Communist bloc countries; all tended to confirm the
worst fears of Dutchmen as to where the country was heading. And from
1950 on, the Netherlands also had the outspoken support of Australia,
largely on strategic grounds, for maintaining its position in the disputed
territory.

Throughout the decade, the West New Guinea policy of the Dutch
government had the overwhelming endorsement of both parliament and
public. But from the beginning, there were significant voices in dissent.
The Labor Party, for example, which formed a major component in
cabinet coalitions down to late 1958, was initially badly split on the issue,
with its parliamentary group mostly favoring the eventual restoration of
the territory to Indonesia but reluctant to precipitate a cabinet crisis over
the question. Labor Party criticism subsided during the middle years of
the decade, as opinion across the political spectrum turned more decidedly anti-Indonesian, but became vocal again after 1957. The notion
of somehow "internationalizing" the problem, perhaps through a United
Nations trusteeship, gained credence among some Labor spokesmen as a
possible way out. Following a cabinet crisis in December 1958, the Labor
Party went into opposition and its criticism became correspondingly
stronger. It was soon joined by the small Pacifist Socialist Party, which
gained parliamentary representation for the first time in the 1959 elections,
and of course by the Communists, who had opposed the government on
this issue almost from the beginning. Otherwise the parties in parliament
continued until the end of the decade to support the official policy of
maintaining Dutch control over West New Guinea until the Papuans could
safely exercise the right of self-determination.

The majority of Dutch nationals remaining in Indonesia after the Round
Table Conference settlement saw clearly that their future in the country
was jeopardized by The Hague's stubborn determination to hold onto the
territory, but they had little, if any, effective influence on the formulation
of policy. Missionary leaders of the Dutch Reformed and other Protestant
churches active in Indonesia were similarly troubled, while their colleagues
in West New Guinea generally supported government policy. Despite this
split, the missionary headquarters of the Dutch Reformed Church even-

tually reached a consensus critical of that policy; and in June 1956, the General Synod of the church, at the instigation of its Missionary Council, issued a public Call to Reflection which expressed its concern as to "how the development of affairs concerning New Guinea had led to critical tension between the Dutch people and the Indonesian people," [4] and also cast serious doubt as to the moral defensibility of the the government's course without, however, proposing any specific solution for the problem. Lijphart comments that the Call to Reflection was "the first of a series of developments that led to a reorientation and eventually a complete change" of government policy on West New Guinea, and "the turning-point in Dutch domestic politics" concerning the issue.[5]

Within the business community, companies having significant interests in Indonesia and the pressure groups representing them always understood the long-term implications of government policy, and tried hard but unsuccessfully to bring about its modification. The socalled Rijkens Group, a small, informal, and private association of leading businessmen organized in 1953 by a former managing director of Unilever to promote better relations with Indonesia, and which advocated the retrocession of West New Guinea as an essential step in this direction,[6] subsequently played a significant role in maintaining contacts between the two governments after diplomatic relations had been broken off in August 1960. Following the seizure of Dutch properties in December 1957, the business community continued to see rapprochement as the only prospect for obtaining some compensation for these losses, and for ultimately restoring the once lucrative trade between the two countries. By and large, the press supported the government on West New Guinea throughout the 1950s, although a measure of opposition continued, especially from leftist publications and, toward the end of the period, occasionally from Catholic newspapers as well.

In the closing years of the decade, a variety of factors began to tend toward a change of policy. Perhaps most important was the simple passage of time. Memories faded; the shock and bitter disappointments engendered by the unexpected loss of empire abated with the years. Even the catastrophic events of December 1957 and thereafter, when Dutch properties and enterprises in Indonesia were sequestered and subsequently

---

[4]Quoted in *ibid.*, p. 203.

[5]*Ibid.*, p. 200.

[6]"The Rijkens group believed that the Dutch policy of retaining West New Guinea would prove disastrous, partially because of the grave danger of war with Indonesia and partially because the aim of Dutch policy, an independent West New Guinea, was deemed wholly unrealistic in view of the territory's undeveloped state." Van der Kroef, "The West New Guinea Settlement," *loc. cit.,* p. 131.

nationalized, and most Dutch citizens expelled from the country, paradox-
ically hastened this evolution by severing the last remaining ties of
material interest and personal involvement. Almost inevitably, the Dutch
began to develop a sense of detachment and objectivity in their reading of
Indonesian events, and to appraise more realistically the proper place of
West New Guinea in the spectrum of national interests. During the 1950s,
moreover, new opportunities opened up for the Netherlands to play a
creative and fruitful role in the affairs of Western Europe through participation in the movement for economic integration which culminated in the
European Coal and Steel Community, Euratom, and the European
Economic Community (the "Common Market"). The undoubted historical significance of these undertakings helped to salve the loss of
imperial grandeur, and to divert attention from Indonesia to the evolving
politics of European unity. This whole process was immeasurably facilitated, finally, by the general economic prosperity of the Netherlands
during this period. Holland weathered the loss of its East Indian diadem,
and absorbed the refugees of empire, without serious economic difficulty.[7]

With respect to West New Guinea, the disadvantages of continued possession were increasingly apprehended as time went by. The dispute with
Indonesia had already exacted a fearful toll in terms of the Netherlands'
material interests in and political ties with that country. On the basis of
hard experience, the economic potential of the territory was now seen to
fall far short of the bright expectations of earlier enthusiasts, while the
present costs of administration imposed a heavy burden on the Dutch
budget. Furthermore, there was a growing danger that the controversy
might ultimately involve the Netherlands in war with Indonesia. While
this prospect might have been laughed away in earlier years, Jakarta's
striking success in dealing with the regionalist rebellions, and the massive
arms buildup carried out after 1958, forced a much more sober estimate
of the risks involved. The material cost of prosecuting such a war, in a
territory so remote from the metropolitan Netherlands, could well impose
a prohibitive financial burden on the country and an intolerable strain on
its human resources. In any case, the Dutch people had precious little
stomach for another colonial war in the Indies.

Moreover, anticolonialist sentiment in the international community was
rising steadily, as witness the debates of the United Nations, and especially
the action of the fifteenth session of the General Assembly in December

---

[7]". . . the severance of ties with Indonesia has meant little or no long-range
economic damage to the Netherlands . . . even before it came to a complete rupture
of Dutch-Indonesian relations at the close of 1957 over the West New Guinea dispute, Dutch capital had rapidly begun to move out of Indonesia." *Ibid.*, p. 132,
fn. 37, citing Wytze Gorter.

1960 in adopting unanimously the socalled Declaration on the Granting of Independence to Colonial Countries and Peoples.[8] It was highly unlikely that the Dutch could count on significant support in a struggle with Indonesia over West New Guinea, even from their closest allies. But the strategic problems of waging war in the territory without the support of the Netherlands' principal allies would have been enormous; and in the face of their active obstruction, these problems would have been insuperable.

However compelling the sense of moral obligation to the autochthonous population, West New Guinea was a heavy burden and potentially a dangerous responsibility. Lijphart suggests that the evolution of Dutch opinion as to how to deal with this dilemma went through two distinct stages:[9]

Persistent anti-Indonesian feelings and disillusionment about New Guinea drove the Dutch into attempting to shed their responsibility for the territory as long as two conditions could be fulfilled: (1) a firm guarantee for the right of self-determination of the Papuans, and (2) the denial of Indonesian aspirations in West New Guinea. The Dutch were still strongly committed to the principle of self-determination, and they were absolutely convinced that this principle would never be respected by the Indonesians. This was not the only reason why the Dutch wanted to deny Indonesian claims to New Guinea. Even in the absence of presumed incompatibility between Papuan self-determination and Indonesian sovereignty over the territory, the Dutch would have been spitefully unwilling to make concessions to the country that had treated them so badly. As a result of these factors Holland embarked on a policy of accelerating the political development of the Papuans — trying to achieve the self-determination stage at an early date and thus rid itself of New Guinea and all its problems. The effort to make the United Nations shoulder the responsibility for the territory was in line with this policy.

After about 1960 the desire to withdraw from the island even at the expense of the self-determination principle and even in spite of the anti-Indonesian sentiments became stronger and stronger, especially among opinion leaders, and later played a significant role in 1961 and 1962. It was manifested in two ways: (1) the tendency to take a closer look at the principle of self-determination in order to interpret it as a more flexible instrument in Dutch policy, and (2) the

---

[8]For an account of the consideration and adoption of this Declaration by the fifteenth session of the General Assembly, see *Yearbook of the United Nations 1960* (New York: United Nations, 1961), pp. 44-50. The text of the Declaration may be found on pp. 49-50.

[9]Lijphart, *The Trauma of Decolonization*, pp. 195-196.

tendency to deemphasize the unattractiveness of the Indonesian solution to the New Guinea problem. The usual rationalization of this complex of preferences was the argument that West New Guinea could have a future only as part of Indonesia and that the Papuans' only sensible choice would be the Indonesian solution. This argument became even more acceptable when external pressure in the form of the Indonesian military offensive and United States intervention could be blamed as the *force majeure,* making a change of policy and a violation of Holland's moral commitments inevitable.

But the maturation of such attitudes took time. As late as October-November 1961, a public opinion poll showed that, while only five percent of those expressing opinions still thought that the Netherlands should remain in West New Guinea permanently, a total of 67 percent continued to favor Dutch retention of the territory, whether alone or in collaboration with the United Nations, until such time as the Papuans had decided their own future, and only 14 percent wanted to get out as soon as possible. (The balance favored other solutions.)[10]

A Decade of Modest Achievement

Throughout most of the 1950s, Dutch rule in West New Guinea was cast in the traditional colonialist mold, despite official protestations that the ultimate objective of policy was self-determination for the Papuans.[11] Van der Veur characterizes this period in the following terms:[12]

The Dutch colonial policy of the 1950-1962 period can be divided politically into one of neo-colonialism (1950-1960), developing into one of terminal colonial democracy (1959-1962). Initially, the atmosphere was colonial and utterly bureaucratic. The prevailing view was that the best Papuan was the one who quickly carried out orders without question. Colonial rule was considered a matter of a generation, if not longer. Everything was hierarchically organized: the administration, economic activities, the Church. Criticism of official policy was frowned upon and quickly interpreted as a sign of pro-Indonesian inclinations.

[10]Adapted from *ibid.,* p. 247.

[11]For official views and statistical data on the internal development of West New Guinea during the 1950s, see the annual reports submitted by the Dutch government to the United Nations, entitled *Report on Netherlands New Guinea for the Year* —. Especially useful analyses may also be found in van der Kroef, *The West New Guinea Dispute,* pp. 11-18; the same author's article, "West New Guinea in the Crucible," *loc. cit.,* pp. 521-531; and van der Veur, "Political Awakening in West New Guinea," *loc. cit.,* pp. 54-62.

[12]Van der Veur, "Political Awakening in West New Guinea," *loc. cit.,* p. 60.

In such an environment, relatively little progress was made in the creation of popular legislative institutions. Advisory councils were appointed in some of the larger towns, and the Dutch government described them as a training ground for the establishment of politically automonous communities;[13] but in practice, they were "rarely consulted and almost always ignored." [14] An elective council for the Biak-Numfur region, in the northern part of the territory, was set up in 1959. The indirect elections for this body stimulated a remarkable turnout, and gave some indication that detribalized Papuans in the settled coastal and offshore island districts might be ready for more rapid political evolution than the Dutch had hitherto envisaged.

The fact was that, despite the autocratic style of the colonial government, developments in several fields were encouraging the gradual emergence of a modern Papuan consciousness. World War II had had a powerful and disruptive impact, especially among tribes along the northern coast. After the war, the processes of social change were given further impetus by the slow but steady penetration of colonial authority into the more remote areas of West New Guinea. More than three quarters of the population, which was estimated at just over 700,000, had been brought within the orbit of Dutch administration by 1961.[15] With the administration came schools, medical facilities, agricultural and other services. Expenditures on public education quadrupled during the 1950s, and the number of students in all categories grew apace. In 1960, there were 32,686 pupils in primary schools, 2,734 in continuation schools, 430 in junior high schools, 616 in teacher training and technical schools, and over 400 undergoing some kind of medical training.[16] A few students were being sent to Holland for higher education. A special School of Administration, originally established in 1944 after the expulsion of the Japanese, accelerated the training of Papuan officials. More than half of the 8,700 officials serving the colonial regime in 1960 were Papuans; while for the most part they still occupied the lower grades, elementary schools were increasingly staffed by Papuan teachers, and 35 of the territory's 74 districts were administered by Papuan officers.[17] Thus, by the end of the decade, the Papuanization of the public services was proceeding slowly but steadily.

The work of Protestant and Catholic missionaries, building on prewar foundations, also served as a powerful catalyst for change, especially

[13]See *Report on Netherlands New Guinea for the Year 1958*, p. 12.
[14]Van der Veur, "Political Awakening in West New Guinea," *loc. cit.*, p. 60.
[15]See *Report on Netherlands New Guinea for the Year 1961*, Appendix IV-A.
[16]See *Report on Netherlands New Guinea for the Year 1960*, Appendix XL.
[17]See *ibid.*, Appendices XL-XLIII; and van der Kroef, "The West New Guinea Settlement," *loc. cit.*, p. 124.

through an expanding system of mission schools that supplemented the publicly-supported school system. The Protestant churches of West New Guinea were reorganized in 1956 into an independent Evangelical Christian Church that relied heavily on a locally-trained Papuan leadership.[18] A Protestant labor association, the Christian Trade Union of New Guinea, founded in 1952 primarily to protect the interests of Dutch and Eurasian employees, became progressively more Papuanized after 1957, and by 1960 had 3,000 members.[19] It was especially strong in towns along the northern coast, while a smaller, more conservative Catholic group, the General Roman Catholic Association of Officials, had support primarily in the southern part of the colony.[20] The membership of these unions came both from government and from private enterprise. While they had little, if any, influence on government policy,[21] the associations did afford their Papuan members valuable experience in the techniques of organizational activity, and also the opportunity to acquire a measure of political sophistication.

The economic development of West New Guinea proceeded slowly during the decade. Expenditures of the colonial government rose dramatically, from 36.2 million florins in 1950 to 143.7 million in 1960 (at the time, one florin equalled approximately $ .28); revenues increased from 20.6 million florins to 59.9 million; and the deficit from 15.6 million to 91.5 million.[22] The deficits reflected the extent to which the administration of the territory was subsidized by the Netherlands, which additionally met directly the costs of the governor's function, the military establishment, and certain economic pilot projects.[23] Most of the colonial government's expenditures went to support the administrative apparatus and the expanding services it provided; relatively little was earmarked for capital investment. Capital outlays by the private sector were even smaller. Accord-

[18]"Thus, it was in the religious field that the Papuan 'was first entrusted with the promotion of his own interests via a democratic system,'" Van der Veur, "Political Awakening in West New Guinea," loc. cit., p. 61, quoting C. S. I. J. Lagerberg.

[19]See ibid., p. 61.

[20]See Justus M. Van der Kroef, "Nationalism and Politics in West New Guinea," Pacific Affairs, vol. 34, no. 1 (Spring 1961), pp. 47-48. This division corresponds to the historical focus of Protestant and Catholic missionary effort in the north and south, respectively.

[21]"The true importance of labor organization may be judged from a recent incident. A group of Papuans and Dutch who belonged to the influential Protestant trade union engaged in a public demonstration on the occasion of a visit by the Dutch Secretary of State for West New Guinea Affairs. It was simply ignored by the visitor." Van der Kroef, "West New Guinea in the Crucible," loc. cit., p. 529. This refers to a visit by T. H. Bot early in 1960.

[22]See Report on Netherlands New Guinea for the Year 1961, pp. 79-80.

[23]See Lijphart, The Trauma of Decolonization, p. 43.

ing to one estimate, capital investment by the government in the closing years of the decade was averaging only 27 million florins *per annum,* and private sector investment was running at about 16 million.[24] Most private capital investment went into mining, mainly oil production.[25] But by the end of the decade, the Vogelkop fields were drying up,[26] and exploration for other mineral resources was just getting under way.

Commercial agriculture made some progress. By 1960, the principal export crops were cocoanuts, nutmeg, mace, and resins, with cocoa beans beginning to have some significance. The development of coffee and rubber was also starting up. Truck gardening was expanding in the neighborhood of the larger towns. Experimental rice cultivation at Merauke showed encouraging results, and there were plans to increase the rice acreage substantially. The exploitation of West New Guinea's timber resources was being stepped up rapidly. In the industrial sector, there were at the end of the decade (in addition to oilfield installations) a mechanical sawmill at Manokwari and several smaller mills elsewhere; small shipyards at Manokwari, Sorong, and Merauke; an oxygen plant at Manokwari; a printery at Hollandia; soft drink factories at Hollandia and Sorong; repair shops for motor vehicles, agricultural and other machinery in several towns; a copra plant; and several electric generating stations.[27] In 1960,

[24]See van der Kroef, "Nationalism and Politics in West New Guinea," *loc. cit.,* p. 50, citing the Dutch economist C. A. Cannegeiter.

[25]See *ibid.,* p. 50.

[26]Crude oil production reached a peak of 554,000 metric tons in 1954, and declined to 248,000 tons in 1960, and 167,000 tons in 1961. See *Statistical Yearbook 1962* (New York: United Nations, 1963), p. 148.

[27]See Khan and Taylor, *op. cit.,* pp. 4-5. The composition of West New Guinea's exports during the last four years of the decade is shown in the following table, taken from Lijphart, *The Trauma of Decolonization,* p. 44.

Composition of West New Guinea's Exports, 1957-1960, By Value
(in thousands of Dutch florins)

	1957	1958	1959	1960
Crude oil	20,831.8	16,336.5	13,719.5	12,468.8
Copra	2,194.2	2,907.0	3,236.2	3,072.1
Nutmeg	2,069.2	1,680.1	2,527.9	2,576.4
Crocodile skins	1,782.9	1,026.5	1,317.3	1,791.4
Copal	807.3	1,012.4	1,025.9	768.2
Mace	702.6	607.2	764.7	872.5
Shells	409.2	386.8	207.4	181.8
Scrap	384.5	135.8	382.7	298.6
Dammar	37.2	59.4	105.9	35.1
Timber	5.1	12.5	429.1	1,118.7
Cocoa beans	—	6.5	55.5	90.8
Other	18.6	21.4	3.4	0.7
	29,242.6	24,192.1	23,775.5	23,275.1

a total of 15,910 Papuans were registered as wage earners, of whom 9,093 were employed in government installations, and 6,817 by private enterprise.[28]

During the 1950s, developments such as those briefly recounted above accelerated the processes of social change throughout West New Guinea. Almost everywhere, even in the more remote areas, the Western impact was beginning to erode the traditional patterns of Papuan life. In van der Kroef's words:[29]

> The further entrenchment of Dutch administrative control, the spread of the Gospel, the introduction of educational, medical and other social welfare services, the gradual monetization of economic life and the spread of wage labor in the oil industry and government establishment — all these have brought a revolution in the life of the Papuan, characterized by cases of severe individual and collective frustration and upheaval. In some areas the penetration of foreign influences has produced a sweeping and all-levelling enmity; in others the Papuan is anxious to throw the whole of his own culture in the dustbin of history and accept *in toto* the white man's ways; elsewhere autochthonous and Western traits exist side by side, unintegrated, the Papuan changing roles as the situation demands, and then again one sees the acculturation process accompanied by so-called "Messianic" movements and upheavals, in which the Papuan community organizes itself for action, often destructive, on the basis of apocalyptic expectations revolving around some ancestral hero whose imminent return will bring about a new age of plenty and in which the Papuan will be the equal of the white man.

In relatively advanced areas along the coasts, the detribalization and urbanization of the population was proceeding fairly rapidly by the end of the decade. The main towns were Hollandia (17,000), Biak (9,000), Manokwari (10,500), Sorong (9,100), and Merauke (6,000).[30] Having absorbed a smattering of Western education, and no longer content with the narrow horizons of village life, Papuans were setting out in growing numbers for the imagined promise and excitement of the coastal centers

---

[28]See Lijphart, *The Trauma of Decolonization*, p. 54.

[29]Van der Kroef, *The West New Guinea Dispute,* pp. 12-13. On this general subject, see also H. G. Barnett, "Peace and Progress in New Guinea," *American Anthropologist,* vol. 61 (1959), pp. 1013-1019; J. van Baal, "Erring Acculturation," *American Anthropologist,* vol. 62 (1960), pp. 108-121; Justus M. van der Kroef, "Patterns of Cultural Change in Three Primitive Societies," *Social Research* (Winter 1957); and by the same author, "Culture Contact and Culture Conflict in Western New Guinea," *Anthropological Quarterly,* vol. 32 (1959), pp. 134-160.

[30]There were also a number of smaller "Westernized" towns.

where, however, the slow pace of development did not always permit their absorption into the modern sector of the economy. One consequence was the appearance of shanty towns inhabited largely by "young bachelors who wish to become acquainted with modern life in a place such as Hollandia and above all with the material welfare prevailing there, the fame of which has penetrated far into the interior." [31] With the slums and the inevitable disillusionment came frustration, criminality, and incipient political unrest.

While it is difficult to appraise the alignment of political loyalties among the emancipated segment of the Papuan population in 1960, in view of the close supervision which the colonial government exercised over the press and other forms of public expression, it would appear that disaffection from the Dutch had not yet reached significant proportions. Sharp criticisms of Dutch policy were heard from time to time, especially in relation to the inadequacy of economic development;[32] but there was little evidence of widespread subversion among the Papuans. Undoubtedly a measure of pro-Indonesian sentiment existed in various places.[33] Support for union with Indonesia was undercut, however, both by ethnic antagonism, which derived from traditional Indonesian highhandedness toward the Papuans in precolonial times, and more recently as petty functionaries of the Dutch administration; and by some realization that prospectively the Indonesians could not possibly do as much for the territory as its present rulers.[34] From the point of view of West New Guinea's internal political evolution, the real significance of the 1950s was that the overall processes of modernization laid the basis for the emergence of a distinct sense of Papuan self-consciousness among the slowly increasing although still relatively minuscule indigenous elite. This became apparent after the Dutch initiated in early 1960 a new plan for hastening the development of

[31]"Trek naar de Stad," *Nederlands Nieuw Guinea,* vol. 7, no. 6 (November 1959), p. 29, quoted in van der Kroef, "West New Guinea in the Crucible," *loc. cit.,* p. 524.

[32]"An example is Nicolas Jouwe, a prominent Papuan leader, who recently formed his own wood export company . . . During a journey to the Netherlands not long ago he was outspoken in his criticism of the slowness with which the Dutch were developing West New Guinea and the resultant lack of employment opportunities for the rapidly increasing number of educated and emancipated Papuans." Van der Kroef, "West New Guinea in the Crucible," *loc. cit.,* p. 525. This article appeared in December 1960.

[33]See, for example, van der Veur, "Political Awakening in West New Guinea," *loc. cit.,* pp. 66-67.

[34]See van der Kroef, "West New Guinea in the Crucible," *loc. cit.,* pp. 530-531; and Justus M. van der Kroef, "Toward 'Papua Barat,'" *Australian Quarterly,* vol. 34, no. 1 (March 1962), pp. 20-21.

the territory, a step which was soon followed by the flowering of a kind of Papuan nationalism whose main emphasis was on the separate identity of the autochthonous population and its right to determine its own political future.

A New Program for the Development of West New Guinea

In March 1959, a new cabinet took office under the prime ministership of J. E. de Quay. One of its principal objectives was to accelerate the political development of West New Guinea; and a year later (April 1960), the government made public the details of a bold program for this purpose.[35] The plan called for establishment of a central New Guinea Council having a Papuan majority, initially to exercise primarily advisory powers but with a measure of real legislative authority as well;[36] hastening the training of Papuans to participate in various representative bodies and for service in the administration; creation of a small Papuan military corps; and implementation of greatly expanded economic and social development programs for the territory.

The announcement reflected a major shift in Dutch policy. While ultimate self-determination for the Papuans had long been the official objective of Dutch administration in the territory, hitherto the emphasis was always placed on the backwardness of the population, and the lengthy period to be envisaged before the Papuans could intelligently exercise the right of free choice. One formulation of this perspective was to link the duration of Dutch control over West New Guinea to the termination of Australian administration in the Trust Territory of (East) New Guinea; as T. H. Bot, the Secretary of State responsible for West New Guinea affairs, reportedly put it, "as soon as the General Assembly's trusteeship committee says that the Australian-administered part is ready for self-determination there is no question of our hesitation in withdrawing." [37] This was really another way of emphasizing that the Dutch might have to remain for a long while, since it was well known that Australia at that time foresaw the necessity of a prolonged tutelege over its half of the island.

But the April 1960 proposals, if seriously implemented, indicated a

[35]For details, see especially van der Kroef, "West New Guinea in the Crucible," loc. cit., p. 535; by the same author, "Nationalism and Politics in West New Guinea," loc. cit., p. 38; and van der Veur, "Political Awakening in West New Guinea," loc. cit., pp. 62-63.

[36]The proposed council was described in the Dutch parliament as "a training ground in which the members can learn the tricks of the political trade," and as a step toward self-determination. Quoted in The New York Times, April 6, 1960.

[37]Quoted in Christian Science Monitor, March 7, 1960.

clear intention to speed up the whole process, so that the Netherlands might decently relinquish its now increasingly irksome responsibility at a much earlier date than hitherto contemplated, without the necessity, however, of yielding control to Indonesia. When the program was presented to the Dutch parliament, it struck a responsive chord across the political spectrum (except from the Pacifist Socialists and the Communists), which indicated the growing popular desire to be rid of the burden of West New Guinea as quickly as possible; in the more powerful Second Chamber, the plan to set up a New Guinea Council was approved by the overwhelming vote of 108 to 5.[38]

At the time the new program was announced, the Dutch government probably did not have a precise conception as to the objective toward toward which the political evolution of the territory should move. In presenting the plan to parliament, T. H. Bot, for example, still spoke of the "real possibility of linking western New Guinea and the eastern part of the island in a Melanesian union." [39] But it is doubtful whether this was still considered a realistic alternative. Soundings in Canberra had made clear that the Australian government "was not prepared to commit itself to a common solution," [40] largely because of misgivings as to the wisdom of Dutch policy in accelerating the pace of political development in West New Guinea, and the manifest determination of the Australians to preserve their own dominion over the eastern half of the island for an indefinite period.[41] Nor were the Dutch themselves yet prepared to fix a firm date for the actual exercise of self-determination by the Papuans.

Political life in the colony quickened almost immediately. Within a few months, several new groupings or "parties" took shape to contest elections for the proposed New Guinea Council and for several new regional councils as well.[42] Perhaps the most important was the "radical" Nationalist Party, organized at Hollandia in August, whose inaugural program called for rapid progress toward self-government, Papuanization of the administrative services, and greater educational opportunities for the autoch-

[38]See Lijphart, *The Trauma of Decolonization*, pp. 270-273, for an analysis of Dutch parliamentary consideration of the new proposals.

[39]*The New York Times*, April 6, 1960.

[40]Watt, *op. cit.*, p. 254.

[41]See Mackie, "The West New Guinea Argument," *loc. cit.*, pp. 38-39; and, by the same author, "Australia and Indonesia, 1945-60," *loc. cit.*, p. 310.

[42]On the emergence of these parties, see the two articles by van der Kroef, "Nationalism and Politics in West New Guinea," *loc. cit.*, pp. 38-53, and "Recent Developments in West New Guinea," *loc. cit.*, pp. 279-291; and also van der Veur, "Political Awakening in West New Guinea," *loc. cit.*, pp. 62-63.

thonous population.[43] The more conservative Democratic People's Party, which included many Eurasians, was an older but moribund group which was revived at the capital in the same month; it looked to a long period of continued Dutch tutelege, and also supported the concept of an eventual Melanesian federation. Three parties founded in the Manokwari area in September and October all favored independence for West New Guinea in constitutional partnership with the Netherlands; two were Papuan and the third multiracial in composition. Two additional parties were set up in November, and still another in February 1961.

While due allowance had to be made for the small size and rudimentary character of these organizations, their narrowly-based clientele and shifting membership, and the close identity which most of them had with particular localities or ethnic groups,[44] their emergence and the platforms they formulated did indicate a perhaps surprising political awareness among the emancipated segment of the population, and a growing indigenous interest in the colony's constitutional future. Encouraged by the Dutch, the new parties took a lively part in the campaign leading to elections in February 1961 for the New Guinea Council; and the colonial government also carried out an extensive educational and informational program to

[43]The Nationalist Party was reputed to have some pro-Indonesian inclinations. See van der Veur, "Political Awakening in West New Guinea," loc. cit., p. 64. At the party's organizational meeting, its principal leader, Frits Kirihio, "warned against those Indonesian elements in West New Guinea who might be looking for armed intervention from Indonesia. These people, he continued under the reported applause of his listeners, would do well to take care that they are not chased out of the country . . . the time for being 'pro' something, i. e., 'pro-Dutch' or 'pro-Indonesian,' is past. 'Now we are only for our own country.'" Van der Kroef, "Nationalism and Politics in West New Guinea," loc. cit., p. 40. In November 1960, the party proposed a tripartite conference among the Netherlands, Indonesia, and Papuan party leaders to consider the political future of the territory. In April 1961, it called for independence for West New Guinea in 1970. See van der Kroef, "Recent Developments in West New Guinea," loc. cit., p. 281, including fn. 6.

[44]". . . it must not be thought that the Papuan political groupings are as yet particularly powerful. The comparatively small size of the electorate, the low level of ideological partisanism, and the indirect system of elections—all have the tendency to encourage a kind of 'circulating' Papuan elite, the members of which are chosen more for their personal qualities than for their particular party affiliation; indeed, party affiliation and party formation in West New Guinea may well develop the characteristics of the political processes common to other underdeveloped countries: a small elite, ceaselessly making and unmaking parties, counting more on personal qualities, ethnic identity or a particular subcultural orientation for support rather than on over-riding ideological unity in the country as a whole." Van der Kroef, "Nationalism and Politics in West New Guinea," loc. cit., p. 47.

stimulate popular interest. The 16 elective seats [45] were contested by some 90 candidates, and more than 50,000 Papuans participated in the various polls. In addition, 12 councillors were appointed to represent areas considered too backward for meaningful elections. Papuans comprised an overwhelming majority of the Council as installed in April 1961; of the 28 members, only three were Dutchmen and two Eurasians. The elections were reportedly conducted in a free and open atmosphere devoid of overt racial antagonism.[46] The results appeared to be a stunning success for the Dutch experiment in accelerating Papuan political development.

At ceremonies inaugurating the new Council on April 5, the Dutch government expressed the hope that the road to West New Guinea's independence would be short, and called on the councillors to give their advice within a year on the methods and possibly also the date of self-determination.[47] Some leaders of the Nationalist Party were already demanding a complete transfer of sovereignty by 1970, in part out of concern lest the territory be transformed into a United Nations trusteeship, a step which might delay the date of independence.[48] This demand was too radical for the other parties; and on April 25, the Council unanimously adopted a more conservative motion calling on the Netherlands to "continue its task" in the colony "regardless of political pressures at home or from abroad." [49] Appraising the first session of the Council, which lasted until August, van der Kroef states:[50]

A sober realization of the long road that still lies ahead was evident from the discussions in the Council on the 1962 budget for the area, and the obvious preoccupation of the members with the humdrum "bread and butter" problems of government, as well as their responsiveness to local problems of economic development, would seem to preclude the possibility that more sweeping nationalistic sentiments will soon be dominant in the Council chamber . . . Both from the

[45]In Hollandia and Manokwari, seats were filled by direct elections employing paper ballots. An indirect system was used in other, less advanced districts, with the voting done by "whispering ballot." See *The New York Times,* March 6, 1961.

[46]The election "was held in an atmosphere so devoid of racial feeling that many whites voted for Papuan candidates and many Papuans voted for whites." *Ibid.,* March 29, 1961. On the elections, see *Papuans Building Their Future* (The Hague: Government Printing Office, 1961); and the articles cited in fn. 40, above.

[47]See *The New York Times,* April 6, 1961.

[48]See *ibid.,* April 3, 1961; and van der Kroef, "Recent Developments in West New Guinea," *loc. cit.,* p. 281.

[49]Quoted in van der Kroef, "Recent Developments in West New Guinea," *loc. cit.,* p. 280.

[50]*Ibid.,* pp. 281-282. 191.

Council debates as well as from local press reports concerning partisan political activity one senses the momentum of a new Papuan consciousness.

The farreaching proposals of the Dutch government in September 1961 to relinquish authority over West New Guinea to the United Nations[51] spurred a more vigorous assertion of Papuan nationalism. An *ad hoc* National Committee met at Hollandia on October 19, and speedily adopted a national flag, an anthem, and a new name for the territory, Papua Barat. A special session of the New Guinea Council was convened several days later to ratify these steps; and they were formally approved by the colonial government earlier in November. The new Papuan flag was officially flown for the first time, next to the Dutch tricolor, on December 1.[52] These developments, which had the obvious backing of the Dutch, aroused a good deal of controversy among members of the Papuan elite, however, many of whom — especially in areas outside of Hollandia — were still not prepared for such drastic and highly symbolic action.[53] The whole episode further exacerbated the squabbling that already scarred political life in the colony, both between parties and among the leaders of various groupings as well.[54] One observer concludes that while sentiment among the educated segment of the population "definitely began to shift to a 'pro-Papuan' rather than a pro-Indonesian or a pro-Dutch viewpoint," nevertheless "personal conflicts among leaders and followers still prevailed, tribal differences remained marked, and no united 'Papuan front' emerged." [55]

[51]See pp. 103 ff., below.

[52]On this episode, see van der Veur, "Political Awakening in West New Guinea," *loc. cit.*, pp. 64-66.

[53]See *ibid.*, pp. 65-66.

[54]For evidence of this, see van der Kroef, "Recent Developments in West New Guinea," *loc. cit.*, pp. 280-281.

[55]Paul W. van der Veur, "The United Nations in West Irian: A Critique," *International Organization*, vol. 18, no. 1 (Winter 1964), p. 57.

Elsewhere, van der Veur argues that "the change in Dutch policy in 1960 was effectively undermining pro-Indonesian sentiments. By 1962, several pro-Indonesian Papuans admitted that their followers were becoming charmed with the 'pro-Papua' trend, and one prominent pro-Indonesian Papuan acknowledged to the author that he 'would be happier with an independent state of *Papua Barat,* if such was only possible.' " The author continues:

> An important segment of the younger group of Western-educated men, although not necessarily pro-Indonesian, initially viewed the Dutch colonial regime in almost the same terms as the pro-Indonesian group. Their doubts and many of their grievances began to melt away, however, after 1959 when Dutch promises were implemented and political, social and educational advance took place. Now, they felt, there was proof of Dutch intentions . . .

Those Papuans who were still attending school (above the elementary level) in the early 1960s knew neither the prewar nor the immediate postwar period. They were familiar only with the Indonesians from hearsay and — as President Soekarno would exclaim — 'Dutch hearsay at that!' To gain insight into the thinking of these pupils the author carried out a questionnaire survey in various towns of West Irian. Preliminary findings among pupils above the second year of secondary education (a total of 329) indicate a considerable degree of political awareness, contrasting with an abysmal ignorance of economic matters. Most pupils were not afraid to give their views on the crucial question of the future of West New Guinea. This was true even for those in one town where the test had to be given shortly after the dropping of Indonesian paratroopers some 20 miles away. The overwhelming majority of the pupils accepted Dutch tutelege toward self-government and eventual independence; indicated a desire for close ties with Australian New Guinea; and rejected a transfer from Dutch to Indonesian authority. These pupils appear to provide a reasonably accurate picture of what these pupils thought about the matter at that particular time. Van der Veur, "Political Awakening in West New Guinea," *loc. cit.*, pp. 66-67.

Chapter Seven

A Serious International Crisis

The notion of some kind of "international" solution for the West New Guinea problem, as a device for relieving the Netherlands of exclusive responsibility for the territory, was advanced from time to time during the 1950s, and gained increasing support in Dutch political circles as the decade drew to a close. Thus the independent Socialist daily *Het Parool* declared in June 1956 that:[1]

Because of the developments in the world and in Indonesia itself since the transfer of sovereignty (in 1949), a cession of New Guinea to the Indonesian republic is out of the question. Therefore, an internationalization of the problem in the form of a trusteeship under the supervision of the United Nations offers the best solution in our judgment.

In September 1958, several Labor members of the Second Chamber introduced a motion, which was ultimately defeated by a vote of 78 to 45, inviting the government to comment on "the possibilities, the conditions, and the perspectives of the conclusion of a trusteeship agreement for New Guinea between the Netherlands and the United Nations;"[2] and in February 1960, the Labor group in the Second Chamber, now in opposition, offered a more detailed plan along the same lines which provided that the Netherlands would continue to administer West New Guinea as a United Nations trust territory for a period of ten years, after which the Trusteeship Council would make proposals to the General Assembly as to the future of the territory.[3] By 1961, the concept of internationalization had become a staple of Dutch political discussion on the West New Guinea problem.[4]

[1]*Het Parool*, June 23, 1956, quoted in Lijphart, *The Trauma of Decolonization*, pp. 228-229.

[2]Quoted in *ibid.*, p. 256.

[3]See *ibid.*, pp. 269-270.

[4]See *ibid.*, pp. 232 ff.

The Dutch government was inevitably affected by this shift in opinion.[5] As late as February 1960, the Dutch Foreign Minister, J. M. A. H. Luns, still emphatically rejected the idea of involving the United Nations in any kind of supervision of Dutch administration in the territory;[6] but the tide was already changing. In June, with relations between Indonesia and the Netherlands deteriorating alarmingly following the Dutch announcement of a new program for the development of West New Guinea, and the decision to send the aircraft carrier *Karel Doorman* to Far Eastern waters, The Hague for the first time invited the United Nations Secretary-General to send an observer to investigate conditions in the colony at first hand.[7] This invitation was subsequently renewed, apparently on several occasions;[8] but it was never taken up by the United Nations. In September, the press carried reports that the Dutch government had decided to place West New Guinea within the United Nations trusteeship system.[9] The stories were promptly denied; but it was nevertheless clear that The Hague was giving serious consideration to some form of international solution.

The fact of an impending shift in Dutch policy was confirmed by Foreign Minister Luns in an address to the General Assembly in October, during the opening debates of the fifteenth session. Almost at the end of his remarks, Luns turned to the West New Guinea problem, and stated:[10]

> Our administration has no other aim than to prepare the population of the Territory, within the shortest possible time, for the exercise of its right of self-determination . . . (The population) should decide for itself whether it wishes to be an independent country, or to join up with the eastern part of the island, or to become part of Indonesia, or to opt for any other form of political existence . . .
>
> Our intentions are clear, unequivocal and open to verification. We have no secrets, and we invoke no immunity on account of domestic jurisdiction . . . the Netherlands is prepared to subject its policy and its actions, aimed at the speediest possible attainment of self-determination by the Papuan people, to the continuous scrutiny and judgment of the United Nations.

[5]"Until the beginning of 1961 the Dutch government received wide support from the press. This situation underwent drastic changes during the years 1961 and 1962, however. The changes in editorial opinion were a major political factor behind subsequent changes in Dutch policy. They had a profound influence on public opinion." *Ibid.,* p. 232.

[6]See van der Kroef, "Recent Developments in West New Guinea," *loc. cit.,* p. 288.

[7]See van der Kroef, "The West New Guinea Settlement," *loc. cit.,* p. 134.

[8]See, for example, *The New York Times,* January 5, 1961.

[9]See *ibid.,* September 6, 1960.

[10]*GAOR,* Fifteenth Session (1960), A/PV. 886.

Luns gave no indication as to how he thought the world organization might exercise its "scrutiny and judgment" with respect to the policy and actions of the Netherlands in West New Guinea. The same formulation was employed in the joint communique issued during the visit of Tengku Abdul Rahman, the Malayan Prime Minister, to The Hague in late November 1960. Rahman initially took this to mean that the General Assembly would be given the power to decide on the future of the territory; and Luns was obliged to inform him that the Netherlands did not intend that the question of Dutch sovereignty over West New Guinea be submitted to the world organization.[11]

Exactly what the Dutch did have in mind at this stage is not entirely clear from the available evidence; the ambiguity is perhaps due to the fact that Dutch policy on West New Guinea was passing through a period of rapid evolution. Luns explained in February 1961 that his General Assembly proposal, together with the Dutch government's invitation to the Secretary-General to send observers to West New Guinea, were designed to bring "the presence of the United Nations" to the territory.[12] No doubt The Hague was also giving the most serious thought to more formal modes of internationalization. Tengku Abdul Rahman's whole mediation effort was obviously based on his belief, which he said was derived from earlier conversations with the Dutch, that the Netherlands might be prepared to see West New Guinea transformed into a United Nations trusteeship. In March 1961, the Dutch government made public that it had been "willing to accept a three-nation trusteeship" as proposed by Rahman, "but that the proposal had foundered on Indonesia's demand that the territory become Indonesian after one or two years of trusteeship."[13] The announcement insisted that the Indonesian condition was "contrary to the United Nations Charter which requires that the subject nation of the trusteeship will eventually have the right of self-determination."[14] A month later, Luns reiterated that the Netherlands would not oppose the establishment of a United Nations trusteeship over West New Guinea, subject to the single reservation that the "right of self-determination of the people must be guaranteed;"[15] and in May, he declared to the

---

[11]See p. 72, above.

[12]Quoted in Lijphart, *The Trauma of Decolonization*, p. 274.

[13]*The New York Times*, March 21, 1961.

There is no question that this was, in fact, the Indonesian condition *sine qua non*. A month previously, Subandrio had stated publicly that Indonesia would accept United Nations mediation on the condition that "complete power" over West New Guinea was transferred to Indonesia "within a year to two." Quoted in *ibid.*, February 25, 1961.

[14]Quoted in *ibid.*, March 21, 1961.

[15]Quoted in *ibid.*, April 5, 1961.

First Chamber of the Dutch parliament that he did "not exclude any reasonable internationalization" as a solution to the problem.[16]

It would appear that by Spring 1961, at the latest, the Dutch were prepared to accept a solution based on a United Nations trusteeship, provided that the Papuans were assured of the ultimate right to decide their own political future. The Dutch were confident that, when faced with the necessity of choice, the autochthonous population would reject the alternative of union with Indonesia. On the other hand, The Hague would not yet accept any formula which might deny the right of self-determination to the Papuans, or which in other respects seemed likely to lead to absorption of the colony by the Indonesians. For the Dutch, the road to Canossa was long and hard.

A concrete formulation of what constituted a "reasonable internationalization" from the Dutch point of view was presented at the sixteenth session of the General Assembly in September 1961 by Foreign Minister Luns. The socalled Luns Plan represented the boldest initiative yet taken by the Netherlands government to bring about a solution of the West New Guinea dispute on terms that were, however, still basically compatible with its professed devotion to the principle of self-determination for the Papuan people.

The Luns Plan.

The main elements of the Luns Plan, as outlined in the Foreign Minister's address during the general debate, were as follows:[17]

First, the Netherlands is prepared to bring the administration and the development of the Territory under the active supervision of the United Nations and is prepared to accept a decision of the General Assembly which clearly guarantees the right of self-determination of the population.

Second, to this end the Netherlands is prepared to relinquish sovereignty to the people of Netherlands New Guinea.

Third, in this connexion the Netherlands is prepared to transfer its present powers, to the extent required by the above purpose, to an organization or international authority established by and operated under the United Nations, which would be vested with executive powers and which could gradually take over tasks and responsibilities and thus prepare the population for early self-determination under stable conditions.

[16]Quoted in Lijphart, *The Trauma of Decolonization,* p. 274.
[17]*GAOR,* Sixteenth Session (1961), A/PV. 1016.

In order to assist the General Assembly in examining these proposals, which he characterized as embodying "an entirely new concept in the history of decolonization," Luns also suggested that a United Nations commission be set up to investigate conditions in the territory at first hand, including "the possibilities for organizing an early plebiscite . . . in order to register the wishes of the inhabitants of the territory;" and to make concrete recommendations to the General Assembly within the framework of the Luns Plan.[18]

In outlining his proposals, Luns rather ostentatiously associated Dutch policy with the provisions of the famous Declaration on the Granting of Independence to Colonial Countries and Peoples, which had been adopted by the General Assembly in December 1960 without a dissenting vote, and especially its stipulations on self-determination and the necessity for "immediate steps . . . to transfer all powers to the peoples of these territories" which had not yet attained independence.[19] But the principle of self-determination had long since come to form the official basis of Dutch policy on West New Guinea. The new elements in the Luns proposals were the explicit statement that The Hague was prepared to relinquish sovereignty to the people of the territory, the proposal for a plebiscite, and the concept of transferring administrative responsibility for any necessary interim period to an international executive authority under the auspices of the United Nations.

The plan was hedged by the condition that the Netherlands government would only accept a General Assembly decision "which clearly guarantees the right of self-determination of the population," with The Hague presumably acting as sole judge in this respect. Luns subsequently stated that the Netherlands would "fully respect whatever decision the Papuan people may take, including, of course, a decision to join Indonesia;" [20] and, indeed, it had long been The Hague's official posture that the right of self-determination obviously implied that the Papuan people could opt for Indonesia. In an explanatory memorandum submitted to the General Assembly in November, the Netherlands government envisaged a choice

[18]On October 9, 1961, the Dutch submitted a draft resolution which focussed on the proposal for a United Nations commission and its possible terms of reference. See *GAOR*, Sixteenth Session (1961), Annexes, A/L. 354. An explanatory memorandum placed the proposed commission in the larger framework of the Luns Plan as outlined in the Foreign Minister's speech to the General Assembly. See *GAOR*, Sixteenth Session (1961), Annexes, A/4915. The Dutch submitted an additional explanatory memorandum early in November. See *GAOR*, Sixteenth Session (1961), Annexes, A/4954.

[19]See pp. 86-87, above.

[20]*GAOR*, Sixteenth Session (1961), A/PV. 1049.

among three possible alternatives: integration with Indonesia, independence, or association with the eastern half of New Guinea and other Pacific islands.[21] But since the Dutch were persuaded that the Papuans would never voluntarily choose union with Indonesia, such professions did not reflect any weakening of the Dutch resolve to keep West New Guinea out of Indonesian hands. On the contrary, the Luns Plan was really an imaginatively designed proposal to relinquish an increasingly irksome and even dangerous colonial responsibility to the United Nations in circumstances that minimized the possibility that West New Guinea would ultimately be handed over to the Indonesians. Unhappily for the Dutch, it was not sufficiently attractive to win the support of the General Assembly.

In the ensuing debate,[22] all the old arguments were rehearsed anew. But the central theme of the discussion involved the question of self-determination. Everyone agreed that the "Indonesian people" had the right of self-determination. Did the Papuans of West New Guinea? Indonesia insisted that the territory was, and always had been, an integral part of the republic; its population was as much Indonesian as the inhabitants of the other islands. In this connection, Subandrio cited with approval the dictum previously enunciated to the General Assembly by Doudou Thaim, the Foreign Minister of Senegal:[23]

> From the very instant that a colonized territory accedes to independence, its new sovereignty must be exercised within the boundaries where colonial sovereignty extended.

Hence the population of West New Guinea had definitively exercised the right of self-determination when the "Indonesian people" declared their independence from the Dutch in August 1945. To impute an alleged "right" of self-determination to the socalled "Papuan people" was simply a device to dismember the republic. The Indonesian Permanent Representative, Ali Sastroamidjojo, put the case in the following terms:[24]

> West Irian . . . is an integral part of the Republic of Indonesia. The people living in West Irian are Indonesians, who have already exercised their right of self-determination, together with their compatriots of the other islands of Indonesia, on 17 August 1945. To speak now of the sacred right of self-determination for a part of the Indonesian territory which the Netherlands has been able to control only by force of arms is merely to cloak the "divide and rule" policy

[21]*GAOR,* Sixteenth Session (1961), Annexes, A/4954.

[22]For the debate, see *GAOR,* Sixteenth Session (1961), A/PV. 1016, 1030, 1049-1050, 1052, 1054-1061, 1064-1066.

[23]*GAOR,* Sixteenth Session (1961), A/PV. 1030. For Thaim's speech, See *GAOR,* Sixteenth Session (1961), A/PV. 1012.

[24]*GAOR,* Sixteenth Session (1961), A/PV. 1016.

of colonialism. This kind of self-determination is nothing else but fragmentation of Indonesia and the Indonesian people, which is a flagrant violation of the principles embodied in resolution 1514 (XV), on the ending of colonialism, referred to by the Minister of Foreign Affairs of the Netherlands.

Doubtless with some relish, the Indonesian Ambassador then quoted back at the Dutch the paragraph of the Declaration on the Granting of Independence to Colonial Countries and Peoples which reads:

Any attempt aimed at the partial or total disruption of the national unity and the territorial integrity of a country is incompatible with the purposes and principles of the Charter of the United Nations.

The Dutch position, of course, was exactly the reverse. They maintained that West New Guinea had never been part of the Republic of Indonesia; that the autochthonous population of the territory comprised a separate and unique people who had an inalienable right of self-determination; that the Papuans had not participated in any meaningful way in the Indonesian declaration of independence; and that the Dutch had a duty to safeguard the right of self-determination for the Papuans until such time as the latter could exercise it freely and intelligently.

As it turned out, the General Assembly was still badly divided on the issue. A group of nine countries supporting the Indonesian position, led by India, introduced a draft resolution [25] which significantly ignored the question of self-determination and simply called on the two parties to "engage themselves in further negotiations under the aegis of the President of the General Assembly." Thirteen Black African countries, all formerly ruled by France, sponsored a competing draft [26] which insisted that "any solution . . . must be based on the principle of self-determination of peoples." It called for further bilateral negotiations with the assistance of the Secretary-General; and proposed a United Nations commission to investigate the situation in the event of the failure of bilateral negotiations, and in particular to examine the possibilities of an interim international administration without prejudice to the ultimate right of the local population to decide its own status.

Several delegations which generally supported the Dutch draft considered that it did not sufficiently recognize the special interest of Indonesia in the dispute. The 13-member draft had the virtue of combining the principle of self-determination with the concept of direct bilateral negotiations; and the Dutch indicated that they could accept this approach.

[25]*GAOR*, Sixteenth Session (1961), Annexes, A/L. 367/Rev. 1.
[26]*GAOR*, Sixteenth Session (1961), Annexes, A/L. 368.

In the voting, the 13-member draft failed of adoption by a vote of 53 in favor, 41 against, and nine abstentions. Support for the resolution came primarily from its sponsors (plus Nigeria and Somalia in Africa), and the Western and Latin American countries, while most other Afro-Asian countries and the Soviet bloc opposed it. For the first time, the United States took a position in the debate, and voted to support the 13-member draft.[27] While falling short of the necessary two-thirds majority, the draft did gain the affirmative vote of more than half the membership of the United Nations. The Dutch chose to interpret this as a vindication of the right of the Papuans to self-determination, and "a proof that in trying to internationalize the administration of West New Guinea, we have taken the right direction." [28] In view of the vote on the 13-member draft, they decided not to press their own resolution to a formal vote. The nine-power draft then failed by a vote of 41 to 40, with 21 abstentions. The pattern of the voting was roughly the reverse of the poll on the 13-member draft. The 41 affirmative votes represented only 40 percent of the votes cast, which (if the nine-member draft be considered as favoring the Indonesian position) was markedly worse than Indonesia had done in 1957.

"All Means At Our Disposal".

While the Dutch may have taken satisfaction from the outcome of the General Assembly debate, in which a clear majority of members voted to sustain the right of self-determination for the Papuans, the immediate consequence was further to escalate the West New Guinea dispute toward the level of a serious international crisis. Jakarta inevitably interpreted the whole episode as a warning that time was running out, and that prompt action was required lest Indonesia forfeit all opportunity of reclaiming the lost territory in the foreseeable future. The upshot was a series of measures that dangerously increased the prospect of large-scale hostilities.

The Dutch program for the political and economic development of West New Guinea, officially announced in April 1960, had turned out to be much more than a catalog of pious platitudes. Significant progress was made in the political field during 1960 and 1961 in advancing the autochthonous population toward eventual self-government. The Papuanization

[27]See pp. 125-127, below.

[28]GAOR, Sixteenth Session (1961), A/PV. 1066. In a preliminary vote, the clause of the 13-member draft which provided that "any solution . . . must be based on the principle of self-determination of peoples" failed of adoption by a vote of 53 in favor, 36 against, and 14 abstentions. Hence the draft resolution as finally voted on did not include this provision.

of the administrative services was going forward steadily. Elections had been held, and a central New Guinea Council (together with several new regional councils) brought into existence. In the economic sector, the Dutch government submitted to parliament in March 1961 a farreaching ten-year development program for the territory. It called for annual expenditures starting at 100 million guilders (approximately $30 million) in 1961, and increasing to a level of 120 million guilders (approximately $36 million) in 1964.[29]

The infant legislature at Hollandia soon demonstrated a vigor that was remarkable in the circumstances, while the Papuan elite at large plunged enthusiastically into the controversies of an authentic political life. All the evidence seemed to indicate the emergence of a new Papuan nationalism, and a powerful sentiment for eventual independence. On December 1, in solemn ceremonies at Hollandia, a new Papuan flag was raised to fly with the Dutch tricolor, and the name of the colony changed (unofficially, pending amendment of the Netherlands constitution) to Papua Barat, or West Papua.[30] Responding to developments at the United Nations, the New Guinea Council passed a series of resolutions supporting the Luns Plan and calling on all nations to respect the right of the Papuans to self-determination.[31]

If this trend continued, it might soon appear to many governments that West New Guinea actually was approaching independence. Given the sentiment of the United Nations as manifested in the recent votes, and the prospect that a growing number of Afro-Asian countries might come to support the concept of Papuan independence, especially if it were once proclaimed, the developing situation in the territory must have been judged as increasingly unfavorable to Indonesian aspirations. There was, perhaps, a sense of forboding behind the bombast of Subandrio's warning before the General Assembly:[32]

[29]See *Facts on File,* vol. 21, no. 1063 (March 9-15, 1961), p. 94.

[30]See *The New York Times,* December 1, 1961.

[31]See *Christian Science Monitor,* November 29, 1961. It is difficult to appraise the extent to which these resolutions accurately reflected the views of the Papuan elite. The Dutch, of course, would have strongly encouraged such activities; and the whole environment was favorable to the expression of pro-Dutch, pro-independence, and anti-Indonesian sentiments. The tenor of Papuan political statements changed remarkably after the Indonesians took over the territory on May 1, 1963. But the Papuan nationalism that began to emerge during the period 1960-62 was certainly not a fraud.

Perhaps we may conclude that the views exemplified in the text reflect, at the least, the main currents of articulate Papuan opinion *at the time.* On the other hand, it should be remembered that, even then, a measure of pro-Indonesian sentiments certainly continued in the territory, especially in the far west.

[32]*GAOR,* Sixteenth Session (1961), A/PV. 1050.

For Indonesia, at least this much is clear: once the Netherlands makes the separation of West Irian an accomplished fact, once it proclaims the independence of this territory, . . . we shall be compelled to use all the means at our disposal to annul such a proclamation, even if it means war with the Netherlands. The sole responsibility for such a situation will rest upon the shoulders of the Netherlands. Every nation would do the same as Indonesia. The proclamation of independence of a part of its national territory, at the instigation of a foreign Power, will be met with force.

Shortly after the votes in the General Assembly, President Sukarno declared that the "decisive moment" for the liberation of West New Guinea was at hand. "We do not want to wait any longer," he said. "I will give my command in the near future." [33]

On December 12, a new National Defense Council was announced. A week later Sukarno, having assumed the title of Commander-in-Chief of the Forces for the Liberation of West Irian, ordered the Indonesian armed forces to be prepared to "carry out the duty of liberating" West New Guinea "from the shackles of Dutch colonialism at any moment I shall decide;" [34] and also issued his famous "Trikora" or Triple Command calling for the total mobilization of the Indonesian people, and ordering them to "wreck Dutch efforts to set up a Papuan puppet state," and to "fly the red and white flag (of Indonesia) over the West Irian territory." [35] Shortly thereafter, the National Defense Council proclaimed a new province of West Irian incorporating the territory of the Dutch colony. India's seizure of Goa and the other Portuguese enclaves on the subcontinent on December 17, to which the international community offered scant rebuke and no effective opposition, doubtless acted as a further stimulus to Indonesia's appetite for resolving the issue once and for all by armed invasion. Meanwhile, the infiltration of small guerrilla units into West New Guinea was stepped up. In mid-January 1962, Dutch destroyers exchanged fire with Indonesian motor torpedo boats off the southern coast. One Indonesian boat, apparently loaded with troops, was sunk with heavy loss of life. The Deputy Chief of Staff of the Indonesian Navy, Commodore Jos Sudarso, was among those lost in this action. This engagement, which was the first between regular naval units, sharply intensified the sense of crisis that now enveloped the controversy over West New Guinea.

Despite all the bombast of public statements, however, and the pin-

---

[33]Quoted in The New York Times, December 1, 1961.
[34]Quoted in ibid., December 20, 1961.
[35]Quoted in ibid., December 19, 1961.

pricks of guerrilla raids, the ultimate military intentions of the Indonesian leadership remained obscure. Until the archives are finally opened, we shall probably not know whether a large-scale invasion of the disputed territory was ever seriously planned, much less irrevocably decided upon. To be sure, the military buildup initiated in 1958 was shifted into high gear during 1961, following General Nasution's mission to Moscow in January (which resulted in a mammoth arms deal with the Soviet Union), and a subsequent visit by Sukarno and Nasution in June. Early that year, the United States embassy in Jakarta already considered the situation to be alarming. Former Ambassador Howard P. Jones has written:[36]

Regardless of how the rest of the world viewed these developments — the general reaction was to write them off as typical Sukarno bluster — it was clear to us in Djakarta that the Indonesians were not bluffing, that we had the makings of a major military crisis on our hands.

By the beginning of 1962, however, the buildup was apparently far from complete; in particular, Indonesia's ability to transport a substantial force over several hundred miles of open water from staging bases in South Celebes, to provide continuous air cover thereafter, and to keep the force adequately supplied while campaigning in the immensely difficult terrain of West New Guinea, was open to serious question. An informed report from Canberra early in the year concluded that:[37]

---

[36]Jones, op. cit., p. 191.

[37]London Times, January 26, 1962. The report presented a careful estimate of the military situation in West New Guinea at the time. "To dominate the whole territory, which is more than three times the size of England, the Indonesians would have to take Biak, which is believed to be defended by one battalion of Marines comprising 850 regular officers and men. Another 500 soldiers in anti-aircraft units at Biak are equipped with 3.7 in., 41 mm., and 105 mm. high-angle guns and twin-barrelled machine guns. Shore-based sailors and aircraft ground crew at Biak total another 500 . . . About 1,075 more soldiers, mainly conscripts, are stationed in company and platoon strength at Hollandia, Manokwari, Sorong, Fakfak, Kaimana, Kokenau and Merauke. A Papuan battalion which began training only in November last year is at Manokwari. In addition, there are about 200 Dutch in the 1,400-strong mixed Dutch-native police force scattered throughout the territory."

Air strength consisted of 21 Hawker Hunter fighters, with three more expected; four Neptune reconnaissance planes, with five expected; 12 Firefly strike bombers; and several Dakotas, Herons, and Otters. Naval units included one destroyer and two frigates.

"It is understood that Indonesia's Mig fighters, of which she has 75, would not be able to stay more than a useless few minutes over Biak even if they flew from Morotai, and Indonesia's bombers alone would be no match for the Hunters. Indonesia has the amphibious craft to transport army assault units, but lacks the protection which maritime reconnaisance aircraft would give. However, if the Indonesians managed to land in battalion or even company strength the Dutch would find it

The present Dutch forces in West New Guinea, acting alone, could almost certainly prevent the Indonesians taking all but isolated and small parts of the 161,000 square mile territory . . . The forces could continue to do so until at least the end of this year.

Commenting on "the enormous logistic problems facing the Indonesians in any major military operation against" the territory, *The New York Times* reported from Macassar (South Celebes) in January that "current operations in (that city) must be classified as only a beginning in a long preparation needed for any full-scale amphibious exercise." [38] A month later, Subandrio informed a closed session of the Indonesian parliament that the country would not be prepared to invade West New Guinea before the end of 1962.[39]

Feith asserts that there were "major divisions of opinion" among the Indonesian leadership as to the most desirable strategy for resolving the West New Guinea tangle. He continues:[40]

In general the army appeared to favor a "clear-cut" solution, either diplomatic or military. For much of 1961 its leaders seemed to stake their hopes on a diplomatic victory gained as a result of United States and other Western pressure on Holland. In the second quarter of 1962 the emphasis changed, with a highly influential group of officers arguing, "Now that our preparations are so far advanced as this, let us fight with all we have and win decisively." President Sukarno on the other hand argued for a "rallying the people" approach. Rather than seek a victory which would seem to be a gift from the imperialists, and rather than run the risks of all-out warfare, he advocated mass rallies, the enlistment of volunteers, and the sending of small numbers of soldiers and volunteers to West Irian — but without the abandonment of diplomatic avenues.

---

difficult to reinforce hard-pressed local garrisons because they lack coastal shipping The Indonesian Navy, at present 14,000 strong, has two fast Italian destroyers which are built for coastal work and could not reach Biak, four Russian Skory destroyers, and about 10 frigates. The Navy has had two of the Skory destroyers about two years and they may now be well manned, but the efficiency of the other ships is doubtful. The delivery of the Russian cruiser Sverdlov early this year will only increase the Navy's immediate manning difficulties . . . Six Russian W class submarines have just arrived for the Indonesian Navy and these could carry a useful number of soldiers if a landing were attempted."

See also the military estimate in *U.S. News & World Report*, April 23, 1962. pp. 55-60; and Maude, *op. cit.*, pp. 167-168.

[38]*The New York Times*, January 26, 1962.

[39]See Pauker, "The Soviet Challenge in Indonesia," *loc. cit.*, p. 616.

[40]Feith, *op. cit.*, pp. 353-354.

In the event, Sukarno's strategy proved sufficient to assure victory in 1962. As the year progressed, it became apparent that the United States had abandoned its neutral posture in the dispute and begun to exert heavy pressure on the Dutch to yield; and that the latter were, in fact, preparing to capitulate, provided only that they obtained the merest facesaving gestures to cover their retreat. Until a settlement was finally reached in August, the Indonesians kept up the military pressure in order to exact the most favorable terms possible, but the level of military activity never escalated beyond small-scale infiltrations and isolated engagements.

Given this outcome, it is perhaps superfluous to speculate as to whether the Indonesians would ultimately have attempted more decisive military measures if the political stalemate had persisted throughout 1962 and beyond. The arms buildup did continue for several years thereafter, and the time might doubtless have come when Jakarta would have risked a large-scale invasion of the territory with some assurance of success. But it never came to this. Maude questions whether the Indonesian leadership "ever contemplated a successful operation to take the whole of West Irian by force." In his view:[41]

What was probably planned was an invasion to occupy a beachhead: once the flag had been planted on Irian the immediate claims of honour would have been satisfied, and an interminable wrangle would have developed in the United Nations until perhaps the Dutch would have tired of the whole business.

Something like this seems a reasonable hypothesis.[42] But still the situation was dangerous enough. It was conceivable that the conflict might burgeon beyond the will or ability of either side to control it; and no one could safely predict the outcome when once the clasp of war was closed. At the least, continued hostilities, even at the low level of sporadic landings and parachute drops, might have served to stiffen Dutch resolve — or stubborness — at precisely the time that they were getting ready to give way. Especially where the outcome is still uncertain, it is often more difficult to yield when blood has been spilled and honor become engaged. On the Indonesian side, the frustration of continued stalemate might have exacerbated an already precarious domestic situation, and possibly led to political

[41]Maude, *op. cit.,* p. 168.

[42]Compare, for example, the following view: "Indonesian idea . . . is to make enough landings so that the Dutch cannot eliminate them all, thus planting the Indonesian flag on the soil of West New Guinea. Then, as the Indonesians figure it, the United Nations would demand a cease-fire and the Dutch would be forced to capitulate in the U. N. Security Council." *U. S. News and World Report,* April 23, 1962, pp. 58-59.

collapse at home. A case could be made that, in such circumstances, the likely beneficiaries would be the Indonesian Communist Party and the Soviet Union.

These were among the fears that eventually led the United States to intervene decisively in the dispute.

Chapter Eight

The Evolution Of United States Policy

At the 1949 Hague Round Table Conference, the formula finally adopted for dealing with the West New Guinea question was suggested by the United Nations Commission for Indonesia. The membership of the Commission consisted of Australia, representing the interests of Indonesia; Belgium, designated by the Netherlands; and the United States, chosen by Australia and Belgium as impartial third party. According to Taylor's exhaustive account, the general outlines of this temporary solution were first advanced informally by the Australian representative, T. K. Critchley, to his colleagues on the Commission; and later formally proposed in more specific terms by the Commission as a whole after its assistance in the matter had been requested by the three negotiating parties.[1]

The dominant figure on the Commission, however, was the United States member, H. Merle Cochran. During the preliminary negotiations leading to the Round Table Conference, Taylor comments that:[2]

... it was to Cochran that the ... parties ... turned as *primus inter pares* within the Commission. They did so because of his negotiating skill, his strategic position as the "middle" or "neutral" member of the U.N.C.I., and his Government's role in world affairs.

Cochran gave a comparable performance at The Hague, where his services were especially valued by the Dutch. Many of the compromises adopted by the Round Table Conference apparently originated with him rather than the Commission. Indeed, Critchley feared that Cochran's paramount influence might jeopardize the acceptability of Conference decisions among the Indonesians, and that it might also enable the U.S.S.R. to sustain the charge that the overall outcome was largely the result of United States intervention.[3] Hence it is probable that Cochran had a decisive part in putting across the West New Guinea compromise, even if he did not formulate its precise terms.

[1]See Taylor, *op. cit.*, p. 238.
[2]*Ibid.*, p. 409.
[3]See *ibid.*, p. 412. Feith speaks of the "largely American-steered Round Table Conference," Feith, *op. cit.*, p. 350.

114

We can only speculate as to why the United States supported a solution which preserved Dutch control over the disputed territory, subject to the stipulation "that within a year from the date of transfer of sovereignty . . . the question of the political status of New Guinea be determined through negotiations." Even then, it must have been fairly apparent that subsequent negotiations on the issue would be extremely difficult, and that the Round Table Conference compromise probably meant the indefinite perpetuation of Dutch control. Considerations of military strategy may have played a part in the decision,[4] as well as an intention to safeguard West New Guinea from the tide of communism then widely thought to threaten the newly independent countries of Asia. On the other hand, the Netherlands had taken an inflexible stand on West New Guinea, in part because of an appreciation that the Dutch parilament would not approve the balance of the Round Table Conference settlement unless the territory were retained. In these circumstances, a pro-Dutch compromise on the issue might reasonably have been construed as the price necessary to salvage everything else. Finally, the Netherlands was a partner of the United States in the newly organized North Atlantic Treaty alliance. Having exerted a decisive influence on The Hague to concede independence to Indonesia, Washington might understandably have hesitated to repeat the exercise in an attempt to persuade the Dutch to relinquish this last remnant of their once vast Asian empire.

But whatever the correct interpretation, the United States clearly bore a responsibility for the West New Guinea compromise, and for the long controversy that ensued from it.

Studied Neutrality.

In so far as United States support for the West New Guinea compromise reflected primarily an assessment of what was necessary to rescue the main elements of the Dutch-Indonesian settlement at the Round Table Conference, there seems little doubt that Washington would thereafter have welcomed a speedy and permanent resolution of the dispute. Following the collapse of the special ministerial conference at The Hague in December 1950, the United States made known its disappointment and concern, and urged both sides to resume bilateral discussions.[5] But the situation was undeniably awkward. This country had played an important part in Indonesia's successful struggle for freedom, fortunately without lasting damage to our traditional friendship with the Netherlands. Further

4See pp. 36-38, above.
5See *The New York Times,* January 8, 1951.

intervention in their quarrels was bound to complicate relations with one party or the other, and perhaps with both, while there was every reason of policy to maintain friendly ties all around. A case could now be made for disengagement and a posture of studied naturality in the residual disputes that were the inevitable aftermath of decolonization, especially if such issues could be kept within manageable limits. And in 1950, it was not yet apparent that West New Guinea would ultimately become so serious a problem in Dutch-Indonesian relations, or that it would eventually occupy so preeminent and destructive a place in Indonesian politics.

In any event, Washington did try to steer clear of further overt involvement in the dispute for more than a decade after The Hague agreements. While the question was certainly discussed in diplomatic channels from time to time, there is little evidence of American initiatives during the 1950s to facilitate the search for settlement, and every effort was made to avoid the appearance of taking sides. When Indonesia brought the controversy to the United Nations for the first time in 1954, the American delegation remained silent during the debate and carefully abstained in the voting. The same course was followed in 1956 and 1957. Nor did the blandishments of Sukarno's direct diplomacy weaken the determination of the Eisenhower administration to maintain a neutral posture. In his address to a joint session of the Congress during a state visit to Washington in May 1956, the Indonesian President made an eloquent plea for his country's claim to West New Guinea:[6]

> The return of West Irian is for us the remaining part of our national political aspiration. It is the final installment on the colonial debt. We see our brothers still in chains, who joined with us in proclaiming our common independence, and so our own freedom is not yet complete. The salt of liberty cannot have its full savor for us until all of Indonesia is again united under the freedom which is the birthright of all men.

The problem was canvassed in private conversations as well, but Sukarno "failed to obtain support" for the Indonesian case.[7] The public statements of Eisenhower and other senior officials at the time maintained a discreet silence on the issue.

Fifield asserts that throughout the history of the controversy, "there were divided counsels in Washington concerning the attitudes that the United States should assume in the General Assembly."[8] In practice, the

---

[6]Quoted in *Department of State Bulletin*, vol. 34, no. 884 (January 4, 1956), p. 930.

[7]Pauker, "General Nasution's Mission to Moscow," *loc. cit.*, p. 13.

[8]Russell H. Fifield, *Southeast Asia in United States Policy* (New York: Praeger, 1963), p. 354.

alternative of noninvolvement was scrupulously followed by the Eisen-hower administration. Secretary of State John Foster Dulles sought to explain this posture at a press conference in April 1956 in the following terms:[9]

We expect to continue to take a position of neutrality because that is our general policy with relation to these highly controversial matters which involve countries both of whom are friends and where we ourselves are not directly involved.

And when the issue was again before the General Assembly in November 1957, he stated at another press conference that:[10]

Our position on (West New Guinea) is similar to that which we took last year. That is a position of neutrality. The arguments pro and con are closely balanced. We do not see a clear case to be made for either side sufficient, we think, to enable us to take a positive position on one side or another. So that we will continue, I expect, this year to abstain on the resolution.

But there was more involved in the American posture than the justifi-cations advanced by Secretary Dulles. For one thing, the Netherlands was an ancient friend and now an ally in N.A.T.O.; there was little dis-position to subject this relationship to undue strain. By 1957, moreover, Washington had come to harbor serious misgivings about the Jakarta regime. Relations had cooled perceptibly as the stridency of Sukarno's nationalism sharpened and political and economic conditions in the island republic deteriorated. Informed observers increasingly forecast the possi-bility of a complete collapse and an eventual Communist takeover. The decision to abstain on the resolution before the General Assembly in 1957, which called for the resumption of negotiations between the two parties, reflected in part an assessment of the impact of alternative courses of action on Indonesia's domestic political situation. Shortly after the vote, in which the resolution failed to obtain the two-thirds majority necessary for adoption, a "State Department spokesman" was reported to have offered a detailed explanation of the official posture. He cited first the arguments already made by Dulles, namely, that this country was "the friend of both the Dutch and the Indonesians," and that "the points in controversy are not as clear as the two parties in interest regard them." But, in addition, he stated that the United States, in its efforts to maintain links with the island republic, had the assistance of "powerful nationalist groups" in Indonesia, "all stoutly anti-Communist and some opposed to President Sukarno." To have voted against the resolution (that is, against

[9]Quoted in *Department of State Bulletin*, vol. 34, no. 877 (April 16, 1956), p. 643.
[10]*Ibid.*, vol. 37, no. 963 (December 9, 1957), p. 918.

the Indonesian position) would have undermined the strength of these groups. Conversely, "to have voted for the resolution (with its implication that the Netherlands should cede its sovereignty over West New Guinea as a condition precedent to new negotiations) would have given vast prestige to Sukarno and the influences around him, which include Communists and fellow-travelers." Faced with this dilemma, "abstention was the only wise diplomacy." [11]

The extent to which strategic considerations helped to shape policy at this juncture is unknown. The Indonesians certainly had a point when they protested that the consequence, if not the intent, of neutrality was pro-Dutch because it tended to support the status quo. Among other things, it removed the prospect of effective American pressure on The Hague to seek an accommodation on the issue. No doubt the United States still hoped for an eventual resolution of the controversy. But one has the impression that by the mid-1950s, if not before, Washington was satisfied for the time being not to disturb the existing situation in the disputed territory. Conditions in Indonesia were becoming increasingly worrisome. Washington was shocked by the violent retaliatory measures initiated against the Dutch in December 1957 following the defeat of Indonesia's appeal to the twelfth session of the General Assembly for United Nations support. Dulles expressed his disquiet at a press conference in mid-December: [12]

> That situation does give us concern. It raises a question as to the maintenance of law and order in the area. We have . . . expressed to the Indonesian Government our view that moderation should prevail and forces of law and order kept in control of the situation.

Following a N.A.T.O. Heads of Government meeting several days later, the allies also expressed their "concern" over the "recent serious events" in Indonesia.[13] This was hardly the climate in which a change in the status of West New Guinea might have won favorable consideration in Washington.

During the previous summer, the United States Ambassador in Jakarta, John M. Allison, who was alarmed by the tensions then being whipped up over West New Guinea, devised a tentative scheme for settlement of the dispute based on ultimate transfer of the territory to Indonesian control. After discussing it informally with various Indonesian officials, who ap-

---

[11]*The New York Times,* December 3, 1957. (Parentheses in quoted portion are in original).

[12]Quoted in *Department of State Bulletin,* vol. 37, no. 966 (December 30, 1957), p. 1027.

[13]See p. 57, above.

parently expressed some interest, Allison submitted his plan to the State Department for consideration. There the proposal died. Dulles was not prepared to sponsor a program favorable to Indonesia's claim; and nothing came of Allison's initiative.[14]

When the regionalist rebellions broke out in February 1958 with the proclamation of a Revolutionary Government of the Republic of Indonesia at Padang, there was little doubt that Washington's sympathies lay with the Padang regime; and substantial, not-so-covert material assistance was, in fact, channelled to the rebels by the Central Intelligence Agency. It is idle to speculate as to whether official views on the West New Guinea question might have changed if the regionalist cause had triumphed. The fortunes of war went otherwise; and during the spring, the United States had to reconsider its Indonesian policy. The upshot was a series of modest steps to improve relations with the Jakarta government. Allison was soon replaced by Howard P. Jones, who "decided that the nature of Indonesian nationalism had not been correctly understood," [15] and who came to

[14]News of this episode became known to the press. At a press conference in mid-December, Dulles was asked whether Allison had offered United States mediation at any stage. Dulles replied that Allison "was not authorized to offer mediation or good offices in the dispute between Indonesia and the Netherlands." *Department of State Bulletin,* vol. 37, no. 966 (December 30, 1957), p. 1027. In fact, Allison never offered mediation, although his plan, if it had been accepted, would have involved American mediation.

The Indonesians were disappointed at the failure of Allison's initiative. At another press conference several days later, Subandrio asserted that prior to his departure for the United Nations in November, "information conveyed to me by the United States ambassador in Jakarta indicated the possiblity of active and constructive American participation in endeavors to solve the West Irian dispute." But when he discussed the matter with Dulles in Washington a day before the opening of the General Assembly debate, the latter "for an unknown reason very firmly stated to me that the United States would continue to take a 'strictly neutral' policy and would abstain from voting on the resolution" calling for a resumption of Dutch-Indonesian negotiations. *The New York Times,* December 22, 1957.

Further details on Allison's initiative may be found in Jones, *op. cit.,* pp. 178-179. Jones was Allison's successor as United States Ambassador to Indonesia. See also van der Kroef, *The West New Guinea Dispute,* p. 30; and *Antara Daily News-bulletin,* January 6, 1958.

Kahin states: "The conviction among Indonesians that the United States sided with the Netherlands was reinforced shortly (after the General Assembly vote in December 1957) when Secretary of State Dulles abruptly recalled and transferred the American Ambassador, John Allison; for they understood that Allison had just recommended that the United States support the Indonesian claim to West Irian." Kahin, "Indonesia," *loc. cit.,* p. 682.

[15]Roger Hilsman, *To Move A Nation* (Garden City, N. Y.: Doubleday, 1967), p. 372. For Jones' own account of the West New Guinea dispute and its ultimate settlement, see Jones, *op. cit.,* pp. 174-215. His account reflects a decidedly pro-Indonesian estimate of the problem.

symbolize a more friendly attitude toward the Sukarno regime. On Jones'
recommendation, Washington agreed to the sale of substantial supplies of
light arms to the Indonesian forces, a policy "designed both to head off
the Communists and to strengthen the responsible elements of the new
Indonesian society." [16] Jones went on to establish a close personal relationship with Sukarno, although the Eisenhower administration was "less
responsive to (his) subsequent recommendations" for improving relations
with Indonesia.[17]

As for West New Guinea, the policy remained unchanged until after
Eisenhower left the White House. When Tengku Abdul Rahman, the
Malayan Prime Minister, visited Washington in October 1960 to seek
"moral support" for his plan for resolving the dispute (on the basis of
an eventual transfer of the territory to Indonesian control *via* a temporary
international trusteeship), he won only the assurance that his proposal
would be studied, while press reports indicated that the United States was
still determined to stay officially neutral.[18]

Almost inevitably, the United States position managed to satisfy neither
party to the dispute. Both sides coveted the support of so powerful a
champion, and both were disappointed when it was not forthcoming. It
was the Indonesians, however, who felt most aggrieved by the American
posture of neutrality, since the undoubted effect of this policy was to help
sustain the status quo. As time went on, this rankled more and more; and
Indonesian criticism grew correspondingly sharper. Following Indonesia's
defeat in the General Assembly in November 1957, Prime Minister Djuanda expressed his "regret" that the United States had not supported his
country in the debate.[19] Editorial comment in Indonesia was especially
caustic, and there were reports that American prestige was "collapsing"
because of Washington's neutrality on West New Guinea.[20] The usually
temperate former Vice President, Mohammad Hatta, placed much of the
blame for the failure of the United Nations to take action in the dispute
squarely on the United States:[21]

> The United States stand of neutrality . . . does, in fact, give support
> to the Dutch. Because of it, and its adoption by various other states,
> Indonesia's suggestion in the General Assembly of the United Nations
> for the opening of discussions with the Netherlands regarding West
> Irian was never able to muster the necessary two-thirds vote and

[16]Hilsman, *op. cit.,* p. 372.
[17]*Ibid.,* p. 372.
[18]See p. 71, above.
[19]*The New York Times,* December 19, 1957.
[20]*New York Herald Tribune,* December 19, 1957.
[21]Mohammad Hatta, "Indonesia Between the Power Blocs," *loc. cit.,* p. 486.

failed to pass. It has been rejected three times . . . Indonesians cannot understand why the United States should assume such a half-hearted posture in this matter.

Hatta was undoubtedly correct in suggesting that Washington's neutrality influenced the position taken by other countries in the United Nations. Two years later, the *Times of Indonesia* commented that "the intransigence of the Netherlands has only been made possible by overt Australian backing and covert American support." [22]

The Dutch, too, found cause for complaint from time to time. The government professed to be "shocked and disappointed" by comments made by Secretary of State Dulles during a visit to Jakarta in March 1956, which were construed as unduly friendly to the Indonesians and, in the case of the West New Guinea dispute, as suggesting that they adopt a more belligerent attitude toward the Dutch.[23] Foreign Minister Luns stated his "disappointment" when the United States abstained in the General Assembly vote in November 1957;[24] and a month later, he protested at American "inaction" with respect to the takeover of Dutch properties in Indonesia and the expulsion of Dutch nationals from the country.[25]

On the other hand, the Dutch must have recognized that, on balance, American neutrality favored their position. Indeed, they occasionally tried to read more into that posture than the facts warranted. In October 1958, for example, following discussions in Washington, Luns made a statement — reportedly with the approval of Dulles — to the effect that "the United States adhered strictly to the principle that violence must not be used to effect territorial changes and that this policy applied to Taiwan as much as to New Guinea." [26] After returning to The Hague, Luns claimed that the parallel between Taiwan and New Guinea had come from American officials; and he made little effort to modify the impression that he had "brought back . . . a moral commitment by the United States to oppose

[22]Quoted in L. P. Singh, "Bases of Indonesia's Claim to West New Guinea," *Australian Quarterly*, vol. 34, no. 1, (March 1962), p. 15.

[23]Quoted in *The New York Times*, March 23, 1956. Dulles had referred to the slogan "Fifty-four Forty or Fight," which was current in the United States during the dispute with Great Britain over the Oregon territory. American officials dutifully had to explain that the point of the Secretary's remark was that territorial disputes could be settled by peaceful means.

[24]Quoted in *ibid.*, November 30, 1957.

[25]Quoted in *ibid.*, December 24, 1957. Without being specific as to timing, Jones reports that there "had been only slightly veiled threats from the Dutch that they would pull out of NATO if we intervened in any way concerning West Irian." Jones, *op. cit.*, p. 180.

[26]*The New York Times*, October 26, 1958.

Indonesia if that nation should use force" against the territory.[27] When T. H. Bot, the Dutch Secretary of State for West New Guinea Affairs, visited Washington in February 1960, he reported that his government's program for the political development of the colony had been "especially favorably and positively received" by government officials; this brought forth an Indonesian expression of "anxiety," and the State Department had to explain that "no change has come in the American policy of strict neutrality towards West New Guinea." [28] Three months later, S. H. Visser, the Minister of Defense, asserted that the Netherlands "could count" on foreign help if the territory were attacked, although he did not specify where that help might come from.[29] The fact was that The Hague had no commitment of military support from any quarter in such circumstances, and certainly not from the United States. But during the Eisenhower years, it did have Washington's benevolent neutrality, and that counted for a lot.

Enter Kennedy

On the whole, the new administration of John F. Kennedy, which took office in January 1961, appeared to have a more compassionate interest than its predecessor in the manifold problems of the Afro-Asian countries, and a deeper understanding of even the more aberrant manifestations of their sensitive and volatile nationalism. There is little doubt, moreover, that the leadership of many emerging nations, including Indonesia, initially responded to the youthful President with more enthusiasm than had typically characterized their relations with the previous administration, and with greater confidence that their views would at last receive a sympathetic hearing. Not a few of them were generous in their advice as to how Kennedy might improve things. At a press conference early in February, for example, Subandrio urged the United States to "detach itself from obligations" to its N.A.T.O. allies in dealing with the West New Guinea dispute, and not to permit its military ties with the Netherlands to stand in the way of opposition to colonialism.[30] But this was a bit stiff for openers.

Washington was, however, sincerely anxious to improve relations with the Jakarta government, and to get on with the task — as the new administration saw it — of steering Sukarno and Indonesian nationalism

---

[27]*Ibid.,* October 26, 1958.
[28]Quoted in van der Kroef, "West New Guinea in the Crucible," *loc. cit.,* p. 533.
[29]Quoted in *ibid.,* p. 537.
[30]Quoted in *The New York Times,* February 12, 1961.

"into constructive channels." [31] On the recommendation of Ambassador Jones, Kennedy soon invited Sukarno to visit the White House in the course of an upcoming world tour. President Eisenhower had failed to include Indonesia in the itinerary of his 1960 trip to the Far East, and the proposed visit would serve, in part, to make up for that alleged insult.[32]

Sukarno's visit, which duly took place in April, was probably responsible in part for another apparent snub that outraged the Dutch. Early that month, the New Guinea Council was inaugurated at Hollandia with considerable fanfare. Alone among the members of the Southwest Pacific Commission, the United States declined an invitation to send a representative to the ceremonies.[33] Unofficial explanations seemed quite straightforward. While prepared to hear the views of both sides in the West New Guinea dispute, Washington was determined not to become involved at this juncture; and in particular, it wished to avoid giving offense to Sukarno on the eve of his visit to the White House. The government apparently believed that it should stay aloof from the controversy at the time in the hope of someday playing a useful role in efforts to resolve it.[34] Perhaps understandably, however, the Dutch were greatly annoyed. "The United States seems to take us for granted," Luns complained at The Hague. "Particularly in regard to Indonesia, America has slighted our views again and again." [35] Luns was in Washington shortly thereafter, and conversations with United States officials appeared to reassure him. Reporting subsequently on a meeting with the new American President on April 10, Luns stated in Rotterdam that Kennedy had endorsed the Dutch policy of self-determination for West New Guinea.[36]

While too much should not be read into this incident, it was possibly significant as indicating an incipient predisposition in Washington to lend a hand in working out a settlement at some later date. The idea certainly

[31]Hilsman, op. cit., p. 373.

[32]Throughout the period 1960-62, Jones had "continually hammered away at Washington, urging that positive action be taken to settle the West Irian dispute." Jones, op. cit., p. 189. He looked on the Sukarno visit as a step in this direction. Jones strongly concurred with the view that "the only way (the dispute) will ever be settled will be if Indonesia gets it." He was convinced not only of the "inevitability of West Irian going to Indonesia, but that it was in the United States' interest to do something to implement it." Ibid., p. 189.

[33]The membership of the Southwest Pacific Commission included Australia, France, the Netherlands, New Zealand, the United Kingdom, and the United States.

[34]See The New York Times, April 1, 1961, and April 6, 1961.

[35]Quoted in ibid., April 5, 1961. See also Richard P. Stebbins, The United States in World Affairs 1961 (New York: Harper, 1962), p. 138.

[36]See Facts on File, vol. 21, no. 1072 (May 11-17, 1961), p. 176.

came up during Kennedy's talk with Luns; and the President's reaction, even at this early stage of his administration, would appear not to have been entirely negative. At a press conference two days after his meeting with Luns, Kennedy was asked whether the United States could usefully extend its good offices in controversies such as the West New Guinea dispute. He replied:[37]

> Well, we are going to see Mr. Sukarno, and I am sure that that will be one of the matters we will discuss. I did not have a chance to — that was one of the matters touched upon by the Foreign Minister of the Netherlands. It is rather difficult for the United States to offer its good offices unless we were asked by both parties to do so. To the best of my knowledge, we have not been asked by both parties to mediate that dispute.

In short, Kennedy appeared to have an open mind on the prospect of eventual involvement; and if this were so, it represented a perceptible change of mood from the Eisenhower era. But for the present, the new administration was almost overwhelmed by other, more pressing problems in the international arena. April was the month of the Bay of Pigs; Laos was a major preoccupation; and the clouds were gathering over Berlin again. There could have been little time as yet to focus on West New Guinea; and in any case, the dispute had not yet matured to the point where intervention might have proved effective.

The visit of the Indonesian President came in late April. There are conflicting reports as to how his meetings with Kennedy went.[38] The West New Guinea problem was discussed at length, but the joint communique issued at the close of the visit was silent on the subject.[39] Jones and Brackman report that Sukarno made much of the supposed relationship between

[37]Quoted in *Public Papers of the Presidents, John F. Kennedy, Containing the Public Messages, Speeches, and Statements of the President, January 20 to December 31, 1961* (hereafter cited as *Public Papers . . . 1961*) (Washington: Government Printing Office, 962), p. 265.

[38]Hilsman states that the meeting "went well. Kennedy recognized the politician and dedicated nationalist in Sukarno, while Sukarno came away with a growing sense of Kennedy's statesmanship and his empathy for the striving peoples of the world." Hilsman, *op. cit.,* p. 373. Jones also states that the visit "went off well." For his fairly detailed account, see Jones, *op. cit.,* pp. 194-197. Brackman also supports this general appraisal. See Arnold C. Brackman, *Southeast Asia's Second Front* (New York: Praeger, 1966), pp. 101-102. Schlesinger, on the other hand, asserts that the meeting was "no great success. The Indonesian leader's vanity was unconcealed, and his interest in reasoned exchange seemed limited." Arthur M. Schlesinger, Jr., *A Thousand Days* (Boston: Houghton Mifflin, 1965), p. 533.

[39]For the full text of the communique, see *Department of State Bulletin,* vol. 44, no. 1142 (May 15, 1961), p. 713.

the dispute and the rise of Communist influence in Indonesia, and that he presented himself to the new American President as his country's "best bulwark" against communism.[40] Grant asserts that Sukarno received an assurance from Kennedy to the effect that the United States was interested in a "fresh approach" to the issue;[41] if true, this possibly reflected a renewed concern in Washington to assist at some point in the search for an eventual settlement. But here, as on other matters, "nothing concrete was accomplished." [42] For the next several months, the United States continued to adhere in practice to a public posture of passive neutrality not unlike the Eisenhower period. President Kennedy was not yet prepared to alter policy on the issue.[43]

When the West New Guinea issue again came before the United Nations in Fall 1961, the United States for the first time chose to support one of the resolutions introduced. The debate at the sixteenth session of the General Assembly revolved around a Dutch proposal to place the territory under a United Nations trusteeship, subject to the condition that the right of the Papuan population to ultimate self-determination be suitably guaranteed; a counterproposal supported by Indonesia which did not mention the principle of self-determination, and simply called on the two parties to resume negotiations under the aegis of the President of the General Assembly; and a compromise sponsored by 13 Black African countries which also called for further negotiations (with the assistance of the Secretary-General), but significantly insisted that the eventual solution be based on the principle of self-determination.[44] The position of the United States was elaborated by the American representative, Jonathan B. Bingham, in a statement which laid great stress on the importance of safeguarding the right of self-determination for the Papuans:[45]

> My Government regards as imaginative and constructive the initiative which the Government of the Netherlands has taken in proposing its relinquishment of control over West New Guinea, with a United Nations administration for an interim period. The basic condition set by the Government of the Netherlands is that the inhabitants of the territory be afforded the right to exercise freedom of choice with regard to the ultimate disposition of the area. The position of

[40]Quoted in Jones, *op. cit.,* p. 197; and Brackman, *op. cit.,* p. 101.
[41]Quoted in Grant, *op. cit.,* p. 140.
[42]Hilsman, *op. cit.,* p. 373.
[43]See Jones, *op. cit.,* p. 197. But Kennedy did initiate an exchange of correspondence with Sukarno thereafter that continued throughout his administration. See *ibid.,* p. 198.
[44]See pp. 103-107, above.
[45]*GAOR,* Sixteenth Session (1961), A/PV. 1061.

the United States on the principle of self-determination is well known, and we perceive no valid reason why an appropriate expression of the will of the people should be denied the inhabitants of West New Guinea.

On the other hand, the Netherlands draft did "not sufficiently recognize the intense Indonesian interest in the territory" and Jakarta's claim to sovereignty over it. The General Assembly should not be asked to decide between the rival claims to sovereignty. Any resolution adopted by the General Assembly should provide that the administration of West New Guinea be turned over to the United Nations for an interim period.

We believe that such a U. N. administration, leading to the expression of choice by the people of the area, should provide to Indonesia every reasonable opportunity to pursue its objective of achieving the integration of West New Guinea with Indonesia . . .

. . . in our view, adoption of a simple appeal to the parties to negotiate would amount to rejecting, or at least ignoring, the idea that the people of the area should be given the right of self-determination.

The right of self-determination was a basic right under the Charter of the United Nations and under the Declaration on the Granting of Independence to Colonial Countries and Peoples, and would appear to apply in cases where sovereignty was "open to dispute, as in the present instance."

Indonesia claims sovereignty, and its claim is supported by a number of delegations . . . the Netherlands also claims sovereignty, and its claim is likewise supported by a number of delegations. Thus, this would seem to be a case in which the principle of self-determination is entirely appropriate and indeed offers the only practical and just way out of an impasse which has now continued for more than a decade.

This first American intervention in United Nations debate on the West New Guinea issue, after so many years of silence, appeared to be an important development. While the United States might still insist that it remained neutral on the merits of the dispute, the fact was that Bingham's statement lent encouragement and support to the real objectives of Dutch policy as it had now evolved. In this respect, the substance of his speech was a logical extension, in changing circumstances, of Washington's previous posture of noninvolvement, the effect of which had also been pro-Dutch in the sense that American neutrality served to buttress the status quo. The Indonesian position was that the Papuans had long ago exercised their right of self-determination when they "joined" with "other Indonesians" in the August 1945 declaration of independence. By inescapable implication, the United States now rejected this interpretation when it espoused the view that the right was still available "in cases where sovereignty is open to dispute, as in the present instance." To be sure, the Jakarta government ought to have "every reasonable opportunity" during the interim period of United Nations administration to persuade the Papuans to integrate with Indonesia. But even the Dutch were prepared to concede this, precisely because they were confident that the Papuans would never voluntarily choose to do so. Hence the Dutch were delighted with what seemed to be a public expression of Washington's support for the main trend of their policy; while the Indonesians, bitterly disappointed, accused the United States of having abandoned neutrality on West New Guinea.[46]

But the most intriguing aspect of the affair was that it occurred just as the Kennedy administration was preparing a major shift of policy on the issue, the substance of which was to repudiate the spirit, if not the letter, of Bingham's earnest asseverations. One has the impression that his statement was a last reflection of "orthodox" State Department thinking on Dutch-Indonesian relations: that is, instinctively pro-Dutch in deference to traditional ties of friendship and the vital importance of the N.A.T.O. link; concerned over the course of Indonesia's internal evolution and the tendencies of its foreign policy; unwilling to appease Sukarno's nationalist megalomania; yet alive to the dangers of war and anxious to make a contribution to peaceful settlement of the dispute. In this context, it is hardly surprising that the Department, traditionally devoted to the principle of self-determination for dependent peoples, should have been impressed by the apparent fairness of the Dutch proposal and taken the initiative to support its main thesis before the General Assembly, although every effort was made in Bingham's speech to preserve the appearance of impartiality as between the protagonists.[47] But this approach was increasingly out of touch with the changing appraisal of Kennedy's inner circle as to how best to deal with the island republic; and Bingham's speech had little, if any, long-term significance as an authoritative articulation of United States policy on West New Guinea.[48]

[46]See *The New York Times,* December 1, 1961, and December 19, 1961.

[47]Jones asserts that he subsequently learned at the State Department that the United States delegation had acted on this occasion without instructions and on its own initiative. See Jones, *op. cit.,* p. 201. This may be correct; but the thrust of the American intervention was to support the "orthodox" view of the problem.

[48]Interestingly enough, the annual *U. S. Participation in the UN, Report by the President to the Congress for the Year 1961* (Washington: U. S. Government Printing Office, 1962) reports in detail on Bingham's interventions, but has nothing to say about the new initiatives launched late in the year by the Kennedy administration to settle the dispute. See *ibid.,* pp. 165-175.

Chapter Nine

The Decision To Intervene

The Kennedy administration brought a sense of urgency to United States relations with the socalled Third World of Asia, Africa, and Latin America. Kennedy himself believed that in the global confrontation with communism, the struggle for Western Europe was essentially won. The battleground had now shifted to the Third World countries.[1] "Today's struggle does not lie (in Western Europe)," he said in 1963, but rather in Asia, Latin America, and Africa.[2] What were the implications for policy?

Kennedy recognized, and was prepared to accept, that most of the emerging nations were determined to keep free of the entangling alliances of Cold War politics. He once remarked that the desire for independence "carries with it the desire not to become engaged as a satellite of the Soviet Union or too closely allied to the United States."[3] But this was no obstacle to effective cooperation. From the standpoint of American interest, the important thing was not to make unwilling allies of the newly independent countries; overt alignment offered little concrete advantage to the United States, and was usually a highly divisive issue in the domestic politics of the emerging nations. What really mattered was that these countries preserve their independence as against the Communists, and their own passion for freedom afforded the common ground for a fruitful collaboration. The object of policy should be to assist these countries to develop sufficient political cohesiveness and economic strength to survive as independent states. Cooperation to this end served the larger purposes of the United States in the struggle with communism far more than the quest for meaningless alliances. Schlesinger summarizes this aspect of the Kennedy administration's approach in the following terms:[4]

Where (Secretary of State John Foster) Dulles divided the world on the question of whether nations would sign up in a crusade against communism, thereby forcing the neutrals to the other side of the line,

[1]For a brief discussion of Kennedy's views on the Third World countries, see Schlesinger, *op. cit.*, pp. 506-509.
[2]Quoted in *ibid.*, p. 507.
[3]Quoted in *ibid.*, p. 507.
[4]*Ibid.*, pp. 507-508.

Kennedy, by making national independence the crucial question, invited the neutrals to find a common interest with us in resisting communist expansion.

Kennedy was determined to make a fresh start with the neutralist countries, and he abandoned forthwith the moralizing that often seemed to characterize Washington's approach during the tenure of Secretary Dulles. In his brief inaugural address, Kennedy spoke directly to "those new states whom we welcome to the ranks of the free," and his eloquence evoked a universal response. "We shall not always expect to find them supporting our view," he continued. "But we shall always hope to find them strongly supporting their own freedom." [5]

While the record of the Truman and Eisenhower years reflected a responsible concern for developments in the emerging nations, the spokesmen of the New Frontier often professed a deeper sympathy and broader understanding. There was, in particular, a sensitivity to the "pride of nationalism" among the newly independent countries, an awareness of its origins, respect for its aspirations, a more tolerant acceptance of its bluster and importunities. [6] Before he took office, Kennedy had remarked that "more energy is released by the awakening of these new nations than by the fission of the atom itself." [7] The task of policy was not to frustrate this surge of nationalist feeling, but rather to guide it onto constructive pathways.

The President "was not sentimental about these peoples or their flamboyant leaders." [8] He accepted that they would cause trouble, and that at times they would have to be dealt with firmly. But he also acknowledged the right of each nation to "develop its own full potential peaceably, preserving and cultivating the essence of its own culture and way of life." [9] According to Hilsman, his general guidelines for policy toward the newly independent countries were understood within the administration to be as follows: [10]

> The effort to project oneself into the other fellow's position, to develop an understanding of the new nationalisms should be made. The United States, where it could without injury to other interests and with regard to our own friends and obligations, should try to find a way to provide the new nationalisms all the help we could in develop-

[5]Quoted in *Public Papers . . . 1961*, p. 1.

[6]For an analysis of nationalism in the emerging nations by a prominent member of the Kennedy administration, see Hilsman, *op. cit.*, pp. 363-366.

[7]Quoted in Hilsman, *op. cit.*, p. 362.

[8]*Ibid.*, p. 366.

[9]*Ibid.*, p. 367.

[10]*Ibid.*, p. 367.

ing economically, in assuming the responsibility that was rightfully theirs for maintaining peace in their own region, and in finding the voice in world affairs to which they were entitled. Our purpose, in a word, was to help them achieve their legitimate aspirations.

In particular, the consequences of frustrated nationalism had to be guarded against. Here the danger was not so much that the Communists might capture the leadership of these nationalist movements, although this had happened before (for example, in Vietnam during the 1940s and 1950s). Rather it was that the emerging nations might be misled into a "grand alliance with the Communists against the West," even though they were not converted to communism.[11] Such an alliance could gravely threaten the world position of the United States.

The Problem of Indonesia

In the case of Indonesia, implementation of these concepts posed special difficulties. The Jakarta government had already travelled far down the road toward a "grand alliance" with the Communist countries.

Almost from the beginning, the Indonesian republic had espoused a neutralist posture in world affairs; as early as 1950, "the symbol of an independent foreign policy was an integral part of Indonesian nationalism."[12] In the early years, this did not imply a strong anti-Western or anti-American orientation. But during the middle 1950s, Indonesian neutralism grew more assertive and militant, as Jakarta staked out a claim to leadership of the world's anticolonialist forces. Relations with the West, including the United States, deteriorated steadily. Foreign business enterprises operating in Indonesia "found the political climate increasingly unsympathetic."[13] While it is difficult to judge the relevance of the West New Guinea controversy to this general development, there seems little doubt that mounting frustration over Jakarta's inability to resolve the question satisfactorily, and resentment at the failure of most Western countries to support the national claim, were significant contributing factors. For the United States, a low point was reached in 1958 when Washington undertook to supply arms and other material support to the regionalist rebels, a step which understandably infuriated the Sukarno regime. Some progress was made thereafter in restoring a measure of normality to United States relations with Indonesia, largely through the patient efforts of Am-

[11]Ibid., p. 366.
[12]Feith, op. cit., p. 350. For an authoritative statement on this subject, see Mohammad Hatta, "Indonesia's Foreign Policy," Foreign Affairs, vol. 31, no. 3 (April 1953), pp. 441-452.
[13]Feith, op. cit., pp. 350-351.

bassador Jones. But a thousand irritants remained; and, despite the continuation of some assistance programs, Washington found itself in 1961 with little effective influence on the course of Indonesian developments.

Meanwhile, Sukarno was turning more and more to the Communist bloc for material aid and diplomatic support. Rapprochement with the Communists got under way in the early 1950s, with the first accreditation of Indonesian ambassadors to Peking and Moscow in 1953 and 1954. Trade with the bloc countries increased substantially thereafter. For some years, the Indonesian leadership was disinclined to accept military or economic assistance from the Communists, in large part in order to avoid dependence on Communist sources of supply, but also because of the prestige that might accrue thereby to the already powerful Indonesian Communist Party (P.K.I.). In 1956, the Indonesian parliament declined to take up a $100 million line of credit offered by the Soviet Union. But after the United States rejected an Indonesian request for arms the following year, Jakarta overcame its scruples and in 1958 began to accept both military and economic assistance from the bloc. In the years that followed, a series of aid agreements was concluded, of which perhaps the most important was the arms deal negotiated by General Nasution in January 1961. By 1962, credits from bloc countries exceeded $1.5 billion, of which more than half was for military assistance.[14] The massive military buildup thus set in motion was publicly justified largely in terms of the West New Guinea dispute, especially after suppression of the regionalist revolts.

In view of the previous aversion of the Indonesian armed forces to become dependent on military assistance from the Communists, the Nasution deal in particular must have appeared to presage a major shift toward the bloc countries.[15] Jakarta's foreign policy pronouncements took on a strongly anti-Western bias, which seemed to reflect "a somewhat uncritical acceptance of Communist claims and an overly positive evaluation of (Soviet) proposals on pending international problems."[16] Cordial relations with the Soviet Union were supplemented by progressively closer ties with the People's Republic of China, especially after 1960. For some years previously, the relationship had been shadowed by Jakarta's assault on the

[14]See Pauker, "The Soviet Challenge in Indonesia," loc. cit., pp. 613-614.

[15]See, for example, Pauker's analysis in ibid; and in his earlier article, "General Nasution's Mission to Moscow," loc. cit. Van der Kroef's conclusions were less pessimistic. See his article, "Nasution, Sukarno and the West New Guinea Dispute," loc. cit.

[16]Stebbins, The United States in World Affairs 1961, p. 211.

Overseas Chinese community in Indonesia.[17] While Sukarno did not trumpet the concept of a Jakarta-Peking axis until later, by 1961 it was apparent that the two countries were swinging into close alignment on most issues. Treaties of friendship and cultural cooperation were signed that year, and both sides renewed pledges of mutual support for their respective territorial claims to West New Guinea and Taiwan. Thereafter, Sukarno frequently elaborated on the doctrine, which he first developed at the Belgrade Conference of Non-Aligned Countries in September 1961, of a world divided into two hostile camps representing the socalled Old Established Forces and Newly Emerging Forces (the OLDEFO and NEFO, in Sukarno's identifying acronyms); and he proudly proclaimed Indonesia's leading position in the ranks of the latter.

By 1961, a current if pessimistic view of Soviet policy in Indonesia held that Moscow stood on the threshold of a major breakthrough. Pauker's estimate, for example, was as follows:[18]

Indonesia has become a major target of Soviet aid and influence, and only massive Western efforts can now prevent its gradual incorporation into the Communist bloc. All the instrumentalities available to the Kremlin — overt and covert, domestic and international — are concentrated on the elimination of Western influences from Indonesia, its isolation from the new nations of Asia and Africa, erosion of the will of domestic anti-Communist political forces to resist capture of the government by the Communist Party, and eventual alignment with the Soviet Union.

The analysis was that Soviet diplomacy skillfully fostered a fundamental reorientation of Indonesia's international position through support for Jakarta's foreign policy objectives (in particular, the recovery of West New Guinea), and by the apparent generosity and effectiveness of its aid programs. The massive scope of this assistance encouraged a growing Indonesian dependence on Communist sources of supply, especially for arms, and at the same time mortgaged foreign exchange earnings to ser-

---

[17]On this subject, see Donald E. Willmott, *The National Status of the Chinese in Indonesia, 1900-1958* (Ithaca: Modern Indonesia Project, Cornell University, 1961); G. William Skinner, "The Chinese Minority," in McVey, *op. cit.*, pp. 97-117; and, for brief accounts of the Sino-Indonesian rapprochement, Lea E. Williams, "Sino-Indonesian Diplomacy: A Study of Revolutionary International Politics," *China Quarterly*, no. 11 (July-September 1962), pp. 184-199; and Brackman, *op. cit.*, pp. 257-266.

[18]Pauker, "The Soviet Challenge in Indonesia," *loc. cit.*, p. 612. The article was published in July 1962, before settlement of the West New Guinea dispute. An established authority on Indonesia, Pauker was then head of the Asia section of the Social Science Department of the RAND Corporation.

vice a mounting debt to the bloc countries. Aid programs also opened channels for the exercise of more subtle influence by Soviet technicians and military advisers. Meanwhile, the arms buildup exacerbated an already chaotic economic situation, fomented runaway inflation, and enhanced the prospect of an eventual economic collapse.

In this context, Moscow was pictured as deliberately pushing for a military showdown between Indonesia and the Netherlands. Pauker reports that just before preliminary negotiations between the two sides began in March 1962, the Soviet Ambassador in Jakarta "expressed to Foreign Minister Subandrio his displeasure at Indonesia's efforts to achieve a peaceful solution of the West New Guinea dispute after receiving massive Soviet military aid and political encouragement to take West New Guinea by force." [19] Large-scale hostilities presumably would polarize the support of Western countries behind the Dutch, and thereby hasten Indonesia's definitive alignment with the Communist bloc; while, at the same time, the economic costs and the political tensions engendered by prolonged conflict would inevitably accelerate the processes of decay within the country.

The P.K.I. was often assumed to be a major beneficiary of all this. The party had made a remarkable recovery since the abortive Madiun uprising in 1948 and the ruthless suppression that followed it. By 1961, the P.K.I. was reputed to be the largest or second largest Communist party outside the bloc countries, and it was almost certainly the strongest political grouping within Indonesia. As the system of guided democracy developed in the late 1950s, political power was effectively shared in uneasy partnership between Sukarno and the armed forces, especially the Indonesian Army. But while Sukarno had considerable influence over the government bureaucracy, he lacked an organizational base of his own to sustain the precarious equilibrium with the military. He was "in permanent danger of becoming more dependent on the army than it (was) on him unless he (could) balance . . . other groups against it." [20] He thus courted the backing of various political parties, including the P.K.I., to buttress his own position. The Communists, in turn, were prepared for many reasons to give Sukarno their support. The association afforded the party a measure of political legitimacy in the shadow of Sukarno's towering prestige, while at the same time providing some protection against suppression by the military (which since 1958 had imposed progressively more stringent restrictions on the activities of the Communists). In addition, the P.K.I. secured at least potential access to a share of government

[19]*Ibid.*, p. 613.
[20]Feith, *op. cit.*, p. 337.

134 WEST NEW GUINEA

authority. Thus far, the Communists had not obtained places in the cabinet, despite Sukarno's most diligent efforts to overcome Army opposition to this step. But the party was represented on such symbolically important bodies as the Supreme Advisory Council and the National Planning Council; and the two top figures, D. N. Aidit and M. H. Lukman, were awarded quasi-cabinet status (although without administrative responsibility) in March 1962 with their appointment to the newly-formed State Leadership Consultative Body.

From this perspective, Communist bloc programs of military and economic assistance to Indonesia, and diplomatic backing for Jakarta's foreign policy objectives, further strengthened the P.K.I. "Soviet maneuvers (helped) the party by making the Indonesian cabinet so dependent on communist-bloc economic, military and diplomatic support that it dare not alienate Communist good will." [21] All-out party endorsement of Sukarno's West New Guinea policy was an obvious political tactic. If the territory were at last recovered from the Dutch, the P.K.I. would share in the general acclaim. Meanwhile, the deterioration of the economy and, indeed, of the whole fabric of Indonesian society, which had already asumed alarming proportions and which might be greatly speeded up by the outbreak of war with the Netherlands, could presumably set the stage for a Communist accession to power. In Pauker's judgment, P.K.I. strategy was: [22]

... to create so compelling an image of strength, purposefulness and dedication to the national cause, under the protection of President Sukarno, that eventually all other political forces will be discredited and the P.K.I., standing as a tower of strength in the midst of chaos, will be brought to power by acclamation. Naturally, the more that Soviet military assistance weakens the military's will to resist Communism, the easier would be the takeover.

To be sure, aspects of this general analysis were disputed by some observers. Writing shortly after settlement of the West New Guinea dispute, Feith argued that Soviet objectives in Indonesia were "probably more modest" than sometimes thought: [23]

Moscow may indeed have hoped to contribute to the likelihood of an Indonesian-Dutch war. However, its principal goal for the foreseeable future is likely to be to maintain the advantages it now enjoyed in Indonesia, rather than to seek new gains. Large-scale Russian

[21]Guy J. Pauker, "Current Communist Tactics in Indonesia," *Asian Survey,* vol. 1, no. 3 (May 1961), p. 28.
[22]Pauker, "The Soviet Challenge in Indonesia," *loc. cit.,* p. 624.
[23]Feith, *op. cit.,* p. 356.

military and other aid could thus be interpreted as an attempt to keep President Sukarno in power, and to make sure of a continued flow of friendly words from him, to forestall a major repressive action against the PKI, and to maintain influence vis-a-vis Peking within both the Indonesian government and the Indonesian Communist party.

As for the P.K.I., Feith conceded the growing organizational strength of the party, in contrast to the plight of most other political groupings under the system of guided democracy. But these gains were "heavily outweighed by the losses the party has sustained" in the process. In face of the growing hostility of the armed forces and the "damocles sword of banning" that constantly hung over its head, the P.K.I. had been forced to accept increasingly severe restrictions on its activities. The influence of Communist sympathizers in the officer corps had been "steadily reduced since 1958;" and despite the honorific posts to which some leading members and sympathizers had been appointed, the party had not yet gained "a significant foothold" in the bureaucracy.[24] Feith concludes:[25]

By its policy of support for President Sukarno, the party has saved itself from being banned, but it has paid for this freedom by accepting considerable emasculation . . . It is true that the PKI's good organization, its freedom from evident clique conflict, its members' moral discipline and dedication to the task, and its popularity among peasants, workers, artisans, petty traders, and teachers are remarkable and widely admired. It seems highly improbable, however, that such admiration alone could bring the party to power; the latter could happen only if international or other developments induced a major loss of the will to power on the part of the ruling groups of the present period.

Estimates on this and other matters varied a good deal. But most observers were generally agreed on a pessimistic appraisal of Indonesia's current situation; and the long-term propects often looked to be immensely disquieting.

The Relevance of West New Guinea

It seemed clear, moreover, that the West New Guinea issue had become a key element in the dynamics of Indonesian politics. One could reasonably argue that Jakarta's changing international orientation, its drift toward the Communist bloc and growing dependence on military and economic assistance from bloc sources, were in large measure the con-

[24]*Ibid.*, p. 340.
[25]*Ibid.*, pp. 340-341.

sequence of frustration arising out of its persistent inability to resolve the dispute satisfactorily. By the same token, Indonesia's economic decline and the dissensions of domestic politics, which appeared to some analysts to open up the possibility of an ultimate P.K.I. takeover, could also be attributed in some degree to preoccupation with West New Guinea. Both strands converged in the threat of large-scale war with the Netherlands, which by the end of 1961 seemed increasingly likely.

President Kennedy regarded Indonesia as "one of the potentially significant nations of Asia;" and he was "anxious to slow up its drift toward the communist bloc." [26] The President's confidant and younger brother, Attorney-General Robert F. Kennedy, later summarized one dimension of this significance in the following terms: [27]

> The Communists, both Russian and Chinese, have realized the importance of this new nation. Capture of Indonesia by the Communists would enable them to flank the whole of Southeast Asia, an area barely holding onto freedom by its fingertips. Not only would such an achievement have world-wide implications; it would give to the Communists tremendous natural resources of oil and rubber.

There was real danger that Indonesia might precipitate a major war with the Netherlands over West New Guinea, and such a development could only redound to the advantage of the Communists. In the Attorney-General's words: [28]

> As the Communists saw it, if hostilities were begun by Indonesia, the West, including the United States, would end up on the side of the Dutch, opposing the military action of the Indonesians. The lineup would then be described as a struggle between the colonial nations, supported by the United States, against the new nations of the world, supported by the Communists. This was a conflict which would be unpleasant at best and would, over an extended period of time, be virtually impossible for us to win. The Communists would become far more entrenched in Indonesia, the anti-Communists would have their position undermined, and Southeast Asia would have been encircled by the Soviet Union and China.

According to Brackman, Sukarno skillfully exploited the communism issue during his visit to Washington in April 1961 in order to encourage a shift of United States policy on West New Guinea. He acknowledged the growing strength of the Communist movement in Indonesia, but insisted

[26]Schlesinger, *op. cit.*, p. 533.
[27]Robert F. Kennedy, *Just Friends and Brave Enemies* (New York: Harper & Row, 1962), pp. 4-5.
[28]*Ibid.*, p. 6.

that the territorial dispute with the Netherlands "played into the hands of the PKI." [29] Describing himself as the "best bulwark in Indonesia against Communism," he urged the new President to give him support.[30] The implication presumably was that once Indonesia "recovered" the lost territory, Jakarta would at last turn to the urgent tasks of domestic reconstruction; and that thereafter, the Communists could no longer take advantage of the dispute, or of worsening political and economic conditions resulting from it, to consolidate their own position in the country. Sukarno's "apparent sincerity" in all this was reported to have "impressed" Kennedy.[31]

Other considerations were involved in the President's evolving estimate. Apart from the consequences of war on Indonesia, he was determined that the dispute should not "develop to the point of a great-power confrontation in the Banda Sea with Moscow and Peking backing Indonesia while America backed the Dutch; . . . West New Guinea did not seem to him a part of the world in which great powers should be rationally engaged." [32] But this was precisely what might occur if the situation were allowed to deteriorate much further. Throughout this period, Kennedy was preoccupied with the problem of Laos; if the issues at stake in that unhappy country were not worth a showdown among the superpowers, West New Guinea must have seemed a peripheral concern at best.

Kennedy was, moreover, anxious for a fresh beginning with the neutralist countries. The task of building satisfactory relations with them, and of encouraging their development along non-Communist lines, was difficult enough without the bitter diversion of disputes left over from the liquidation of colonialism. He felt that West New Guinea was "the kind of pointless colonial issue which only exacerbated relations between the West and the emergent Afro-Asian world . . . by removing a source of nagging irritation between Indonesia and the West, both parties would profit." [33] Ambasador Jones once commented on:[34]

> . . . the overriding influence of the West Irian dispute in shaping the views of the Indonesian people toward the outside world. It cast its shadow over the whole range of Indonesia's relations with the

[29]Brackman, op. cit., p. 102.

[30]Quoted in ibid., p. 101.

[31]Ibid., p. 102. It is clear from Ambassador Jones' account that he, too, vigorously supported this general point of view in his advices to Washington. See Jones, op. cit., pp. 174-215, passim.

[32]Schlesinger, op. cit., p. 534.

[33]Brackman, op. cit., pp. 102-103.

[34]Quoted in Department of State Bulletin, vol. 47, no. 1221 (November 19, 1962), p. 768.

Western World, including the United States . . . (and) stood as a major barrier between us.

Indeed, a case could be made for the hypothesis that the evolution of a more constructive relationship with the Jakarta government hinged on a prior settlement of the dispute along lines acceptable to Indonesia. Nor could this passion for West New Guinea be dismissed as a crotchet peculiar to Sukarno. In Hilsman's judgment, "it was the new nationalism itself that was the driving force of Indonesia;" even if Sukarno disappeared from the scene, "the basic thrust of Indonesian aspirations would remain the same." [35]

Within the New Frontier it was often argued, too, that Sukarno and his colleagues would never turn their attention to urgent problems of political and economic reform until the West New Guinea controversy was settled to their satisfaction; or conversely, that the territory was in truth the "final installment on the colonial debt" which, when once redeemed in full, would remove the last barrier to a grand assault on Indonesia's overwhelming domestic difficulties. Shortly after the 1962 settlement, for example, Jones spoke in almost lyrical terms about the prospects opened up thereby. During the preceding 20 years, he said: [36]

> . . . an almost unbroken succession of disasters and other disturbances — foreign invasion, military occupation, revolution, internal rebellion, and the mobilization brought about by the West Irian dispute . . . (had) had their depressing influence on the nation's ability to concentrate its efforts on bringing to its people the fruits of their rich land. Now . . . these disturbances are all things of the past. Indonesia has at last reached the stage of opportunity to develop its great resources and to turn the energy and genius of its people wholeheartedly to the task of creating a just and prosperous society.

In retrospect, it seems clear that this hope was in vain. Indonesia's problems were more profound than West New Guinea; some of them, and the relationship of the territorial dispute to these deeper maladjustments of Indonesian society, were discussed in an earlier chapter.[37] Writing shortly after settlement of the dispute in 1962, Hanna summarized this perspective as follows:[38]

[35]Hilsman, op. cit., pp. 370-371.

[36]Quoted in Department of State Bulletin, vol. 47, no. 1221 (November 19, 1962), p. 769.

[37]See pp. 26-33, above.

[38]Willard A. Hanna, "The Irian Barat Settlement," American Universities Field Staff Reports Service, Southeast Asia Series, vol. 10, no. 18 (Indonesia) (New York: American Universities Field Staff, 1962), p. 7.

The Irian Barat settlement . . . like the Irian Barat dispute and crisis, centered not upon Irian Barat at all, and the consequences are likely to be felt least of all within Irian Barat itself. The dispute, the crisis, the settlement, and the consequences center, rather, upon Indonesia. The whole unhappy Irian Barat episode can best be regarded as an evidence of long and profound disturbance within Indonesia, not the cause but the symptom of a chronic national illness.

But President Kennedy presumably shared — or, at least, he was prepared to test — the hypothesis that resolution of the West New Guinea dispute was an essential preliminary to diverting the force of Indonesian nationalism into constructive channels.[39]

It was apparent, moreover, that the settlement would have to be formulated largely on Indonesian terms. Jakarta now pursued the national claim with unexampled passion, and the threat of war could not be taken lightly. At this late date, it was highly improbable that Sukarno would settle for anything less than full control over the disputed territory. The zeal of the Dutch, on the other hand, was steadily weakening. According to Schlesinger, Kennedy "was sure that the Dutch, having declined to fight over Java and Sumatra, would hardly go to war over this last barren fragment of their Pacific empire." [40] This was apparent not only from the trend of discussion in press and parliament, but also from the shifting policies of the government itself. Dutch proposals to the General Assembly in Fall 1961 made manifest their determination to get rid of the albatross of West New Guinea as quickly as possible through the expedient of international trusteeship, although at the time The Hague was still not prepared to turn the territory over to Sukarno. All that remained was to persuade the Dutch to swallow this last bitter pill as well, and to hand over the colony "under an appropriate face-saving formula." [41]

To be sure, the implication of this approach was that the achievement of almost any settlement acceptable to Indonesia was more important than the particular issues involved in the dispute, including the question of self-determination for the Papuans. But this judgment was congruent with

---

[39]See Brackman, op. cit., p. 103; and Hilsman, op. cit., pp. 371-372.

[40]Schlesinger, op. cit., p. 533-534.

[41]Ibid., p. 533. Stebbins points out that since "the declared U. S. objective was not to impose a particular solution but simply to bring about some adjustment that would prevent a military clash, its influence tended almost automatically to be exerted in the direction of trying to satisfy the more militant of the two parties. Under these circumstances, the essential problem in the negotiations was to find a way of meeting Indonesia's demands while still retaining such safeguards as might be possible for the benefit of the Netherlands, its Papuan subjects, and world opinion." Richard P. Stebbins, The United States in World Affairs 1962 (New York: Harper & Row, 1963), p. 208.

the New Frontier's general assessment as to the significance of Indonesia
in world affairs, and the impact of the controversy on that country's
domestic politics and international orientation. As Hilsman states:[42]

> The spectacle of the Soviet Union and the other Communist coun-
> tries supplying Indonesia with a billion dollars of military arms and
> equipment and the increasing Communist influence that was the
> logical resultant of this aid had given the United States cause to
> worry about the wisdom of continuing this policy of passive neutral-
> ity. But the prospect of war between Indonesia and the Netherlands
> made it even worse.

It was also recognized that if the United States abandoned its neutral
posture in the dispute, which "inevitably favored the *status quo* and thus
the Dutch," [43] in order to work for a settlement of this kind, a serious
strain would inevitably be placed on relations with the Netherlands. No
one relished this necessity; Hilsman, for example, observes:[44]

> The Kennedy administration took pride in its sympathy and under-
> standing for the emerging nations, but the American friendship for
> the Netherlands was old and treasured. It was also interconnected
> with the problems of NATO and the defense of Europe, and this
> was at a time when the Soviet Union was renewing its threats on
> Berlin.

But this was a price that had to be paid, and presumably the assessment
was that no irretrievable damage would be done to ties with The Hague.

Prelude to Intervention

The decision to play a more active role in the Dutch-Indonesian controversy, and to assist positively in the search for a peaceful settlement,
apparently took shape late in 1961. Kennedy discussed West New Guinea
with Sukarno during the latter's visit in April, but without specific result.
For several months more, Washington continued to straddle the issue.
When the dispute came before the General Assembly in Fall 1961, the
United States rather unexpectedly joined in the debate for the first time
in the long history of United Nations consideration of the issue. By and
large, the position taken on this occasion generally supported the Dutch
approach to a solution, although not the specific proposals put forth by
The Hague; and the seeming shift greatly disquieted the Indonesians.

It has already been suggested that American policy on this occasion

---

[42]Hilsman, *op. cit.*, pp. 374-375.
[43]*Ibid.*, p. 374.
[44]*Ibid.*, p. 375.

probably reflected "orthodox" State Department thinking on how to deal with the controversy. The socalled Europeanists, those who assigned high priority to United States interests in Europe, have often exercised a dominant influence in the counsels of the Department; and it is sometimes alleged that they have, on occasion, led this country to misconceive or neglect its proper interests in other parts of the world. Hilsman states that during this period, "the 'old Europe' group, supported by strong voices inside the CIA, were decisive" on questions relating to Indonesia, and that they opposed a shift from the policy of neutrality on West New Guinea. ". . . the Far Eastern Bureau, weakened in the McCarthy era, lacked the strong leadership that it would have to have to carry weight in Washington." [45] Schlesinger adds that the "Europeanists at State saw little point in satisfying Sukarno's imperialistic ambitions at the expense of a NATO ally; and throughout most of 1961 the Department kept threatening to align us with the Dutch against the Indonesians in the UN." [46] This momentarily happened in the Fall. It should be remembered that at the time, the Russians were again exerting heavy pressure on Berlin, and the importance of maintaining the solidarity of N.A.T.O. seemed manifest. An obvious implication was that the Dutch had to be supported on West New Guinea, or at least not opposed, in order to avoid disrupting the alliance at a critical juncture.

The Defense Department usually supported the Europeanists on colonial questions.[47] In the case of Portugal, for example, the importance of the American base in the Azores for N.A.T.O. logistical support determined the Pentagon's attitude when issues involving Portuguese territories in Africa arose. This calculus apparently did not apply, however, with respect to the Netherlands and West New Guinea. On the contrary, Pentagon influence tended to emphasize "the friendliness side in a policy of 'firm friendliness' " toward Indonesia.[48] There were special reasons for this which seem to have outweighed an undoubted concern for the Netherlands and its significance for N.A.T.O. Over the years, the American military had forged close ties with the Indonesian armed forces through the implementation of two little publicized but highly successful aid programs: a civic action program to assist Indonesian military units in carrying out civil reconstruction projects (which helped to generate popular support for the military, and also served to justify the maintenance of a large army in peacetime); and an officer training program, as a result of which "one-

[45]Hilsman, op. cit., p. 377. See also Jones, op. cit., pp. 202-203.
[46]Schlesinger, op. cit., p. 534.
[47]On the Defense Department's position on the West New Guinea issue, see Hilsman, op. cit., pp. 376-377; and Jones, op. cit., p. 203.
[48]Hilsman, op. cit., p. 377.

third of the Indonesian general staff had had some sort of training from Americans" by 1961, and "almost half of the officer corps." [49] These programs had given the Pentagon "an opportunity to develop an understanding of Indonesia." Hilsman continues:[50]

As a result of (them), the American and Indonesian military had come to know each other rather well. Bonds of personal respect and even affection existed, as a matter of fact, that gave the Pentagon an understanding of Indonesian motives and aspirations that was better than any other agency in Washington.

Presumably the Pentagon had also appraised the dimensions of the Communist danger in Indonesia. A major purpose of the civic action and military training programs was to strengthen the Indonesian military for an eventual showdown with the Communists.

However strong the influence of the Europeanists, there were always voices at State to support a fresh approach on West New Guinea. No doubt the dissidents took heart with the advent of the Kennedy administration; and we may assume that proposals for a more active United States role were frequently advanced during 1961 in the normal course of policy planning and discussion. From Jakarta, Ambassador Jones strove diligently "to make Washington understand that the time had come to change our policy of passive neutrality . . . and take positive steps to settle the question." It seemed obvious to Jones that, "as military hardware continued to pour in from Russia and the bloc, . . . it was only a matter of time before Indonesia would be sufficiently well-equipped militarily to challenge the Dutch." [51]

But the task of effecting a change of policy is time-consuming at best, and usually involves the slow erosion of resistance to change rather than sudden and dramatic conversion. A shakeup at the State Department in late November, which brought W. Averell Harriman to the Far Eastern Bureau as Assistant Secretary of State for Far Eastern Affairs, appears to have been a decisive development in leading the United States to intervene in the West New Guinea dispute. Harriman "understood the new nationalisms intuitively, both the need for firmness when their ambitions soared and the equal need to provide them an honorable alternative;" he also "had personal prestige and power," and he knew how to use them.[52] When he "became convinced that there was a real threat to peace in the West Irian issue and that the United States was, at this juncture, the only

[49]*Ibid.*, p. 377.

[50]*Ibid.*, p. 377.

[51]Jones, *op. cit.*, p. 202. Jones insists that Sukarno's threat of war "was not a bluff." *Ibid.*, p. 203.

[52]Hilsman, *op. cit.*, p. 378.

nation with sufficient leverage to do anything about it, things began to happen."[53] Harriman promptly undertook to "redress the balance" of opinion in the State Department with respect to the Dutch-Indonesian controversy.[54] Thereafter, "United States policy began to move from 'passive neutrality' to a more active role in trying to head off actual hostilities and in bringing the two disputants into face-to-face negotiations." [55]

Kennedy was certainly aware of the main lines of debate within the government, but he hesitated for many months before deciding on a change of policy. By December, the deteriorating situation in the territory and the darkening prospect of war must have persuaded him that something had to be done. According to Schlesinger, it was Robert Komer, then on the staff of the National Security Council, who actually proposed to Kennedy that the United States "take the initiative in trying to settle the West New Guinea argument;" and the President was reportedly "immediately responsive" to Komer's suggestion.[56] Harriman's presence at the Far Eastern Bureau greatly simplified the task of overcoming opposition within the State Department and translating the concept into firm policy. Thus the stage was set for Washington to play the "more active role" it had so long preferred to avoid.

The United States as Mediator

In ordinary circumstances, diplomatists are properly chary of gratuitous involvement in the quarrels of other countries. However well-intentioned, the role of the third-party intermediary has usually been thankless, and always lonely. It is a measure of the changed environment of world politics since World War II — not least, the transformed position and vastly increased responsibilities of the United States in the international arena—that Washington should have determined in the national interest to intervene in a dispute over territory physically so remote from our shores as West New Guinea, and involving principals with whom we sought only to maintain friendly relations. The calculations of national interest which led to this decision have been reviewed above. At this point, it remains to consider briefly the assets and liabilities that this country brought to the role of self-appointed mediator in the controversy between Indonesia and the Netherlands.

[53]Jones, *op. cit.*, p. 202.
[54]Schlesinger, *op. cit.*, p. 534.
[55]Hilsman, *op. cit.*, p. 378.
[56]Schlesinger, *op. cit.*, p. 533.

Perhaps even more extraordinary, by the standards of prewar experience, was the decision to implement this policy in close coordination
with the parallel initiative of the United Nations Secretary-General to
assist in the search for settlement. Goodrich introduces his thoughtful
study of United States participation in the Korean War with the following
comments:[57]

> Thirty years ago if the United States had found it necessary to defend
> an important national interest in Korea, it would have acted inde-
> pendently of the world organization then in existence — the League
> of Nations — and any miiltary action that it might have taken would
> have been carried out independently of the purposes, principles and
> procedures of that organization. The need, even the propriety of thus
> accommodating the policies of the United States to those of other
> powers because it was in the national interest to have their approval
> and support would not have been admitted.

During the interwar period, a proposal for joint mediation with the League
of Nations in an international dispute of the time would have seemed
scarcely less exceptional. But by the 1960s, all this had changed. Cooperation with the Secretary-General of the United Nations for peacekeeping
purposes had become established practice. The United States suffered
from certain disabilities as a potential intervenor in the Dutch-Indonesian
controversy over West New Guinea, and a unilateral effort to mediate the
dispute might have proved difficult if not impossible. The prospects of
the enterprise were greatly enhanced by the alternative of working with
and through the United Nations, a strategy made feasible by the evolving
function of the Secretary-General in the years since 1945 and especially
during the tenure of Dag Hammarskjold.

In his remarkable study on the role of third-party intermediaries in
international crises, Young defines third-party intervention as "any action
taken by an actor that is not a direct party to the crisis, that is designed
to reduce or remove one or more of the problems of the bargaining relationship and, therefore, to facilitate the termination of the crisis itself." In
Young's analysis, the term "intervention" does not apply to "entry into a
situation for the purpose of self-interested manipulation;" the emphasis is
on the "regulation and termination of crisis and conflict situations." [58]
The basic objectives of the intervening third party are "to facilitate the

[57]Leland M. Goodrich, *Korea, A Study of U.S. Policy in the United Nations*
(New York: Council on Foreign Relations, 1956), p. 1.

[58]Young, *op. cit.,* pp. 34-35. While a good many case studies are available, almost
nothing has been published on the theory of third-party intervention in international
crises. Young's book represents an impressive first attempt to formulate a general
theoretical framework, and his insights are heavily relied on here.

realization of common interests and to promote the control of crises,"
rather than to serve its particular national interests.[59] Young then ex-
amines the "resources and capabilities required for successful third-party
intervention" in his sense of the term, and the "actors in the present international system which appear to be candidates for potential interventionary
roles in various types of crisis." [60] Measured against Young's criteria, at
first glance there would appear to be decisive reasons for ruling out the
United States as a potential intervenor in the West New Guinea dispute,
even though this country does seem reasonably well qualified for the role
in some respects.

Young asserts that the "basic qualities" of impartiality and independence "come very close to being defining characteristics of a third party,"
and are "prerequisites for the launching of a successful program of intervention." [61] The quality of impartiality raises immediate problems. Young
states:[62]

> In most situations the existence of a meaningful role for a third party
> will depend on the party's being perceived as an impartial participant
> (in the sense of having nothing to gain from aiding either protagonist
> and in the sense of being able to control any feelings of favoritism)
> in the eyes of the principal protagonists . . . Impartiality refers to a
> situation in which the third party favors neither side to a crisis and
> remains indifferent to the gains and losses of each side.

It may be questioned whether the United States was, or was perceived to
be, impartial in this sense. Young's analysis suggests that the difficulty
should have come from the Indonesian side. He asserts, with reference to
crises arising in the Third World, that an aligned state as potential intervenor "is likely to face several obstacles to the achievement of . . .
impartiality" in the eyes of one or another protagonist "that are often
virtually insurmountable;" and he cites in particular "the inevitable imperialist legacy, which tends to create problems whenever the flow of
influence is from developed to underdeveloped areas." [63] But interestingly

---

[59]*Ibid.*, p. 43.
[60]*Ibid.*, p. 80.
[61]*Ibid.*, p. 81.
[62]*Ibid.*, p. 81. Material in parentheses in original.
[63]*Ibid.*, p. 104. Young adds: "Then too, many recent cases of intervention by
aligned states (even when accompanied by fine declaratory statements) have turned
out to be more or less straightforward programs aimed at helping either the East or
the West to achieve its favored outcome. Examples in recent years would include
the activities of both sides in the Congo, Chinese intervention in Cuba, American
participation in the Guatemalan affair in 1954, Chinese activities in Laos, and Soviet
intervention in the Suez crisis. Finally, the risks of transforming an extrabloc crisis

enough, in the concrete circumstances of the West New Guinea dispute the situation was the other way round. Washington was aware that the only settlement acceptable to Indonesia involved the transfer of the territory to its control, although presumably the Jakarta government would accede to some kind of facesaving formula for the Dutch. On the other hand, the estimate was that the Netherlands could be induced to give up West New Guinea, provided that such a formula was agreed to. From the beginning, therefore, Washington worked for a settlement favorable to Indonesia. Its intervention was designed to bring about a gain for Indonesia and a loss for the Netherlands, and both protagonists were doubtless aware of this.[64] Further, it should be noted that United States support for this outcome derived primarily from an assessment of national interest. That is to say, the "restoration" of West New Guinea to Indonesian control was deemed an essential preliminary in persuading the Sukarno regime to abandon its increasingly adventurous foreign policy and turn at last to massive problems of political and economic reconstruction at home; such an evolution was considered likely to serve the particular interests of the United States.[65]

As for *independence,* which Young defines as being "free from attachment to or dependence on a political entity that has a stake in the outcome of the crisis," [66] the case was again mixed. To be sure, there is no doubt that the United States was free of any meaningful subordination to either party in the dispute. But strong ties of sentiment and interest bound

into an interbloc crisis and of inducing escalation are sufficiently great whenever a bloc member (under any guise) enters such an affair to make all sides rather wary of such developments." *Ibid.,* p. 104. Material in parentheses in original.

[64]Both sides would have sensed the shift in Washington's position from discussions with American officials in Washington and their respective capitals. Ambassador Jones, for example, was an enthusiastic supporter of an outcome that insured the transfer of West New Guinea to Indonesia. He writes that "cables flew back and forth between our embassy in Djakarta and Washington, as well as The Hague, in an effort to find a formula that might promise a peaceful solution." Jones, *op. cit.,* p. 206. He would certainly have hinted to the Indonesians which way the wind was blowing. Furthermore, President Sukarno, Foreign Minister Subandrio, and their colleagues were themselves astute enough to sense the change from their own soundings in Washington. No doubt it was something of a gamble to go along with the American initiative, in view of the tangled history of United States relations with Indonesia since World War II (including Washington's support for the regionalist rebels against Sukarno's government); but it was a gamble with loaded dice.

[65]Hammarskjold once remarked that the international civil servant had an "obligation to observe . . . neutrality," which he defined as meaning that he "must remain wholly uninfluenced by national or group interests or ideologies" in the performance of his function. Quoted in Wilder Foote, ed., *Dag Hammarskjold: Servant of Peace* (New York: Harper & Row, n. d.), p. 338.

[66]Young, *op. cit.,* p. 83.

Washingon to The Hague, especially their partnership in the N.A.T.O. alliance; and this relationship might have implied a bias in favor of the Netherlands. In retrospect, however, it cannot be maintained that this greatly affected the Kennedy administration's role in the search for settlement, since in practice the United States worked for a pro-Indonesian solution and ultimately brought heavy pressure to bear on the Dutch to accept it.

With respect to what he calls "ascribed resources," Young seems to conclude that in principle a major aligned power such as the United States would lack *salience* in the eyes of Indonesia and the Netherlands as "a neutral actor toward which to turn" in the controversy and "as a probable source of useful assistance." [67] He states: [68]

> It is difficult for an aligned state to achieve any real salience as a potential intervenor in (Third World crises). This possibility tends to lie outside the convergence of expectations of the parties to crises and it certainly lacks any quality of prominence or naturalness in most contexts. One simply does not turn to a member of either major bloc for help of (this) kind.

On the other hand, both Indonesia and the Netherlands seem to have ascribed decisive importance to Washington's posture in the West New Guinea dispute; over the years, both sides had frequently consulted the United States and sought its support in the controversy. It should also be remembered that this country had played a key role in negotiations leading to Indonesia's independence from the Dutch, so that renewed participation in the West New Guinea dispute had the element of precedent. To be sure, the Washington government had so long eschewed an active role in the controversy, and so assiduously maintained a posture of studied neutrality, that by 1961 its salience as a potential intervenor was perhaps less apparent. But the record shows that both sides still considered the United States as "a natural actor toward which to turn" in the search for settlement.

The ascribed qualities of respect and continuity would appear to cause fewer difficulties. As for *respect,* the United States doubtless possessed "prestige or repute in the eyes of the parties" resulting primarily from its preeminent political position and historical role in world affairs; and, as we have seen, we may assume that both protagonists conceded "a certain propriety or naturalness" to the United States' playing a major part in the search for settlement.[69] On the Indonesian side, we may also infer what

[67]*Ibid.*, p. 84.
[68]*Ibid.*, pp. 104-105.
[69]*Ibid.*, p. 84.

Young calls "affectual respect" for this country arising out of Jakarta's expectation that United States intervention would be basically favorable to its claims;[70] the Dutch could hardly have shared this sentiment. The quality of Washington's *continuity* as "an established factor in international politics" was obviously unquestioned.[71]

The United States also did well in terms of Young's personnel and physical resource categories.[72] As a potential intervenor in the West New Guinea dispute, Washington certainly had the requisite *knowledge of politico-military affairs,* the *skill,* and (under the Kennedy administration) the *initiative* to play the part; it also possessed the *physical resources* (such as negotiating personnel and facilities, communications, and so forth) necessary, and the capability for their rapid *mobilization.* Here the relevant question was whether the unilateral utilization of these resources was feasible in the circumstances of the Dutch-Indonesian controversy.

Commenting on "the problems faced by aligned or semialigned states" in performing third-party functions, Young concludes:[73]

> They are often reasonably well prepared in terms of the various personnel qualifications and physical resources, but they are apt to score very poorly in terms of basic qualities and ascribed capabilities. (With respect to Third World crises), the aligned states are almost bound to encounter enormous difficulties in achieving any semblance of subjective or perceived impartiality. And independence tends, for the most part, to be out of the question unless the aligned state is for one reason or another in the process of changing the quality of its alignment and therefore able to point to its new status. In addition, there is little evidence that these states have any real salience or prestige as potential intervenors in the eyes of parties which might be involved in relevant crises.

Yet there is no doubt that the United States did play an effective part in the settlement of the Dutch-Indonesian controversy over West New Guinea. How are we to resolve the apparent dilemma?

The United States role could perhaps be dismissed as not being "intervention" in the sense of Young's definition, but rather an example of "entry into a situation for the purpose of self-interested manipulation." The element of manipulation was certainly present. A major objective of United States policy — which was derived from a reasonable assessment of national interest — was to deflect the course of Indonesia's future

---

[70]*Ibid.,* p. 85.
[71]*Ibid.,* p. 85.
[72]See *ibid.,* pp. 87-91.
[73]*Ibid.,* p. 103.

political and economic development into constructive channels; and the transfer of West New Guinea to Indonesian control was conceived as a necessary inducement to this end. But this analysis should not blind us to the fact that the United States had a valid, and perhaps even greater, interest in the orderly functioning of the international system; and that the "action" taken by Washington was also designed to "facilitate the termination of the crisis" and thereby to safeguard international peace and security, which is at the heart of Young's concept of essentially disinterested intervention. In short, the United States role had the qualities both of manipulation and of intervention in Young's sense. It may be that Young's theory of third-party intervention as it relates to Third World crises should be broadened, and in certain respects modified, in order to take into account cases of obviously self-interested manipulation by major aligned powers which also reflect elements of disinterested intervention, and where the particular solutions arrived at are consistent with the objectives of intervention as Young defines them.

Suffice to say at this juncture that a major reason for the success of the American initiative was the decision to work with and through the Acting Secretary-General of the United Nations in the search for settlement, rather than to attempt unilateral mediation of the West New Guinea dispute. The Washington government seems to have understood from the start that it lacked certain of the attributes necessary to perform effectively as third-party intermediary, and that its disabilities in this respect might be made up through partnership with the chief executive officer of the world organization. We turn, therefore, to a brief consideration of the role of the Secretary-General in peacekeeping activities generally, and to the circumstances of his intervention in the controversy between Indonesia and the Netherlands.

Chapter Ten

The Role of the United Nations

By 1961, concepts of United Nations peacekeeping had gone through a substantial evolution.[1] The system written into the Charter assigned primary responsibility for such activities to the Security Council, and more especially to its five permanent members; and "depended for its effectiveness on recognition by the permanent members that they had a common interest in keeping the peace and that they should compromise their differences in order that they might cooperate in furthering this common interest."[2] But the assumption of great-power solidarity for peacekeeping purposes proved illusory, and the Charter system never really got off the ground. In Young's words:[3]

> (The system) . . . foundered basically on the rocks of great-power disunity and the antagonisms of the cold war. The competitive interests of the great powers began to obscure their common interests, and the newness and sharpness of the Soviet-American split made any movement toward cooperation virtually unthinkable in many contexts. In fact, there was a tendency for these powers to oppose each other on principle, even in cases where the opposition of their concrete interests was by no means clear-cut.

On the other hand, the United Nations was not wholly paralyzed by great power rivalries. Even in its early years, the new world organization found means to undertake a variety of peacekeeping activities in relation to Greece, Indonesia, Palestine, Kashmir, and other crisis areas, often with considerable success, although the action taken in specific cases usually did not fit into a coherent or widely accepted conceptual framework.

The socalled Uniting for Peace approach to peacekeeping, which was formally embodied in a resolution adopted by the General Assembly early in November 1950, sought to transfer primary responsibility for the main-

---

[1]The brief summary which follows relies heavily on Young's analysis. See Young, *op. cit.*, pp. 115-156. See also Leland M. Goodrich, "The Maintenance of International Peace and Security," *International Organization* vol. 19, no. 3 (Summer 1965), pp. 429-443.

[2]Leland M. Goodrich, *The United Nations* (New York: Crowell, 1959), p. 162.

[3]Young, *op. cit.*, pp. 122-123.

tenance of international peace and security from the Security Council to the General Assembly, where the Soviet veto did not apply and where the Western bloc then had a safe majority of votes.[4] Thus presumably the paralysis of Soviet obstruction in the Security Council would be overcome, and the United Nations enabled to discharge its Charter responsibilities in the security field. This was in line with Washington's view that "the United Nations ought to be able to act, even, if necessary, in the face of Soviet opposition."[5] While theoretically universal in application, the Uniting for Peace resolution was really a device to enable the Western bloc, led by the United States, to utilize the world organization for Cold War purposes. But support for this approach declined very rapidly as its full implications became more apparent, especially following Communist China's massive intervention in the Korean War. Indeed, as Young points out, the Korean experience "appears to have opened the eyes of many to the dangers and disadvantages of United Nations peacekeeping more than it set an influential precedent for future activities on the part of the Organization."[6] At the same time, the Western countries were themselves coming to place increasing reliance on regional alliance systems to safeguard their own security, and to minimize the potentialities of the United Nations in this respect. Moreover, the decline of Western influence in the policymaking organs of the world organization, which was accelerated by the influx of new members after 1955, and a growing apprehension of the limits of Western power, steadily undermined the utility of the Uniting for Peace procedure as a reliable instrument of Western policy. By Fall 1956, this "image of international peacekeeping was clearly a thing of the past."[7]

The Hammarskjold Approach

It was the genius of Dag Hammarskjold, who assumed office as Secretary-General in April 1953, to realize the potentialities that still remained for effective United Nations peacekeeping in a world divided by Cold War, and to elaborate in concrete cases the techniques and procedures that gave substance to his concepts. In Hammarskjold's view, it was "extremely difficult for the United Nations to exercise an influence on problems which are clearly and definitely within the orbit of present day

[4]Western control of the General Assembly disappeared with the wholesale admission of new members to the world organization after 1955.

[5]I. L. Claude, Jr., "The Containment and Resolution of Disputes," in Francis O. Wilcox and H. Field Haviland, Jr., eds., *The United States and the United Nations* (Baltimore: John Hopkins University Press, 1961), p. 122.

[6]Young, *op. cit.*, p. 132.

[7]*Ibid.*, p. 134.

conflicts between power blocs." But the United Nations might still make a substantial contribution through the conduct of a "preventive diplomacy" outside the main arena of Cold War politics. In particular, "conflicts arising within the non-committed areas offer opportunities for solutions which avoid an aggravation of big Power differences and can remain uninfluenced by them." In such activities, the efforts of the United Nations should always "aim at keeping newly arising conflicts outside the sphere of bloc differences." [8] In addition, Hammarskjold envisaged the possibility that "conflicts on the margin of, or inside, the sphere of bloc differences" might be brought "out of this sphere through solutions aiming, in the first instance, at their strict localization." [9]

Unlike the original Charter system and the Uniting for Peace approach, both of which focussed on collective enforcement measures to prevent or contain aggression in the context of the Cold War, Hammarskjold's concept of peacekeeping emphasized facilitative procedures while downgrading the possible use of coercive restraints. In the words of U Thant, who succeeded Hammarskjold after the latter's death: [10]

> There has been a tacit transition from the concepts of collective security, as set out in Chapter VII of the United Nations Charter, to a more realistic idea of peace-keeping. The idea that conventional military methods — or, to put it bluntly, war — can be used by or on behalf of the United Nations to counter aggression and secure the peace seems now to be rather impractical.

No doubt this was a less heroic concept of peacekeeping than that envisaged by the Charter, and it confined the United Nations role largely to Third World crises, or at least to those in which the great powers were not directly involved. Moreover, the perspective was essentially neutral in relation to great power interests; the objective of peacekeeping was primarily to "underwrite the maintenance of at least minimal stability in the international system and to support the processes of peaceful change." [11] A basic assumption of this whole approach was that the two superpowers would, in fact, "acquiesce to exclusion from the immediate realm of peace-

[8]Quoted in Foote, op. cit., pp. 302-303. On this point, Claude comments that preventive diplomacy "involves the use of the (United Nations) for politically impartial intervention into a troubled area peripheral to the Cold War, for purposes of forestalling the competitive intrusion of the major Cold War antagonists," I. L. Claude, Jr., "Implications and Questions for the Future," International Organization, vol. 19, no. 3 (Summer 1965), p. 840.
[9]Quoted in Foote, op. cit., p. 303.
[10]Quoted in United Nations Review, vol. 10, no. 7 (July 1963), p. 54.
[11]Young, op. cit., p. 137.

keeping activities and to the reduction of opportunities to score Cold War gains in specific crisis situations."[12]

Hammarskjold's approach also dramatized the potential of executive actions by the Secretary-General, whether or not specifically authorized by the policymaking organs of the United Nations. In this connection, he once remarked:[13]

> I (believe) that it is in keeping with the philosophy of the Charter that the Secretary General also should be expected to act without guidance from the Assembly or the Security Council should this appear to him necessary toward helping to fill any vacuums that may appear in the systems which the Charter and traditional diplomacy provide for the safeguarding of peace and security . . . Were (the policymaking organs of the United Nations) to disapprove of the way these intentions were to be translated by me into practical steps, I would, of course, accept the consequences of your judgment.

In short, Hammarskjold "proposed to exercise or to accept personal responsibility as Secretary-General for initiating and for carrying out . . . preventive measures" [14] whenever he considered such steps necessary and feasible; and in practice, no serious restrictions were placed on the energetic initiatives taken by the Secretary-General.

As elaborated in concrete situations, Hammarskjold's concepts of peacekeeping demonstrated substantial utility in a succession of crises occurring in the Third World: the aftermath of Suez, Lebanon, Jordan, the dispute between Thailand and Cambodia over Preah Vihear, Laos, and the Congo. The diversity of instrumentalities and procedures employed in these episodes attested to Hammarskjold's resourcefulness and ingenuity. By 1961, his approach to peacekeeping had become an established feature of the diplomatic landscape. If not yet routine, intervention by the Secretary-General in serious Third World crises had gained an important measure of acceptability. Two years earlier, Hammarskjold himself commented that "the Organization has begun to gain a certain independent position, and

[12]*Ibid.*, p. 140. See also Brian Urquhart, "United Nations Peace Forces and the Changing United Nations," *International Organization*, vol. 17, no. 2 (Spring 1963), pp. 338-354.

[13]Security Council, *Official Records*, 837th meeting, July 22, 1958.

Hammarskjold made this statement in explaining his decision to enlarge the United Nations Observer Group in Lebanon without specific authority from the Security Council.

[14]Goodrich, "The Maintenance of International Peace and Security," *loc. cit.*, p. 437.

. . . this tendency had led to the acceptance of an independent political and diplomatic activity on the party of the Secretary-General as the 'neutral' representative of the Organization." [15]

The Secretary-General as Mediator

In terms of Young's inventory of resources and capabilities, Acting Secretary-General U Thant presumably ranked high as a potential intervenor in the Dutch-Indonesian controversy over West New Guinea, although he was not without some important disabilities as well. Above all, the impartiality of his office as between the protagonists could not be seriously questioned. By 1961, the cumulative record of successive incumbents, especially Hammarskjold, had established their capacity to afford to the parties to a dispute "a truly third party . . . who was not judicial but political, representing no government but at the same time not bound by rules of law or by preference for the *status quo*;" [16] or, in Hammarskjold's words, their "neutrality in relation to interests," which is the essence of impartiality.[17] The standing of the Secretary-General among Third World countries was attested by the "development in recent years of an informal constituency composed of small and nonaligned states" [18] which supported the expanded function of his office. As for the Dutch, they were already on record as having requested on several occasions the intervention of the Secretary-General in various phases of the West New Guinea dispute.

The political independence of the Secretary-General was similarly unquestioned. But the reverse side of this coin was the limited leverage available to him for exerting pressure on the parties to a dispute at appropriate stages of the mediatory process. To be sure, the possibilities in this respect should not be minimized, in view of the substantial prestige which his office has acquired over the years. But, as Young points out:[19]

. . . the absence of a recognizable political base of support leads to weakness . . . (The Secretary-General) is not analagous to a government. And he has no formal constituency or party to lend force to his attempts to exercise pressure.

From this point of view, there might be significant advantages to associating a United Nations role in the Dutch-Indonesian controversy over West

[15]Quoted in Foote, *op. cit.*, p. 210.
[16]Lincoln P. Bloomfield, *The United Nations and U.S. Foreign Policy*, revised edition (Boston: Little, Brown, 1967), p. 173.
[17]Quoted in Foote, *op. cit.*, p. 352.
[18]Young, *op. cit.*, p. 275.
[19]Young, *op. cit.*, pp. 274-275.

New Guinea with an initiative by the United States to intervene in the search for settlement, since in the circumstances Washington was strategically placed to bring timely pressure to bear on both parties to the dispute, and especially the Netherlands. The feasiblility of this approach hinged, of course, on the congruence of United States objectives with the solution likely to emerge from negotiations in which the United Nations played a part.

As for the salience of the Secretary-General as a potential intervenor in the dispute, the respect likely to be accorded his participation, and the continuity of his office in the performance of this role, little additional comment seems necessary. Indeed, Young goes so far as to conclude that the West New Guinea crisis "generated" a situation "in which no leading participant would have seriously thought of leaving the Secretary-General out of the resultant negotiations."[20] To be sure, in the Fall of 1961 Thant was still relatively new at his post, which he then held only in an acting capacity; and there must have been some uncertainty as to how he would exercise the powers of his office in this particular situation. On the other hand, it was at least a reasonable presumption that he would choose to follow Hammarskjold's concept of the expanded function of the Secretary-General for peacekeeping purposes.[21]

In terms of personnel and physical resources, the Acting Secretary-General and his staff clearly had the knowledge and diplomatic skills necessary to play the mediator's part in the West New Guinea dispute. Nor did access to adequate physical resources constitute a critical obstacle to effective United Nations participation. Despite the range of his responsibilities elsewhere, Thant was able to improvise almost overnight the means and facilities necessary to implement the settlement ultimately

[20]*Ibid.*, pp. 279-280.

[21]Commenting on the early years of Thant's tenure as Secretary-General, Young asserts that almost from the beginning he displayed a tendency to "rely heavily . . . on the authority of executive initiatives in his activities dealing with the maintenance of international peace and security." *Ibid.*, p. 297.

Speaking in 1965, Thant declared that "the Secretary-General must always be prepared to take an initiative, no matter what the consequences to him or his office may be, if he sincerely believes that it might make the difference between peace and war . . . It follows that the powers and possibilities of the Secretary-General must husbanded so that they can be used to the best possible advantage in the common interests of all nations. I have no intention of using them for any other purpose, nor yet of failing to use them to the full if I believe the situation demands it." Quoted in *U. N. Monthly Chronicle*, vol. 2, no. 6 (June 1965), pp. 103-104.

It seems clear, however, that with the passage of years, Thant came to embrace a more passive concept of the Secretary-General's function than that implemented so successfully by his predecessor.

agreed upon by Indonesia and the Netherlands; and in the process, he added significantly to the inventory of techniques and practices available for United Nations peacekeeping activities in the future.

United Nations Peacekeeping and United States Policy

Writing in 1961, Claude comments somewhat critically on the fact that "the bulk of (United States) policy with regard to the United Nations has been directed toward enhancing its usability as a Western instrument." [22] Without examining the merits of this general policy approach, there was little doubt that during the preceding 15 years, Washington had often found the new world organization a helpful partner in a variety of difficult circumstances. Haviland, for example, after reviewing the record of United Nations peacekeeping activities since 1946, concludes that:[23]

... most of the United Nations peacekeeping operations have been consistent with the United States' interests ... the United States has found the United Nations to be a useful instrument, despite all of its limitations, for dealing with a substantial portion of major postwar conflicts of all kinds, not in deference to abstract ideals but in recognition of practical assets.

This was true even with respect to some crises directly related to the Cold War, such as Greece, Korea, and Hungary, in which the "conditions affecting United Nations involvement ... were sufficiently favorable to enable the Organization to make substantial contributions." [24] On the other hand, Washington did not turn to the United Nations in most Cold War situations precisely because it was unable to marshal sufficient support among the membership to utilize the resources of the organization, despite

---

[22]Claude, "The Containment and Resolution of Disputes," loc. cit., p. 122. In expanding this point, Claude states that the United States "lost little time after San Francisco in repudiating the implication of the veto rule, which is that the organization should not be capable of taking major political action opposed by a major power as contrary to its interests. In a nutshell, the history of the United Nations is a record of American attempts to destroy or reduce the meaningfulness of the Soviet veto power, and of efforts by the Soviet Union to maintain or increase the efficacy of its veto. Having created an organization with a built-in, and deliberately designed, impediment to its operating in situations of great-power disunity, we have persistently undertaken to make it operable in just such situations. Our evaluation of the United Nations has rested heavily upon its potentiality for being transformed into an agency capable of acting with Western support, regardless of possible Soviet objections." Ibid., pp. 122-123. Italics in original.

[23]H. Field Haviland, Jr., "The United States and the United Nations," International Organization, vol. 19, no. 3 (Summer 1965), p. 657. It should be noted that Haviland's comments refer to the first 20 years of United Nations history.

[24]Ibid., pp. 645-646.

Soviet obstruction in the Security Council, for purposes considered advantageous to the national interest.

Controversies occurring in the Third World often posed hard choices for United States policy. With respect to disputes arising out of the liquidation of colonialism, Washington was frequently inhibited from taking a firm stand in the United Nations because of traditional ties of friendship and alliance with the European countries concerned. But in the abstract, the long-term interests of the United States in colonial issues of this kind were usually conceived to be in facilitating an orderly transition to independence, while damping down impending or actual conflict, and in preventing the Communists from taking advantage of the situation meanwhile. The impact of United Nations intervention in such instances as Indonesia, Suez, the French North African territories, Laos, and the Congo was to support these purposes. As for conflicts between Third World countries, substantial American interests were usually involved on both sides of these controversies; and the United States generally encouraged United Nations participation in cases such as Palestine, Kashmir, the 1958 Middle East crisis (including the Lebanon and Jordan episodes), the Thai-Cambodian dispute, and the controversy over Buraimi Oasis. Here, too, the influence of the United Nations was toward isolating and pacifying conflict, although not usually to bring about a permanent solution. The achievement of these proximate objectives was certainly congruent with United States interests in the particular circumstances.[25]

This is not to suggest that the Washington government has unfailingly supported the possibilities of United Nations peacekeeping in all circumstances. As indicated above, we have been chary of United Nations involvement in many Cold War controversies, and we have often chosen to stand aside on questions relating to decolonization. Again, the United States has usually discouraged intervention by the world organization in Latin American conflicts, preferring to keep such issues within the preserve of hemispheric diplomacy. It is nevertheless true, as Young points out, that:[26]

[25]For the United States attitude on United Nations intervention in Third World disputes, see ibid., pp. 648-655.

[26]Young, op. cit., pp. 190-191. Writing in 1966, Young adds this important comment: "It should not, however, be assumed that this orientation is ironclad and unshakable. The changing nature of the Organization is generating some frictions with important United States interests, and there is a growing amount of criticism and skepticism directed toward the United Nations in American policy-making circles. Among the factors which can be associated with these developments are: (1) the influx of new members into the Organization and the consequent fear of being outvoted or overwhelmed by 'irresponsible' powers (often defined as those that flout

. . . the generally stabilizing programs and impact of the United Nations, as well as its influence in favor of peaceful and planned change — or at least not very violent change — have tended to fit in well with the basic interests of the United States . . . (With respect to) peacekeeping operations, the United States has a record of support and crucial backing in many instances.

Increasingly during the 1950s, the peacekeeping activities of the United Nations came to involve executive initiatives on the part of the Secretary-General; and by and large, the United States strongly supported Hammarskjold's enlargement of the range of responsibilities which he assumed as his proper function in the years after 1953. Here again, the American posture was motivated primarily by "strong national-interest considerations." [27] When Hammarskjold came under heavy attack from the Soviet Union for his conduct of United Nations intervention in the Congo, the United States vigorously defended both the man and the broadened concept of his office. Washington led the fight to defeat the Russian "troika" proposals for reorganizing the United Nations secretariat, which if accepted would have emasculated the potentialities for executive action in the future. Writing in Fall 1961, Harlan Cleveland, then Assistant Secretary of State for International Organization Affairs, declared that a principal objective of American policy in the United Nations was to "press for the further strengthening of the executive capacities" of the world organization.[28]

The Rationale of a Joint Approach

Washington's decision to work with and through the Acting Secretary-General in the search for an acceptable settlement of the West New Guinea dispute was in line with this general orientation. The record of previous United Nations peacekeeping activities suggested that Thant would support a solution consistent with the purposes of United States policy as they had come to be formulated by late 1961. While it could not be alleged that the Acting Secretary-General had a stake in any

American interests); (2) a feeling that many United Nations actions are inefficacious and rather peripheral; (3) a growing insistence that the American financial burden associated with the United Nations is either too great or disproportionate compared to the contributions of other members; and (4) a general fear of loss of control in the United Nations and a consequent fear that the Organization will act in various ways that are harmful to American interests." *Ibid.*, pp. 190-191.

[27]*Ibid.*, p. 192.

[28]Harlan Cleveland, "The Road Around Stalemate," *Foreign Affairs*, vol. 40, no. 1 (October 1961), p. 36.

particular outcome, he certainly had no vested interest in the preservation of the status quo. In the circumstances of the West New Guinea dispute, moreover, it seemed clear that the most feasible means of safeguarding international peace and security (which was the overriding objective of United Nations involvement in such controversies) would be to turn the territory over to Indonesia, subject to certain safeguards and facesaving formulae deemed important by the Dutch. There was, finally, broad international acceptance of the view that some such solution was the almost "inevitable" ending of a decolonization crisis of this kind. The assumed congruence of United Nations perspectives on West New Guinea with American aims in relation to the dispute (an hypothesis that could readily be verified through routine diplomatic consultation) presumably formed the basis of Washington's determination to collaborate with the Acting Secretary-General in what ultimately became a kind of joint undertaking in third-party mediation.

There were substantial advantages for both the United States and the United Nations in such an approach. From Washington's point of view, cooperation with the Acting Secretary-General would tend to invest the enterprise with precisely those qualities that a unilateral American initiative would most conspicuously lack, namely, the prestige of salient international sponsorship and the cloak of unquestioned impartiality. This much may have been necessary even to get the negotiations started. Moreover, the terms of a viable compromise might prove unacceptable to both parties if advanced by the United States alone. No doubt the Dutch would be required to accept a public humiliation, and Washington was alive to the importance of saving Dutch face in the process. As for the Indonesians, they would resent even a favorable settlement received at the hands of the United States, and especially one that temporarily delayed the transfer of administrative control and indefinitely postponed the definition of legal sovereignty over the disputed territory. For both parties, the Acting Secretary-General's endorsement of the outcome might provide the necessary coating to render a distasteful compromise politically palatable at home; and his public responsibility would also tend to alleviate the onus that the United States would inevitably bear as prime mover of the settlement. Finally, the United Nations could presumably be counted on to supply the military forces and improvise the administrative machinery that might be required to implement the terms of a settlement.

Thant's perspective, on the other hand, may have focussed on the opportunity to enlist the power of the United States in support of the Charter purpose of the United Nations to "bring about by peaceful means" the "adjustment or settlement of international disputes." It is, perhaps, a truism to state that the Secretary-General cannot perform successfully in

the mediator's role if the configuration of power and interests in a particular conflict is not favorable to his intervention. Young is doubtless
correct, moreover, when he asserts that "the probability of success for an
intervening party in any given crisis will be related to the existence of at
least a rough parity of power" between the parties;[29] and that in the discharge of his function, the mediator must rely on "basically persuasive
activities" rather than force "to help both sides realize their common
interests while at the same time preventing consequences that might prove
disruptive for the international system as a whole." [30] But the Secretary-
General is also free to frame his initiatives in accordance with the realities
of a given situation; and, indeed, he would be foolhardy if he did not take
them into account. In the case of West New Guinea, Thant was certainly
made aware at an early stage of the objectives of United States policy and
of the sincerity of Washington's determination to work for a peaceful
resolution of the controversy. This knowledge greatly strengthened his own
hand. To be sure, the Acting Secretary-General would necessarily act at
all stages as if his intervention were an independent initiative; to do
otherwise would seriously undermine his credibility as an impartial third
party. But it is clear that the posture of the United States virtually insured
the effectiveness of his own role in the search for settlement, since he
could reasonably rely on the tendency of Washington's influence as the
mediatory process unfolded.

As nearly as one can judge from the available evidence, the impulse for
joint intervention came primarily from the American side. Having concluded that the United States should involve itself in the West New Guinea
dispute in order first to deal with a rapidly worsening situation, and
eventually to foster a peaceful resolution of the controversy, Washington
formulated a plan calling for direct negotiations between the parties, but
in the presence of a ranking American diplomat as "disinterested" third
party, and on the basis of proposals advanced by the United States. In
order to insure an appropriately impartial atmosphere for these proceed-
ings, the formal sponsorship of the United Nations was considered essential, with the American mediator to act officially as representative of the
Acting Secretary-General. Both Indonesia and the Netherlands were
obviously consulted on this scenario, and their assent obtained. Neither
party could have labored under any illusions as to what was actually
going on, in particular the decisive part played by the United States. But
all sides apparently understood the importance of protective coloration for
the actual negotiations, and of United Nations involvement in the terms

[29]Young, *op. cit.*, pp. 43-44.
[30]*Ibid.*, p. 45.

of settlement. This is not to minimize the part played by the Acting Secretary-General. In the early stages, Thant exerted himself to bring about direct negotiations; and it was a tribute to his flexibility at this time that he fell in with the American plan and agreed to provide the impartial cover so necessary for the success of the undertaking.

Chapter Eleven

Toward Negotiations

In late November 1961, the United States abandoned its long-preserved silence in United Nations debates on the West New Guinea issue to support a position basically favorable to Dutch policy on the question of self-determination for the Papuans.[1] The Indonesians were shaken by this development, which they interpreted as a departure from Washington's previous posture of "studied neutrality" in the dispute; and Foreign Minister Subandrio declared at a press conference in Jakarta that West New Guinea had now "become a problem between Indonesia and the United States." [2] The possible implications of this episode were soon forgotten, however, in the wake of a wholly new initiative by the United States to sponsor direct negotiations between Indonesia and the Netherlands.

Despite the extreme bitterness that now characterized Dutch-Indonesian relations, the prospects for fruitful intervention by an outside power were not unpromising. Young points out that international crises "tend to have a very distinct competitive-cooperative flavor" in Boulding's sense that both sides would probably be better off with any of a range of possible solutions to a crisis than with its continuation (and possible escalation into open warfare), while the actual distribution of advantages as between the two parties hinges on the particular solution within this range that is ultimately agreed to.[3] This was certainly the case in the West New Guinea dispute. The Dutch had already made public their decision to relinquish control over the territory, and for them the only remaining question concerned the terms of their withdrawal. It is hard to conceive an issue over which war would have been less in the Dutch interest; and yet the Netherlands might well have fought if the only alternative were the acceptance of an outrageous national humiliation. As for the Indonesians, the struggle for West New Guinea had doubtless assumed great importance by late 1961, and eventually Jakarta might have mounted a large-scale invasion in an attempt to take the territory by force. But in view of Indonesia's

---

[1]See pp. 125-127, above.

[2]Quoted in *Christian Science Monitor,* December 13, 1961.

[3]Young, *op. cit.,* pp. 25-26. The Boulding reference is to Kenneth Boulding, *Conflict and Defense* (New York: Harper, 1962), p. 314.

already precarious domestic political and economic situation, the resulting conflict — whose duration and outcome were highly uncertain — might have proved a national disaster. Hence there were also strong incentives on the Indonesian side to seek a peaceful solution, provided that it insured ultimate control over the disputed territory.

For an intervening third party, this convergence of interest in a peaceful solution afforded significant common ground on which to search for a mutually acceptable settlement. The mediator's art was to assist the protagonists "to realize their common or overlapping interests" [4] in a situation where both sides had long since assumed intransigent public positions, and where neither would talk directly with the other. Aside from its intrinsic interest as a significant episode in recent diplomatic history, the effort of the United States jointly with the United Nations to promote a settlement of the West New Guinea dispute affords an instructive example of effective third-party intervention in controversies of this kind.[5]

First Steps

At the outset, the most important thing was to bring the protagonists together in a meaningful diplomatic contact. Several years had passed since the Netherlands and Indonesia had attempted to negotiate over West New Guinea; and even diplomatic relations between the two countries had been broken off in 1960. Despite the growing danger of war, both sides seemed incapable of breaking the impasse. Hence the first task of the intermediary was to move the two parties off dead center and in the direction of significant negotiations. The mediatory process began with intense efforts on the part of the United States and the United Nations to persuade Jakarta and The Hague that their interests lay in the avoidance of war over West New Guinea, that a basis for settlement could be found, and that discussions to this end should be undertaken forthwith. In his discussion of what he calls the mediator's "repertory of practice," [6] Young gives pride of place to the tactic of "persuasion," which he defines as "the processes through which conflicting parties can become aware of common or overlapping interests and ways of capitalizing on them through contact with representatives of a third party." [7] This was a difficult busi-

[4]Young, op. cit., p. 35.

[5]In the course of the mainly chronological analysis that follows, the historical data will also be employed to illustrate and comment on various aspects of the mediator's role considered in more theoretical terms. For this purpose, extensive use will be made of Young's model of third-party functions and tactics in international crises. See ibid., pp. 34-79.

[6]Ibid., p. 49.

[7]Ibid., p. 51.

ness in the circumstances of the Dutch-Indonesian controversy. The utility of persuasion implies "a certain assumption of rationality" on all sides,[8] while tempers in Jakarta and The Hague had long since reached the breaking point and strong emotional commitments inhibited the acceptance of reasonable argument.

On December 14, it was reported that President Kennedy had sent parallel letters to Sukarno and Prime Minister Nehru of India "asking them not to use force to gain territory they regard as parts of their own country." [9] His letter to Sukarno offered "to help find a solution by direct negotiations." [10] In the case of India, the President's appeal was unsuccessful in forestalling that country's seizure of Portugal's tiny enclaves on the subcontinent three days later. Sukarno's reply on December 18 was more hopeful. To be sure, he warned that Indonesia "could not remain idle while (the) Netherlands took steps to create an independent government" in West New Guinea, and that his country would be "compelled to use force to settle the dispute" unless Dutch provocations ended immediately.[11] But he also "begged the United States, in effect, to abandon its policy of passive neutrality and to take positive measures to bring the Dutch to accept negotiations." [12] Following discussions at the State Department the next day, the Indonesian Ambassador to the United States, Zairin Zain, informed reporters that his government was "willing to accept the helping hand of the United States," although he had not formally requested American good offices in the dispute between his country and the Netherlands.[13] Through all this, there was no indication that Jakarta had modified its view that the only subject open to negotiation concerned the modalities of transferring administration over the disputed territory to Indonesia.[14]

Kennedy also wrote to Jan Eduard de Quay, the Dutch Prime Minister, stressing the importance of avoiding war over West New Guinea and urging a peaceful solution of the controversy.[15] Here, too, his appeal struck a responsive chord. On December 19, the Foreign Ministry, while deploring the issuance of Sukarno's spectacular Triple Command for the

[8]*Ibid.*, p. 53.

[9]*The New York Times*, December 15, 1961.

[10]Schlesinger, *op. cit.*, p. 534.

[11]*The New York Times*, December 19, 1961.

[12]Hilsman, *op. cit.*, p. 375.

[13]Quoted in *The New York Times*, December 20, 1961.

[14]On December 26, Sukarno reiterated that his country would "only negotiate with the Dutch on the basis of handing back West Irian to the Republic of Indonesia. We reject any talk of self-determination. Do not try to persuade us." Quoted in *ibid.*, December 28, 1961.

[15]See *ibid.*, December 20, 1961, and December 21, 1961.

liberation of the territory, indicated that "negotiations would have to take place" at some point.[16] The Hague's Ambassador in Washington, J. H. van Roijen, informed the State Department on the same day that his government was indeed prepared to talk with the Jakarta regime. But he stipulated an important condition. "Basic to the approach of the Netherlands," he said, "was the right of the Papuan people to self-determination, and the Netherlands Government was willing to negotiate only on that basis." In short, the principle of self-determination for the Papuans was apparently still a breaking point for the Dutch. Van Roijen also indicated that the discussions would have to be held in the presence of a third party; and it was known that the Dutch were especially interested in some form of United Nations participation in the proposed talks. Finally, the Dutch Ambassador stated that his government "had not asked for United States assistance in reaching agreement;" [17] although four days later, The Hague did announce that it was seeking American help in arranging an "open discussion" with the Indonesians.[18]

Meanwhile, the Acting Secretary-General of the United Nations, U Thant, sent identical cables to Sukarno and de Quay on December 19 "expressing his deep concern over the possibility of a serious situation arising between Indonesia and the Netherlands and expressing his sincere hope that the two parties might come together to seek a peaceful solution to the problem." [19] Thant made no suggestions as to detailed arrangements, nor did he refer to the conflicting conditions that both sides still maintained for negotiations.[20] The Hague replied promptly to Thant's appeal, stating that it was "actively investigating ways and means of reaching a solution compatible with our responsibilities and if possible, also acceptable to Indonesia;" [21] and promising as well to refrain from steps that might aggravate the situation.[22] On the other hand, there is no public record that Jakarta ever responded specifically to the Acting Secretary-General's cable. Throughout this period of intense diplomatic activity relating to West New Guinea, Thant met on several occasions with Dutch and Indonesian representatives at the United Nations. But one has the

[16]Quoted in *ibid.*, December 20, 1961.

[17]*Ibid.*, December 20, 1961.

[18]Quoted in *ibid.*, December 24, 1961.

[19]*Everyman's United Nations*, 7th edition (New York: United Nations, 1964), p. 97.

[20]See *The New York Times*, December 20, 1961.

[21]Quoted in *ibid.*, December 27, 1961.

[22]See *ibid.*, January 3, 1962. The Dutch replied to Thant's cable on December 23, 1961.

distinct impression that the more important discussions were going forward in Washington.

To be sure, the State Department consistently understated the United States role in the enterprise. A spokesman acknowledged on December 20 that the government was trying "to get the two sides together for a peaceful settlement." [23] But Washington repeatedly denied that it would act as a third party in any Dutch-Indonesian discussions.[24] The role of the United States, it was said, was simply "to persuade the two nations to begin talks." [25] At a press conference early in January 1962, Secretary of State Dean Rusk put it this way:[26]

> . . . we have not at any time formally offered our services as mediator. This is one of those many, many issues which come to our desk because, when friends of ours in different parts of the world find themselves in disagreement with each other, each comes to us to ask if we can be of some assistance in the dispute . . . We see no reason why this matter cannot be effectively discussed between the two Governments and some sort of peaceful settlement reached; but we're not in a position of formal mediation.

Technically, this was undoubtedly an accurate statement. For reasons already indicated, the United States wished to avoid the complications of "formal mediation" in the Dutch-Indonesian controversy. But there was ample evidence from press statements and the frequency of diplomatic contacts that the Washington government was now actively promoting negotiations between the two parties, and that both sides were responding positively to the American initiative. On January 2, Ambassador Zain commented that the United States was "being very helpful" in the situation.[27]

It may be observed at this point that the intermediary activities of the United States and the United Nations had already brought about a significant change of climate. Young comments on this aspect of the mediator's function in the following terms:[28]

> At a minimum the very presence of a third party in the bargaining process is likely to have a noticeable effect on the behavior of the principals. Such a presence very often affects expectations and attitudes concerning acceptable behavior patterns.

[23]Quoted in *ibid.*, December 21, 1961.
[24]See, for example, *ibid.*, December 27, 1961, and December 28, 1961.
[25]*Ibid.*, December 28, 1961.
[26]Quoted in *Department of State Bulletin*, vol. 46, no. 1178 (January 22, 1962), p. 125.
[27]Quoted in *The New York Times*, January 3, 1962.
[28]Young, *op. cit.*, p. 36.

While the decibel range of mutual accusations and recriminations remained high throughout this period (and, indeed, until a settlement was finally reached in August 1962), it no longer sufficed the protagonists simply to shout past each other's ears. The rational initiatives of Washington and New York compelled the attention of both sides. Their entry into the dispute could not be ignored, and their proposals had to be responded to. In the process, channels of indirect communication were established between the parties, and negotiations "about negotiations" set in motion. This represented considerable progress.

A major obstacle to direct discussions was the fact that both Jakarta and The Hague stipulated conditions precedent to negotiations that the other could not accept. Here, too ,the intervention of the United States and the United Nations was central to resolving the dilemma. Stevens points out that "the mere fact of a mediator's entrance into a dispute provides the parties with a means for rationalizing retreats from previously held positions, particularly if the mediator can be made to appear to take part of the 'responsibility' for any settlement." [29] Under urgent pressure from Washington and New York to begin negotiations, it was increasingly difficult for the two protagonists to remain adamant on the question of preconditions, and contrariwise less embarrassing for them to back down in this respect.

In particular, the Dutch must have realized at a very early stage that the self-determination argument no longer carried the day in Washington, and that the weight of United States intervention would be in the direction of a settlement basically favorable to Indonesia. Young observes that a mediator's disapproval of a policy or stand "will have an effect, in many cases, on the certainty with which a party holds its position and on its ability to appeal to outside standards for support." [30] In any event, the Dutch soon gave way on the question of self-determination as a precondition to negotiations. Early in January, Prime Minister de Quay informed the Netherlands parliament that his government was dropping its demand that Indonesia accept the principle of self-determination for the Papuans before talks began. De Quay coupled his announcement with the assurance that this decision did "not detract from our conviction that in the discussions we must first consider the interests of the population;" [31] but the extent of the Dutch retreat could scarcely be disguised. Hitherto, the presumed right of the Papuans to determine their own political future had

[29]Carl Stevens, *Strategy and Collective Bargaining Negotiation* (New York: McGraw-Hill, 1963), p. 130.

[30]Young, *op. cit.*, p. 37.

[31]Quoted in *The New York Times*, January 3, 1962.

not been open to discussion; indeed, the duty of preserving that right formed the main defense of Dutch policy on West New Guinea. But in order to get talks under way, The Hague now conceded, in effect, that the question was no longer foreclosed; and it remained to be seen how tenaciously the Dutch would defend in actual negotiations the official cornerstone of their policy.

In his announcement to parliament, the Dutch Prime Minister commented that "it might be expected that Indonesia also would be willing to negotiate without confronting the Netherlands with prior conditions." [32] De Quay referred here to Jakarta's claim to sovereignty over West New Guinea, and its insistence that the only subject to be discussed related to the terms of transfer to Indonesian control. According to press reports, Washington had already informed the Dutch government that Jakarta's position was "less uncompromising" than appeared from official statements.[33] But the initial response to de Quay's concession was hardly promising. Subandrio declared that his government would negotiate only if the Dutch agreed in advance to hand over the territory; otherwise Jakarta would resort to force. "We do not object to bilateral negotiations," he added rather grandly, "with the purpose of transfer of the administration of West Irian to Indonesia." [34] Throughout this period, the Indonesians showed much less flexibility on fundamental issues than the Dutch. Young notes that the interjection of third-party views and evaluations in a bargaining situation "may affect the expectations of each party concerning the commitment of its opponent to its position." [35] Undoubtedly the Jakarta government already sensed which way the wind was blowing, and understood that the impact of United States and United Nations intervention would be to undermine the resolution of the Dutch. The Hague's abandonment of the principle of self-determination as a precondition to negotiations would have been read as an unmistakable signal in this respect. In the developing circumstances, the Indonesians must have felt less constrained to offer significant substantive concessions of their own in order to get a settlement.

On the other hand, there were indications that the Sukarno regime was prepared to consider various facesaving formulae that might afford the Dutch a graceful line of retreat. Early in January, government sources

[32]*Ibid.*, January 3, 1962.

[33]*Ibid.*, December 31, 1961.

[34]Quoted in *ibid.*, January 4, 1962. If the Netherlands declined to meet this condition, "we will not negotiate," Sukarno declared in a public speech. "If the Dutch refuse to negotiate we will continue our struggle until West Irian has returned to Indonesia." Quoted in *ibid.*, January 4, 1962.

[35]Young, *op. cit.*, p. 37.

suggested that Indonesia would be willing to defer the question of formal, legal sovereignty over West New Guinea if the actual administration of the disputed territory were turned over to it. This meant that Jakarta would not insist on The Hague recognizing its claim to sovereignty in the terms of settlement. In this connection, it was pointed out that in recent speeches, Sukarno had "deliberately stressed a change of 'administration' rather than 'sovereignty' as the paramount issue." [36] Further, the process of transfer might be spread out over "two or three years," [37] and Dutch officials might remain in the territory until an orderly change of adminis- tration had been effected. Finally, Indonesia would consider the eventual possibility of some kind of vote by the Papuan population as to their political future, but only after a period of Indonesian rule.[38]

While these concessions were more in form than substance, they did begin to sketch out a program for covering Dutch withdrawal from West New Guinea with reasonable dignity and without the requirement of complete capitulation. Government spokesmen acknowledged the effective- ness of United States pressure in the formulation of Jakarta's more moderate approach, which was at the same time characterized as "'the most liberal" position that Indonesia could take.[39] In all probability, the specific proposals also came from the American side, just as Dutch abandonment of their condition relating to self-determination was almost certainly the result of Washington's urging. In short, the diplomacy of the Kennedy administration was having some success in bringing the two protagonists closer together, although a good many obstacles still had to be overcome before direct discussions were eventually agreed to.

New Alarums

Meanwhile, Jakarta continued to mix the carrot with the stick. Bombas- tic speeches filled the air, and dire threats of force took on meaning against the backdrop of ostentatious preparations for war. Following a meeting of the Supreme Command for the Liberation of West Irian on January 9, Subandrio indicated that Indonesia's patience was wearing thin. "Within a week or ten days," he said, "we will have arrived at a conclusion and will

---

[36]*The New York Times,* January 5, 1962.

[37]Quoted in *ibid.,* January 5, 1962

[38]Late in December, Subandrio had indicated that Jakarta was willing to discuss giving the people of West New Guinea "a great measure of autonomy" if the terri- tory were turned over to Indonesia. Quoted in *ibid.,* December 29, 1961. On the softening of Indonesia's negotiating position, see *ibid.,* January 4, 1962, and January 5, 1962; and also *Christian Science Monitor,* January 4, 1962.

[39]Quoted in *The New York Times,* January 4, 1962.

have certainty (sic) whether steps in the diplomatic field with the Dutch can be of help in solving the West Irian issue." [40] The Foreign Minister professed to be especially concerned that The Hague, while offering to negotiate without preconditions, continued to press the view that the future of the territory should be resolved on the basis of self-determination.[41] Meanwhile, Indonesian attempts to infiltrate guerrilla forces into West New Guinea continued; and in mid-January occurred the naval engagement in which an Indonesian motor torpedo boat was sunk with the loss of many troops drowned or captured.[42]

In the atmosphere of crisis that now surrounded the Dutch-Indonesian controversy, U Thant immediately cabled both governments expressing his concern over this latest clash and urging them to "seek a peaceful solution of the problem." [43] Two days later, on January 17, he issued another strong appeal calling on both sides "to refrain from any precipitate action" and requesting that their permanent representatives in New York "be instructed to discuss with me the possibilities of a peaceful settlement of the whole question in conformity with the purposes and principles of the Charter." [44] The Netherlands accepted Thant's bid the next day, and Indonesia on January 20. The Acting Secretary-General had, in fact, been conducting a series of informal talks for some time with the representatives of both parties at the United Nations, in a parallel initiative with Washington to arrange direct discussions.[45] The favorable response to his Jan-

---

[40]Quoted in ibid., January 10, 1962.

[41]See ibid., January 10, 1962. At this meeting of the West Irian Liberation Supreme Command, Brigadier Suharto, the present President of Indonesia, was appointed theater commander to direct possible operations against the disputed territory.

[42]See p. 109, above.

[43]Quoted in The New York Times, January 16, 1962.

[44]Quoted in ibid., January 18, 1962.

[45]In this connection, see New York Herald Tribune, January 5, 1962.

Referring to the intervenor's tactic of persuasion, Young comments that "the Secretary-General of the United Nations and his staff are in an almost unique position to undertake such activities during many crisis situations. Rather high-level representatives of both sides are often readily available. Here the development of strong permanent missions to the United Nations has been a key factor. Facilities are available for private or behind-the-scenes activities and for consultations with representatives of the various parties concerned either separately or together. And the forum provided by the United Nations system is one in which such activities appear to be gaining a certain acceptance in the flow of mutual expectations." Young, op. cit., p. 51.

In view of the quality of diplomatic representation usually accredited to the United States, comparable opportunities are, of course, also available to the Washington government as well.

uary 17 appeal had the effect of placing these talks on a somewhat more formal basis.

The concept of negotiations under United Nations auspices was increasingly mentioned. When the Dutch announced early in January that they were dropping the principle of self-determination for the Papuans as a precondition to direct talks, they also indicated the desirability of Thant participating as a third party;[46] and his acceptability in this respect was emphasized by The Hague in subsequent communications.[47] Following a meeting with Assistant Secretary of State Harriman in Washington the same day (January 2), Indonesian Ambassador Zain commented to reporters that it would be very useful if the Acting Secretary-General sat in on negotiations between the two parties; he thought it better not to embarrass the United States by asking it to play the role of mediator.[48] At press conferences in mid-January, just after the Dutch-Indonesian naval incident, both President Kennedy and Secretary Rusk endorsed Thant's efforts to arrange negotiations, and incidentally underlined the concern of the United States to bring about a peaceful settlement of the West New Guinea dispute. The President said:[49]

We have been extremely anxious that a peaceful accommodation be reached in this matter, and have used our influence to bring that about. I am particularly glad that the Secretary-General of the United Nations, Mr. U Thant (sic), has been occupying himself with a good deal of energy to try to see if there is a possibility for peaceful settlement. I am hopeful that both parties will respond to his efforts, and that we can prevent an outbreak of hostilities between Indonesia and the Dutch. Great responsibility rests on both of these countries, and I am hopeful that they will give Mr. U Thant every cooperation.

Kennedy's statement was interpreted by informed sources as indicating that the Acting Secretary-General was "Washington's candidate to mediate the dispute." In the view of State Department officials, "the Burmese diplomat is acceptable to both sides and can thus spare the United States direct involvement in the expected negotiations." [50] Following Thant's

[46]See *The New York Times*, January 3, 1962, and January 17, 1962; and also *Christian Science Monitor*, January 18, 1962.

[47]See, for example, the Dutch reply to Thant's January 15 appeal, referred to in *The New York Times*, January 18, 1962.

[48]See *ibid.*, January 3, 1962.

[49]Quoted in *Public Papers . . . 1962*, p. 17.

[50]*The New York Times*, January 17, 1962.

January 17 appeal, the State Department issued a release welcoming "this commendable initiative;" [51] and the next day, Rusk declared:[52]

> The Secretary-General of the United Nations has a basic responsibility to do what he can to maintain the peace, and his initiative in this matter is most welcomed by the United States Government. We hope that the two Governments concerned will give heed to his appeal to them to avoid further incidents and to establish contact with him to explore the possibilities of negotiation and a possible peaceful settlement of this situation. We think this is entirely in accord with not only his privileges but his obligations under the charter. We would support him fully in this peacekeeping effort which he has undertaken.

More than two months were to pass, however, before Dutch and Indonesian representatives finally met at the conference table. Throughout this period, Thant conducted intermittent but separate discussions with both parties at the United Nations. In an effort to remove one obstacle to direct talks, he appealed to the Netherlands government on January 29 to release Indonesian prisoners taken in the naval engagement earlier that month "as a humanitarian gesture which might help in easing tensions all round." [53] The Hague responded favorably, and repatriation of the prisoners was completed on March 11. Prime Minister de Quay expressed the hope that "this voluntary gesture may contribute to easing the present tension and thus improve the climate for negotiations between the parties under (the Acting Secretary-General's) auspices." [54] However much this may have helped, the atmosphere of mutual hostility and pervasive distrust that subsisted between the two parties always constituted the main barrier to more rapid progress in the now active search for settlement.

The Dutch and Indonesian Positions Summarized

As they had evolved by February 1962, the respective positions of the two parties had moved perceptibly closer, but were still in conflict on important points. The Dutch had dropped their insistence that the right of the Papuans to ultimate self-determination be recognized by Indonesia as a precondition for direct discussions. This demand was totally unacceptable to Jakarta, and it is hard to see how significant progress could have been made until the Dutch yielded on this point. On the other hand, The

[51]Quoted in *ibid.*, January 18, 1962.
[52]Quoted in *Department of State Bulletin,* vol. 46, no. 1180 (February 5, 1962), p. 203.
[53]Quoted in *Everyman's United Nations,* 7th edition, p. 97.
[54]Quoted in *The New York Times,* March 12, 1962.

Hague still publicly supported the principle, and was apparently determined to defend it in actual negotiations. The Netherlands also favored a period of international administration for West New Guinea, preferably by the United Nations itself, during which time the autochthonous population would be prepared for self-determination, and at the end of which they would have the right to decide their own political future. Having dropped self-determination as a precondition for negotiations, the Dutch now held out for talks without preconditions from any quarter. In particular, they still would not agree to negotiate on the basis of any formula which provided *a priori* that control of the territory would eventually be turned over to Indonesia, even if after an interim period of joint or neutral administration, since such a procedure would effectively deny the principle of self-determination for the Papuans. Finally, The Hague wanted negotiations to take place in the presence of a third party, and their preference for United Nations participation in this respect was well known.[55]

As for the Indonesians, they would enter negotiations only if there were prior agreement on the ultimate transfer of West New Guinea to Indonesian administration. Provided this point were conceded, Jakarta intimated that it was prepared to be reasonable on almost everything else. Thus the Sukarno regime had now dropped its former demand that the Netherlands formally acknowledge Indonesian sovereignty over the territory, which was a measure of humiliation that the Dutch might not have been able to accept. Moreover, the actual process of transfer might be spread out over two or three years; and during this interval, administrative responsibility might be shared by the two parties, with Dutch officials working side-by-side with Indonesians. Indeed, a variety of other alternatives might be feasible for the transition period. Jakarta seemed mistrustful, however, of the concept of United Nations trusteeship as an interim arrangement, except on the understanding that Indonesia would assume full authority over the territory within a stated time. Presumably this was because the principle of international trusteeship implied that the Papuans should have the opportunity to decide on their political future *before* a transfer of authority to Indonesia.[56] But Jakarta did indicate that it would agree to a plebiscite *after* it had exercised control over West New Guinea for a number of years. The breaking point, in short, was the requirement

[55]For discussion of the Dutch position, see especially *New York Herald Tribune,* January 5, 1962, and January 23, 1962; and *The New York Times,* February 13, 1962, February 26, 1962, and March 10, 1962.

[56]For the views of Secretary-General Dag Hammarskjold on this point as expressed to Prime Minister Tengku Abdul Rahman of Malaya in November 1960, see p. 71, above.

that there be a "clear understanding" that any negotiations would lead to Indonesian administration of the disputed territory.[57]

This summary of the respective positions may clarify why Thant's initial efforts to arrange direct discussions under his auspices and "without prior conditions" were unsuccessful. In talks at the United Nations early in January, Jan Polderman, then acting head of the Dutch delegation, informed Thant that The Hague accepted his proposal "to enter into direct negotiations without any prior conditions by either side;" but Emile Jossis Lapian, the acting head of the Indonesian delegation, indicated that Jakarta "could not enter into direct negotiations without first knowing what these negotiations would be concerned with," that is, unless there was "a prior agreement that the talks would deal with the transfer of the administration of West New Guinea to Indonesia."[58]

Following his appeal to both parties on January 17, requesting that their representatives at the United Nations be instructed to discuss with him "the possibilities of a peaceful settlement," Thant reportedly advanced a compromise formula for resolving the substance of the Dutch-Indonesian controversy. According to this plan, West New Guinea would be transformed into a United Nations trust territory to be administered jointly by two Asian countries friendly to Indonesia "pending final decision regarding its future." [59] Thant proposed Malaya and either India or Burma as joint administrators. The Permanent Representative of the Netherlands, C. W. A. Schurmann, promptly informed the Acting Secretary-General that his government would accept the plan, subject to the negotiation of details; but Sukardjo Wirjopranoto, Indonesia's chief delegate at the United Nations, expressed reservations. The "ideal solution," according to him, would be to hand over the territory directly to Indonesia; if West New Guinea "must" become a trust territory for a transitional period, Jakarta wanted to be sole administrator.[60] This, of course, was unacceptable to the Dutch. Sukardjo's reaction did make clear again, however, that Indonesia would be disinclined to accept any scheme that might be construed as leaving in question the final disposition of the territory.

On February 8, the Dutch parliament was informed that favorable re-

---

[57]Quoted in *The New York Times*, February 1, 1962, from a press interview with Foreign Minister Subandrio. Discussion of the Indonesian position may be found in *New York Herald Tribune*, January 5, 1962, and January 23, 1962; and *The New York Times*, January 21, 1962, February 1, 1962, and March 10, 1962.

[58]*New York Herald Tribune*, January 5, 1962.

[59]*Ibid.*, January 23, 1962.

[60]*Ibid.*, January 23, 1962.

sults from Thant's efforts to arrange negotiations were "by no means sure."[61] Jakarta's precondition was seemingly an insuperable obstacle to direct discussions.

Preliminary Talks Arranged

Meanwhile, Washington continued to press for talks between the two parties. During February, Attorney-General Robert F. Kennedy visited Indonesia and the Netherlands in the course of a world tour. His unique stature as the President's brother and confidant lent special significance to his mission. Kennedy brought a Presidential letter to Sukarno "urging the Indonesians to come to the conference table without preconditions;" [62] and in conversations with the Indonesians, he emphasized the deep interest that the United States had in their country and in a peaceful solution of the West New Guinea dispute.[63] For Sukarno and his colleagues, these discussions must have confirmed their already strong impression that the weight of Washington's influence would be for a settlement basically favorable to Indonesia's claim.[64] In any event, they decided to go along with the American program. Hilsman states that before Kennedy left Jakarta, the Indonesian leadership "had agreed to drop their most onerous preconditions for negotiations." [65] According to Brackman, however, Sukarno had not budged to the issue of the transfer of West New Guinea to Indonesia:[66]

The question of whether or not there would be a transfer was simply beyond debate. As for the question of a plebiscite, which Kennedy raised, Sukarno promised to abide by a referendum *after* the transfer of West New Guinea's administration. Sukarno knew that he was

[61]Quoted in *ibid.*, February 9, 1962.
[62]Schlesinger, *op. cit.*, p. 534.
[63]See *New York Herald Tribune*, February 14, 1962.
[64]"In a television interview on March 4, 1962, shortly after his return to the U. S. Robert Kennedy indicated support for the Indonesian position and rather severely criticized Dutch policy, particularly the Dutch educational effort in West New Guinea . . . In retrospect, the U. S. attorney general's television remarks were perhaps the first unequivocal indication that Washington meant to exert increasing pressure on The Hague in the coming months." Van der Kroef, "The West New Guinea Settlement," *loc. cit.*, p. 139.
Among other things, Kennedy said in the course of the interview that Indonesia had "a strong argument" in laying claim to West New Guinea. He also expressed the view that Jakarta "was going to take over" the territory, and that the Dutch really wanted to leave, although not on Indonesian terms. Quoted in *Facts on File*, vol. 22, no. 1113 (February 22-28, 1962), p. 76.
[65]Hilsman, *op. cit.*, p. 379.
[66]Brackman, *op. cit.*, p. 105. Italics in original.

negotiating from a position of strength — i. e., the weakness of the great powers in Southeast Asia.

But, at least, the Indonesians did agree to talk directly with the Dutch. Kennedy himself summarized the results of his visit in the following terms:[67]

> . . . we came to an agreement that (Indonesia) would send negotiators to meet with the Dutch to determine if the matter could be solved amicably. This was at least a step forward, although I could see many hurdles in the future. We were not dealing with completely reasonable men on either side of this controversy.

The Attorney-General's subsequent call at The Hague came at a difficult moment. Early in February, a K.L.M. Royal Dutch Airlines plane carrying soldiers in civilian dress had refueled in Alaska, Hawaii, and Wake Island en route to West New Guinea. In protest, a mob of Indonesian youths stoned the United States embassy in Jakarta, possibly at the instigation of the government. Washington thereupon withdrew "for the time being" all landing rights on United States territory for commercial aircraft carrying Dutch troop replacements to the disputed territory. According to the State Department, this step was taken "in the interest of a peaceful solution" of the Dutch-Indonesian controversy, and before the attack on the embassy;[68] but it inevitably caused a good deal of resentment in the Netherlands. While in Indonesia, Kennedy found occasion to remark publicly on the traditional friendship between the Netherlands and the United States, and to say that "we intend to continue as friends." [69] His gesture served to improve somewhat the atmosphere for his visit to The Hague, where he was received with much anticipation. There is unfortunately little on the public record to indicate the upshot of Kennedy's discussions with the leaders of the Dutch government, although we may assume that he urged them to meet with the Indonesians on whatever basis the United States could ultimately work out for direct discussions. Brackman reports that Kennedy "engaged the Dutch in a 'frank exchange' and curtly warned that they could not depend on American support (presumably the Seventh Fleet) should the conflict escalate;" and he adds that

[67]Kennedy, op. cit., p. 134.

[68]Quoted in The New York Times, February 6, 1962. On this incident, see also Brackman, op. cit., p. 104; and Malcolm E. Smith, Jr., Kennedy's 13 Great Mistakes in the White House (New York: National Forum of America, 1968), pp. 147-148.

Other nations were also reacting to the heightened intensity of the dispute. Japan suspended landing rights for Dutch troop flights; while, on the other side of the fence, the British halted the shipment of arms to Indonesia. See London Times, February 6, 1962.

[69]Quoted in The New York Times, February 15, 1962.

the Dutch were "disturbed" by the Attorney-General's "brusqueness." [70] Kennedy himself commented later that he "came up against a number of Dutch leaders who were as intransigent in their position regarding West New Guinea as were some of their opposite numbers in Indonesia." [71]

Shortly thereafter, Foreign Minister Luns flew to Washington for conferences with President Kennedy, Secretary of State Rusk, and other leaders. By all accounts, Luns was "the most stubborn Dutchman of them all" on the West New Guinea issue,[72] and "opposed the mediation effort." [73] His visit apparently went badly. In Brackman's words:[74]

Luns learned that young (Robert) Kennedy had spoken with authority. The Americans told the Dutch that they had created the Irian impasse at a time when moderate, constructive governments like those of Hatta and Natsir were in power. Now they were unable to see the crisis to a conclusion without U. S. help. Since the Dutch had already informed the U. N. General Assembly of their readiness to "terminate sovereignty over Netherlands New Guinea at the earliest possible date," there was no point in resisting the transfer to Djakarta and risking an East-West confrontation over a "colonial" issue which would bring the Afro-Asian world down against the West.

Schlesinger gives a brief but vivid account of one meeting which Luns had with the President:[75]

Luns was so carried away by the injustice of it all that he waved a flabby forefinger in Kennedy's face, a gesture which Kennedy courteously ignored. To all such manifestations Kennedy's response was direct: "Do you want to fight a war about West New Guinea?"

He made it clear that the Dutch were free to blame the United States for the outcome if only they would permit the problem to be settled.

According to Schlesinger, it was "Robert Kennedy's pressure on Sukarno and the President's and Harriman's on Luns (that) finally brought the principals reluctantly to the conference table." [76]

Young speaks of the "role of an intervening party in dramatizing the dangers of failure to reach a positive termination" of an international crisis. He has in mind primarily the "possibly disastrous consequences of

[70]Brackman, op. cit., p. 105. Material in parentheses in original.

[71]Kennedy, op. cit., p. 15. At a press conference at The Hague on February 26, Kennedy commented that both Indonesian and Dutch political leaders were taking an "emotional" rather than a practical approach to the West New Guinea dispute. Quoted in Facts on File, vol. 22, no. 1113 (February 22-28, 1962), p. 76.

[72]Hilsman, op. cit., p. 374.

[73]Schlesinger, op. cit., p. 534.

[74]Brackman, op. cit., p. 105.

[75]Schlesinger, op. cit., p. 534.

[76]Ibid., pp. 534-535.

an outcome of mutual loss," that is, a conflict whose costs to both sides outweighed the advantages that even the supposed winner might claim.[77] No doubt the Washington government pointed forcefully to the real possibility of such a conclusion in the West New Guinea controversy if both sides persisted in maintaining intransigent positions up to the point of war. But in addition to this, the two antagonists could not have failed to weigh the implications of quiet suggestions that Washington might wash its hands of the whole affair if they did not show an increasing measure of reasonableness. Here the consequences of failure would be to sacrifice as well the efforts and energies of the United States in the search for settlement, in circumstances where American involvement offered the last, best hope of a peaceful solution.

Only rarely did pressure take overt, public form, as in the case of the ban on Dutch troop flights. With respect to the Dutch, moreover, Washington certainly made clear that they would not have the support of the United States in the event of large-scale hostilities that could be traced to Dutch intransigence over negotiations. After agreement was finally reached in August, Prime Minister de Quay declared that the Netherlands had been "forced into it against our will and against everything we honor;" he explained that The Hague "could not count on the support of its allies, and for that reason we had to sign." [78] De Quay was doubtless overstating the case, although he probably did feel that his country had been let down by the United States. In any event, it made good political sense to shift as much of the blame as possible onto the shoulders of the Washington government; and indeed, President Kennedy had specifically invited the Dutch authorities to do so.[79] As for the Indonesians, Washington held out the prospect of further economic assistance as an inducement to moderation. During Sukarno's visit to Washington in April 1961, Kennedy had praised Indonesia's new eight-year development plan; and he subsequently appointed a special economic mission to study how the United States might assist this effort. But no decisions had been made in this respect by early Spring 1962.

[77]Young, op. cit., pp. 38-39.

[78]Quoted in The New York Times, August 17, 1962. The significance of United States support for the Dutch is perhaps indicated in Schlesinger's comment that "Dean Rusk gave Luns some incautious assurances during another NATO meeting at Athens in May which stiffened the Dutch for a moment and probably resulted in worse terms for them in the end." Schlesinger, op. cit., p. 535.

[79]Attention has already been called to Stevens' observation that a mediator often "provides the parties with a means for rationalizing retreats from previously held positions, particularly if the mediator can be made to appear to take part of the 'responsibility' for any settlement." Both Kennedy and de Quay understood the name of the game.

During March, the intensive efforts of the Kennedy administration to arrange direct discussions between the two parties began to yield public results. As reported in the press, the scenario envisaged by the United States involved the device of "preliminary" talks as a first step, to be held without prior conditions in the presence of a third party, and for the purposes of exploring possible areas of agreement and drawing up an agenda for later negotiations.[80] Hopefully this technique would circumvent the problem posed by Jakarta's insistent demand that the Netherlands accept as a precondition to negotiations that West New Guinea be turned over to Indonesia, and by the refusal of The Hague to capitulate to this demand before discussions started. The talks were to be conducted in secret at an undisclosed location near Washington, D. C. On March 12, Prime Minister de Quay announced that the Dutch cabinet had unanimously agreed to go forward with the United States-sponsored discussions. The mission was entrusted to the Dutch Ambassador to Washington, J. H. van Roijen, and the Netherlands Permanent Representative at the United Nations, C. W. A. Schurmann. Two days later, Indonesia also agreed to take part; and Sukarno dispatched Adam Malik, then Jakarta's Ambassador to Moscow, and Sudjarwo Tjondronegoro, a high official in the Foreign Ministry, to lead the Indonesian team. Negotiations actually began on March 20 at a private estate in Middleburg, Virginia, about 30 miles from Washington.

The whole program had obviously been worked out in consultation with U Thant; and the talks were, in fact, formally conducted under the auspices of the United Nations. The United States submitted a list of ten names simultaneously to Jakarta and The Hague as candidates for the role of disinterested third party. Eventually both sides settled on Ellsworth Bunker, a then-retired American diplomat,[81] who was thereupon invited by Thant to act as "mediator representing the Acting Secretary-General" at the talks;[82] and officially, Bunker served in this capacity rather than as the representative of Washington.

[80]See *The New York Times,* March 10, 1962.

[81]Jones reports: "The selection of a man acceptable to both sides took some time. Ten names were submitted simultaneously to the Indonesian and Dutch governments. I took the list to Sukarno, who wanted to be sure that the mediator — or 'Third Party,' as he was called — was a man who had some understanding of the specific problems of people in new nations. He was most favorably impressed by Bunker's record. Could I guarantee, he asked me, that Ambassador Bunker, whom he had not met, had a sympathetic approach to Asian peoples and the problems arising from colonialism? I said I could. Would he understand the Indonesian position? I assured him that he could count on Bunker's being an impartial, fair-minded man who understood the forces at work in the world today." Jones, *op. cit.,* p. 207. fn. 5.

[82]*Everyman's United Nations,* 7th edition, p. 98.

Chapter Twelve

Negotiations Under
United Nations Auspices

The role of the third party in international crises, and the opportunities open to the skillful mediator in promoting a settlement, vary a great deal from case to case. On the one hand, there may be little if any potential for useful involvement. Young states:[1]

> It is possible . . . to imagine severe crises in which the nature of the dilemmas is such as to negate virtually all possibilities of successful intervention. In fact, there might even be cases in which attempts at intervention would contribute to an exacerbation of the original crisis. Neither side may be willing to consider seriously accepting the intervention of a third party, and suspicions, difficulties over impartiality, emotional distortions, lack of information, and various irrationalities may make the idea of intervention an empty suggestion.

Even where involvement by a third party is welcomed (or, at least, accepted), the range of his activities in the process of settlement will exhibit much diversity, depending on his own conception of his role, his qualifications, and the circumstances of a given case. In particular, a mediator may or may not take part in direct negotiations between the parties. By the time Indonesia and the Netherlands finally met at the conference table on March 20, 1962, the United States and the United Nations had already contributed significantly to the search for settlement. Their role in reestablishing communications between the protagonists, in persuading both sides that a reasonable basis for settlement could be found, and in developing a mutually acceptable program for initiating direct (if "informal") discussions between the parties, were models of the mediator's art. Had nothing more been attempted, this measure of joint intervention by the United States and the United Nations would have been judged a successful diplomatic initiative.

But the Kennedy administration intended a great deal more. From the beginning of the enterprise, Washington apparently envisaged direct in-

[1]Young, *op. cit.*, p. 49.

volvement in the negotiating sessions; and in practice, the United States asserted an effective leadership over the course of the actual discussions, which took place in the presence of Ambassador Bunker as mediator "representing" the Acting Secretary-General of the United Nations.

First Round

The first round of discussions began on March 20 and ended March 22, after three days of continuous exchanges. The round had been billed in advance as a "preliminary session" to last only a few days,[2] and which was presumably to lay the basis for more formal negotiations at a later stage. After the session ended, a communique stated that the discussions had been conducted "in an atmosphere of cooperation," and that they would be resumed after both sides had had an opportunity to consult their respective governments.[3] A State Department spokesman declared that "the talks had gotten off to a good start and . . . the outlook for a peaceful solution of the dispute appeared encouraging." [4]

In fact, the talks had not gone well at all. The Indonesians sought to confine discussions to the modalities of a transfer of administration, while the Dutch still strove to safeguard the presumed right of the Papuans to self-determination. Both sides "had rigid instructions as to their positions on self-determination, and there was no give on either side." [5] Confronted with the possibility that the negotiations would collapse at this early stage, Bunker "called for a recess to enable the two delegations to obtain more flexibile instructions." [6] Three days later, Jakarta abruptly announced that Indonesia's representatives were withdrawing from the negotiations. A government spokesman denied, however, that the door was closed to future talks. "We are awaiting further diplomatic developments," he said. "If there is a further move from the Dutch, the door is still open." [7] According to Jones, the Indonesians had "decided not to return to the conference table until the Dutch had agreed to surrender control of West New Guinea's administration." [8]

2*The New York Times,* March 20, 1962.
3Quoted in *ibid.,* March 27, 1962.
4Quoted in *ibid.,* March 27, 1962.
5Jones, *op. cit.,* p. 208.
6*Ibid.,* p. 208.
7Quoted in *The New York Times,* March 27, 1962.
8Jones, *op. cit.,* p. 208.
In a press interview, Subandrio cited the following reasons for the breakdown of the talks: "The Jakarta government had entered the talks 'with the fair hope that the Netherlands would not reject in principle the transfer of administration (of West New Guinea) under certain conditions which would reflect' Dutch 'commit-

But Jakarta had accurately judged which way the wind was blowing. Now the game was to insure the best possible terms in the hard bargaining that lay ahead. To this end, the Indonesians employed a twofold strategy. On the one hand, they sought to project a posture of openmindedness and accommodation with respect to further talks, and to blame Dutch intransigence for the delay in resuming negotiations. At the same time, they continued to increase the military pressure in West New Guinea; there was to be no let-up until the Dutch gave in. While this overall strategy was presumably aimed primarily at The Hague, it was doubtless also designed to affect Washington's perception of the evolving situation and to encourage the United States to intervene more decisively along lines favorable to Indonesia.

Thus on March 27, a day after the announcement that Indonesia was withdrawing from the talks, Sukarno stated that his government "was awaiting a reply on whether the Netherlands was prepared to enter formal negotiations on the transfer of the administration of the disputed territory to Indonesia." [9] Three days later, President Kennedy was sufficiently disturbed by the impasse to write the Indonesian leader urging that negotiations be resumed. Kennedy's letter prompted Foreign Minister Subandrio to comment piously that "there was a deep desire on the part of the United States for a resumption of secret talks and a peaceful settlement," [10] leaving the implication that only the stubbornness of the Dutch stood in the way of this happy consummation.

Simultaneously, Jakarta stepped up military activities against the territory, a process that continued right down to the final settlement in August. On March 25, Indonesian planes attacked a small Dutch naval vessel off the western tip of the island, wounding three crewmen. Repeated attempts

ments' to Indonesia before 1950; 'instead, even before the negotiations started, the Netherlands moved its warships from the Caribbean Sea to the Pacific Ocean, obviously on the first lap of their journey to West Irian; Dutch 'preparations in West Irian for the proclamation of a so-called independent Papuan State have been intensified;' the negotiations had 'lost their secrecy and informality when the Netherlands . . . announced more than once, . . . as if real negotiations had been started and as if the negotiators 'need not necessarily talk about the transfer of administration to Indonesia;' 'the Indonesian delegate (Adam Malik) was told on more than one occasion (during the talks) that the Netherlands was not prepared to transfer administration over West Irian to Indonesia under any conditions;' 'these combined factors compelled Indonesia to arrive at the conclusion that the meeting had been used by the Dutch as a tactical manouver . . . to placate public opinion at home and to win support from the outside world . . . in their struggle against Indonesia.' " *Facts on File,* vol. 22, no. 118 (March 29-April 4, 1962), p. 107.

[9]*The New York Times,* March 28, 1962.

[10]Quoted in *ibid.,* March 31, 1962.

were made to infiltrate guerrilla bands both by coastal landings and increasingly by parachute drops; and the number of armed clashes between Dutch and Indonesian forces rose accordingly. Moscow chose this moment to expand its military aid program to the Sukarno regime. Subandrio declared in the Soviet capital that the new arms were meant "purely to liberate West Irian." [11] After an especially large parachute drop near Fakfak in May, General Nasution, the Indonesian Minister of Defense, promised that the offensive would continue. The government "had no more faith in negotiations with the Netherlands," he said. "We have only one reply now — to step up our policy of confrontation . . . especially in the military field." [12] On May 17, the Dutch announced that they had shot down an Indonesian plane carrying paratroops to West New Guinea. A day later, the Indonesian representative at the United Nations, Sukardjo Wirjopranoto, asserted that the paratroop landings marked the beginning of the "liberation" of the territory, and that the movement would not be halted unless there was a "peaceful solution" of the dispute on Indonesian terms.[13] On the whole, Jakarta did an effective job in creating the impression of growing military commitment, although in reality the fighting never reached major proportions. According to a report in late May, the number of invaders up to that time totalled less than 600;[14] and generally the available Dutch forces managed to choke off the frequent coastal landings and parachute drops without too much difficulty.

The Bunker Plan

Ambassador Bunker now resorted to something approaching shock treatment. On April 2, he submitted to both parties a set of proposals as a suggested basis for subsequent negotiations that, in fact, comprised a comprehensive program for resolving the West New Guinea dispute in its entirety. The text of the Bunker Plan, as released by the United Nations late in May, was as follows:[15]

[11]Quoted in *Antara Daily Newsbulletin*, May 9, 1962.

[12]Quoted in *The New York Times*, May 16, 1961.

[13]Quoted in *ibid.*, May 19, 1962.

[14]See *Facts on File*, vol. 22, no. 1126 (May 24-30, 1962), p. 173.

[15]Quoted in *Department of State Bulletin*, vol. 46, no. 1200 (June 25, 1962), pp. 1039-1040. It is not entirely clear how closely the text of the Bunker proposals made public by the United Nations in late May corresponds to the draft presented to the Dutch and Indonesians early in April. Some modifications were introduced as the result of subsequent diplomatic exchanges. *The New York Times* reported, for example, that on April 18, "Mr. Bunker added a sentence to make the condition of a plebiscite and respect for Papuan rights more explicit." *The New York Times*,

Proposals for Negotiations Between the Governments
of Indonesia and the Netherlands

1. The Government of Indonesia and the Netherlands would each sign separate agreements or a single agreement which would be presented to the Acting Secretary-General of the United Nations.

2. The Government of the Netherlands would stipulate the transfer of administrative authority over West New Guinea to a temporary executive authority under the Acting Secretary-General of the United at a specified date. The Acting Secretary-General of the United Nations would appoint a mutually acceptable, non-Indonesian administrator who would undertake to administer the territory for a period of not less than one year but not more than two. This administrator would arrange for the termination of Netherlands administration under circumstnces that will provide the inhabitants of the territory the opportunity to exercise freedom of choice in accordance with paragraph 4 below. This administrator would replace top Dutch officials with short-term, one year non-Indonesian and non-Dutch officials hired on a contract basis.

3. The temporary executive authority under the Acting Secretary-General of the United Nations would administer West New Guinea during the first year with the assistance of non-Indonesian and non-Dutch personnel, Beginning the second year the Acting Secretary-General of the United Nations would replace United Nations officials with Indonesian officials, it being understood that by the end of the second year full administrative control would be transferred to Indonesia. United Nations technical assistance personnel will remain in an advisory capacity and to assist in preparation for carrying out the provisions of paragraph 4.

4. Indonesia agrees to make arrangements, with the assistance and participation of the Acting Secretary-General of the United Nations and United Nations personnel, to give the people of the territory the opportunity to exercise freedom of choice not later than __ years after Indonesia has assumed full administrative responsibility for West New Guinea. The Government of the Netherlands would agree to transfer administration in accordance with this proposal on condition that the Government of the Netherlands would receive, as a result of formal

June 2, 1962. This is confirmed in Jones, *op. cit.,* p. 209. See also van der Kroef, "The West New Guinea Settlement," *loc. cit.,* p. 140. Jones also asserts that Bunker submitted "revised proposals" to the two parties late in May, but he gives no details as to the extent of the revisions. See Jones, *op. cit.,* p. 209. But presumably the final version of the Bunker Plan did not differ greatly from the original draft.

negotiations, adequate guarantees for safeguarding the interests, including the right of self-determination, of the Papuans.

5. Indonesia and the Netherlands agree to share the costs of the foregoing.

6. Once this agreement has been signed, the Governments of Indonesia and the Netherlands will resume normal diplomatic relations.

The Bunker Plan speaks for itself, and little additional commentary seems necessary. In essence, it provided for a plainly pro-Indonesian solution. The plan stipulated definitely that "full administrative control" over West New Guinea would be transferred to Indonesia within two years, in line with Jakarta's insistent demand that the main point be resolved *ab initio*. In order to save Dutch face, the transfer would not be direct but rather *via* an interregnum of temporary United Nations administration; and the vexed problem of sovereignty over the disputed territory would be dealt with by the simple expedient of ignoring it. Also in deference to Dutch sensibilities, elaborate lip service was given to the presumed right of the Papuans to self-determination, but under a formula that virtually assured an ultimate choice favorable to Indonesia. In short, the Dutch were spared the humiliation of abject surrender, but little else. Finally, at a time when the United Nations was already overburdened financially, especially by the extraordinary expenses of the Congo intervention, Bunker disposed of the problem of costs with the novel suggestion that they be shared equally by the principals. This proposal had the additional virtue of obviating the necessity for approval (and hence discussion) of the agreement by a United Nations organ prior to its going into effect.

From another perspective, the Bunker Plan made abundantly clear that the Kennedy administration had embraced the broadest possible definition of the mediator's function in working toward a settlement of the West New Guinea dispute. There can be little doubt that the Bunker proposals were drafted by the State Department after extensive prior consultation with both principals, and that the plan represented Washington's best judgment as to the outlines of a viable solution. Having succeeded in bringing the two parties together, the United States might have envisage the mediator's role at the actual negotiations in narrow terms, confining Bunker's participation primarily to "procedural points concerning methods for solving dilemmas" and limiting his involvement in formulating the "actual substance of possible termination or settlement arrangements." [16] Washington chose instead to take responsibility for sponsoring a comprehensive settlement program through the proposals tabled

[16]Young, *op. cit.*, p. 56.

by the American diplomat who was acting as United Nations mediator.

Iklé comments that the "mediator's suggestions are influential mainly because they create focal points" around which negotiations can proceed.[17] He defines this concept in the following terms:[18]

Among the many alternatives for settling an issue, there are often a few which seem particularly prominent to the parties. These focal points are like a notch where a compromise might converge, a resting place where rising demands might come to a halt, or a barrier over which an initial proposal cannot be budged . . . focal points serve to reduce the alternatives that the parties must consider.

The Bunker Plan provided just such focal points. In particular, it dealt squarely with the two main stumbling blocks in the way of resolving the West New Guinea dispute: the nonnegotiable Indonesian demand that control of the territory be turned over to them, and Dutch preoccupation with the principle of self-detemination for the Papuans. In both instances, Bunker's proposals afforded a reasonable way out of the dilemma. Moreover, the Bunker Plan made extensive use of ideas that had long been discussed as possible components of a settlement, including the concept of temporary United Nations administration and an eventual plebiscite for the autochthonous population (both of which could be found in the Luns Plan, for example). In essence, its terms comprised a unique formulation of mostly familiar elements. To use Young's terminology, the Bunker Plan had "saliency." that is, "prominence in the perceptions of the parties, uniqueness, simplicity, and a certain naturalness imparted by the structure of the situation itself." [19] From this point forward, it became the basis of subsequent bargaining between Indonesia and the Nethrlands, and its terms were substantially adopted in the final settlement.

This is not to suggest, however, that the Bunker Plan immediately commended itself to Jakarta and The Hague. In many respects, its provisions must have come as a shock to both sides. For the Dutch especially, it represented a humiliating defeat; and diplomatic legerdemain could not disguise the reality of what was proposed. The Netherlands was asked to go far beyond the concessions of the Luns Plan and agree to an Indonesian takeover of West New Guinea, an outcome they had fought bitterly for more than a decade. While the Bunker proposals did not

[17]Fred Charles Iklé, *How Nations Negotiate* (New York: Harper & Row, 1964), p. 214. Schelling also discusses the power of the mediator to "make potent suggestions." See Thomas C. Schelling, *The Strategy of Conflict* (Cambridge: Harvard University Press, 1960), pp. 143-144.

[18]Iklé, *op. cit.,* p. 213.

[19]Young, *op. cit.,* pp. 40-41.

require direct transfer to Indonesia, the device of temporary United Nations administration was obviously a facesaving formula pure and simple; and even the contemplated interval of international control was much shorter than that adumbrated in the Luns Plan.[20] Further, and perhaps even more important, the provisions for safeguarding the right of self-determination for the Papuans were largely window dressing, in that the proposed exercise of "freedom of choice" was not to take place during the period of United Nations administration, but only *after* Jakarta had exercised control for a number of years.

As for the Indonesians, they were given the assurance of ultimate control, but they were denied the direct transfer of authority so urgently required by patriotic *amour propre*. Despite Sukarno's threats and bluster, he would have to wait at least a year, and possibly two, before the national claim was finally redeemed. Even then, Jakarta would have to recognize, albeit implicitly, that the question of sovereignty remained moot, and would not be legally resolved until after the Papuans had exercised "freedom of choice" under some kind of United Nations supervision. On April 9, Sukarno indicated that the Indonesian government accepted the terms of the Bunker Plan in principle. "We approve of the broad outlines of American attempts to solve" the West New Guinea problem peacefully, he said.[21] But a day later, Sukarno declared that he would reject the "two-year condition" in the proposal for transferring the territory to Indonesian control.[22] And he repeated a previously given pledge that the national claim would be redeemed before the end of the year. The Netherlands "has less than nine months to return West Irian to Indonesia," he warned; otherwise, "We will fight for our rights with all our means." [23]

A Test of Wills

Not surprisingly, the Bunker Plan provoked a good deal of resentment in Dutch government circles. The Hague had long since faced up to the necessity, even the desirability, of relinquishing control over West New

[20]While the Luns Plan did not specify a term of years for United Nations administration, the implication of the plan was that several years of international administration would be required for its proper implementation.

[21]Quoted in *The New York Times,* April 10, 1962.

[22]Quoted in *Christian Science Monitor,* April 10, 1962.

[23]Quoted in *ibid.,* April 10, 1962. On several occasions Sukarno boasted that "before the cock crows on January 1, 1963," West New Guinea would be Indonesian. See, for example, *Antara Daily Newsbulletin,* April 12, 1962, and May 22, 1962.

Guinea. But this had hitherto been thought of in terms of a transfer of authority to an international trusteeship of indefinite duration, at the end of which the Papuans would be given the right to determine their own political future. The mediator's proposals called for much more far-reaching concessions to the Indonesians, and this was bitter medicine indeed — even, or perhaps especially, when proffered by a presumed friend and ally. Dutch officials complained that Bunker had really become "a party to the dispute." [24] In addition, the Dutch were annoyed by indications that, prior to the preliminary talks in March, Washington had discussed the main outlines of the plan with the Indonesians at much greater length than with themselves.[25] At a N. A. T. O. ministerial conference in Athens early in May, Foreign Minister Luns was reported to have "sharply criticized" United States involvement in the Dutch-Indonesian controversy.[26]

Within the Dutch cabinet, Luns appears to have argued vigorously against acceptance of the Bunker proposals. Van der Kroef reports:[27]

Luns . . . seemed to believe that the Dutch should avoid any outright commitment to a resumption of negotiations on the relatively narrow basis of the Bunker plan; he was reported to favor a more flexible and "open" approach, in which any question might be raised during negotiations. The strategy was based, according to certain informed circles, on Luns' conviction that the political and especially the economic situation in Indonesia would deteriorate so rapidly in the near future as to produce important changes in Indonesia's West New Guinea policy. Hence protracted discussions, i. e., discussion based on an "open" agenda, which might prolong the talks indefinitely or cause them to break down and thus buy the Dutch and the Papuans more time, seemed the wiser course.

But the tide was running the other way. During the early months of 1962, criticism of the government's still cautious approach became more vocal in parliament, and especially in the Dutch press. The inevitability of surrendering sovereignty over West New Guinea was now widely accepted, and in such circumstances the prospect of war over the principle of self-determination for the Papuans seemed increasingly anachronistic. On March 28, the Socialist newspaper *Het Parool* echoed a growing popular sentiment when it commented editorially that "our country is neither

[24]Quoted in *Christian Science Monitor*, April 10, 1962.

[25]See *ibid.*, April 10, 1962; and *The New York Times*, April 14, 1962, and April 15, 1962.

[26]*The New York Times*, May 5, 1962.

[27]Van der Kroef, "The West New Guinea Settlement," *loc. cit.*, pp. 140-141. The author cites "an official in the New Guinea section of the Interior Affairs Ministry

willing nor able to conduct war over New Guinea." [28] This was the reality, and the more militant jingoism of the right-wing press carried less and less conviction. As a matter of practical politics, the Dutch government now had little choice but to settle for the best terms it could get.

To be sure, there was a general feeling of frustration and disappointment over the impending outcome, and considerable bitterness with respect to the role of the United States. In official circles, Luns was certainly not alone in his opposition to the Bunker Plan. The cabinet apparently debated it at great length over a period of weeks, in the face of mounting pressure from Washington and New York and the insistent threat of further military action by the Indonesians. After a marathon session on April 13, it was reported that the cabinet had decided "not to reject" the mediator's program, while at the same time making clear that it could not accept all of Bunker's proposals, and that the main stumbling block related to the inadequate guarantees for the Papuans' right to self-determination.[29] Weeks of diplomatic discussion ensued, and gradually the Dutch were worn down to the point where they agreed to consider the prospect of a plebiscite after transfer of West New Guinea to Indonesian control.

Meanwhile, The Hague continued to react strongly to Indonesian military moves against the beleaguered territory. However unfavorable the tendency of diplomatic developments, the Dutch had no intention of capitulating on the battlefield. Late in March, de Quay informed parliament that some naval units and "limited" troop reinforcements were being sent to West New Guinea;[30] and by May, Dutch strength in the area had risen to about 8,000 men.[31] There were also reports that the government was considering a limited mobilization of civilian reservists in the territory, and the evacuation of women and children from certain especially vulnerable areas, such as Fakfak.[32]

The Dutch also attempted to mobilize international sentiment against the Indonesian offensive. On May 5, C. W. A. Schurmann, the Permanent Representative of the Netherlands at the United Nations, addressed a letter to the Acting Secretary-General charging that Indonesian military operations against West New Guinea were a "direct threat to the peace."[33] Later that month, Prime Minister de Quay called on Thant to urge Indo-

---

of the Netherlands" as his confidential source for this report. *Ibid.*, p. 141, fn. 55.

[28]Quoted in Lijphart, *The Trauma of Decolonization*, p. 242. On shifts in Dutch political and press opinion during 1962, see *ibid.*, pp. 227-249 and 277-284.

[29]*The New York Times*, April 15, 1962.

[30]*Ibid.*, March 28, 1962.

[31]See *ibid.*, May 5, 1962.

[32]See *ibid.*, May 18, 1962.

[33]Quoted in *ibid.*, May 5, 1962.

nesia to halt "all aggressive action against Netherlands New Guinea." He asserted that recent paratroop landings were "part of an act of aggression clearly prepared and intended as such," and he again requested the dispatch of United Nations observers to prevent "further aggression." [34] Thant's reply must have been a disappointment. The Acting Secretary-General said that he could not direct such an appeal to Indonesia because it would "imply that I was taking sides in the controversy, which I believe would not be in the best interest of all concerned." [35] He also rejected de Quay's request for United Nations observers on the ground that he could consider sending such personnel to West New Guinea only if the Jakarta government also asked for them.

At the same time, Thant did send identical messages to de Quay and Sukarno calling for the resumption of negotiations. "In view of the serious developments during the past few days," he appealed to both governments "to resume urgently the discussions which had been undertaken through the good offices of Ambassador Bunker." [36] The Acting Secretary-General said that it would be "most regrettable if the situation were allowed to deteriorate further, particularly as it is my firm belief that the question is capable of an acceptable solution at an early date on the basis of the proposals already communicated to your excellency by Ambassador Bunker." [37] A day later, Bunker "announced revised proposals, which had been submitted simultaneously to Indonesia and the Netherlands." [38] The Indonesian Foreign Minister, Subandrio, commented promptly on Thant's message to the effect that any call for the resumption of negotiations should be directed to the Dutch.[39] On May 25, two days after the Acting Secretary-General's appeal, de Quay finally announced to parliament that the Dutch government "was prepared unequivocally to resume negotiations 'on the basis' of the Bunker proposals." [40]

De Quay's statement proved not to be sufficient, however, to bring about a cessation of hostilities in West New Guinea, or even a prompt resumption of the suspended talks. Obviously attempting to put this latest Dutch concession to constructive use, Thant sent identical messages to Sukarno and de Quay on May 29 stating that he "was grateful for their agreement

[34]Quoted in *ibid.*, May 22, 1962.

[35]Quoted in *New York Herald Tribune*, May 24, 1962.

[36]Quoted in *The New York Times*, May 24, 1962.

[37]Quoted in *New York Herald Tribune*, May 24, 1962.

[38]Jones, *op. cit.*, p. 208. It is not clear from Jones' account just how much these "revised proposals" differed from the original terms of the Bunker Plan, but the probability is that they did not vary much from the original text.

[39]See *The New York Times*, May 25, 1962.

[40]Van der Kroef, "The West New Guinea Settlement," *loc. cit.*, p. 141.

to negotiate on the basis of" the Bunker proposals, and calling for an immediate cease-fire in the disputed territory pending further negotiations.[41] The press carried optimistic reports on the outlook;[42] and the Netherlands government quickly informed the Acting Secretary-General that it "fully share(d)" his desire for an end to the hostilities.[43] But another six weeks were to pass before both parties were again brought to the conference table.

It soon became apparent that the Indonesians were holding out for a more definitive commitment from the Dutch with respect to the Bunker Plan. The Hague's agreement to resume discussions "on the basis" of the mediator's proposals could be construed as an attempt to preserve a more flexible negotiating position than would be the case if it accepted those proposals "in principle." Van der Kroef states that:[44]

Few know this better than the members of the De Quay cabinet. Acceptance as a "basis" could still be interpreted as permitting a relatively "open ended discussion" that might range — and break down — over many tangential issues, whereas acceptance "in principle" meant, in effect, that West New Guinea in one way or another would come under Indonesian control. As early as May 28 Indonesian Foreign Minister Subandrio asserted that Dutch acceptance of the Bunker proposal would mean "that West New Guinea has already been returned to Indonesia."

On May 31, Sukarno complained that the Netherlands had still not shown "a clear and firm attitude" toward the Bunker Plan;[45] and a day later, Subandrio declared that his government would not reply to Thant's latest appeal until Jakarta had received "further information." [46] When Sukarno finally replied on June 5, it was to inform the Acting Secretary-General that Indonesia planned to intensify military action against the Dutch in West New Guinea. His country had always favored a peaceful solution of the problem, and had "accepted promptly the principles of the Bunker proposals." The Netherlands, on the other hand, "did not react favorably" to them, but instead had moved to strengthen its armed forces in the disputed territory. "It is for this reason that we have to step up our military activity," although Indonesia "still supports all efforts to settle this problem of West Irian along the principles of the Bunker proposals." [47]

[41]The New York Times, May 30, 1962.
[42]See ibid., June 2, 1962; and Christian Science Monitor, June 2, 1962.
[43]Quoted in The New York Times, June 3, 1962.
[44]Van der Kroef, "The West New Guinea Settlement," loc. cit., p. 142.
[45]Quoted in ibid., p. 142.
[46]The New York Times, June 2, 1962.
[47]Quoted in ibid., June 6, 1962.

Thant, who professed to see little difference between the two positions,[48] immediately cabled back to the Indonesian President that since the Dutch had agreed to further talks, "I feel that I should now appeal to you to agree to a resumption of negotiations as early as possible."[49] But the Indonesians knew what they wanted, and they were determined to get it. On June 9, Subandrio commented that his country was not eager for another round of talks unless "there is a positive and clear-cut similarity of approach by both sides" to the Bunker Plan. This was a roundabout way of saying that the Dutch had to accept the proposals in principle before negotiations could begin again. For "if there is no similarity of attitude, talks will only lead to a lengthy discussion and even end in jeopardy." [50] A week later, the Dutch swallowed their pride again, and made the concession that Jakarta demanded. On June 16, C. W. A. Schurmann, the Netherlands representative at the United Nations, informed the Acting Secretary-General that his government accepted the Bunker Plan "in principle." Thant cabled Sukarno the news a day later, and added that "In the circumstances I hope that there will be no further delay in the resumption of negotiations." [51]

But still the Indonesians professed to be dissatisfied. On June 20, Sukarno insisted in a message to Thant that Dutch acceptance of the Bunker Plan "should stipulate the sequence of actions constituting the solution of the West Irian problem. This means that the free choice for the West Irian people will be executed after transfer of administration." [52] The Acting Secretary-General replied that the Dutch had indeed accepted "the principle of the phased operations" embodied in the mediator's proposals,[53] and that "in my judgment" the Netherlands had met Indonesia's conditions for a resumption of the talks.[54] Sukarno demanded a more explicit capitulation. A week later, he complained to Thant that the Dutch government had not yet confirmed their acceptance of the principle of "phased operations," and that some statements emanating from The Hague seemed to indicate a much less satisfactory posture.[55] The Acting Secretary-General, who by this time must have been growing weary, nevertheless did what was necessary; and on June 28, he was able to inform the Indonesian

[48]See van der Kroef, "The West New Guinea Settlement," *loc. cit.,* p. 142. Jones dismisses all this as "some odd quibbling over words." Jones, *op. cit.,* p. 210.
[49]Quoted in *The New York Times,* June 8, 1962.
[50]Quoted in *ibid.,* June 9, 1962.
[51]Quoted in *ibid.,* June 18, 1962.
[52]Quoted in van der Kroef, "The West New Guinea Settlement," *loc. cit.,* p. 143.
[53]Quoted in *ibid.,* p. 143.
[54]Quoted in *The New York Times,* June 21, 1962.
[55]See van der Kroef, "The West New Guinea Settlement," *loc. cit.,* p. 143.

President that he had received from the Dutch representative at the United Nations a statement to the effect that "the Netherlands Government confirms once more that . . . it accepts the sequence of events as laid down in the Bunker proposals on condition that it will receive, equally in accordance with the Bunker proposals, adequate conditions and guarantees for the rights and interests of the Papuans." [56] This was apparently what Sukarno was waiting for; and on July 3, he announced that Indonesia would send a representative to Washington to resume negotiations with the Dutch.[57]

In the protracted negotiations that followed the preliminary talks in March and the submission of the Bunker Plan to both sides early in April, it seems clear that the Dutch were, in fact, trying desperately to preserve some freedom of maneuver for the climactic negotiations to come, while the Indonesians wanted to tie them down as tightly as possible beforehand to the Bunker principles. On balance, Jakarta emerged as the decisive winner of this contest of wills. When direct discussions were finally resumed in July, little of substance remained to be agreed upon except the facesaving formulae to cover The Hague's retreat.

Throughout this period, the Indonesians kept up the military pressure in West New Guinea, both to maintain a sense of impending crisis as background for the diplomatic maneuvering, and to influence directly the results of the bargaining.[58] On June 24, for example, between 150 and 200 Indonesians paratroopers were dropped near Merauke, a town on the southern coast of the disputed territory.[59] This was more than a week after the Dutch representative at the United Nations had informed Acting Secretary-General Thant that his government accepted the Bunker Plan "in principle;" and the attacking force was described as "much stronger and (more) unified than previous Indonesian forays." [60] The Hague imme-

[56]Quoted in *ibid.,* p. 143.

[57]See *The New York Times,* July 4, 1962.

[58]"The objectives of these new infiltrations were soon apparent. For one thing, Indonesia hoped to force concessions because of the growing numbers of her military forces in the territory: toward the close of July . . . it was reported, for example, that Indonesia demanded a considerable shortening of the period of UN interim administration envisaged by the Bunker plan because, the Indonesians argued, 'a new factor' had entered the West New Guinea crisis — the growing number of Indonesian forces on the disputed territory's soil. Undoubtedly another objective of the continuing infiltrations, however dubious their real military value, was to prevent a possible Papuan coup d'etat facilitated by the unusually quick withdrawal of Dutch forces from West New Guinea as provided for under the . . . (final) agreement." Van der Kroef, "The West New Guinea Settlement," *loc. c·t.,* pp. 145-146.

[59]See *The New York Times,* June 25, 1962.

[60]*Ibid.,* June 26, 1962.

diately protested to the United Nations; and an authoritative government source indicated that the Netherlands was "playing with the idea of bringing the New Guinea issue before the United Nations Security Council." [61] This step was never taken, although the Indonesians continued their military harassment after negotiations were resumed in mid-July, and, indeed, even after the final agreement was signed on August 15.

About 30 infiltrators landed near Sausapor, on the extreme northwest coast, on July 18; [62] and there were larger landings on Was and Misool islands, near the western tip of the territory, on August 7 and August 9.[63] A day later, the Netherlands Ambassador to the United States, J. H. van Roijen, again protested to the United Nations.[64] Then on August 13, only two days before a settlement of the dispute was formally agreed to, the Indonesians dropped several hundred paratroopers in the vicinity of Merauke, Sorong, and other coastal towns.[65] In still another note to Thant, the Dutch representative in New York, C. W. A. Schurmann, expressed his regret "at having to report once again on new Indonesian acts of hostility, committed with utter disregard for the fact that the current Dutch-Indonesian negotiations conducted under the guidance of the Acting Secretary-General already seem close to completion." [66] But these protests had no discernible effect on the course of events. Thant was powerless to stop the Indonesians; and a Dutch appeal to the Security Council or the General Assembly would probably have foundered in face of the predominant "anticolonialist" sentiment in both bodies. Additional Indonesian landings were reported on August 21, several days after signature of the Dutch-Indonesian settlement.[67] When the agreement was taken up by the General Assembly in September, Schurmann called attention to the inability of the United Nations to stop the fighting before a settlement was reached and while negotiations were going forward. "The Netherlands Government regrets," he said, "that in this instance no effective remedy was to be found against the use of force, contrary to the obligations of States under the Charter of the United Nations." [68]

---

[61]Quoted in *ibid.*, June 27, 1962.

[62]See van der Kroef, "The West New Guinea Settlement," *loc. cit.*, p. 145.

[63]See *The New York Times*, August 11, 1962.

[64]See *ibid.*, August 11, 1961.

[65]See *ibid.*, August 14, 1962, and August 15, 1962.

[66]Quoted in *ibid.*, August 15, 1962.

[67]See van der Kroef, "The West New Guinea Settlement," *loc. cit.*, p. 145.

[68]*GAOR*, Seventeenth Session (1962), A/PV. 1127.

The Role of the Mediator

The public record does not fully reveal the extent of United States pressure on the two principals in the period between the first round of talks in March and the resumption of negotiations in July. But we may assume that Washington kept the heat on both sides to return promptly to the conference table, and that its influence was heavily felt in The Hague. The United States apparently took an especially strong line as to what its position would be in the event that large-scale hostilities should develop because of the reluctance of the Dutch to come to terms with the Indonesians.

As we have seen, Jakarta's military activity against West New Guinea never reached major proportions; and to the end, the Dutch were able to cope with Indonesian landings and paratroop drops without undue difficulty. But the danger of escalation was very real. The Dutch Foreign Minister, J. M. A. H. Luns, subsequently admitted in a television interview that the threat of war had been a decisive factor in the outcome of the dispute.[69] No doubt he had partly in mind the fact that, by Summer 1962, the Dutch government and people simply had no stomach for a fight over the future of West New Guinea. But Washington had also made clear that the United States would not support the Netherlands in the event of war. Indeed, the Kennedy administration seems to have gone a good deal further than this. The columnist Arthur Krock reported that Washington "let the Dutch know in advance that the United States would close the channels through which their forces in that distant area would have to be supplied; and also that it had obtained pledges from the British to follow the same policy." [70] In short, the Dutch were to be deprived of the military means to fight if war should come. Presumably the Indonesians were also admonished to avoid a conflict. The presence of numerous American missionaries in the disputed territory would have given Washington a valid pretext to assert that it could not stand idly by in the event of hostilities. But arm twisting in The Hague was probably a lot more forceful. Prime Minister de Quay had grounds for lamenting that his

[69]See *The New York Times*, August 17, 1962. Ambassador Jones was also seriously worried about the military situation. "In Djakarta, we knew that . . . the Indonesians were continuing their preparations for a major military assault on West Irian. I became convinced that war was just around the corner, for we in the embassy knew what was happening as a result of an operation that was then top secret — direct observation by U-2 planes, a fact later publicly revealed by Sukarno. The Indonesians had the troops and the equipment, and public opinion had been whipped up to the high-tension level." Jones, *op. cit.*, p. 210.

[70]*The New York Times*, August 17, 1972.

government "had to sign" the August 15 agreement because it "could not count on the support of its allies."

Washington's role was, in fact, a difficult and thankless one. Whether wisely or not, the Kennedy administration had decided on a policy for resolving the West New Guinea dispute, and the Dutch had to pay the higher price. But it was not a pleasant business. Shortly after the preliminary talks in March, the President was asked at a press conference to clarify the United States position in the dispute, and to comment on reports that "proposals put forward by the United States were not fair to the Netherlands." Kennedy's reply underlined, perhaps inadvertently, the extent of Washington's involvement in Ambassador Bunker's mediation:[71]

> I think everybody is displeased, really, with our role, because our role is an attempt — Ambassador Bunker's role has been, under the direction of U Thant, to try to see if we can bring some adjustment to prevent a military action which would be harmful to the interests of both countries, with which we desire to be friendly. So I suppose it's hard to think of any proposal that we could make which would be welcome on both sides.
>
> I'm hopeful that if we can be useful, we'll continue to try to be. If both sides feel that we cannot be, then perhaps others can take on this assignment, or perhaps it can be done bilaterally . . . the role of the mediator is not a happy one, and we've prepared to have everybody mad, if it makes some progress.

Late in May, when the Indonesians were increasing their military pressure against West New Guinea, and the Dutch had not yet publicly accepted the Bunker Plan even as a basis for further talks, Kennedy was asked at another press conference to comment on the prospect for future negotiations. The President replied:[72]

> Well, as you know the United States has been working very hard, with the help of Ambassador Bunker, to attempt to work out a solution which would make the kind of military action which is now taking place unnecessary. We have not had success . . . But I hope that the proposals of Ambassador Bunker would be considered very carefully by both sides, because we would be very concerned if the situation in that section of the world disintegrated or degenerated into a complete military conflict between these two countries.

It has already been pointed out that, in formulating and espousing the Bunker proposals, the Kennedy administration had chosen to define its mediatory role in very broad terms. This concept of the mediator's func-

---

[71]Quoted in *Public Papers . . . 1962*, p. 320.
[72]Quoted in *ibid.*, p. 437.

tion continued to inform the United States approach until agreement between the two principals was finally reached in August. After the preliminary talks in March, the first task was to persuade both sides to agree upon the outlines of the mediator's program, and this proved especially difficult in the case of the Dutch. But the force of persistent American diplomacy, supported when necessary by the Acting Secretary-General of the United Nations, eventually moved The Hague to acceptance of the plan, first as a basis for further negotiations, and finally "in principle" as the Indonesians insisted. The utility of the Bunker proposals in facilitating this series of Dutch concessions cannot be overstated. Schelling observes that:[73]

> If one is about to make a concession, he needs to control his adversary's expectations; he needs a recognizable limit to his own retreat.
> If one is to make a finite concession that is not to be interpreted as capitulation, he needs an obvious place to stop.

The mediator's program may have been hard to take, but at least it set limits: both as to how far the Dutch would have to retreat, and as to how much the Indonesians could expect to achieve.

We may assume that during this period, the United States resorted to the whole arsenal of mediatory tools and tactics in promoting the Bunker Plan as a reasonable basis for settlement. Stevens comments, for example, that "one of the most important aspects of the mediation process is the mediator's control over the communications structure in the negotiation situation."[74] To be sure, Washington did not have anything like complete control over communications between Jakarta and The Hague. Thus, both sides continued to issue a stream of public statements throughout the course of the negotiations, and also to convey "messages" through unilateral actions such as the escalation of Indonesian military pressure in West New Guinea and the Dutch response thereto. Even in the narrow sense of the formal exchange of verbal or written messages, other channels, including the United Nations, were also available to both protagonists. But the United States government was the principal point of contact for such exchanges, and this afforded substantial opportunities for affecting the course of negotiations. In part, it made possible a go-between function which, while modest in scope, may nevertheless have rendered an important contribution to the success of the negotiations. Boulding points out in this connection that the third party, being outside the "emotional field" created by the conflict, "can both receive and give messages to either of the parties without the kind of distortion to which direct messages are

[73]Schelling, *op. cit.*, p. 71.
[74]Stevens, *op. cit.*, p. 129.

subject." [75] But in addition, a strategic position in the line of communications between the principals "generally facilitates attempts at persuasion and also coercion," [76] especially where the mediator opts at the same time for an active role in the negotiations and specifically purposes to exert influence in a particular direction.

In the West New Guinea case, the United States not only formulated the principles of settlement which, after the preliminary talks in March, became virtually the exclusive basis for further bargaining; it also vigorously supported the Bunker program in private and in public.[77] There was ample occasion, in the course of innumerable diplomatic exchanges with both parties, to spell out the meaning and implications of the mediator's proposals, to clarify for each side the position and problems of the other with respect to them; and in the process, to inject Washington's own views on the various issues involved. A careful elucidation of the consequences of a breakdown in negotiations would have been a major weapon in persuading both sides, and especially the Dutch, as to the wisdom of timely compromise.[78] In short, forceful participation in the bargaining process permitted the "generation and application of various types of pressure" [79] by means of which the United States in time managed to nudge both parties back to the conference table and ultimate agreement.

Ambassador Bunker seems to have carried the main burden of managing the negotiations;[80] and in practice, he worked much more closely with

[75]Boulding, op. cit., p. 316.

[76]Stevens, op. cit., p. 129.

[77]Early in June 1962, for example, The New York Times, reported that the Kennedy administration, "in warm support of Mr. Bunker's proposals, has been pressing the Dutch to reach a settlement on what it believes are the available terms. At the same time it is urging the Indonesians to bear with the Dutch through another round of preliminary talks." The New York Times, June 2, 1962. At a press conference in late May, Secretary of State Dean Rusk commented that "We . . . believe that (the Bunker proposals) are a reasonable basis for discussion and that they can open the way to a negotiation which could find out whether (Indonesia and the Netherlands) could not come together and agree on a solution." Quoted in Department of State Bulletin, vol. 46, no. 1199, p. 975.

[78]Writing in late May 1962, Krock states that the Dutch "got a strong hint that, if they refused to 'negotiate' what obviously was a formula for the eventual triumph of Indonesia's military aggression, the Kennedy Administration would withdraw as intermediary and put the issue before the U. N., where, by all indications, the prospect of any curb at all on Sukarno is even less." The New York Times, May 29, 1962.

[79]Young, op. cit., p. 59.

[80]A press report early in June commented that Bunker had been "working ceaselessly" since the preliminary talks in March to bring about a resumption of negotiations. Christian Science Monitor, June 2, 1962.

Washington than with New York in the discharge of his responsibilities. While he was frequently in touch with the Acting Secretary-General, he apparently did not operate under detailed insructions from Thant, nor did he report to New York on a day-to-day basis. By comparison, his liaison with the Department of State was more continuous, and he had the regular assistance of U.S. Foreign Service personnel. On the other hand, every effort was made to preserve Bunker's public posture as an impartial mediator representing the United Nations. To the extent possible, American involvement in the negotiations was played down; and except for occasional comments by the President and Secretary of State at news conferences, spokesmen for the United States generally maintained a discreet silence on the whole subject.

Thant played a much more prominent public role. He gave his open and active support to the mediation at all stages, and he frequently took part personally in diplomatic exchanges with both protagonists. Moreover, the weight of his influence was cast in directions parallel to the objectives of United States policy. After the preliminary talks in March, Thant placed the prestige of his office behind the Bunker Plan; and he thereafter made clear to the parties — and especially the Dutch — that they could expect little help from the United Nations unless they were prepared to negotiate along the lines of the mediator's proposals. In short, the Acting Secretary-General provided the formal leadership and the necessary cover, and the impartiality of his sponsorship made the enterprise acceptable to both sides.

Chapter Thirteen

Settlement

On July 13, the Acting Secretary-General announced that talks between Indonesia and the Netherlands had been resumed the day before. The negotiations were again being conducted in the presence of Ambassador Bunker, and were going forward "on the basis of the principles of the Bunker plan." [1] The Indonesian team was headed by Adam Malik, then Jakarta's Ambassador to the Soviet Union, while J.H. van Roijen and C.W.A. Schurmann again represented the Netherlands.

Last Flurry

Contrary to some expectations, these final discussions were by no means limited to the perfunctory endorsement and routine elaboration of points already agreed upon during the previous weeks of intense diplomatic maneuvering. The Indonesians knew, of course, that they had won the game. But they were determined to extract additional concessions from the Dutch, and they were prepared to push hard in order to get them. As for the Dutch, the will to resist further demands was eroding rapidly, although they were still grimly resolved to hold onto at least the face-saving formulae of the tentative settlement.

Malik's first task was apparently to make sure that The Hague's announced concessions up to that moment still held. The point was soon verified to his satisfaction; van Roijen gave renewed assurances as to his government's "acceptance in principle of (the) proposals put forward" by Ambassador Bunker, and that it also "accepted the sequence of events" laid down in the proposals.[2] Thereupon, President Sukarno immediately announced (on July 17) that he was sending Foreign Minister Subandrio to the United States in order, as he rather ungraciously put it, "to explore whether there is a possibility of holding formal talks" with the Dutch on the future of West New Guinea.[3]

[1]Quoted in *New York Herald Tribune*, July 14, 1962.
[2]*The New York Times*, July 18, 1962. See also Jones, *op cit.*, p. 211.
[3]Quoted in *ibid.*, July 17, 1962.

Indonesia's new demands centered on three main issues. The Bunker Plan provided that West New Guinea would be administered under United Nations auspices "for a period of not less than one year but not more than two." Subandrio now insisted that the duration of United Nations administration be drastically foreshortened, and that the transfer of authority to Indonesia be completed by January 1, 1963. This would serve to fulfil President Sukarno's rash but frequently repeated boast that West New Guinea would be Indonesia's before the end of 1962. Subandrio also demanded that the actual role of the world organization during the brief interval of international administration be "largely symbolic."[4] Finally, on an issue not covered by the Bunker Plan, he proposed that Indonesian military forces infiltrated into the disputed territory over the preceding several months be allowed to remain and even "given functions to perform" during the interim period of United Nations administration.[5]

While these demands were formulated within the framework of the mediator's proposals, their net effect if agreed to would have been to undermine the utility of the Bunker Plan as a restraint on future Indonesian policy, especially with respect to the question of ultimate self-determination for the Papuans. In addition, acceptance of the demands would also have tended to depreciate whatever value the plan had as a device for safeguarding Dutch prestige in the process of relinquishing control over a former colony. Almost inevitably, therefore, the Dutch negotiators balked at these further concessions; while Subandrio, in the face of their recalcitrance, threatened to break off the talks and return home.

These were days of almost constant diplomatic activity in Washington and New York relating to West New Guinea. The press carried reports of numerous meetings that the plenipotentiaries on both sides had with President Kennedy, Secretary of State Rusk, Ambassador Bunker, and Acting Secretary-General Thant, among others. Having come so far in the search for settlement, it was clear that the United States and the United Nations as third-party intermediaries in the dispute were now determined to find the additional compromises necessary to bring their joint effort to a successful conclusion. Nor did the Indonesians have things wholly their way in this last flurry of negotiation. Both Thant and Kennedy were reported to have warned Subandrio that if war resulted in consequence of Jakarta's latest demands, Indonesia "would be widely condemned by world

[4]*Ibid.*, July 27, 1962.

[5]*Ibid.*, July 27, 1962.

opinion." [6] The Acting Secretary-General also made clear to Subandrio that the United Nations would have to exercise effective — as contrasted with merely symbolic — authority in West New Guinea during the interim period of international administration, and that its task could not be completed by January 1, 1963.[7] Finally, we may assume that both the Americans and the United Nations pointed out once again that there were limits beyond which the Dutch could not be pushed. As if to underline this fact, the Netherlands government announced that it had begun the evacuation of 7,000 women and children from the disputed territory "as a precaution in the face of possible Indonesian invasion." [8]

If we are to judge by the outcome, however, once more the balance of pressure seems to have been exerted against the Dutch. Throughout the months of the Washington talks, the United States continued to supply Indonesia with arms and economic assistance pursuant to previously negotiated agreements.[9] Nearly 20 cargoes of wheat were delivered to Indonesian ports under the Food for Peace progarm during the period from January to May 1962.[10] Even more striking, the Indonesian Air Force made extensive use of C-130 cargo planes obtained earlier from the United States for air operations against West New Guinea, despite original assurances that the aircraft would not be employed for such purposes.[11] There is no public evidence that the Washington government ever attempted to exert the leverage that might have been afforded by these assistance programs to influence Jakarta's strategy in the negotiations, although admittedly — in view of Sukarno's intransigence on the whole question — this would probably not have been an especially productive tactic. Even the prospect of massive economic assistance held out by President Kennedy in the event of a successful settlement of the dispute

[6]*Christian Science Monitor,* August 1, 1962. "President Kennedy minced no words (in the conversation with Subandrio). In effect, he told the Indonesian foreign minister that the United States was 'through' with Indonesia unless Subandrio was prepared to be reasonable. Subandrio told (Ambassador Jones) later, making a gesture of wiping his brow, 'Whew! Your President certainly laid down the law.'" Jones, *op. cit.,* p. 211.

[7]See *The New York Times,* July 31, 1692. "U Thant apparently also made clear that the onus of the breakdown in negotiations would be laid at Indonesia's door and that under no circumstances would he agree to a UN stewardship that was not a genuine one." Jones, *op. cit.,* p. 211.

[8]Quoted in *Christian Science Monitor,* August 1, 1962. See also *The New York Times,* July 31, 1962.

[9]See Brackman, *op. cit.,* p. 107.

[10]See *ibid.,* p. 308, fn. 15, quoting Indonesian sources.

[11]See *ibid.,* p. 107.

does not seem to have ameliorated significantly the rigidity of Indonesia's position. On the other hand, as we have already seen, the United States made it crystal clear to the Netherlands that it could not count on American military support in the event of large-scale warfare over the territory, and Washington also took steps to impede the movement of Dutch reinforcements to their beleaguered colony.

In any event, the Indonesians once more succeeded in extracting major concessions from the Dutch. On July 31, it became known that the two parties had at last reached agreement on "all essential points." [12] As these were subsequently spelled out, the duration of full United Nations administration was foreshortened to end on May 1, 1963, instead of after "a period of not less than one year but not more than two" as provided for by the Bunker Plan. Thereafter the United Nations Administrator was given discretionary power to transfer authority to the Indonesian government either immediately or in stages. Taking into account the time necessary to prepare the international administration of the territory, and the probability that the United Nations Administrator would be disposed to hand over his authority early rather than late, this compromise meant that full United Nations control would last for only a few months. To be sure, the United Nations would exercise real authority during this period, and not confine itself to a "largely symbolic" role. But it seemed unlikely that, in so brief an interval, the international administration could have much lasting impact on the long-term political evolution of the territory. By way of compensation, the Dutch successfully insisted upon fairly detailed provisions relating to an ultimate act of self-determination by the Papuans. But since this event would now take place only after several intervening years of Indonesian rule, the efficacy of these provisions was open to serious doubt.

On the question of the Indonesian guerrillas previously infiltrated into West New Guinea, Jakarta won hands down. The final agreement provided that Indonesian armed forces in the territory would be "under the authority of, and at the disposal of" the Acting Secretary-General, and that the United Nations Administrator might "use" them at his discretion "to maintain law and order." [13]

---

[12]Quoted in *Christian Science Monitor*, August 1, 1962.

[13]The text of the Dutch-Indonesian agreement is reproduced in the Appendix. The text of the agreement, and of four related "understandings," may be found in *GAOR*, Seventeenth Session (1962), Annexes, A/5170.

Alone

The formulation and conduct of Dutch policy with respect to West New Guinea during 1962 must have been an immensely frustrating and painful business. Having fought for so long to maintain the Dutch position in the territory, de Quay, Luns, and their colleagues in the cabinet were now condemned by the exigencies of time and events to preside over the liquidation of that position, and in circumstances that offered few concessions to their pride and patriotism.

After rejection of the Luns Plan by the General Assembly in Fall 1961, both popular and parliamentary opinion in the Netherlands shifted rapidly in favor of a peaceful settlement of the controversy on almost any reasonable terms. When the main points of the Bunker Plan became known in the Netherlands early in April 1962, the terms of the suggested settlement were greeted with widespread approbation. The Socialist newspaper *Het Parool* published an article on April 11 entitled, "Yes for the Bunker Plan;" [14] and Lijphart estimates that by late May, "more than two-thirds of the political forces in the Second Chamber (of parliament) now favored a settlement following the broad outline" of the mediator's proposals.[15] In the face of this trend, no cabinet could have maintained an intransigent posture on the issue; and in any event, few of its members (except for diehards like Foreign Minister Luns) any longer cared to try.

The erosion of international support for Dutch policy was even more striking. To be sure, at the General Assembly debate on the West New Guinea question in Fall 1961, a 13-member draft resolution supporting a solution "based on the principle of self-determination of peoples" did win a majority of the votes cast (although not the two-thirds majority required for adoption); and the Dutch publicly interpreted this as an endorsement of the main thesis of the Luns Plan, which was not pressed to a vote. But to a great extent, this was mere whistling in the dark. As the Dutch must have realized at the time, the 53 votes for the 13-member draft were not translatable into firm backing for Dutch policy in the event of a major crisis. This became apparent when the Indonesians deliberately set out to provoke just such a crisis following Sukarno's Triple Command on December 19, 1961.

In this respect, the reaction of the United States (which had supported the 13-member draft) undoubtedly had the most decisive impact on Netherlands policy in the months ahead. But Washington's substantial abandonment of The Hague was hardly unique. The British, too, proved unwilling to stand with the Dutch in the gathering crisis, despite the long

---

[14]See Lijphart, *The Trauma of Decolonization*, p. 281.
[15]*Ibid.*, p. 283.

traditions of friendship that bound the two countries together and their current partnership in the N.A.T.O. alliance. During the 1950s, the United Kingdom had "followed a policy of neutrality (in the West New Guinea dispute) very similar to that of the United States;" [16] and in like manner, the net result had been to help sustain the Dutch position in the territory. But by 1961, the London government and British opinion no longer had any wish "to be tied to support . . . what were widely regarded as the outmoded colonial policies of . . . the Netherlands." [17] Already well advanced in the process of divesting the greatest colonial empire the world had ever seen, the British presumably thought that they knew something about the business, and that the Dutch were going about it in entirely the wrong way. Moreover, Britain had an important economic stake in Indonesia, and was "anxious to expand her trade with Indonesia and to safeguard her oil and estate interests there" [18] In such circumstances, and at a time when the British were systematically circumscribing their overseas responsibilities to match their diminished military capacity and straitened economic position, the prospect of conflict in support of Dutch policy in West New Guinea must have seemed anachronistic indeed.

As early as June 1961, J. B. Godber, then Under-Secretary for Foreign Affairs, stated in the House of Commons that Britain had "no direct interest" in the West New Guinea question beyond the maintenance of peace in Southeast Asia.[19] It is true that the United Kingdom voted for the 13-member draft resolution in the General Assembly that Fall, but this proved to be no more indicative of British policy in the immediate future than the similar American vote. Soon after President Kennedy launched his mediatory effort in late 1961, he asked for assistance from Harold Macmillan "to persuade (both) the Dutch and the Australians toward a greater flexibility on the issue." [20] The British Prime Minister readily agreed. His government was in fundamental accord with Kennedy's assessment of the West New Guinea problem. Whatever the merits of the Dutch case, the United Kingdom — like the United States — was not prepared "to mount firm opposition to Indonesian claims, because in the climate of the times such a policy would have been disadvantageous in the Cold War and an obstacle to fostering good relations with the newly established

[16]Justus M. van der Kroef, "The West New Guinea Problem," *The World Today,* vol. 17, no. 11 (November 1961), p. 501.
[17]D.C. Watt, *Survey of International Affairs 1961* (London, New York, Toronto: Oxford University Press, 1965), p. 55.
[18]Van der Kroef, "The West New Guinea Problem," *loc. cit.,* p. 501.
[19]Quoted in *Hansard,* vol. 643, no. 134, col. 166.
[20]Schlesinger, *op. cit.,* p. 534.

states." [21] In the negotiations that followed, the British were especially helpful in convincing the Australians that the time had come to modify their longstanding opposition to Indonesian control over the disputed territory.

By the end of 1961, Australian policy on West New Guinea had reached a dead end. Over the years, Canberra had consistently supported the Dutch position in the territory, both in repeated public statements and through energetic diplomatic activity, especially at the United Nations. On the other hand, the Australians were never willing to underwrite that position by entering into a military alliance with the Dutch. Watt states that "the Menzies Government throughout its period of office resisted Dutch pressure in this direction." [22] No doubt Canberra canvassed the feasibility of such a course more than once. But Dutch and Australian policy required above all the "support of a Great Power able and willing to back it up, in the last resort, by armed force;" and since such assurances were not forthcoming from either Great Britain or the United States, Australia "could not risk" the military alternative on its own.[23]

Indeed, the prospect of having to give military support to the Netherlands "must have been most unpleasant for military authorities to contemplate." [24] The mission was probably beyond the capacity of the Australian armed forces as then constituted. Nor was Canberra prepared to undertake the military buildup that might have been necessary to enforce a policy of resisting Indonesian encroachment against West New Guinea.[25] Even in the field of administrative cooperation between Dutch and Australian territories on the island, the Canberra government consistently dragged its feet. The 1960 Dutch program for the accelerated political development of West New Guinea seriously alarmed the Australians as premature; and when Dutch spokesman "spoke approvingly" that year of the concept of a Melanesian federation as an "ultimate solution" for the political future of both territories, Canberra was simply not prepared to "accept the implications" of this policy.[26] And in June 1960, Paul Has-

---

[21]Greenwood, "Australian Foreign Policy in Action," *loc. cit.*, p. 92.

[22]Alan Watt, *op. cit.*, p. 258. Menzies served as Prime Minister continuously during the years 1949-66.

[23]*Ibid.*, p. 257.

[24]Millar, *loc. cit.*, p. 282.

[25]See B. D. Beddie, "Some Internal Political Problems," in J. Wilkes, ed., *Australia's Defence and Foreign Policy* (Sydney: Angus and Robertson, 1964) p. 136; and Millar, *loc. cit.*, p. 282.

[26]Mackie, "Australia and Indonesia, 1945-60," *loc. cit.*, p. 324, fn. 96; and p. 310.

luck, then Minister for Territories, declared that the Australian half of the island would not be ready for self-government for another 30 years.[27]

In the absence of significant support from Australia (or any other country) except in the diplomatic arena, the Netherlands began to examine seriously the possibilities of internationalizing the West New Guinea problem as a way out. Later in 1960, it became known that The Hague was considering a United Nations trusteeship for the territory, although the Luns Plan was not formally put before the General Assembly until Fall 1961. This departure must have caused the Australians serious misgivings, but it did not bestir them to advance any imaginative alternatives of their own. During General Nasution's visit to Canberra in April 1961, Prime Minister Menzies strongly restated his government's support for the Dutch position in West New Guinea and for the principle of self-determination for the Papuans. He also declared, however, that Australia would accept any settlement of the dispute freely negotiated between the two parties, and this probably reflected a dawning realization that the objectives of Australian diplomacy might not be safeguarded over the long term. But until late 1961, when the Indonesians suddenly intensified their "confrontation'" of the Dutch in response to the Luns Plan, Australian policy was still fundamentally oriented toward keeping the Indonesians out of the territory.

Thereafter, Australian diplomacy was simply outdistanced by events; and clearly the decisive factor was the intervention of the United States, in collaboration with the United Nations, to mediate a negotiated settlement basically favorable to Indonesia. Canberra had no real choice but to accept what Washington ordained. On January 12, 1962, Prime Minister Menzies publicly faced up to the realities. He said:[28]

Having regard not only to our treaty rights and responsibilities but also to the hard facts of international life, we act in close collaboration with the great free Powers, particularly Great Britain and the United States of America. No responsible Australian would wish to see any action affecting the safety of Australia on the issues of war and peace in this area except in concert with our great and powerful friends.

A month later, Menzies put the case even more strongly when he labelled as "crazy and irresponsible" the suggestion that "without regard to what

[27]See Alan Watt, op. cit., p. 261.

[28]Quoted in Gavin Souter, New Guinea: The Last Unknown (New York: Taplinger, 1966), p. 228. On this period, see also Charles Grimshaw, "Problems of Australian Foreign Policy, January-June, 1962," The Australian Journal of Politics and History, vol. 8, no. 2 (November 1962), pp. 139-142.

might be the attitude or action of the Great Powers, Australia should in the event of armed Indonesian aggression against Dutch New Guinea, declare war against Indonesia." [29] He also emphasized that the Australian government had "on very many occasions" made clear "in relevant quarters" its support for the principle of self-determination for the Papuans;[30] but to no avail.

Any lingering hope that the United States might be persuaded to change its approach was apparently dashed at a regular meeting of the A.N.Z.U.S. Council, held in Canberra in May, where Secretary Rusk reportedly made it crystal clear that there was to be "no support, diplomatic or otherwise, for the Nethrlands or for Australia, apart from pressure to secure a settlement by discussion rather than by arms."[31] Nor was significant backing to be obtained from any other quarter. Menzies had earlier observed that "every nation in Asia supported the Indonesian claim." [32] Japan, in fact, had followed the American lead in denying transit rights for Dutch military reinforcements en route to West New Guinea.

In short, Australia had no effective choice but to accept the unpalatable settlement being worked out under the joint auspices of the United States and the United Nations. It is true that the Australian Minister for External Affairs, Sir Garfield Barwick, visited Indonesia twice during this period, in May and again in early July. But in so far as they related to the West New Guinea dispute, his efforts were confined to attempting to persuade the Jakarta government "to abandon threats of force, to return to the conference table and to recognize a right of self-determination." [33] There was no longer the possibility of gaining even a respectful hearing for more substantive alternatives. When the Dutch-Indonesian settlement was finally concluded in August, most Australian spokesmen assessed its terms as a major diplomatic defeat. Barwick himself remarked sourly that

[29]Quoted in Vandenbosch, op. cit., pp. 68-69.

[30]Quoted in ibid., p. 69.

[31]Greenwood, "Australian Foreign Policy in Action," loc. cit., p. 91. The final communique of the meeting stated simply that the assembled ministers "noted with approval the efforts of the Acting Secretary-General of the United Nations to promote a settlement by peaceful negotiation. They appealed to both of the parties to the dispute to give the Acting Secretary-General their maximum support and to refrain from the use or threat of force." For the text of the communique, see Department of State Bulletin, vol. 46. no. 1196 (May 28, 1962), pp. 869-871.

[32]Quoted in Vandenbosch, op. cit., p. 69.

[33]Greenwood, "Australian Foreign Policy in Action," loc. cit., p. 91. Barwick's own account may be found in his statement to the Australian House of Representatives on August 21, 1962, in which he summarized Australia's role during the last months of the dispute. See Commonwealth of Australia, Parliamentary Debates, House of Representatives, August 21, 1962.

the outcome was a "part of history with which Australia must live" in the future. But he admonished his auditors in the Australian House of Representatives that "if any should have contemplated a military adventure, it is worth remembering that none of the countries of the West, and particularly of those with whom Australia has the closest association, were at any relevant time willing to maintain a Netherlands administration by military means." [34]

A Settlement At Last

On July 31, Acting Secretary-General U Thant announced that "a preliminary agreement has been reached by the Indonesian and Netherlands representatives in regard to the modalities of the transfer of authority over West New Guinea." [35] Press reports the next day, citing "official sources" in Washington, confirmed that "all essential points" had been agreed upon.[36] The chief negotiators thereupon returned to The Hague and Jakarta to report to their respective governments and to obtain approval of the main terms of settlement; while second-level teams continued to discuss technical and financial details.

There were still a few bad moments to be surmounted during the following two weeks. The Indonesians kept up the military pressure in West New Guinea with additional troop landings at various points; and Jakarta managed to table a few final demands, mostly on procedural points. A dispute as to "what flags should fly over the territory and when . . . threatened to upset the entire program" until Bunker proposed a satisfactory compromise. The Dutch were understandably outraged by the renewed Indonesian landings, which they must have regarded as gratuitous provocations. They lodged strong protests with the United Nations against the Indonesian actions, which came "at a time when negotiations between the Netherlands and Indonesia are taking place," [37] and "with utter disregard" for the fact that these negotiations "already seem close to completion." [38] But The Hague refrained from an appeal to the Security Council, which doubtless would have been fruitless anyway, although apparently some thought was given to this alternative.

[34]Commonwealth of Australia, *Parliamentary Debates, House of Representatives,* August 21, 1962.

[35]Quoted in *Everyman's United Nations,* 7th edition, p. 98.

[36]See *Christian Science Monitor,* August 1, 1962; and *The New York Times,* August 1, 1962.

[37]Quoted in *The New York Times,* August 13, 1962.

[38]Quoted in *ibid.,* August 15, 1962.

The last stage of the negotiations took place at the United Nations, with Thant taking a personal hand in talks with the plenipotentiaries for both sides (who had now returned from hasty consultations in their respective capitals). At length, the last snag was satisfactorily unravelled, the last hurdle overcome; and the two governments gave their assent to the completed agreement. The plenipotentiaries affixed their signatures to the text in a ceremony at United Nations headquarters in New York on August 15, in the presence of the Acting Secretary-General. It was a moment for congratulations all round. Foreign Minister Subandrio and Ambassador van Roijen joined in fulsome praise and thanks to Thant and Ambassador Bunker for their tireless efforts during the protracted negotiations, now at last brought to successful fruition. The Acting Secretary-General, in turn, felicitated both governments on "this historic agreement which, in line with the principles of the Charter, has settled peacefully a longstanding problem, with benefit to all concerned." [39]

The text contained few surprises. As a first step, it called for the General Assembly to "take note" of the agreement and to authorize the Acting Secretary-General to "carry out the tasks entrusted to him therein." Immediately thereafter, the Nethelands was to transfer the administration of West New Guinea to a United Nations Temporary Executive Authority (U.N.T.E.A.), to be established in the territory by and under the jurisdiction of the Acting Secretary-General. This was one of the novel aspects of the settlement, in so far as it constituted the first time that the United Nations had assumed responsibility for directly administering a territory and population anywhere in the world. A United Nations Administrator "acceptable to Indonesia and the Netherlands" was to be appointed by the Acting Secretary-General, and provided with such administrative personnel and security forces as deemed necessary to discharge his functions.

U.N.T.E.A. administration of West New Guinea was to be in two phases. During the first phase, which was to be completed by May 1, 1963, "top Netherlands officials" were to be replaced by non-Netherlands, non-Indonesian officials, although Netherlands nationals could be retained in other posts; and U.N.T.E.A. was also given authority to employ "personnel provided by Indonesia" in such posts. Then "at any time after the first phase," the United Nations Administrator could at his discretion transfer "all or part" of the administration to Indonesia; and U.N.T.E.A. authority was to cease "at the moment of transfer of full administrative control to Indonesia." United Nations security forces were also to be replaced by Indonesian forces after the first phase had been completed. A second novel feature of the agreement provided that Indonesia and the

[39]Quoted in *ibid.*, August 16, 1962.

Netherlands were to "share on an equal basis" the cost of the U.N.T.E.A. administration.

The agreement contained fairly detailed provisions for enabling the Papuan population to exercise the "right to self-determination." After the transfer of full administrative authority to Indonesia, the latter was to make the necessary arrangements "to give the people of the territory the opportunity to exercise freedom of choice." The precise methods to be followed "for ascertaining the freely expressed will of the poulation" were left to further determination; but it was stipulated that the inhabitants were to have a choice as to "(a) whether they wish to remain with Indonesia; or (b) whether they wish to sever their ties with Indonesia." The "act of self-determination" was to be completed before the end of 1969. In due course, the Secretary-General was to appoint a representative to "advise, assist and participate in arrangements which are the responsibility of Indonesia for the act of free choice." This representative and his staff were to assume their duties in the territory "one year prior to the date of self-determination;" and ultimately, both Indonesia and the United Nations representative were to submit final reports to the Secretary-General, who was to "report to the General Assembly on the conduct of the act of self-determination and the results thereof."

The most important of four related "understandings" supplementary to the main agreement provided for a cessation of hostilities in West New Guinea, to take place on August 18, 1962; and for the necessary arrangements to make the cease-fire effective. Another "understanding" stipulated that on December 31, 1962, "the Netherlands flag will be struck, and the Indonesian flag will be hoisted side by side with the United Nations flag;" and also provided that the "transfer of authority to Indonesia will be effected as soon as possible after May 1, 1963." Sukarno had won. The Indonesian flag would fly over West New Guinea before the cock crowed on the New Year; and within a few months thereafter, Indonesian control would be complete.

Instruments of ratification were exchanged between the two parties at the United Nations on September 20, 1962.[40] On the following day, the General Assembly interrupted its annual General Debate to act on a resolution jointly sponsored by Indonesia and the Netherlands (and called for in their agreement) whereby the General Assembly took formal note of the

---

[40]*GAOR*, Seventeenth Session (1962), Annexes, A/5170, Add. 1. The agreement had been approved unanimously by the Indonesian parliament on September 1; by the Second Chamber of the Netherlands parliament on September 7 (by a vote of 129 to 9), and by the First Chamber on September 13 (by a vote of 63 to 3). See van der Veur, "The United Nations in West Irian: A Critique," *loc. cit.,* p. 58, fn. 14.

settlement and authorized Thant to carry out the responsibilities assigned to him pursuant to its terms.[41] The resolution was speedily adopted by a vote of 89 to none, with 14 abstentions.[42] The interminable West New Guinea dispute was at last officially settled.

[41]*GAOR*, Seventeenth Session (1962), Annexes, A/L. 393.

[42]France, Haiti, Rwanda, and 11 former French African colonies abstained. Their refusal to endorse the Dutch-Indonesian agreement reflected serious concern as to whether it adequately safeguarded the Papuans' right of self-determination. Later in the General Debate, the representative of the Central African Republic denounced the agreement as an "absolute violation of the principle of self-determination." He roundly criticized the General Assembly for having participated in "the spectacle—astonishing in our era of decolonization—of a territory being handed over by one colonial Power to another with the blessing of the United Nations." *GAOR*, Seventeenth Session (1962), A/PV. 1151.

Chapter Fourteen

Epilogue

With the signature of the Dutch-Indonesian agreement on August 15, 1962, and the subsequent action of the United Nations General Assembly "taking note" of the settlement, the long dispute over the future of West New Guinea was at last resolved. Subsequent developments in the territory, with the important exception of Indonesia's implementation of the "act of free choice" in 1969, are outside the scope of this study. In order to complete the chronological record, however, it may be worthwhile to recount briefly the evolution of West New Guinea (or Irian Barat, as the Indonesians called it) under United Nations administration and subsequently under Indonesian rule.

The U.N.T.E.A. Phase

The United Nations Temporary Executive Authority was to have full powers, as from October 1, 1962, "to administer the territory of West New Guinea (West Irian), to maintain law and order, to protect the rights of the inhabitants and to ensure uninterrupted, normal services during a period of several months until, in turn, the administration of the territory was transferred to the Indonesian Government." [1] Even before assuming this responsibility, however, the first task was to implement the cease-fire agreed to by Indonesia and the Netherlands, which was to take effect on August 18. This task was assigned to Brigadier-General Indar Jit Rikhye, Military Advisor to the Secretary-General, assisted by 21 military observers seconded by Brazil, Ceylon, India, Ireland, Nigeria, and Sweden, and with aerial support provided by the United States and Canadian air forces. The military observer team moved with dispatch to discharge its mandate, aided by the ready cooperation of both sides. By September 21, Rikhye was able to report that "all actions concerning the

---

[1]*GAOR*, Eighteenth Session (1963), Supplement No. 1, A/5501, *Annual Report of the Secretary-General on the Work of the Organization, 16th June 1962 - 15 June 1963* (hereafter cited as A/5501), p. 35. In addition to Thant's report, another official account of the U.N.T.E.A. experience may be found in *The United Nations in West New Guinea* (New York: United Nations, 1963).

213

cessation of hostilities, including the concentration of the Indonesian forces, in four main areas, the provision to them of emergency supplies, and the repatriation of over 500 Indonesian detainees had been completed without incident." [2]

Meanwhile, a United Nations Security Force (U.N.S.F.) was hastily organized in accordance with Article VII of the Dutch-Indonesian settlement. Major-General Said Uddin Khan of Pakistan, who was named Commander of U.N.S.F., arrived in Hollandia on September 4, 1962; an advance party of 340 men landed in the territory early in October; and eventually U.N.S.F. was built up to a total strength of approximately 1,600.[3] The main task of this force was defined in the Dutch-Indonesian agreement as "primarily (to) supplement exisiting Papuan (West Irianese) police in the task of maintaining law and order." [4] This involved not only the ordinary police function, but also the more delicate responsibilities of standing as a buffer between Dutch and Indonesian contingents in the territory, and also "ensuring that any vacuum caused by the withdrawal of the Dutch was adequately filled by the UN Force." [5] U.N.S.F. performed effectively throughout the period of United Nations administration. Fortunately, the situation was "generally calm" everywhere in the territory. Only two significant incidents occurred, "involving the police and a small group of Indonesian troops," and resulting in one fatality and four other casualties. But in both instances, order was "immediately restored" by units of the United Nations force.[6]

[2]A/5501, p. 35. Apparently the main problem was to inform Indonesian infiltrators of the cease-fire. "This was accomplished by radio broadcasts and pamphlets dropped from the air. As soon as they were informed of the end of hostilities, they proceeded to the four main centers where they were assembled." David W. Wainhouse *et al.*, *International Peace Observation* (Baltimore: Johns Hopkins University Press, 1966), p. 418.

[3]See Rosalyn Higgins, *United Nations Peacekeeping, 1946-1967, Documents and Commentary, II, Asia* (London: Oxford University Press, 1970), p. 125. The figures are as of February 7, 1963. This book contains the most comprehensive study so far published on the work of the military observer team and U.N.S.F., with emphasis on the legal and constitutional aspects. See pp. 91-149. For other, briefer accounts, see D. W. Bowett, *United Nations Forces* (New York: Praeger, 1964), pp. 255-261; Ruth B. Russell, *United Nations Experience with Military Forces: Political and Legal Aspects* (Washington: Brookings, 1964), pp. 126-133; Jack Citrin, *United Nations Peacekeeping Activities* (Denver: University of Denver, 1965), pp. 47-52; and Wainhouse, *op. cit.*, pp. 414-421.

[4]See Article VII of the Dutch-Indonesian agreement, in the Appendix.

[5]Higgins, *United Nations Peacekeeping, 1964-1967, Documents and Commentary, II, Asia*, p. 139.

[6]A/5501, p. 37. These incidents occurred at Sorong and Doom. Van der Veur speaks of "some minor but vicious incidents in Merauke, Sorong-Doom, and Sentani" which were "directly attributable" to the presence of Indonesian troops in the

The main function of U.N.T.E.A. was to supervise and facilitate transfer of the territorial administration from the Dutch to Indonesian control. José Rolz-Bennett of Guatemala, Thant's Deputy Chef de Cabinet, was appointed as his Temporary Representative in West New Guinea, and arrived in the territory on September 21 (the same day that all actions relating to the cease-fire were reported as completed) to work out with Netherlands officials the details of the transfer of authority to U.N.T.E.A. The ceremony of transfer took place on October 1 (the Netherlands Governor having departed three days earlier), and the United Nations flag raised to fly side by side with the Dutch flag. On the same day, Indonesia and the Netherlands established liaison missions to the United Nations administration in the territorial capital. A permanent United Nations Administrator, Djalal Abdoh of Iran, was named on October 22, and took up his post in West New Guinea on November 15.

A major problem was to recruit the personnel necessary to staff the transitional administration. This was made especially difficult by the hasty departure of large numbers of Dutch civil servants (in addition to the 18 top officials whose posts were to be vacated pursuant to the Dutch-Indonesian agreement) before and after the transfer of authority to the United Nations.[7] The fact that U.N.T.E.A.'s life expectancy was predictably short also complicated the problem of recruitment. The problem was met by persuading as many Dutch officials as possible to stay on the job temporarily, by utilizing Papuan personnel where possible, and by internationally recruited staff. As might have been expected, Indonesia "responded with speed" to the United Nations request for personnel assistance.[8] Indeed, the Indonesian takeover of the administration proceeded very rapidly: [9]

The influx of Indonesian personnel was accelerated towards the end of February 1963 and increased with the approaching date of transfer of administration to Indonesia. By the beginning of April, fewer than a dozen Netherlands nationals remained while the total number of Indonesians in the service of UNTEA had reached 1,600. As regards Papuan officials, at the time of transfer of administration to

territory. Van der Veur, "The United Nations in West Irian: A Critique," *loc. cit.*, p. 60. He also states that several "beatings by pro-Indonesian Papuans and some investigations by Indonesian military were reported." *Ibid.*, p. 68. But van der Veur also agrees that U.N.T.E.A. "in general accomplished a remarkably smooth transfer. In this regard the United Nations operation was a major success." *Ibid.*, p. 71.

[7] Of 2,540 Netherlands officials in the colonial administration as of September 1, 1962, all but 775 had departed by October 1; and most of these left soon thereafter. See *ibid.*, p. 59, fn. 16.

[8] A/5501, p. 37.

[9] *Ibid.*

Indonesia on 1 May 1963, they numbered some 7,000, an increase of approximately 600 for the entire period of UNTEA.

The replacement of Dutch military and police forces in the territory was comparably rapid. All naval and land units were withdrawn "without incident" by November 15. By agreement with U.N.T.E.A., large numbers of Indonesian troops who had infiltrated into West New Guinea were replaced by fresh contingents from Indonesia; and it was also agreed "that the number of Indonesian troops in the territory would not exceed the strength of the Pakistan contingent of UNSF, except with the prior consent of the UNTEA administration." [10] Dutch officers and NCO's in the paramilitary Papuan Volunteer Corps (whose strength totalled approximately 350 officers and men) were replaced by Indonesians, and command of the corps transferred to an Indonesian officer on January 21, 1963. As for the Papuan police force, its Dutch officers were replaced, first by Filipinos, and then by Indonesians. By the end of March 1963, the entire police force was officered by Indonesians.[11]

Van der Veur has criticized the United Nations administration of West New Guinea, *inter alia,* on the grounds that there was not "sufficient time to recruit and train personnel" for U.N.T.E.A.;[12] that U.N.T.E.A. was authorized to use Indonesian troops for the maintenance of law and order, which (he says) "sabotaged the task of the United Nations," since the "mere presence of heavily armed Indonesian troops was bound to have a marked psychological effect;" [13] that the departure of the Dutch "disrupted existing services at least temporarily," and that their replacement by Indonesians "immediately jeopardized the development of an independent United Nations administration;" [14] that U.N.T.E.A. was unable to halt a drainage of goods out of West New Guinea "via Indonesian officials and

[10]*Ibid.,* p. 36. Van der Veur states, however, that with "additional Indonesian paratroopers dropped during the last stages of the negotiations in mid-August 1962, the number of Indonesian troops surpassed the Pakistani contingent representing the United Nations security force." Van der Veur, "The United Nations in West Irian: A Critique," *loc cit.,* pp. 59-60.

[11]A/5501, p. 36.

[12]Van der Veur, "The United Nations in West Irian: A Critique," *loc cit.,* p. 58.

[13]*Ibid.,* pp. 59-60. As Higgins has pointed out, this is really a criticism of the Dutch-Indonesian agreement, not of U.N.T.E.A. Higgins, *op. cit.,* p. 141. Moreover, the United Nations Administrator "had no occasion to call on the Indonesian armed forces in connexion with the maintenance of law and order." A/5501. p. 37. This fact does not, however, wholly meet van der Veur's point about the "psychological effect" of the presence of Indonesian forces in the territory during the U.N.T.E.A. phase.

[14]Van der Veur, "The United Nations in West Irian: A Critique," *loc. cit.,* p. 59.

military men . . . to the blackmarkets of Indonesia's urban centers;" [15] that levels of employment declined during the U.N.T.E.A. phase, and "thousands of skilled and semi-skilled workers . . . returned from the 'advanced areas' to their (subsistence) villages;" [16] that "the number of 'public utility projects' planned and initiated by UNTEA (was) negligible;" [17] and especially that the United Nations administration failed adequately to fulfil the terms of the Dutch-Indonesian settlement to "publicize and explain" its terms, and to "inform the population concerning the transfer of administration and the provisions for the act of self-determination." [18]

No doubt there is considerable validity to all of these charges. But they overlook the crucial fact that U.N.T.E.A. was conceived primarily as a device to lubricate the transfer of West New Guinea from Dutch to Indonesian rule, and to do so in a very short period of time. There was simply no prospect that the brief United Nations administration could in other respects significantly affect the course of political evolution in the territory, and still less its economic development. Moreover, so profound a political transformation was bound to set in motion all manner of changes, not all of them happy ones. Thus, the normal functioning of the colonial administrative machinery was inevitably affected adversely, although there was certainly no general breakdown of administrative continuity. The level of economic activity also declined with the withdrawal of the Dutch, and citified Papuan workers in large numbers did flee to the safety of the countryside while awaiting the uncertain future. There was simply not enough time for U.N.T.E.A. to do much about all this; although it did initiate and complete a number of public works projects, and by and large "the economic stability of the territory was maintained." [19] It was also sadly true that the Indonesians often behaved more as conquerors than liberators, and proceeded to loot the territory. Carpetbaggers are apparently a universal phenomenon. Finally, the clauses of the Dutch-Indonesian agreement requiring U.N.T.E.A. to "publicize and explain" its terms to the Papuan population were no doubt sincerely meant, but were

---

[15]*Ibid.*, p. 61. "Not only such 'luxury items' as transistor radios, cameras, typewriters, wristwatches, sunglasses, and dollars but also car tires, babyfood, toiletsoap, medicine, medical instruments, and even sugar and rice have found their way to Djakarta and other Indonesian centers." Paul W. van der Veur, "West Irian in the Indonesian Fold." *Asian Survey,* vol. 3, no. 7 (July 1963), p. 333.

[16]Van der Veur, "The United Nations in West Irian: A Critique," *loc. cit.,* p. 61. Quotations and parentheses in original.

[17]*Ibid.* Quotations in original.

[18]See Article X of the Dutch-Indonesian agreement, in the Appendix.

[19]A/5501, p. 39.

hardly central to the settlement; and in any case, U.N.T.E.A. did make some — even if not enough — effort in this respect.[20]

U.N.T.E.A. assumed responsibility for the administration of West New Guinea on October 1, 1962. Within a month, Indonesia had launched an energetic campaign to shorten the period of international administration. The Indonesian press published a steady barrage of articles on the subject. Letters and petitions to the same effect were forwarded by various Papuan leaders and other groups to Thant and Djalal Abdoh, the United Nations Administrator of the territory. On November 21, members of the New Guinea Council, now staunchly pro-Indonesian,[21] issued a declaration asking for an early transfer of administrative authority to Indonesia; and a public demonstration in Hollandia in January 1963 supported this demand. Also in January, Sudjarwo Tjondronegoro, head of the Indonesian liaison mission to U.N.T.E.A., brought the matter formally to Thant's attention at the United Nations. In his report to the General Assembly on the U.N.T.E.A. experience, Thant subsequently maintained that, after consultations with the Netherlands representative in New York, he came to the conclusion that "any shortening of UNTEA was not feasible;" [22] and he so informed the Jakarta government.

Legge comments that this campaign "was a piece of bad public relations and one wonders what sort of purpose could have been served by it.[23] In fact, it appears to have served the object the Indonesians had in mind, in that it may have been a contributing factor leading the United Nations to abbreviate significantly the period of its administration. The Dutch-Indonesian agreement provided that the "first phase" of U.N.T.E.A., during which the United Nations administration would take over from the Dutch "as rapidly as possible," would be completed by May 1, 1963.[24] Thereafter, in the "second phase," U.N.T.E.A. would have "discretion to transfer all or part of the administration to Indonesia at any time;" [25] and it was also agreed that "the transfer of authority to Indonesia" would be

---

[20]See *ibid*, p. 38. *The United Nations in West New Guinea*, an official account of U.N.T.E.A. published by the United Nations in 1963, devotes exactly six lines to this aspect of U.N.T.E.A.'s work. See pp. 15-16.

[21]See p. 221, below.

[22]A/5501, p. 39. The Indonesian newspaper *Suluh Indonesia* editorialized that Thant was "sticking by the 'dead writings' of the New York agreement and refusing to take notice of fresh evidence." J. D. Legge, "Indonesia After West Irian," *Australian Outlook*, vol. 17, no. 1 (April 1963), p. 7. Quotations in original.

[23]*Ibid*.

[24]See Article IX of the Dutch-Indonesian agreement, in the Appendix.

[25]See Article XII.

effected "as soon as possible after 1 May 1963." [26] It is open to con-
jecture as to precisely what was originally intended by this time frame,
although everyone understood that it would be quite brief. In any event,
Thant and his colleagues now decided to foreshorten the "second phase"
to a matter of hours, and to complete the entire transaction on May 1.
Thant dispatched C. V. Narasimhan, his Chef de Cabinet, to West New
Guinea and Indonesia for consultations; and on February 9, the latter
announced in Jakarta that the transfer of the territory to Indonesian control would take place on May 1, at 12:30 p. m. Narasimhan explained it
this way: [27]

> . . . (The Dutch-Indonesian agreement) contemplated a first phase
> of UNTEA, and a second phase. The second phase could have been
> as long as necessary. Now the second phase we are curtailing on the
> recommendation of the Administrator to a matter of a few hours.
> Because before 1 May, the first phase is not over, and the second
> phase, which was to have been indefinite, has been reduced to a
> matter of a few hours.

Three days earlier, the Indonesian Foreign Minister, Subandrio, had announced (following talks with Narasimhan) that the United Nations had
agreed to an "informal" takeover of West New Guinea by Indonesia before May. [28] Whatever this meant, the fact was that U.N.T.E.A. had "had
to rely from the start on hundreds of Indonesians to carry on daily administration," because of the precipitate departure of the Dutch; [29] and it
was now agreed that the substitution of Indonesian officials "would be
accelerated." [30] By the end of April, some 1,564 Indonesians were working in the administration, and every administrative department had been
taken over by an Indonesian. At the same time, plans were made for the
withdrawal of the United Nations Security Force and for its replacement
by Indonesian units, a process that was completed by the end of April. [31]

---

[26]*GAOR*, Seventeenth Session (1962), Annexes, A/5170.

[27]Quoted in van der Veur, "The United Nations in West Irian: A Critique," *loc.
cit.*, p. 65.

[28]*Washington Post*, February 7, 1963.

[29]Justus M. van der Kroef, "West New Guinea: The Uncertain Future," *Asian
Survey*, vol. 8, no. 8 (August 1968), p. 695.

[30]A/5501, p. 39.

[31]See *ibid.;* also van der Veur, "The United Nations in West Irian: A Critique,"
loc. cit., p. 65. Article XIII of the Dutch-Indonesian agreement provided that
"United Nations security forces will be replaced by Indonesian security forces *after*
the first phase of the UNTEA administration." (Emphasis added.)

Indonesian Rule

In a ceremony at Hollandia, now renamed Kotabaru,[32] on May 1, 1963, full administrative control over West New Guinea was handed over by U.N.T.E.A. to the representative of Indonesia at 12:30 p. m., and the flag of the United Nations taken down. President Sukarno did not attend the ceremony, "preferring to wait until Indonesia had complete authority before making his visit." [33] Nor did the Netherlands government take part. President Kennedy hailed the transfer as "a notable event both for Indonesia and the principle of peaceful settlement of disputes between nations;" [34] while Premier Khrushchev of the U.S.S.R. described it as a victory in Indonesia's "just struggle" for the territory.[35]

The transfer of authority was soon followed by the suppression of the nascent Papuan nationalist movement. During the last few years of Dutch rule, an authentic nationalism had begun to take root and flourish in West New Guinea, stimulated by the bold program announced by the Dutch in 1960 to accelerate the political development of the territory.[36] Its persistent strength was attested to by the Australian scholar, Herbert Feith, who visited West New Guinea in 1964, a year after the Indonesian takeover. "I was jolted," he said. "Papuan nationalism . . . was clearly a more genuine and full-blooded thing that I had expected." [37]

The failure of the Luns Plan in the General Assembly in Fall 1961, the deepening crisis between Indonesia and the Netherlands, and the subsequent negotiations under United Nations auspices, all served to galvanize the Papuan nationalists to new activity. In January and February 1962, the New Guinea Council passed a series of resolutions demanding self-government by 1970, and Papuan participation in any negotiations between Jakarta and The Hague on the future of the territory.[38] Demonstrations occurred in Manokwari and Fakfak. In March, the *ad hoc* National Committee issued an appeal to "fellow Negroids" everywhere to "use your influence to persuade the United Nations Organization that this menace of the Republic of Indonesia will be put to a stop." [39] A month later, a group of Papuan leaders cabled President Kennedy to insist that

[32]Subsequently renamed (1) Sukarnapura; and (2) Jayapura, following Sukarno's downfall.

[33]*The New York Times*, May 1, 1963.

[34]Quoted in *ibid.*

[35]Quoted in *ibid.*

[36]See pp. 94 ff., above.

[37]Quoted in van der Kroef, "West New Guinea: The Uncertain Future," *loc. cit.*, p. 694.

[38]See van der Kroef, "The West New Guinea Settlement," *loc. cit.*, p. 137.

[39]Quoted in *ibid.*

Papuans were not Indonesians, and that "forced participation in Indonesian administration would be equivalent to a slave trade carried on by members of the United Nations." [40]

The August 1962 agreement between Indonesia and the Netherlands came as a great shock to the Papuan nationalists. Van der Veur states:[41]

Papuans who had placed their faith in the Dutch promises for self-determination were stunned and bewildered. Those who had been most directly involved politically felt betrayed and wondered how an agreement which solemnly claimed to have in mind "the interests and welfare of the peoples of the territory . . ." could decide about them without consulting them.

Later that month, the Nationalist Party adopted a program calling for West New Guinea to become an independent republic by 1970. In September, a specially-convened National Congress met to discuss the Dutch-Indonesian agreement. Opinion at the Congress was sharply divided; but a final communique "accepted the . . . agreement as the only possible way to prevent a world war but favored the holding of the plebiscite in 1963; . . . (and) confirmed that the act of self-determination granted to the inhabitants means external self-determination." [42]

After U.N.T.E.A. took over from the Dutch on October 1, the political climate changed dramatically. The shield of Dutch benevolence was suddenly removed. Now the inexperienced Papuan nationalists had to face alone the reality of a rapidly expanding Indonesian military and administrative presence, and the imminent certainty that Jakarta would assume complete control of the territory after May 1, 1963. Some of them fled the country with the departing Dutch. For those who remained, Jakarta quickly brought to bear the instrumentalities of coercion and cajolement to force a sea change in their expression of Papuan sentiment. Unhappily, the United Nations interim administration proved an indifferent champion of Papuan liberties. By November, the New Guinea Council was dutifully calling for an abbreviation of the U.N.T.E.A. phase and a speedier transfer of authority to Indonesia.[43] Jakarta had little difficulty in persuading Papuan leaders to embrace the Indonesian line on such issues as the duration of U.N.T.E.A. and the pointlessness of the proposed "act of free choice." [44] Nationalist demonstrations were forestalled,[45] and pro-Indo-

---

[40]Quoted in *ibid.*

[41]Van der Veur, "Political Awakening in West New Guinea," *loc. cit.,* p. 69.

[42]*Ibid.,* pp. 70-71. See also van der Kroef, "The West New Guinea Settlement," *loc. cit.,* p. 149.

[43]On this development, see also A/5501, p. 39.

[44]For further details, see p. 227, below.

[45]See van der Kroef, "The West New Guinea Settlement," *loc. cit.,* p. 149, fn. 72.

nesian manifestations encouraged.[46] Even before the departure of the
United Nations administration, political life in the territory was being
increasingly stifled; and after the Indonesian takeover, the legitimate expression of Papuan nationalism was silenced altogether. In due course, the
New Guinea Council and the several regional councils set up in the last
years of Dutch rule [47] were "reconstituted" to insure unanimous support
for Indonesian policy. The night of "guided democracy" descended on
West New Guinea. Van der Kroef states: [48]

> Shortly after May 1963 . . . , Indonesia instituted a "political quaran-
> tine" in West New Guinea: partisan political activity was banned
> unless officially approved, controls over the press and all public
> gatherings generally equalled — but in some respects outdid — those
> under the authoritarian system . . . in the rest of Indonesia, and
> severe restrictions were imposed on the movement of persons with-
> in, into, and out of the region.

The suppression of nationalist manifestations continued throughout the
years leading up to the "act of free choice" in 1969. The "political
quarantine," originally imposed (according to the official version) "to
eliminate the remnants of colonialism in the province," [49] was supposedly
lifted in June 1965 to permit Indonesian political parties to function in
West New Guinea.[50] But this did not extend to the espousal of Papuan
separatism. An Australian journalist who visited the territory that month
(one of the rare foreign correspondents to do so during this period)
commented on the "absence of political rights" for the local population.[51]
Three years later, when Fernando Ortiz Sanz took up his responsibilities
as United Nations Representative for the "act of free choice," he pointedly
called to the attention of the Jakarta government "complaints I have
received, both written and oral, from some West Irianese individuals and
organizations, within and outside the territory, about alleged suppression

[46]See A/5501, p. 39.

[47]On the establishment of these regional councils, see Paul W. van der Veur,
"West Irian: A New Era," *Asian Survey*, vol. 2, no. 8 (October 1962), pp. 4-6; and
van der Veur, "Political Awakening in West New Guinea," *loc. cit.*, p. 63.

[48]Van der Kroef, "West New Guinea: The Uncertain Future," *loc. cit.*, p. 695.
For a sympathetic account of the first years of Indonesian rule in West New Guinea,
see M. A. Jaspan, "West Irian: The First Two Years," *Australian Quarterly*, vol. 37,
no. 2 (June 1965), pp. 9-21.

[49]Quoted in van der Kroef, "West New Guinea: The Uncertain Future," *loc.
cit.*, p. 697.

[50]See *Christian Science Monitor*, September 22, 1965.

[51]Quoted in van der Kroef, "West New Guinea: The Uncertain Future," *loc.
cit.*, p. 697.

of the rights and freedoms of the inhabitants." [52] Ortiz tried but largely failed to persuade the Indonesian authorities to ameliorate these conditions prior to implementation of the "act of free choice" in 1969.[53]

Beginning about 1965, reports of unrest and occasional violent outbreaks in West New Guinea began to appear in the Indonesian and foreign press with increasing frequency. According to accounts in Jakarta newspapers, for example, "Free Papuan" rebels rioted in Manokwari and on the island of Biak on the eve of Indonesia's Independence Day (August 17) celebrations that year, and "were subdued only after a battalion of crack Indonesian paratroops had been hastily flown in from Java." The insurgents "had badly mauled paramilitary mobile police, had destroyed hundreds of thousands of gallons of aviation fuel, and had planned to dynamite oil and fresh water installations on Biak." [54] In March 1957, Silas Papare, a Papuan member of the Indonesian Provisional People's Consultative Chamber, "appealed to the government to end Indonesian strafing and rocket attacks on Papuan villages, claiming that as many as one thousand Papuans had already been killed in such action." [55] Foreign Minister Malik subsequently admitted that skirmishes had taken place with rebellious tribesmen of the Vogelkop Peninsula, but said that the number of casualties "was exaggerated, the troops might have killed two hundred." [56] In April, it was officially acknowledged that the Indonesian Air Force had felt it necessary to strafe the town of Manokwari in order to deal with an uprising there, and that 40 persons had been killed.[57] Thereafter Jakarta increased the scale of its security operations, and reported some success in dispersing the rebels.[58] But in May 1968, new outbreaks were reported in the Indonesian press, allegedly the result of a "scarcity of daily necessities." [59]

One estimate of the situation in September of that year held that a "free Papuan" movement "of ungauged strength certainly exists" in West New Guinea, but that it was "actually quite small." [60] Nor was it clear whether the numerous incidents represented anything like a coordinated effort, or simply a number of more or less unrelated riots and other violent outbreaks.

[52]A/7723, Annex I, p. 7.
[53]See pp. 236-237, below.
[54]*Washington Post*, September 16, 1965.
[55]Van der Kroef, "West New Guinea: The Uncertain Future," *loc. cit.*, p. 700.
[56]Quoted in *ibid.*
[57]See *ibid.*
[58]See *ibid.*, p. 701.
[59]Quoted in *ibid.*, p. 707.
[60]*Christian Science Monitor*, September 4, 1968, and September 21, 1968.

The year 1969 was also marked by sporadic dissidence, which was, however, more fully reported in the world press because of the attention focussed on the forthcoming "act of free choice." There was trouble again in Manokwari Regency, where (according to the report subsequently submitted by Ortiz Sanz) "a situation of unrest and turmoil, marked by sporadic armed clashes, had existed" since 1965.[61] Perhaps the most significant incidents occurred in the towns of Enarotali and Waghete, in the central highlands of Paniai Regency. This involved an uprising of rebel tribesmen augmented by about 100 Papuan police deserters. The Indonesians were reported to have used rockets and some 500 paratroopers in order to regain control of the situation.[62]

In June, one press report held that 4,000 Indonesian troops "were hounding tens of thousands of dissident refugees" in the northwest corner of the island. The same report also claimed that there were now "more than a dozen freedom movements operating throughout West Irian." [63] On the other hand, the Indonesian commanding general in West New Guinea estimated rebel strength at that time at "about 50 in the Manokwari area, with a dozen Japanese or American rifles between then; 40 policemen in the Enarotali area, with 40 Mausers and one Bren-gun; and very few on Supiori Island, north of Biak, with a couple of rifles." [64] With 6,000 troops at his disposal, this seemed a manageable situation; and, in fact, few observers argued that the Papuan dissidence posed a serious threat to Indonesian control. It was, however, a painful embarrassment as preparations for the heralded "act of free choice" went forward.

Another evidence of political unrest in West New Guinea was to be found in the increasing numbers of Papuans who crossed the border each year into the Australian-administered eastern half of the island. Between 1963 and 1966, these were numbered at 573; in 1967, 866; in 1968, 801, and up to May 1969, 350.[65] To be sure, much of this involved the normal movement of seminomadic peoples across an artificial international frontier

[61]A/7723, Annex I, p. 14.

[62]See *ibid.*, p. 15; also *The New York Times,* May 6, 1969, May 7, 1969, May 8, 1969, and May 11, 1969; *London Times,* May 7, 1969; *Christian Science Monitor,* May 8, 1969; and *Washington Post,* May 22, 1969. This episode led United Nations Secretary-General Thant to convey his "concern" to the Indonesian government, and to stress "the need for a proper atmosphere in which the Papuans could decide by the planned 'act of free choice' this year if they wished to keep their ties with Indonesia." *The New York Times,* May 10, 1969.

[63]*Washington Post,* June 5, 1969.

[64]*London Times,* June 9, 1969.

[65]See Justus M. van der Kroef, "Australia and the West Irian Problem," *Asian Survey,* vol. 10, no. 6 (June 1970), p. 492.

that had little, if any, significance for them. But the increasing numbers were perhaps significant.[66]

Mention should also be made of the activities of a small group of Papuan exiles in the Netherlands during this period. Led by Nicolas Jouwe and Marcus Kaisiepo, both of whom had played active political roles in West New Guinea toward the end of the Dutch period, and supported by Dutch sympathizers, this group maintained a vigorous propaganda campaign against Indonesian rule of their homeland and in favor of Papuan independence, but without much visible effect. Its relationship to dissident activities in West New Guinea is unclear.[67]

[66]See also *The New York Times,* May 3, 1969, and May 16, 1969; and *London Times,* June 7, 1969.

[67]On this subject, see especially van der Kroef, "West New Guinea: The Uncertain Future," *loc. cit.,* pp. 691-692, 695-696, 701-702.

Sufficient evidence is not at hand to evaluate the social and economic progress of the indigenous population under Indonesian rule. The impression is one of comparative stagnation and neglect during most of the 1960s, although it would appear that the Indonesians did pay some attention to educational development, for example. See *Washington Post,* September 16, 1965. In November 1966, a Papuan delegation complained to Foreign Minister Malik that "the economy was stagnating and the people were complaining about the dire lack of basic necessities." Van der Kroef, "West New Guinea: The Uncertain Future," *loc. cit.,* p. 699. And in March 1967, a Papuan member of the Provisional People's Consultative Chamber, F. Karubuy, "stressed the economic plight of his fellow Papuans, warning that the territory's inhabitants were taking up arms to rebel because of lack of food and clothing and not necessarily because of political motives." *Ibid.,* p. 699. Later in the year, Papuan members of the Indonesian parliament warned that "corruption, economic hardship and general maladministration are alienating the Papuans and that it is by no means to be taken for granted that the Papuan population if given the chance would opt for continued Indonesian control." *Ibid.,* p. 707.

In November 1963, the Secretary-General of the United Nations established, in conjunction with the governments of Indonesia and the Netherlands, a Fund of the United Nations for the Development of West Irian (F.U.N.D.W.I.), and The Hague had promptly pledged $30 million to it. Operations were suspended after Indonesia announced its withdrawal from the United Nations on December 31, 1964, and not resumed until late 1966. Thereafter, a United Nations survey mission submitted a detailed plan for utilization of the fund. See *A Design for Development in West Irian* (New York: United Nations, 1968). Large-scale implementation did not begin until 1969. By mid-1970, seventeen projects obligating $14 million of F.U.N.D.W.I. resources and $55 million of Indonesian support in local currency and facilities, had been approved. It is anticipated that most of F.U.N.D.W.I.'s foreign exchange resources will be utilized by 1973. See *GAOR,* Twenty-fifth Session (1970), Supplement No. 1, A/8001, *Annual Report of the Secretary-General on the Work of the Organization, 16 June 1969 - 15 June 9170,* pp. 190-191.

In April 1969, the Indonesian Ministry of Finance established the West Irian Joint Development Commission "to promote industry, agriculture and other local enterprises, to administer expenditures for social projects, such as schoolhouse construc-

Indonesia and the "Act of Free Choice"

Jakarta's attitude on the "act of free choice" provided for in the Dutch-Indonesian settlement,[68] and to be exercised by the Papuan population by the end of 1969, was at best equivocal. This was one of the few substantial concessions that the Dutch had been able to exact from the reluctant Indonesian negotiators. For the Dutch, it represented at least a *pro forma* vindication of their longstanding demand that the right of the Papuans to political self-determination be safeguarded, even though the proposed exercise of that right only after several years of Indonesian rule practically foreclosed the outcome. The Indonesians, on the other hand, inevitably regarded this aspect of the settlement as tantamount to a denial of the whole basis of their claim to West New Guinea, namely, that the territory was, and always had been, an integral part of the Indonesian state, and that the Papuan population had already exercised its right of self-determination by its presumed participation in the August 1945 declaration of independence. It may be, too, that Jakarta had some misgivings as to what the outcome would be if the "act of free choice" were held under strictly impartial auspices. In this connection, the Dutch-Indonesian agreement provided that the United Nations was to "advise, assist, and participate in arrangements which are the responsibility of Indonesia for the act of free choice;" [69] and it remained to be seen how diligently the United Nations would discharge these responsibilities.

From the beginning, Indonesian spokesmen attempted to qualify the nature and extent of Indonesia's obligation. Thus, in his Independence Day speech of August 17, 1962, President Sukarno argued that the principle of "freedom of choice" stipulated in the agreement really constituted "internal self-determination" rather than "external self-determination," and that Indonesia had accepted the obligation only because there was

---

tion, and to provide a focal point for provincial development." *Ibid.*, p. 191. In November of that year, Indonesia and the Netherlands jointly announced a plan to set up a special fund for the development of West Irian in the Asian Development Bank. The Hague pledged an initial contribution of 17.5 million guilders. See *ibid.*, p. 63.

A major copper strike by the US-owned company Freeport Indonesia Incorporated at Ertsberg, in the Carstensz Mountains, is now being developed rapidly, and entails the investment of several tens of millions of dollars. It is problematical, however, how much of this investment will redound to the benefit of West New Guinea's economy. The operation is highly mechanized and automated, relatively little Papuan labor is required, and the royalties go to Jakarta.

[68]See Articles XVI-XXI of the Dutch-Indonesian agreement.

[69]See Article XVII.

no doubt about the outcome.[70] In January 1963, Max Maramis, the deputy head of the Indonesian liaison mission to U.N.T.E.A., expounded the view that international agreements that infringed upon national interests were null and void. With respect to the promised exercise of self-determination by the Papuans, he said: [71]

> According to logic, . . . the (proposed) plebiscite constitutes the people's voice. When the people decide much earlier that it is no longer necessary to have the aforementioned plebiscite, isn't that also the people's voice?

Two months later, Sukarno declared that the desire to unite with Indonesia was "the wish of all the people of West Irian." [72] Meanwhile, Papuan leaders from all parts of the territory were induced to subscribe to public declarations including four principal points: that Indonesia was "one country with one people and one language;" that the 1945 constitution was the basis of the Indonesian state; that "UNTEA ought to get out of West Irian by January 1, 1963;" and that "the plebiscite is unnecessary." [73]

Such statements generated some international concern that the Jakarta government might be preparing the ground for a repudiation of its obligations respecting the "act of free choice." The Prime Minister of Australia, Robert G. Menzies, declared in parliament in November 1962 that any "idea that the plebiscite should be abandoned is one that strikes directly across the whole principle for which this Parliament has stood, and which was acknowledged in the agreement made between the parties and approved by the United Nations." [74] With the termination of U.N.T.E.A. in May 1963, U Thant felt it necessary to express his confidence that Indonesia "would scrupulously observe" the terms of the agreement, and

[70]Van der Veur, "The United Nations in West Irian: A Critique," loc. cit., p. 63. Presumably this meant that while the Papuans would be allowed to determine their future place within the Indonesian state, they were not free to opt out of the republic. See van der Kroef, "West New Guinea: The Uncertain Future," loc. cit., p. 695.

[71]Quoted in van der Veur, "The United Nations in West Irian: A Critique," loc. cit., p. 63.

[72]Quoted in ibid.

[73]Quoted in ibid. Elsewhere, van der Veur states that Indonesia "employed a variety of persuasive techniques, including expense-paid trips to Djakarta (with numerous attractions provided), promises, flattery, persistent if gentle pressure, veiled threats, and clear intimidation to get its way with politically inexperienced Papuans." Van der Veur, "West Irian in the Indonesian Fold," loc. cit., p. 325.

[74]Commonwealth of Australia, Parliamentary Debates, House of Representatives, November 29, 1962.

"would ensure the exercise by the population of the territory of their right to express their wishes as to their future." [75]

Jakarta's ambivalence on the question reached a peak following Sukarno's decision, announced without warning on December 31, 1964, to withdraw from the United Nations over the issue of Malaysia's election to a two-year term on the Security Council. There was "renewed speculation, fortified by authoritative pronouncements in Djakarta, that Indonesia regarded itself as no longer bound by the . . . requirement" to hold a plebiscite.[76] A few months later, Sukarno was reported to have stated in a press interview that a plebiscite would be "superfluous" because "the whole people of West Irian are in favor of the Indonesian Republic."[77]

The matter came up for discussion in the Australian parliament in March 1965. In reply to a question, the Minister for External Affairs, Paul Hasluck, stated:[78]

The obligation for an act of self-determination in West Irian might perhaps be paraphrased as an obligation to carry out an act of ascertainment. I think "self-determination" does not mean the holding of some sort of plebiscite or direct consultation with the people in that manner. I am doubtful whether the documents would justify that view. There certainly has to be an act of ascertainment — some sort

[75]A/5501, p. 40. During 1964, José Rolz-Bennett visited Jakarta for informal talks with the Indonesian government on holding the "act of free choice" in 1969. See *GAOR,* Twenty-fourth Session (1969), Annexes, A/7723, *Report of the Secretary-General regarding the act of self-determination in West Irian* (hereafter cited as A/7723), Annex II, "Report of the Indonesian Government to the Secretary-General concerning the conduct and results of the act of free choice in West Irian, pursuant to article XXI of the New York Agreement of 1962" (hereafter cited as A/7723, Annex II), p. 22.

[76]Van der Kroef, "Australia and the West Irian Problem," *loc. cit.,* p. 490. ". . . the Djakarta English-language daily, *Indonesian Herald,* which at that time closely reflected the views of the Foreign Affairs Ministry, declared that among the 'great number of advantages' derived from this move was the fact that Indonesia was now 'freed from all commitments made under the auspices of the United Nations. Holding of a plebiscite in West Irian in 1969 is one of them.'" Van der Kroef, "West New Guinea: The Uncertain Future," *loc. cit.,* p. 703. (Quotations in original.)

It is interesting to note that in its 1969 report to the Secretary-General on the act of free choice, even the Suharto government maintained that when Indonesia "withdrew its active participation in the United Nations" after 1964, "future implementation" of the act of free choice "became an unworkable proposition." Presumably it became feasible again, from Jakarta's point of view, after Indonesia resumed its membership in the United Nations. See A/7723, Annex II, p. 22.

[77]*The New York Times,* May 25, 1965.

[78]Commonwealth of Australia, *Parliamentary Debates, House of Representatives,* March 25, 1965.

of attempt to consult the people — but the documents are not perhaps as strong on the means of self-determination as originally we would have liked them to be.

Hasluck was doubtless right as to the facts. The clauses of the Dutch-Indonesian agreement dealing with self-determination nowhere employ the word "plebiscite," but rather use such terms as "self-determination," "act of free choice," "freedom of choice," and "ascertaining the freely expressed will of the population." Hasluck's statement also suggested that Australia accepted the realities of the 1962 settlement, and would probably not stand on too much ceremony as to the procedures ultimately employed to ascertain the views of the Papuan population.

It should be pointed out that at no time, either before or after the fall of Sukarno, did the Jakarta government go so far as formally to repudiate the 1962 settlement or any specific provisions thereof. After General Suharto's accession to power and Indonesia's return to the United Nations, the statements of the new regime relating to the requirements of the agreement on self-determination for the Papuans reflected a significant change of attitude. While in New York in September 1966 to negotiate Indonesia's return to the United Nations, Adam Malik, the new Foreign Minister, indicated that his government "would probably be prepared to honour" the agreement and "implement the act of free choice in 1969;"[79] although he also reported that on a recent visit to West New Guinea, he had been presented with a petition asserting that the Papuan people "wanted to remain in Indonesia." [80] In December, the Indonesian Minister for Home Affairs, Lieutenant-General Basuki Rahmat, caused a brief furor when he remarked that a plebiscite would not be held because the Papuans did not want one.[81] The Netherlands government demanded an "immediate explanation" of Rahmat's statement.[82] Several days later, Malik again affirmed that Indonesia would live up to its obligations: [83]

This is not just a local agreement with which we can do as we wish. We shall carry out the wish of the West Irian people, and if they want a plebiscite we shall hold a plebiscite.

Early in February 1967, the Indonesian Minister of Information, B. M. Diah, again asserted that his government would hold a plebiscite in West

[79]A/7723, Annex II, p. 22.

[80]*The New York Times,* October 1, 1966.

[81]See *ibid.,* December 8, 1966; and van der Kroef, "West New Guinea: The Uncertain Future," *loc. cit.,* p. 704.

[82]Quoted in van der Kroef, "West New Guinea: The Uncertain Future," *loc. cit.,* p. 704.

[83]Quoted in *ibid.*

New Guinea.[84] Two months later, Jakarta's Ambassador to Australia, Major-General Kosasih, declared that Indonesia would "fulfil every agreement made with other countries and the United Nations" relating to West New Guinea; but he also pointed out that the word "plebiscite" did not appear in the agreement, and that Indonesia's obligation was to "ascertain the real feelings of the people of West Irian." [85] Addressing the Indonesian parliament in August, General Suharto referred to Indonesia's "obligation" to afford a "free choice" to the Papuans in 1969. He then added this revealing observation: [86]

> But we ought to help the people in that region in their effort to realize their resolve, affirmed many times in their statements, to remain part of the Indonesian nation and territory, inseparable from the territory of the unitary Republic of Indonesia.

And in a speech to the cabinet a month later, Suharto coupled an assurance that the Papuans would be consulted as to their political future with the estimate that "the people of West Irian will choose to remain within the Republic of Indonesia." [87]

It was apparent from such statements that the obligations imposed by the 1962 agreement as they related to self-determination for the Papuans never ceased to trouble the Indonesians. The reasons for this have already been discussed briefly. It was well nigh impossible for Jakarta to contemplate any form of self-determination process that might possibly result in a Papuan decision to sever ties with Indonesia. Moreover, on a practical level, the Indonesians were fully aware that, whatever their inclinations, talk of a "plebiscite" flew in the face of Papuan realities. The art was to devise some form of consultation that would satisfy the contractual obligation, but whose outcome would never be in doubt. Fortunately for the Indonesians, international opinion — in particular, the Dutch and the Australians — was now prepared to accept the prefigured outcome provided only that sufficient attention were given to the appearance of the formalities. When Malik visited The Hague at the end of October 1967, the usual joint communique stated somewhat vaguely that, in accordance with the 1962 agreement, "arrangements will be made for the people of West Irian to express their wish in 1969 to choose whether or not they

[84]See *ibid.*
[85]Quoted in *ibid.*, p. 705.
[86]Quoted in *ibid.*
[87]Quoted in *ibid.*, p. 706.

will remain part of the Republic of Indonesia." [88] Dutch press reaction to this communique was reported as "generally favorable." [89]

"Self-Determination" for the Papuans

Following a cabinet meeting on April 27, 1967, Foreign Minister Malik announced that Indonesia "would honour its obligations" and "implement the act of free choice for the people in West Irian in 1969." As to the method for doing so, this would have to be arranged "with the assistance of the United Nations Secretary-General." [90] Three months later, José Rolz-Bennett visited Jakarta at the invitation of the Indonesian government to discuss the modalities of implementation. In a memorandum of understanding dated August 1, Indonesia explicitly "reaffirm(ed) its commitment" with respect to the "act of free choice," and further gave its consent to the assignment of United Nations representatives to West New Guinea as provided for in the Dutch-Indonesian agreement.[91]

On April 1, 1968, with the agreement of the Indonesian government, Secretary-General Thant appointed Fernando Ortiz Sanz of Bolivia as his Representative to participate in arrangements for the "act of free choice." After preliminary consultations in New York, Ortiz proceeded to Jakarta in August, and thence to Jayapura (as the capital of West New Guinea was now called) later that month. The Dutch-Indonesian settlement of 1962 had provided that, after the transfer of authority to Indonesia, "a number" of United Nations experts were to remain in the territory to advise and assist in preparations for carrying out the process of self-determination.[92] This provision was never implemented, apparently because of

[88]Quoted in *ibid.*
[89]*Ibid.*
[90]A/7723, Annex II, p. 22.
[91]*Ibid.*, p. 23. Indonesia also agreed to the inclusion of a brief statement on the subject in the Secretary-General's forthcoming annual report. As it subsequently appeared, this statement said: "I am glad to report that the Indonesian Government has assured me that it will fully comply with the remaining responsibilities deriving from the Agreement signed on 15 August 1962 between the Republic of Indonesia and the Kingdom of the Netherlands. The act of self-determination in West Irian will take place in 1969, at a date to be decided upon in due course, and, as called for in the Agreement, one year before the date of the consultation I shall appoint a United Nations representative 'to advise, assist and participate in arrangements which are the responsibility of Indonesia for the act of free choice.'" *GAOR*, Twenty-second Session (1967), Supplement No. 1A, A/6701/Add. 1, *Introduction to the Annual Report of the Secretary-General on the Work of the Organization, 16 June 1966 - 15 June 1967*, p. 1.
[92]See Article XVI.

the noncooperation of the Indonesian government.[93] As Ortiz states in the official report of his mission: [94]

> . . . I therefore had to begin with the collection of basic information about the territory and its population, trying to fulfil in a few months, with a limited staff not well acquainted with the territory, the important and complex functions which under article XVI of the Agreement should have been carried out during the preceding five years by a number of experts.

His authority was even more limited. According to Article XVII of the 1962 agreement, the role of the United Nations Representative was "to advise, assist and participate in arrangements *which are the responsibility of Indonesia* for the act of free choice." [95] Since responsibility for the actual arrangements was so clearly stated to vest in Indonesia, this was interpreted by Ortiz to mean that "the views, counsel, recommendations and suggestions offered in fulfilment of the Secretary-General's responsibilities were not of a binding character" on the Jakarta government.[96] In short, the United Nations Representative could advise, exhort, criticize, and cajole, and even bring to bear the pressure of unfavorable publicity. But in the last analysis, he could not control what happened.

To most observers, moreover, it was apparent that the Indonesian government did not intend to permit much freedom to the Papuans in implementing the "act of free choice." The many public assurances of the Suharto regime had to be balanced against the obduracy of Indonesia's position over the past two decades on the whole question of West New Guinea's political future. In its report submitted to the United Nations

[93]In his *Report,* Thant offers the foillowing explanation: "On 14 May and 2 July 1963, communications were addressed on my behalf to the Government of Indonesia informing it of the names of the persons I had designated as the 'United Nations experts' called for in article XVI of the Agreement. On several occasions, I approached the Government which was in power in Indonesia at that time for the purpose of implementing the provisions of article XVI but failed to obtain a favourable reply. On 7 January 1965, as is well known, Indonesia withdrew its co-operation with the United Nations and it thereafter became impossible to send the United Nations experts to West New Guinea (West Irian)." A/7723, pp. 2-3. (As previously noted, Sukarno announced Indonesia's withdrawal from the United Nations on December 31, 1964.)

[94]*GAOR,* Twenty-fourth Session (1969), Annexes, A/7723, *Report of the Secretary-General regarding the act of self-determination in West Irian,* Annex I, "Report by the Representative of the Secretary-General in West Irian, submitted under Article XXI, paragraph 1, of the Agreement between the Republic of Indonesia and the Kingdom of the Netherlands concerning West New Guinea (West Irian)" (hereafter cited as A/7723, Annex I), p. 4.

[95]Emphasis added.

[96]A/7723, Annex I, p. 4.

after completion of the "act of free choice" in 1969, Jakarta still felt it necessary to point out that it had always "strongly contested" the proposition that the Papuan population should be given the right of self-determination. "Such an act would defy the proclamation of and struggle for independence of Indonesia, which already constituted the exercise of the right of self-determination of all the Indonesian people vis-a-vis the former Netherlands colonial rule in Indonesia." [97] Jakarta had ultimately accepted the relevant provisions of the 1962 settlement only because they "did not appear to be harmful to the national causes since the Government was confident of the satisfactory result of the 'act of free choice' that was to be made after six years," and because "it was the Indonesian Government which would conduct the act of free choice and not the United Nations."[98]

In short, the "act of free choice" was regarded by the Indonesians, not as an obligation to allow the Papuans freely to determine their political future, but rather as a formal procedure that had to be gotten through in order to satisfy the requirements of the 1962 agreement, and which the Indonesians had been willing to accept only because they would have complete control over how it was implemented. The outcome would never be in doubt. President Suharto publicly set the tone for the "act of free choice" when he bluntly stated in February 1969 that a decision by the Papuans to sever their ties with Indonesia would be regarded as "treason." [99] To be sure, the Indonesians did devise a fairly detailed procedure for implementing the "act of free choice," and carried it out with some éclat over a period of several months. But as press reports indicated at the time, even members of the Indonesian government "frankly admit that the entire process is a meaningless formality." [100] As one member of the Indonesian parliament put it, "We are going through the motions of the act of free choice because of our obligations under the New York agreement of 1962. But West Irian is Indonesian and must remain Indonesian. We cannot accept any alternative." [101]

The procedure worked out by Jakarta called, first, for consultations with the representative councils of the eight *kabupaten* or regencies into which the province of West Irian was divided concerning the method to be employed, as required by Article XVII, paragraph (a) of the 1962 agreement. Next, a consultative assembly would be specially constituted in each regency, with one member for every 750 inhabitants, but with a

[97]A/7723, Annex II, p. 21.
[98]*Ibid.*, p. 22.
[99]Quoted in van der Kroef, "Australia and the West Irian Problem," *loc. cit.*, p. 485.
[100]*The New York Times*, July 7, 1969.
[101]Quoted in *ibid*.

minimum membership of 75 and a maximum of 175. The consultative assemblies would have three categories of members: (1) representatives elected from each district of the regency; (2) representatives of organizational and functional groups (political, social, cultural, religious) chosen by their respective groups; and (3) tribal representatives selected by the representative councils in consultation with the tribal peoples concerned. A committee of each representative council "was to organize elections, confirm and install representatives of the people who had been elected members of the consultative assembly, and determine in the best possible way, taking into consideration the conditions and social structure of the community and the inhabitants of the Regency, the number or allocation of each group in the membership of the assembly." [102]

Finally, each of the consultative assemblies thus constituted would be consulted in succession to implement the "act of free choice." The assemblies "would not reach a decision through voting but through *musjawarah*," the traditional Indonesian method of reaching a decision through discussion, understanding, and consensus.[103] The results of these successive consultations would constitute the results of the "act of free choice" for West Irian as a whole.

It is apparent from his final report that this plan did not sit well with Ortiz Sanz, the United Nations Representative. In November, he had informed the Indonesian government that: [104]

. . . in my capacity as United Nations Representative, I could suggest no other method for this delicate political exercise than the democratic, orthodox and universally accepted method of "one man, one vote." However, while maintaining firmly my conviction that the people of West Irian might be given as ample and as complete an opportunity as possible to express their opinion, I recognized that the geographical and human realities in the territory required the application of a realistic criterion. I therefore suggested that the system of "one man, one vote" should be used in the urban areas, where the communications and transportation, the comparatively advanced cultural level of the population and the availability of adequate administrative facilities made it possible, and that this might be complemented by collective consultations in the less acces-

[102]A/7723, Annex 1, p. 12. Deputies of the representative councils who already represented districts or groups referred to in categories (1) and (2) would automatically become members of the consultative assemblies.

[103]*Ibid.*, p. 10. An earlier Indonesian plan for implementing the "act of free choice" had called for a single, province-wide assembly, rather than the eight regency assemblies ultimately decided on.

[104]*Ibid.*, p. 9.

sible and less advanced areas of the interior. A mixed system of that type would have the merit of being the best possible in the circumstances and would enable the Indonesian Government and the United Nations to state that the orthodox and perfect method of "one man, one vote" had been used in the act of free choice to the maximum extent compatible with reality.

But the Indonesians would have none of it. Early in January 1969, during conversations in Jakarta, Ortiz was told that "the suggested mixed system for the act of free choice seemed to be a complex one, not suitable to the existing conditions and the situation in West Irian." [105] A month later, he was officially informed of the procedure that had been decided upon: consecutive consultations with eight specially constituted consultative assemblies, and employing the *musjawarah* process for reaching a decision in each of them. And although he continued to press for his "mixed system," Ortiz had no alternative but to accept Indonesia's choice of method. He explained his position as follows: [106]

> I have no authority to object to, even less to reject, the decision of the Government. By the same token, I have no authority to express agreement with or to co-sponsor the Government's decision. In other words, I will continue to give advice and assistance to the Government. I will participate in the act of free choice, but not in the responsibility of the Government.

The Indonesians went to considerable effort to gain acceptance for the proposed procedure at United Nations headquarters. Sudjarwo Tjondronegoro, then Special Assistant to the Foreign Minister, had visited the United Nations in June 1968, where he had obtained an "understanding" reiterating that arrangements for the "act of free choice" were the "sole responsibility" of the Jakarta government.[107] In January 1969, he was aagin in New York to meet with the Secretary-General. Thant was reported to consider that "the *demokrasi musjawarah* system, upon such a broad and vast forum, and based on elected representatives of the people, (was) not unreasonable in the light of existing conditions." [108] Sudjarwo also obtained an agreement that, "since the question related to an agreement exclusively between Indonesia and the Netherlands, the Secretary-General's later report on the issue (the result of the act of free choice)

[105]A/7723, Annex II, p. 26. Ortiz might have replied that on their half of the island, the Australians had successfully conducted elections on the basis of "one man, one vote."

[106]A/7723, Annex I, p. 10.

[107]A/7723, Annex II, p. 23.

[108]*Ibid.*, p. 26.

would not be subject to the approval or disapproval of the General Assembly." [109]

Sudjarwo visited The Hague in May and June 1968, and twice again in January 1969, where it was reported that the *demokrasi musjawarah* system for the "act of free choice" was "considered reasonable in the light of the prevailing human and socio-cultural conditions in West Irian." [110] To be sure, J. M. A. H. Luns, the Dutch Foreign Minister, was subsequently quoted as observing that the procedure "seemed a very one-sided voting exercise;" [111] and he took the initiative to discuss "the course of events" in West New Guinea with his Indonesian opposite number, Adam Malik, in Rome in May.[112] But The Hague government had long since reconciled itself to the loss of the territory, and had no intention of allowing the procedures of the "act of free choice" to jeopardize the rapprochement carefully built up with Indonesia over the past several years. Australia, too, had successfully cultivated friendlier relations with Indonesia for some time. Whatever its earlier convictions about the alleged right of the Papuans to self-determination, by 1969 Canberra was no longer prepared to pursue the point. In February, the new Minister for External Affairs, Gordon Freeth, spoke understandingly of the proposed *musjawarah* procedure for the "act of free choice," especially in view of the "primitive, Stone Age conditions" in which many of the indigenous people lived.[113] And when a group of Papuan members of the East New Guinea House of Assembly publicly criticized the procedure, the Department of External Territories issued a statement to the effect that East New Guinea's "international relations" were the responsibility of the Canberra government and not of the territorial administration or legislative assembly.[114]

It was perhaps ironic that 1969, the year of the "act of free choice," was marked by widespread unrest in many parts of West New Guinea. In his final report, the United Nations Representative commented at length, if somewhat guardedly, on various aspects of this situation. He noted that he had received a substantial number of petitions during his mission calling for the severance of West New Guinea's ties with Indonesia. The petitioners "often expressed criticism of the Indonesian administration;

[109]*Ibid.* (Parentheses in original.)

[110]*Ibid.*

[111]Quoted in van der Kroef, "Australia and the West Irian Problem," *loc. cit.,* p. 485.

[112]A/7723, Annex II, p. 30.

[113]Quoted in van der Kroef, "Australia and the West Irian Problem," *loc. cit.,* p. 484.

[114]See *ibid.,* p. 497.

complained against acts of repression by the Indonesian armed forces; denounced the lack of guarantees for basic rights and freedoms, including the freedom to organize opposition political parties; (and) requested the release of political prisoners." [115] Ortiz proposed to the Indonesian government in April that it promulgate a general amnesty in order to improve the atmosphere for the "act of free choice." While no such decree was ever issued, some 346 political detainees were in fact released.[116]

Ortiz also reported on outbreaks of violence in the Manokwari Regency, in the towns of Enarotali and Waghete, and along the eastern border with the territories of Papua and New Guinea administered by Australia.[117] The latter incidents resulted from border crossings into East New Guinea that "seem(ed) to show a certain degree of political dissatisfaction on the part of some of the inhabitants." [118] But the United Nations Representative was powerless to intervene in any effective way to ameliorate the causes of the violence.

One has the impression that Ortiz realized the ineffectiveness of his efforts to assure a satisfactory climate for the "act of free choice." Thus he states that he repeatedly advised the Government to create the best possible democratic conditions in the territory prior to, and at the time of, the "act of free choice;" but on his own estimate, his efforts yielded a "fairly negative result." [119] Nevertheless, the United Nations Representative persisted in offering advice whenever he felt it necessary, and (with his staff) in "participating" in the "act of free choice" from start to finish.

The initial consultations with the representative councils of the eight regencies took place between March 22 and April 12, and teams of United Nations observers were present at all the sessions. But Ortiz and his colleagues had no effective part in preparations for the election of members to the special consultative assemblies, which task was the responsibility of committees of the existing representative councils; and the United Nations presence at the actual elections was spotty. By the time the schedules for them were received on May 30, elections had already been completed in two regencies, and partially completed elsewhere. At the insistence of the United Nations representatives, fresh elections were held in a few places; but altogether, United Nations observers attended the election of only 195 members of the consultative assemblies (out of 1026).[120] Indonesia's final report on the "act of free choice" states that

[115]A/7723, Annex I, p. 14.
[116]See ibid., p. 16.
[117]See ibid., pp. 14-16.
[118]Ibid., p. 16.
[119]Ibid.
[120]See ibid., pp. 13-14.

"not only the *musjawarah* system but also the voting procedure was con-
currently applied especially in areas where more candidates had been put
up than the allotted number of seats required." [121] But according to an
American reporter on the scene, most of the members of the consultative
assemblies were "handpicked" by the Indonesian government.[122]

The formal "act of free choice" by the eight consultative assemblies
began at Merauke on July 14, and ended at Jayapura, the capital, on
August 2. The sessions, each of which lasted for about half a day,
followed a similar format. Each was addressed by members of an Indonesian government team headed by the Minister for Home Affairs, and
by the United Nations Representative, following which members of the
assembly took the floor to express their views. At the end of the discussion, the chairman of the assembly summarized the decision reached; and
the members thereupon either rose to signify their assent to the decision
as stated, or so signified by acclamation. José Ortiz Sanz, the United
Nations Representative, was present at all the sessions. Adam Malik, the
Indonesian Foreign Minister, attended three of them; and from the diplomatic corps, the Australian Ambassador attended five, the Netherlands
and Thai ambassadors three each, the Burmese and West German ambassadors two each, and the New Zealand Ambassador one. Representatives of the Indonesian and foreign press were present throughout.[123]

Without exception, all members who addressed their respective consultative assemblies spoke in favor of West New Guinea retaining its ties
with Indonesia; and the decision of each of the eight assemblies on this
point was declared to be unanimous. Following the Jayapura assembly on
August 2, Malik sent a telegram to the United Nations Secretary-General
informing him that the "people of West Irian through their elected representatives have . . . clearly and unequivocally expressed their unanimous
decision to remain within the Republic of Indonesia." [124]

How are we to judge this performance? One may certainly query the
validity of Malik's claim that the "people" of West New Guinea had expressed a "unanimous decision" to remain within the Indonesian state. As
the United Nations Representative points out in his final report: [125]

> The petitions opposing annexation to Indonesia, the cases of unrest
> in Manokwari, Enarotali and Waghete, the flight of a number of
> people to the part of the island that is administered by Australia, and

[121]A/7723, Annex II, pp. 29-30.

[122]*Washington Post,* July 15, 1969.

[123]On the meetings of the eight consultative assemblies, see A/7723, Annex I,
pp. 17-21; and A/7723, Annex II, pp. 31-37.

[124]Quoted in A/7723, Annex I, p. 19.

[125]*Ibid.,* p. 20.

the existence of political detainees, more than 300 of whom were released at my request, show that without doubt certain elements of the population of West Irian held firm convictions in favour of independence.

On the other hand, it does not necessarily follow from these manifestations that a majority of the autochthonous population — or of that proportion of the population who had some understanding of what the "act of free choice" was all about — would have opted for an alternative course in less structured circumstances. Most observers agree that there has always been some measure of support for the Indonesian connexion among the Papuans, although certainly not so much as the "unanimous decision" of the consultative assemblies would suggest. The real problem in appraising the outcome of the "act of free choice" is to form an estimate of the relative strength of these two trends; and on the basis of th available evidence, there is really no way to do so.

Perhaps the most we can say is that the Papuans were not really given a free choice. As Ortiz pointedly remarks in his report, "the (Indonesian) Administration exercised at all times a tight political control over the population." [126] The "act of free choice" was obviously stagemanaged from start to finish; and in such circumstances, the outcome was entirely predictable. To be sure, the conclusion of the United Nations representative was more positive, although hardly free from ambiguity: [127]

. . . it can be stated that, with the limitations imposed by the geographical characteristics of the territory and the general political situation in the area, an act of free choice has taken place in West Irian in accordance with Indonesian practice, in which the representatives of the population have expressed their wish to remain with Indonesia.

On November 19, 1969, the General Assembly of the United Nations adopted a resolution (sponsored by Belgium, Indonesia, Luxemburg, Malaysia, the Netherlands, and Thailand) taking note of the Secretary-General's report on the "act of free choice," and acknowledging fulfilment of the tasks entrusted to him under the terms of the Dutch-Indonesian agreement of 1962.[128] The vote was 84 to none, with 30 abstentions. The large number of abstentions apparently reflected widespread disquiet as the validity of the "act of free choice." During the discussions, which extended over three plenary sessions, several delegations expressed reser-

[126]Ibid.
[127]Ibid.
[128]For the text, see GAOR, Twenty-fourth Session (1969), Annexes, A/L. 574.

vations regarding the procedures used, and questioned whether the people of West New Guinea had been allowed to exercise the right of self-determination within the meaning of the 1962 agreement. A Ghanaian amendment proposed that the Papuans "should be given a further opportunity, by the end of 1975, to carry out the act of free choice envisaged in the Agreement." [129] But it was clear that the majority wished to put the West New Guinea dispute finally to rest; and the amendment failed by 60 votes to 15, with 24 abstentions. The Foreign Minister of the Netherlands, who also expressed doubts about both the procedures and the circumstances of the "act of free choice," perhaps summed up the prevailing sentiment when he said that "it would serve no useful purpose to comment further on the manner in which the act of free choice had taken place or on the outcome." His government now "looked to the future." [130]

[129]For the text, see *GAOR*, Twenty-fourth Session (1969), Annexes, A/L. 576.
[130]*GAOR*, Twenty-fifth Session (1970), Supplement No. 1, A/8001, *Annual Report of the Secretary-General on the Work of the Organization, 16 June 1969 - 15 June 1970*, p. 64.

Chapter Fifteen

Conclusions

It was suggested at the beginning of this investigation that the West New Guinea episode throws significant light on four problems of general interest for the study of contemporary international relations. These concern: (1) the conditions of effective third-party intervention in serious international crises, especially those occurring in the socalled Third World; (2) the prospect for successful great power collaboration in United Nations peacekeeping activities in Third World crises; (3) the usefulness of the United Nations as an instrumentality for promoting United States objectives in certain circumstances; and (4) the relevance of the West New Guinea case for our understanding of the principle of self-determination. This chapter sets forth some tentative conclusions on these four subjects.

The Great Powers as Third-Party Intermediaries

Whatever may be the theoretical obstacles to useful great power intervention as third-party intermediaries in serious international crises involving Third World countries, the historical record seems to show that the United States did play this role with great effectiveness in the later stages of the West New Guinea dispute. Nor would the circumstances appear to be so unusual as to render this episode *sui generis*. What were the factors that enabled the United States to perform so well in the West New Guinea case, despite the undoubted disabilities inherent in its status as one of the world's superpowers?

In the first place, United States objectives were congruent with the orderly functioning of the international system. It is clear that a major purpose of the American intervention was to bring about a settlement basically favorable to Indonesia, in the hope that this would influence the course of that country's internal and international development in ways considered beneficial to the American interest. But the specific outcome envisaged was also consistent with a persuasive interpretation of the more general interest of the international community in the negotiated termination of a dangerous crisis and the peaceful resolution of a protracted and difficult dispute. In short, it could be reasonably argued that the outcome sought by United States policy would serve to safeguard international peace and security. It is perhaps true that the Soviet Union might have preferred to prolong the crisis, and even to provoke large-scale hostilities between Indonesia and the Netherlands, in the hope of reaping significant political advantages therefrom. But the generality of the international community could not possibly have preferred this outcome. For most interested governments — if we are to accept their statements and votes in the General Assembly as reflecting considered policy — the solution espoused by the United States must have appeared, *de minimis,* as a means of preserving the peace and as acceptable in the circumstances; and for many of them, especially among the Third World countries, as essentially fair and reasonable (even if long overdue).

Thus the American solution had the preeminent virtue of acceptability — not because it served United States interests (which the Washington government certainly believed it did), but because it was widely judged as serving the interest of the international community. No doubt there were misgivings in some capitals. But this was a serious problem in only one of them — The Hague; and here the United States was both willing and able to exercise a decisive influence. The nature of this special influence — a second major factor accounting for the success of the American intervention — has already been alluded to. In circumstances where Dutch resolve to "carry on" in West New Guinea was already gravely undermined, Washington made clear to The Hague that its mediation in 1961-62 was the last, best hope of settling the dispute peacefully; that if the effort failed because of Dutch "intransigence" (that is, an unwillingness to accept the essence of the Bunker proposals), the United States would wash its hands of the affair; that thereafter the Netherlands would stand alone for having rejected a solution almost universally accepted as "fair;" and finally, that if large-scale hostilities were to result, the Dutch could not only not count on United States assistance (despite the ties of ancient friendship and the N.A.T.O. alliance), but would have to face positive American (and other allied, especially British) obstruction in their prosecution of the war. This was pressure the Dutch could not stand up to in the circumstances. They had no real choice but to capitulate and settle for whatever facesaving formulae were available.

From this perspective, the success of the American intervention may thus be accounted for by the formulation of a solution acceptable both to the international community and ultimately to the protagonists as well; and by the availability of means to impose the outcome on the one protagonist otherwise reluctant to accept it. In addition, it would appear

that even a superpower such as the United States might in certain circumstances have greater "resources and capabilities" for the role of intermediary in Third World crises than Young seems to believe. Thus, for
example, impartiality — in the sense of favoring neither side and being
indifferent to the gains and losses of each side, and in the sense also of
being recognized by both protagonists as such — seemed less important in
the West New Guinea case than a judicious combination of partiality for
a pro-Indonesian outcome and an ability to force the Netherlands to
accept it. As for "independence" of substantial attachment to either side,
the fact was that Washington had the strongest possible ties with The
Hague, while relations with Jakarta were already chilly and getting worse
all the time. Perhaps the point here is that superpowers can and do
compartmentalize their relationships with smaller powers more frequently
and more effectively than Young would admit. The West New Guinea
dispute and its settlement in no way diminished the American attachment
for the Netherlands or for Europe. It was simply that the United States
did not allow this relationship to control policy in Southeast Asia; and
the balance of forces was such that the Netherlands had no real choice
but to go along. Again, with respect to the salience of a major aligned
power as a potential mediator in Third World crises, Young would appear
to be in error when he concludes that the protagonists in such crises
"simply (do) not turn to a member of either major bloc for help of (this)
kind." In the West New Guinea crisis of 1961-62, both sides responded
with alacrity to the intervention of the United States — whatever their
respective motives; and Washington had no difficulty in commanding
their respectful attention to its initiatives thereafter until a settlement was
reached.

We may conclude that the possibilities for effective great power intervention in Third World disputes — not "for purposes of self-interested
manipulation" but rather "to facilitate the realization of common interests
and to promote the control of crises" — may be somewhat broader than
Young believes. The circumstances of the West New Guinea case were
doubtless unique, in the sense that the environing conditions of every
historical event are always unique; and we should not, therefore, attempt
to draw too many specific lessons from it. But the episode does suggest
that the possible circumstances of future Third World crises — for example, the traditional salience of a particular great power to one or
another of the protagonists, implying thereby its potential utility as a third-
party intermediary, or the special power relationships involved in the case
— may permit great power intervention to assist in controlling dangerous
conflict situations.

The Great Powers and United Nations Peacekeeping

The Hammarskjold approach to United Nations peacekeeping envisaged a specially useful role for the world organization in relation to conflicts arising outside the main spheres of great power rivalry, and primarily in the Third World. Here the United Nations could practice a "preventive diplomacy" aimed at isolating conflicts from Cold War politics and at facilitating solutions unaffected by great power interests. The main objective to be sought in specific cases would be an outcome that preserved at least minimal stability in the international system while at the same time supporting the processes of peaceful change.

Central to this concept was the assumption that the great powers would in fact "acquiesce in a decidedly secondary role in making policy for any given peacekeeping operation" and "forego at least some opportunities to manipulate specific conflicts for cold-war purposes." [1] The Hammarskjold approach also presumed a much greater initiative on the part of the Secretary-General to move to "fill vacuums" even without specific authority from the Security Council or General Assembly, and to accept broad operational responsibilities if necessary.

From one perspective, the role of the United Nations and its Acting Secretary-General in the settlement of the West New Guinea dispute was an important demonstration of peacekeeping in the Hammarskjold mold. Here was a Third World crisis which, if it had been allowed to deteriorate into large-scale hostilities between Indonesia and the Netherlands, might easily have been transformed into a dangerous Cold War confrontation. Despite the tentative nature of his commission as Acting Secretary-General, in this instance U Thant moved energetically to bring about a resumption of negotiations between the protagonists, and lent the prestige of his office to support the long and intricate diplomatic process that followed. Moreover, the eventual settlement of the dispute was made possible by his readiness to assume — without the prior authorization of the policymaking organs of the United Nations — extensive administrative responsibilities in facilitating the transfer of the disputed territory from Dutch to Indonesian control, and by his resourcefulness in implementing almost overnight the instrumentalities necessary for discharging these functions.

The point to emphasize here, however, is that Thant's undoubted success in the West New Guinea case was in large measure due, not so much to his skill in fending off great power involvement in the dispute, nor yet to the self-abnegation of the latter, but rather to Thant's association of

[1]Oran R. Young, *Trends in International Peacekeeping* (Princeton: Center of International Studies, 1966), p. 6.

the United Nations peacekeeping effort with the parallel initiative of the United States. For this was a case in which the most powerful of the superpowers did not stand aside, but rather took the lead both in bringing the protagonists together and in working with the United Nations in negotiating a peaceful settlement. However much this may have been contrary to the assumptions of the Hammarksjold concept as previously understood, Thant grasped the potential for United Nations cooperation with the United States in this case. To put it briefly, such collaboration was made possible by the convergence of United States objectives in the dispute with the general purposes of United Nations peacekeeping according to the Hammarskjold concept: that is, peaceful settlement and peaceful change. However much such an outcome might suit the national interest of the United States as then conceived, it also served the general interest of the international community. As for the Soviet Union, it had no real choice but to stand aside from the whole performance. Its only point of ingress would have been in concert with Indonesia. But the Jakarta government chose to play its hand alone, and to settle for a diplomatic triumph rather than risk the uncertainties of an attempt at military conquest.

From Thant's point of view, moreover, there was a special advantage to this collaboration which more than compensated the undoubted disabilities of great power involvement. In the settlement envisaged by the Bunker proposals, it was not hard to anticipate where the major obstacles would arise. The Indonesians were certainly difficult to deal with on the West New Guinea issue, and it was complicated enough to persuade them to accept anything short of the whole loaf — suitably encrusted with icing. But defeat and humiliation were the lot of the Dutch. To be sure, by 1962 the Netherlands was ready — even eager — to relinquish its thankless responsibilities in West New Guinea. But to a proud and sensitive nation, this was hard to do in the historical circumstances, and especially before the threat of *force majeure* at the hands of a former colonial ward. This is why the modalities of transfer were so important.

There was a limit, however, to what even the most elaborate formulae could conceal; all the provisions for interim international administration, and all the presumed safeguards for Papuan self-determination, could not disguise the extent of the Dutch capitulation. Would they have accepted such a defeat if proffered at the hands of the United Nations alone? We shall never know. For Thant's position was immeasurably strengthened by the United States, which brought heavy pressure to bear on the Dutch to accept the Bunker solution. In Young's terms, Washington provided the Acting Secretary-General with the "constituency" he otherwise lacked "to lend force to his attempts" to bring about a peaceful outcome.

Fruitful collaboration between the Acting Secretary-General and the United States in the settlement of the West New Guinea dispute did not necessarily imply a comparable great power role in other Third World crises. But it was suggestive in this respect. The key variables would appear to be the degree of congruence between great power objectives and those of the international community as expressed through the peacekeeping activities of the Secretary-General; the leverage of such a great power for exerting pressure on one or another of the protagonists, and its willingness to do so (for whatever reason); and the possibility of isolating from the arena of conflict any great power whose interest might be to manipulate the crisis for other purposes. These conditions are not so wholly unusual as to preclude the prospect of future great power collaboration with the United Nations Secretary-General in the resolution of Third World crises.

The United Nations as an Instrument of United States Policy

Little need be added to previous discussion on this point. We are not concerned here with *whether* or *to what extent* the United States should attempt to use the United Nations as an instrument of policy — an important and complex question that is outside the scope of this inquiry, but rather with *why* Washington did so in the West New Guinea case. From the American point of view, of course, the United Nations alternative was feasible because it could be safely assumed that an intervention by the Acting Secretary-General would tend to the same kind of settlement that United States policy had come to favor. This point has already been sufficiently emphasized. But since this was so, there were several positive advantages to working through the United Nations. These may now be recapitulated briefly.

In the first place, referring once more to Young's listing of the necessary resources and capabilities of the third-party intermediary, the United Nations appeared to possess most abundantly precisely those attributes that the United States, as a major aligned power, was presumably most deficient in, namely, impartiality and independence as between the parties in dealing with such crises. By the time of his death in 1961, Hammarskjold had earned a substantial reputation for the success of his "preventive diplomacy;" and this, in turn, had generated a considerable measure of international support for his peacekeeping activities, especially among the Third World countries. While his successor, U Thant, was still largely untried, he had obvious salience as a potential intervenor in the West New Guinea crisis because of the high office he occupied (even if then only in an acting capacity). To be sure, the Dutch must have felt uneasy over the undoubted tendency of the Hammarksjold approach to support the processes of peaceful change; but they cannot seriously have questioned the Acting Secretary-General's essential "neutrality in relation to interests," or the good faith of his initiative to settle the dispute.

The obstacles in the path of a unilateral American intervention were formidable. Relations with Indonesia, for example, were already tense, in part because of Washington's previous failure to support the Indonesian cause in West New Guinea, in part because of a succession of other unhappy incidents in the relationship between the two countries, and in part because of the increasing stridency of Jakarta's "anticolonial" polemics and policy. It would have been politically difficult for the Sukarno regime to accede to negotiations under the aegis of the United States. Even the diplomatic triumph that eventually emerged would have been tainted in Indonesian eyes if the laurels had to be shared with the greatest of the "imperialist" powers. Most of all, Indonesia's victory was not quite complete; the provisions for an interim international administration and the "act of free choice" were limiting factors. In view of the intensity of Indonesian sentiment in the West New Guinea dispute, we may question whether Jakarta could have made these concessions in a negotiation sponsored by the United States, while such compromises were politically feasible in a United Nations setting.

For the Dutch, too, the prestige of the Secretary-General's office offered a measure of balm and dignity to the acceptance of defeat, although The Hague was always acutely (and publicly) aware of the role of its great ally as *deus ex machina*. But the United States certainly had no wish to humiliate or aggrieve an ancient friend more than the absolute minimum necessary to persuade it to accept so painful a settlement; and Washington would have welcomed any palliative for the Dutch, and buffer for itself, in order to minimize the damage done. Moreover, while pressure from the United States was clearly the decisive factor on the Netherlands, the potential of the United Nations for generating political pressure in such circumstances should not be overlooked. After pointing out that the "heart of many contemporary disputes is the desire to alter the *status quo* in a way that existing law is traditionally unable to accommodate or resolve," Bloomfield states: [2]

> . . . the United Nations is incapable of legislating changes in the accepted sense of the word, and in any event it is incapable of enforcing such changes when it does recommend them . . . What the United Nations can do is bring into focus pressures for change that

[2]Bloomfield, *op. cit.,* p. 182.

a majority considers to be legitimate, and to apply a whole variety of measures to bring about such a change.

Unquestionably a majority of the members of the world organization did favor the transfer of West New Guinea to Indonesia. The intervention of the Acting Secretary-General, his sponsorship of a settlement looking to that result, and its subsequent endorsement by an overwhelming majority of the General Assembly, did effectively "bring into focus" the "pressures for change" that Bloomfield speaks of. Again, the United States obviously had no wish to use more "muscle" than absolutely necessary. A helping hand from the United Nations must have been most welcome.

Finally, the Bunker proposals envisaged a solution whose implementation required special means and instrumentalities that in realistic terms could only be provided by the United Nations. The United Nations Security Force, and especially the Temporary Executive Authority, were at the heart of the settlement; they were the modalities that made it possible for the Dutch to give in. It goes without saying that the United States had the technical capacity to perform these functions, and could easily have found the forces and administrative personnel for both tasks. It is just as obvious, however, that they would have been entirely unacceptable, both to the Indonesians and perhaps also to the Dutch. But such instrumentalities could also be improvised by the United Nations, which already had considerable experience in such operations even if the world organization had not previously undertaken responsibility for the direct administration of a major territory; and under the aegis of the United Nations, they were acceptable to both sides. The only alternative might have been a consortium of neutral powers; but this would have been cumbersome in the extreme, and probably unworkable in the end because of the inevitable suspicions of the protagonists. In short, the United Nations was not only ready at hand to provide the instrumentalities required; but its availability for these tasks must also have been decisive in formulating the substance of the compromise sponsored by the United States through Ambassador Bunker.

Evolving Concepts of Self-Determination

In the interminable debate over the future of West New Guinea, both protagonists regularly invoked the principle of self-determination in the presentation of their respective policies on the disputed territory. The Dutch claim was that the indigenous population possessed an inherent right of self-determination in accordance with the terms of the United Nations Charter; and it is true that Article I of the Charter does refer to the "principle of equal rights and self-determination of peoples." Con-

CONCLUSIONS 249

trariwise, the Indonesians insisted that the Papuans had already exercised that right, together with the rest of the Indonesian people, by their presumed participation in the Indonesian declaration of independence on August 17, 1945; and that there could be no question of a second choice or reconsideration of that act.

In fact, there was ample precedent in international usage for both sides of the argument. As Marshall (among others) has succinctly pointed out, the term "self-determination" has customarily been employed to convey two almost diametrically opposed principles; and most governments are "muddled in thought and discourse" on the whole subject.[3] Thus the Dutch really referred to the concept of the self-determination of peoples, that is, the presumed right of distinct ethnic groups of any size to decide their own political future. This is a notion that is "interventionist in tendency," since it justifies intrusion from the outside to assist a people struggling for independence from alien control. The Indonesians, on the other hand, relied on the idea of the self-determination of states, or the presumed right of an existing state to determine its political course without external interference and disruption; a notion that is "noninterventionist in tendency." [4] Since the polemics involved two such contrasting concepts, there was no possibility of agreement between the parties as to what particular "right of self-determination" the Papuans might be entitled to.

A comprehensive, but not very successful, effort to flesh out and give substance to the Charter principle of the "self-determination of peoples" may be found in the Declaration on the Granting of Independence to Colonial Countries and Peoples, adopted unanimously by the General Assembly in December 1960, with only the erstwhile colonial powers (including the Netherlands and the United States) abstaining. A careful reading of its text makes clear that the Declaration simply enshrines rather than attempting to resolve the contradictory concepts of self-determination referred to above. The relevant articles are as follows:

1. The subjection of peoples to alien subjugation, domination and exploitation constitutes a denial of fundamental human rights, is contrary to the Charter of the United Nations and is an impediment to the promotion of world peace and co-operation.

[3]Charles Burton Marshall, "Morality and National Intervention Wars," *Southeast Asian Perspectives,* no. 4 (December 1971), p. 35, fn. 2.
[4]*Ibid.* For standard treatments of the development of the principle of self-determination, see Rupert Emerson, *From Empire to Nation* (Cambridge: Harvard University Press, 1960), especially Part IV; and Alfred Cobban, *National Self-Determination* (London: Oxford University Press, 1945).

2. All peoples have the right to self-determination; by virtue of that right they freely determine their political status and freely pursue their economic, social and cultural development.
3. Inadequacy of political, economic, social or educational preparedness should never serve as a pretext for delaying independence.
4. All armed action or repressive measures of all kinds directed against dependent peoples shall cease in order to enable them to exercise peacefully and freely their right to complete independence, and the integrity of their national territory shall be respected.
5. Immediate steps shall be taken, in Trust and Non-Self-Governing Territories or all other territories which have not yet attained independence, to transfer all powers to the peoples of those territories, without any conditions or reservations, in accordance with their freely expressed will and desire, without any distinction as to race, creed or color, in order to enable them to enjoy complete independence and freedom.
6. Any attempt aimed at the partial or total disruption of the national unity and the territorial integrity of a county is incompatible with the purposes and principles of the Charter of the United Nations.
7. All States shall observe faithfully and strictly the provisions of the Charter of the United Nations, the Universal Declaration of Human Rights and the present Declaration on the basis of equality, non-interference in the internal affairs of all States, and respect for the sovereign rights of all peoples and their territorial integrity.

Article 5 indicates the real object of the Declaration. Articles 1 and 2 (and also Articles 3 and 4) define the right of self-determination of peoples, while Articles 6 and 7 deal with the right of self-determination of states. The authoritative statement of two such contradictory principles in the same document is to be explained, of course, by the special motivations of its mainly Third World sponsors. As Article 5 indicates, they were aiming at the surviving remnants of Western colonialism still to be found in Asia, Africa, and elsewhere; and their intention was to mobilize the influence of the United Nations for the speedy decolonization of these territories. But the governments supporting this measure — especially those Asian and African states that had achieved independence from colonial rule in the recent past — were well aware of the dangers inherent in an unbridled application of the principle of self-determination of peoples. Almost without exception, these states contained significant ethnic minorities — a legacy of the purely political considerations that had so often determined the drawing of boundaries during the colonial period; and all of them faced the incipient problem of separatist movements that could disrupt the precarious unity of the state. Thus the demand for decolonization had to be coupled with safeguards for the preservation of the unity of the newly independent states within their present boundaries.

The special interest of the West New Guinea case in this context was that it epitomized so graphically the dilemmas that the General Assembly attempted to deal with in the Declaration on the Granting of Independence to Colonial Countries and Peoples. In the General Assembly's consideration of the West New Guinea issue in 1961 and 1962, and again in 1969, there is ample evidence that many Third World countries had grave doubts as to whether the right of the Papuans to self-determination, in the sense of the self-determination of peoples, was adequately safeguarded in the various measures placed before that body. At the time of the consideration of the Luns Plan in Fall 1961, for example, thirteen Black African countries sponsored a resolution insisting that any settlement of the dispute "must be based on the principle of self-determination of peoples." After the Dutch-Indonesian settlement was presented to the General Assembly in September 1962, a number of delegates expressed misgivings as to whether the rights of the Papuans were adequately protected by it; although the resolution "taking note" of the agreement was approved by a vote of 89 to 0, but with 14 abstentions. Even more striking was the disquiet manifested during the General Assembly's deliberations in November 1969 on the results of the "act of free choice." It will be recalled that a Ghanaian motion proposing that the Papuans be given a "further opportunity" to carry out the "act of free choice" failed by 60 votes to 15, with 24 abstentions; and that the motion to "take note" of the results was adopted by 84 to 0, but with 30 abstentions.

On the other hand, these votes also demonstrate clearly that the overwhelming majority was not prepared to take measures that might lead to the disruption of what the Indonesians considered as vital to the unity of the state. There — but for the grace of God — went they. It is altogether too simple to dismiss the West New Guinea case merely as a triumph for unprincipled *force majeure*. There was certainly a large element of that in the final outcome. But the Indonesians were also defending the organizing principle of the state, namely, that its boundaries were coterminous with the former colonial domain, and that these boundaries must be maintained inviolate. Almost every newly independent country of Asia and Africa has a vital interest in the preservation of this principle. Thus it is not surprising that, by their votes on the West New Guinea issue, the overwhelming majority of the international community supported the concept of self-determination written into the Declaration on the Granting of Independence to Colonial Countries and Peoples, that is, independence for all from Western colonial rule, but thereafter the preservation of the unity of the newly independent state despite the claims of any ethnic minority.

It may also be argued that the international community at large has a comparable interest in this principle. To be sure, this means that many ethnic groups — even very large ones — will be denied the right of self-determination of peoples. But the alternative of an indiscriminate defense of the latter might be to set in train the dissolution of innumerable ethnically complex states whose main claim to unity derives from the colonial mandate. The consequences of this for the stability of the international system could be incalculable.

In the settlement of the West New Guinea dispute, the Netherlands was doubtless well rid of an irksome colonial responsibility. Indonesia achieved the vindication of its unifying myth. The international community successfully surmounted a potentially dangerous crisis. Perhaps the Papuans were the only losers.

Appendix

AGREEMENT BETWEEN THE REPUBLIC OF INDONESIA AND THE KINGDOM OF THE NETHERLANDS CONCERNING WEST NEW GUINEA (WEST IRIAN)

The Republic of Indonesia and the Kingdom of the Netherlands,

Having in mind the interests and welfare of the people of the territory of West New Guinea (West Irian) hereinafter referred to as 'the territory',

Desirous of settling their dispute regarding the territory,

Now, therefore, agree as follows:

RATIFICATION OF AGREEMENT AND RESOLUTION OF THE GENERAL ASSEMBLY OF THE UNITED NATIONS
Article I

After the present Agreement between Indonesia and the Netherlands has been signed and ratified by both Contracting Parties, Indonesia and the Netherlands will jointly sponsor a draft resolution in the United Nations under the terms of which the General Assembly of the United Nations takes note of the present Agreement, acknowledges the role conferred upon the Secretary-General of the United Nations therein, and authorizes him to carry out the tasks entrusted to him therein.

TRANSFER OF ADMINISTRATION
Article II

After the adoption of the resolution referred to in article I, the Netherlands will transfer administration of the territory to a United Nations Temporary Executive Authority (UNTEA) established by and under the jurisdiction of the Secretary-General upon the arrival of the United Nations Administrator appointed in accordance with article IV. The UNTEA will in turn transfer the administration to Indonesia in accordance with article XII.

UNITED NATIONS ADMINISTRATION
Article III

In order to facilitate the transfer of administration to the UNTEA after the adoption of the resolution by the General Assembly, the Netherlands will invite the Secretary-General to send a representative to consult

253

briefly with the Netherlands Governor of the territory prior to the latter's departure. The Netherlands Governor will depart prior to the arrival of the United Nations Administrator.

Article IV

A United Nations Administrator, acceptable to Indonesia and the Netherlands, will be appointed by the Secretary-General.

Article V

The United Nations Administrator, as chief executive officer of the UNTEA, will have full authority under the direction of the Secretary-General to administer the territory for the period of the UNTEA administration in accordance with the terms of the present Agreement.

Article VI

1. The United Nations flag will be flown during the period of United Nations administration.
2. With regard to the flying of the Indonesian and Netherlands flags, it is agreed that this matter will be determined by agreement between the Secretary-General and the respective Governments.

Article VII

The Secretary-General will provide the UNTEA with such security forces as the United Nations Administrator deems necessary; such forces will primarily supplement existing Papuan (West Irianese) police in the task of maintaining law and order. The Papuan Volunteer Corps, which on the arrival of the United Nations Administrator will cease being part of the Netherlands armed forces, and the Indonesian armed forces in the territory will be under the authority of, and at the disposal of, the Secretary-General for the same purpose. The United Nations Administrator will, to the extent feasible, use the Papuan (West Irianese) police as a United Nations security force to maintain law and order and, at his discretion, use Indonesian armed forces. The Netherlands armed forces will be repatriated as rapidly as possible and while still in the territory will be under the authority of the UNTEA.

Article VIII

The United Nations Administrator will send periodic reports to the Secretary-General on the principal aspects of the implementation of the present Agreement. The Secretary-General will submit full reports to Indonesia and the Netherlands and may submit, at his discretion, reports to the General Assembly or to all United Nations Members.

First phase of the UNTEA administration
Article IX

The United Nations Administrator will replace, as rapidly as possible, top Netherlands officials, as defined in annex A, with non-Netherlands, non-Indonesian officials during the first phase of the UNTEA administration which will be completed on 1 May 1963. The United Nations Administrator will be authorized to employ, on a temporary basis, all Netherlands officials other than top Netherlands officials defined in annex A, who wish to serve the UNTEA, in accordance with such terms and conditions as the Secretary-General may specify. As many Papuans (West Irianese) as possible will be brought into administrative and technical positions. To fill the remaining required posts, the UNTEA will have authority to employ personnel provided by Indonesia. Salary rates prevailing in the territory will be maintained.

Article X

Immediately after the transfer of administration to the UNTEA, the UNTEA will widely publicize and explain the terms of the present Agreement, and will inform the population concerning the transfer of the administration to Indonesia and the provisions for the act of self-determination as set out in the present Agreement.

Article XI

To the extent that they are consistent with the letter and spirit of the present Agreement, existing laws and regulations will remain in effect. The UNTEA will have the power to promulgate new laws and regulations or amend them within the spirit and framework of the present Agreement. The representative councils will be consulted prior to the issuance of new laws and regulations or the amendment of existing laws.

Second phase
Article XII

The United Nations Administrator will have discretion to transfer all or part of the administration to Indonesia at any time after the first phase of the UNTEA administration. The UNTEA'S authority will cease at the moment of transfer of full administrative control to Indonesia.

Article XIII

United Nations security forces will be replaced by Indonesian security forces after the first phase of the UNTEA administration. All United Nations security forces will be withdrawn upon the transfer of administration to Indonesia.

INDONESIAN ADMINISTRATION AND SELF-DETERMINATION

Article XIV

After the transfer of full administrative responsibility to Indonesia, Indonesian national laws and regulations will in principle be applicable in the territory, it being understood that they be consistent with the rights and freedoms guaranteed to the inhabitants under the terms of the present Agreement. New laws and regulations or amendments to the existing ones can be enacted within the spirit of the present Agreement. The representative councils will be consulted as appropriate.

Article XV

After the transfer of full administrative responsibility to Indonesia, the primary task of Indonesia will be further intensification of the education of the people, of the combating of illiteracy, and of the advancement of their social, cultural and economic development. Efforts also will be made, in accordance with present Indonesian practice, to accelerate the participation of the people in local government through periodic elections. Any aspects relating to the act of free choice will be governed by the terms of this Agreement.

Article XVI

At the time of the transfer of full administrative responsibility to Indonesia a number of United Nations experts, as deemed adequate by the Secretary-General after consultation with Indonesia, will be designated to remain, wherever their duties require their presence. Their duties will, prior to the arrival of the United Nations Representative, who will participate at the appropriate time in the arrangements for self-determination, be limited to advising on, and assisting in, preparations for carrying out the provisions for self-determination except in so far as Indonesia and the Secretary-General may agree upon their performing other expert functions. They will be responsible to the Secretary-General for the carrying out of their duties.

Article XVII

Indonesia will invite the Secretary-General to appoint a Representative who, together with a staff made up, *inter alia,* of experts referred to in article XVI, will carry out the Secretary-General's responsibilities to advise, assist and participate in arrangements which are the responsibility of Indonesia for the act of free choice. The Secretary-General will, at the proper time, appoint the United Nations Representative in order that he and his staff may assume their duties in the territory one year prior to the date of self-determination. Such additional staff as the United Nations Representative might feel necessary will be determined by the Secretary-General after consultations with Indonesia. The United Nations Representative and his staff will have the same freedom of movement as provided for the personnel referred to in article XVI.

Article XVIII

Indonesia will make arrangements, with the assistance and participation of the United Nations Representative and his staff, to give the people of the territory the opportunity to exercise freedom of choice. Such arrangements will include:

(*a*) Consultations (*Musjawarah*) with the representative councils on procedures and appropriate methods to be followed for ascertaining the freely expressed will of the population;

(*b*) The determination of the actual date of the exercise of free choice within the period established by the present Agreement;

(*c*) Formulation of the questions in such a way as to permit the inhabitants to decide (*a*) whether they wish to remain with Indonesia; or (*b*) whether they wish to sever their ties with Indonesia;

(*d*) The eligibility of all adults, male and female, not foreign nationals, to participate in the act of self-determination to be carried out in accordance with international practice, who are resident at the time of the signing of the present Agreement and at the time of the act of self-determination, including those residents who departed after 1945 and who return to the territory to resume residence after the termination of Netherlands administration.

Article XIX

The United Nations Representative will report to the Secretary-General on the arrangements arrived at for freedom of choice.

Article XX

The act of self-determination will be completed before the end of 1969.

Article XXI

1. After the exercise of the right of self-determination, Indonesia and the United Nations Representative will submit final reports to the Secretary-General who will report to the General Assembly on the conduct of the act of self-determination and the results thereof.

2. The Parties to the present Agreement will recognize and abide by the results of the act of self-determination.

RIGHTS OF THE INHABITANTS
Article XXII

1. The UNTEA and Indonesia will guarantee fully the rights, including the rights of free speech, freedom of movement and of assembly, of the inhabitants of the area. These rights will include the existing rights of the inhabitants of the territory at the time of the transfer of administration to the UNTEA.

2. The UNTEA will take over existing Netherlands commitments in respect of concessions and property rights.

3. After Indonesia has taken over the administration it will honour those commitments which are not inconsistent with the interests and economic development of the people of the territory. A joint Indonesian-Netherlands commission will be set up after the transfer of administration to Indonesia to study the nature of the above-mentioned concessions and property rights.

4. During the period of the UNTEA administration there will be freedom of movement for civilians of Indonesian and Netherlands nationalities to and from the territory.

Article XXIII

Vacancies in the representative councils caused by the departure of Netherlands nations, or for other reasons, will be filled as appropriate consistent with existing legislation by elections, or by appointment by the UNTEA. The representative councils will be consulted prior to the appointment of new representatives.

FINANCIAL MATTERS
Article XXIV

1. Deficits in the budget of the territory during the UNTEA administration will be shared equally by Indonesia and the Netherlands.

2. Indonesia and the Netherlands will be consulted by the Secretary-General in the preparation of the UNTEA budget and other financial

matters relating to United Nations responsibilities under the present Agreement; however, the Secretary-General will have the final decision.

3. The Parties to the present Agreement will reimburse the Secretary-General for all costs incurred by the United Nations under the present Agreement and will make available suitable funds in advance for the discharge of the Secretary-General's responsibilities. The Parties to the present agreement will share on an equal basis the costs of such reimbursements and advances.

PREVIOUS TREATIES AND AGREEMENTS
Article XXV

The present Agreement will take precedence over any previous agreement on the territory. Previous treaties and agreements regarding the territory may therefore be terminated or adjusted as necessary to conform to the terms of the present Agreement.

PRIVILEGES AND IMMUNITIES
Article XXVI

For the purpose of the present Agreement, Indonesia and the Netherlands will apply to United Nations property, funds, assets and officials the provisions of the Convention on the Privileges and Immunities of the United Nations. In particular, the United Nations Administrator, appointed pursuant to article IV, and the United Nations Representative, appointed pursuant to article XVII, will enjoy the privileges and immunities specified in section 19 of the Convention on the Privileges and Immunities of the United Nations.

RATIFICATION
Article XXVII

1. The present Agreement will be ratified in accordance with the constitutional procedures of the Contracting Parties.

2. The instruments of ratification will be exchanged as soon as possible at the Headquarters of the United Nations by the accredited representatives of the Contracting Parties.

3. The Secretary-General will draw up a *procès-verbal* of the exchange of the instruments of ratification and will furnish a certified copy thereof to each Contracting Party.

ENTRY INTO FORCE
Article XXVIII

1. The present Agreement will enter into force upon the date of the adoption by the General Assembly of the resolution referred to in article I of the present Agreement.

2. Upon the entry into force of the present Agreement, the Secretary-General of the United Nations will register it in accordance with Article 102 of the Charter.

AUTHENTIC TEXT
Article XXIX

The authentic text of the present Agreement is drawn up in the English language. Translations in the Indonesian and Netherlands languages will be exchanged between the Contracting Parties.

IN WITNESS WHEREOF the undersigned plenipotentiaries, being duly authorized for that purpose by their respective Governments, have signed the present Agreement.

DONE at the Headquarters of the United Nations, New York, on this fifteenth day of August 1962, in three identical copies of which one shall be deposited with the Secretary-General and one shall be furnished to the Government of each of the Contracting Parties.

(Signed) SUBANDRIO
For the Republic of Indonesia
J. H. VAN ROIJEN
For the Kingdom of the Netherlands
C. SCHURMANN
For the Kingdom of the Netherlands

ANNEX A

Top Netherlands officials to be replaced as rapidly as possible with non-Netherlands, non-Indonesian officials.

I. *Government*
   Head, Government Information Bureau   1
   Head, Popular Information Service   1

II. *Department of Internal Affairs*
   Director   1
   Divisional Commissioners *(Residenten):*   6
   1—Hollandia
   2—Biak
   3—Manokwari
   4—Fakfak
   5—Merauke
   6—Central Highlands

   Administrative Head of the General Police   1

III. *Department of Finance*
   Director   1

IV. *Department of Social Affairs and Justice*
   Director   1

V. *Department of Public Health*
   Director   1

VI. *Department of Cultural Affairs* (including Education)
   Director   1
   Head, Broadcasting System   1

VII. *Department of Economic Affairs*
   Director   1

VIII. *Department of Transport and Power*
   Director   1

IX. *Department of Public Works*
   Director   1
                                                   ——
                                         TOTAL   18

Bibliographical Note

Research into a problem of contemporary diplomatic history presents the special difficulty that most of the necessary documentation is still buried in the archives and unavailable to the student. In preparing the present study, this difficulty has been partially overcome by interviews with a score of officials, many of them still in the service of the United Nations and the United States and other governments, who played a part in the events discussed. Their candid guidance has been invaluable in informing the text, and the author gratefully acknowledges his debt to the many individuals who helped him so generously. Because these interviews were without exception off-the-record, none of them has been cited in the text. In any case, no specific data gained through interviews have been employed in this study except where independent verification was obtainable from public sources.

The United States government has published very little on the West New Guinea dispute and its role in the search for settlement. Some source material may be found in *Public Papers of the Presidents, John F. Kennedy, Containing the Public Messages, Speeches, and Statements of the President, January 20 to December 31, 1961; ibid., 1962 and 1963; U. S. Participation in the U.N. Report by the President for the Year 1961; ibid., 1962;* and the issues of the *Department of State Bulletin;* as well as in various State Department press releases.

United Nations sources are much more voluminous, especially the *General Assembly Official Records.* These have been extensively employed in the present study, and are fully cited in the footnotes. United Nations press releases were also helpful. The following United Nations serial publications have also been used: *U.N. Monthly Chronicle; United Nations Review; Statistical Yearbook;* and *Everyman's United Nations* (especially the 7th edition, 1964). Two United Nations publications dealing specifically with West New Guinea are *The United Nations in West New Guinea* (1963); and *A Design for Development in West Irian* (1968).

Dutch official sources in English include *Round Table Conference Results as Accepted in the Second Plenary Meeting Held on 2 November 1949 in the "Ridderzaal" at The Hague* (1949); and the reports submitted annually to the United Nations entitled, *Report on Netherlands*

New Guinea for the Year ____; as well as press releases issued by the Netherlands Embassy in Washington, the Permanent Mission of Netherlands to the United Nations, and the Netherlands Information Service, New York. Three pamphlets published by the Dutch government on West New Guinea were also helpful: *Western New Guinea and The Netherlands* (1954); *From the Stone Age to the 20th Century* (n. d.); and *Papuans Building Their Future* (1961).

The main Indonesian official source in English used in this study is *Antara Daily Newsbulletin*. Press releases of the Indonesian Embassy in Washington and the Permanent Mission of Indonesia to the United Nations have also been employed, as well as the serial *Report on Indonesia* and other releases issued by the Indonesian Information Office, New York. Three official pamphlets were also useful: *Some Facts About West Irian* (New York: Permanent Mission of Indonesia to the United Nations, 1957); *Some Questions and Answers Concerning the Dispute Over West Irian* (New York: Permanent Mission of Indonesia to the United Nations, 1957); and *The Question of West Irian* (Jakarta: Ministry of Foreign Affairs).

The government of Malaysia has published two important sources relevant to the West New Guinea problem: *The Territory of the Indonesian State: Discussions in the Meeting of the Investigating Committee for Preparation of Indonesia's Independence,* extracted and translated from the book *Naskah Persiapan Undang-Undang Dasar 1945,* Vol. I (Kuala Lumpur: Federal Department of Information, 1964); and *Malaya/Indonesia Relations, 31st August, 1957 to 15th September, 1963* (Kuala Lumpur: Government Printing Office, 1963). The latter contains important documentary materials on Prime Minister Tengku Abdul Rahman's abortive attempt to mediate the West New Guinea dispute in 1960.

In the absence of more complete documentary sources, heavy reliance has necessarily been placed on press reports relating to the West New Guinea problem. *The New York Times* has been most useful in this respect. Files of the *Christian Science Monitor, London Times, New York Herald Tribune,* and *Washington Post* were also consulted, as well as *Facts on File* and *Keesing's Contemporary Archives.*

The balance of this bibliographical note deals with secondary sources cited in the text of this study. These sources have been grouped under several convenient headings according to subject, although many of them are obviously relevant to more than one of these subjects.

Geographical and Anthropological Aspects.   R. W. van Bemmelen, *The Geology of Indonesia* (The Hague: Government Printing Office, 1949); E. H. G. Dobby, *Southeast Asia,* 7th edition (London: University of London Press, 1960); W. Gordon East and O. H. K. Spate, eds., *The Changing Map of Asia,* 3rd edition (London: Methuen, 1958); D. G. E. Hall, *A History of South-East Asia* (New York: St. Martin's Press, 1955); Leopold Pospisal, *The Kapauku Papuans of West New Guinea* (New York: Holt, Rinehart and Winston, 1965); L. Dudley Stamp, *Asia,* 11th edition (London: Methuen, 1962); Judy Tudor, ed., *Handbook of Papua and New Guinea,* 4th edition (Sydney: Pacific Publications, 1964); M. Halim Khan and Alice Taylor, "Western New Guinea," *Focus,* vol. 12, no. 5 (January 1962); J. P. Kleiweg de Zwaan, "The Papuans of Dutch New Guinea: A Physico-Anthropological Survey," *Antiquity and Survival,* vol. 1 (1955).

General Treatments of the West New Guinea Problem.   Gavin Souter, *New Guinea: The Last Unknown* (New York: Taplinger, 1966) is an excellent introduction to New Guinea as a whole. Two careful studies of the earlier phases of the West New Guinea dispute are Robert C. Bone, Jr., *The Dynamics of the Western New Guinea (Irian Barat) Problem* (Ithaca: Modern Indonesia Project, Cornell University, 1958), written from a pro-Indonesian point of view; and Justus M. van der Kroef, *The West New Guinea Dispute* (New York: Institute of Pacific Relations, 1958), which is moderately pro-Dutch in perspective. The following articles also contain important information: H. G. Barnett, "Peace and Progress in New Guinea," *American Anthropologist,* vol. 61 (1959); Charles A. Fisher, "West New Guinea in its Regional Setting," in George W. Keeton and George Schwarzenberger, eds., *The Year Book of World Affairs, 1952* (London: Stevens, 1952); Willard A. Hanna, "The Irian Barat Settlement," *American Universities Field Staff Reports Service,* Southeast Asia Series, vol. 10, no. 18 (Indonesia) (New York: American Universities Field Staff, 1962); M. A. Jaspan, "West Irian: The First Two Years," *Australian Quarterly,* vol. 37, no. 2 (June 1965); J. A. C. Mackie, "The West New Guinea Argument," *Australian Outlook,* vol. 16, no. 1 (April 1962); L. Metzemaekers, "The Western New Guinea Problem," *Pacific Affairs,* vol. 24, no. 2 (June 1951); and J. van Baal, "Erring Acculturation," *American Anthropologist,* vol. 62 (1960).

266 WEST NEW GUINEA

Justus M. van der Kroef has contributed many articles on the West New Guinea problem, including: "Patterns of Cultural Change in Three Primitive Societies," *Social Research* (Winter 1957); "Culture Contact and Culture Conflict in Western New Guinea," *Anthropological Quarterly,* vol. 32 (1959); "West New Guinea in the Crucible," *Political Science Quarterly,* vol. 75, no. 4 (December 1960); "Nationalism and Politics in West New Guinea," *Pacific Affairs,* vol. 34, no. 1 (Spring 1961); "Nasution, Sukarno and the West New Guinea Dispute," *Asian Survey,* vol. 1, no. 6 (August 1961); "Recent Developments in West New Guinea," *Pacific Affairs,* vol. 34, no. 3 (Fall 1961); "The West New Guinea Problem," *The World Today,* vol. 17, no. 11 (November 1961); "Toward 'Papua Barat,'" *Australian Quarterly,* vol. 34, no. 1 (March 1962); "The West New Guinea Settlement," *Orbis,* vol. 7, no. 1 (Spring 1963); and "West New Guinea: The Uncertain Future," *Asian Survey,* vol. 8, no. 8 (August 1968).

Paul W. van der Veur has also published several articles on the subject: "West Irian: A New Era," *Asian Survey,* vol. 2, no. 8 (October 1962); "Political Awakening in West New Guinea," *Pacific Affairs,* vol. 36, no. 1 (Spring 1963); "West Irian in the Indonesian Fold," *Asian Survey,* vol. 3, no. 7 (July 1963); "New Guinea Annexations and the Origin of the Irian Boundary," *Australian Outlook,* vol. 18, no. 3 (December 1964); and "The Irian Boundary Slumber, 1905-1962," *ibid.,* vol. 19, no. 1 (April 1965).

Indonesia and West New Guinea. The following books on Indonesia also deal with aspects of the West New Guinea problem: Benedict R. O'G. Anderson, *Some Aspects of Indonesian Politics Under the Japanese Occupation: 1944-1945* (Ithaca: Modern Indonesia Project, Cornell University, 1961); P. S. Gerbrandy, *Indonesia* (London: Hutchinson, 1950); Bruce Grant, *Indonesia* (London and New York: Cambridge University Press, 1964); two books by George McTurnan Kahin, *Nationalism and Revolution in Indonesia* (Ithaca: Cornell University Press, 1952); and *The Asian-African Conference* (Ithaca: Cornell University Press, 1956); Angus Maude, *South Asia* (London: Bodley Head, 1966); Ruth T. McVey, ed., *Indonesia* (New Haven: Human Relations Area File, 1963); Leslie H. Palmier, *Indonesia and the Dutch* (London: Oxford University Press, 1962); A. Arthur Schiller, *The Formation of Federal Indonesia, 1945-1949* (The Hague and Bandung: W. van Hoeve, 1955); B. Schrieke, *Indonesian Sociological Studies,* Part One (The Hague and Bandung: W. van Hoeve, 1955); Bernard H. M. Vlekke, *Nusantara, A History of Indonesia,* revised edition (The Hague and Bandung, W. van Hoeve, 1960); David Wehl, *The Birth of Indonesia* (London: Allen and Unwin,

1948); W. F. Wertheim, *Indonesian Society in Transition* (The Hague: W. van Hoeve, 1956); D. E. Willmott, *The National Status of the Chinese in Indonesia, 1900-1958* (Ithaca: Modern Indonesia Project, Cornell University, 1961); and Charles Wolf, Jr., *The Indonesian Story* (New York: Day, 1948).

Informative articles on this subject include: Herbert Feith, "Dynamics of Guided Democracy," in McVey, ed., *op. cit.;* Herbert Feith and Daniel S. Lev, "The End of the Indonesian Rebellion," *Pacific Affairs,* vol. 36, no. 1 (Spring 1963); three essays by Mohammad Hatta, the former Vice President of Indonesia, "Indonesia's Foreign Policy," *Foreign Affairs,* vol. 31, no. 3 (April 1953); "Indonesia Between the Power Blocs," *ibid.,* vol. 36, no. 3 (April 1958); and "Colonialism and the Danger of War," *Asian Survey,* vol. 1, no. 9 (November 1961); Garth N. Jones, "Soekarno's Early Views Upon the Territorial Boundaries of Indonesia," *Australian Outlook,* vol. 18, no. 1 (April 1964); George McTurnan Kahin, "Indonesian Politics and Nationalism," in William L. Holland, ed., *Asian Nationalism and the West* (New York: Macmillan, 1953); George McTurnan Kahin, "Indonesia," in George McTurnan Kahin, ed., *Major Governments of Asia,* 2nd edition (Ithaca: Cornell University Press, 1963); J. D. Legge, "Indonesia After West Irian," *Australian Outlook,* vol. 17, no. 1 (April 1963).

Other useful articles are: Arend Lijphart, "The Indonesian Image of West Irian," *Asian Survey,* vol. 1, no. 5 (July 1961); Guy J. Pauker, "General Nasution's Mission to Moscow," *ibid.,* vol. 1, no. 1 (March 1961); Guy J. Pauker, "Current Communist Tactics in Indonesia," *ibid.,* vol. 1, no. 3 (May 1961); Guy J. Pauker, "The Soviet Challenge in Indonesia," *Foreign Affairs,* vol. 40, no. 4 (July 1962); Karl. J. Pelzer, "Physical and Human Resource Patterns," in McVey, ed., *op. cit.;* L. P. Singh, "Bases of Indonesia's Claim to West New Guinea," *Australian Quarterly,* vol. 34, no. 1 (March 1962); G. William Skinner, "The Chinese Minority," in McVey, ed., *op. cit.;* three articles by Justus M. van der Kroef, "The Eurasian Minority in Indonesia," *American Sociological Review,* vol. 18 (1953); "Decolonization in Indonesia," *United Asia* (February 1958); and "Disunited Indonesia," *Far Eastern Survey,* vol. 27, no. 4 (April 1958); Paul W. van der Veur, "The Eurasians of Indonesia: Castaways of Colonialism," *Pacific Affairs,* vol. 27, no. 2 (June 1954); W. F. Wertheim, "The Indo-European Problem in Indonesia," *ibid.,* vol. 20, no. 3 (September 1947); and Lea E. Williams, "Sino-Indonesian Diplomacy: A Study of Revolutionary International Politics," *China Quarterly,* no. 11 (July-September 1962).

The Netherlands and West New Guinea. Very much less has been published in English on Dutch policy toward West New Guinea. Fortunately, one excellent analysis has been published which focusses precisely on this subject and on the trends of Dutch public opinion with respect to the West New Guinea problem. This is Arend Lijphart, *The Trauma of Decolonization* (New Haven: Yale University Press, 1966). Lijphart's book has been heavily relied on in preparing the present study. The volumes by Robert C. Bone, Jr., and Justus M. van der Kroef, cited above, on the earlier phases of the West New Guinea dispute, were also helpful on the evolution of Dutch policy. Useful articles on this subject include John W. Dykstra, "The Population Problem of the Netherlands," *American Journal of Economics and Sociology,* vol. 17 (1958); and two by Justus M. van der Kroef, "Dutch Opinion on the West New Guinea Problem," *Australian Outlook,* vol. 14, no. 3 (December 1960); and "Indonesia and the Dutch," *Pacific Affairs,* vol. 36, no. 3 (Fall 1963).

The United Nations and West New Guinea. Two short studies dealing with the early phases of United Nations involvement with Indonesia are J. Foster Collins, *The United Nations and Indonesia,* International Conciliation Series no. 459 (New York: Carnegie Endowment for International Peace, 1950); and William Henderson, *Pacific Settlement of Disputes, The Indonesian Question, 1946-1949* (New York: Woodrow Wilson Foundation, 1954). The standard work on this period is Alastair M. Taylor, *Indonesian Independence and the United Nations* (Ithaca: Cornell University Press, 1960).

Various aspects of United Nations intervention in the later stages of the West New Guinea dispute and its settlement are considered in D. W. Bowett, *United Nations Forces* (New York: Praeger, 1964); Jack Citrin, *United Nations Peacekeeping Activities* (Denver: University of Denver, 1965); Rosalyn Higgins, *United Nations Peacekeeping, 1946-1967, Documents and Commentary, II, Asia* (London: Oxford University Press, 1970); Ruth B. Russell, *United Nations Experience with Military Forces: Political and Legal Aspects* (Washington: Brookings, 1964); and David Wainhouse *et. al., International Peace Observation* (Baltimore: Johns Hopkins University Press, 1966). Brian Urquhart, "United Nations Peace Forces and the Changing United Nations," *International Organization,* vol. 17, no. 2 (Spring 1963), is also useful. The only study of United Nations administration in West New Guinea published thus far is Paul W. van der Veur, "The United Nations in West Irian: A Critique," *ibid.,* vol. 18, no. 1 (Winter 1964).

More general treatments of United Nations peacekeeping activities may be found in Wilder Foote, ed., *Dag Hammarskjold: Servant of Peace*

(New York: Harper & Row, n. d.); Leland M. Goodrich, *Korea, A Study of U. S. Policy in the United Nations* (New York: Council on Foreign Relations, 1956); Leland M. Goodrich, *The United Nations* (New York: Crowell, 1959); Rosalyn Higgins, *The Development of International Law through the Political Organs of the United Nations* (London: Oxford University Press, 1963); and in articles by I. L. Claude, Jr., "Implications and Questions for the Future," *International Organization,* vol. 19, no. 3 (Summer 1965); and Leland M. Goodrich, "The Maintenance of International Peace and Security," *ibid.*

The United States and West New Guinea. Roger Hilsman, *To Move A Nation* deals knowledgeably and effectively with the underlying assessments of the Kennedy Administration in its approach to settlement of the West New Guinea dispute. A fairly complete account, as seen from the vantage point of the United States Ambassador in Jakarta, may be found in Howard Palfrey Jones, *Indonesia, The Possible Dream* (New York: Harcourt Brace Jovanovich, 1971); Robert F. Kennedy, *Just Friends and Brave Enemies* (New York: Harper & Row, 1962), provides important insights; while Arthur M. Schlesinger, Jr., *A Thousand Days* (Boston: Houghton Mifflin, 1965) is also useful.

Richard P. Stebbins, *The United States in World Affairs 1961* (New York: Harper, 1962), and *The United States in World Affairs 1962* (New York: Harper & Row, 1963), provides brief accounts of the American intervention; Russell H. Fifield, *Southeast Asia in United States Policy* (New York: Praeger, 1963), also deals briefly with the episode; Arnold C. Brackman, *Southeast Asia's Second Front* (New York: Praeger, 1966), gives a thoughtful analysis of United States policy; and Malcolm E. Smith, Jr., *Kennedy's 13 Great Mistakes in the White House* (New York: National Forum of America, 1968) has a critical chapter on the West New Guinea settlement.

Relevant studies of United States policy on the United Nations are: Lincoln P. Bloomfield, *The United Nations and U.S. Foreign Policy,* revised edition (Boston: Little, Brown, 1967); I. L. Claude, Jr., "The Containment and Resolution of Disputes," in Francis O. Wilcox and H. Field Haviland, Jr., eds., *The United States and the United Nations* (Baltimore: Johns Hopkins University Press, 1961); Harlan Cleveland, "The Road Around Stalemate," *Foreign Affairs,* vol. 40, no. 1 (October 1961); and H. Field Haviland, Jr., "The United States and the United Nations," *International Organization,* vol. 19, no. 3 (Summer 1965).

Australia and West New Guinea.   Australian policy on West New Guinea has been extensively dealt with, especially by Australian writers. This subject was frequently discussed in the Australian parliament. See Commonwealth of Australia, *Parliamentary Debates.* The volume by R. G. Casey (later Lord Casey), who was Minister for External Affairs during the early period, *Friends and Neighbors, Australia and the World* (Melbourne: Cheshire, 1954), is authoritative. The surveys edited by Gordon Greenwood and Norman Harper, *Australia in World Affairs 1956-1960* (Melbourne: Cheshire, 1963), and *Australia in World Affairs 1961-1965* (Melbourne: Cheshire, 1968), contain useful sections on the West New Guinea question. In the first volume, see especially John Andrews, "New Guinea and Nauru," and J. A. C. Mackie, "Australia and Indonesia, 1945-60;" and in the second, see Gordon Greenwood, "Australian Foreign Policy in Action," Norman Harper, "Australia and the United States (with special reference to South-East Asia)," and T. B. Miller, "Australian Defence, 1945-65." Other useful books include Norman Harper and David Sissons, *Australia and the United Nations* (New York: Manhattan Publishing Company, 1959); Amry and Mary Belle Vandenbosch, *Australia Faces Southeast Asia* (Lexington: University of Kentucky Press, 1967); and, in particular, Alan Watt, *The Evolution of Australian Foreign Policy, 1938-1965* (Cambridge: Cambridge University Press, 1967). See also articles by Henry S. Albinski, "Australia and the Dutch New Guinea Dispute," *International Journal,* vol. 16, no. 4 (Autumn 1961); B. D. Beddie, "Some Internal Political Problems," in J. Wilkes, ed., *Australia's Defence and Foreign Policy* (Sydney: Angus and Robertson, 1964); Charles Grimshaw, "Problems of Australian Foreign Policy, January-June 1962," *The Australian Journal of Politics and History,* vol. 8, no. 2 (November 1962); and Justus M. van der Kroef, "Australia and the West Irian Problem," *Asian Survey,* vol. 10, no. 6 (June 1970).

The British were much less preoccupied by the West New Guinea dispute. For very occasional parliamentary discussion, see *Hansard.* See also D. C. Watt, *Survey of International Affairs 1961* (London, New York, and Toronto: Oxford University Press, 1965).

The Theory of Third-Party Intervention.   In dealing with the theoretical aspects of third-party intervention in international disputes, and the relevance of the West New Guinea case thereto, I have relied heavily on the theoretical framework provided in Oran R. Young's seminal study on *The Intermediaries, Third Parties in International Crises* (Princeton: Princeton University Press, 1967). See also his *Trends in International Peacekeeping* (Princeton: Center of International Studies, 1966). Other volumes helpful in this respect are Kenneth Boulding, *Conflict and Defense* (New York: Harper, 1962); Fred Iklé *How Nations Negotiate* (New York: Harper & Row, 1964); Thomas C. Schelling, *The Strategy of Conflict* (Cambridge: Harvard University Press, 1960); and Carl Stevens, *Strategy and Collective Bargaining Negotiation* (New York: McGraw-Hill, 1963).

Self-Determination. Two standard studies of self-determination are Alfred Cobban, *National Self-Determination* (London: Oxford University Press, 1945); and Rupert Emerson, *From Empire to Nation* (Cambridge: Harvard University Press, 1960). The latter's *Self-Determination Revisited in the Era of Decolonization* (Cambridge: Center for International Studies, 1964), discusses the West New Guinea case at some length. See also some interesting comments in Charles Burton Marshall, "Morality and National Liberation Wars," *Southeast Asian Perspectives,* no. 4 (December 1971).

Index

A

Abdoh, Djalal, 215, 218
African Countries, 50, 51, 62, 128, 132, 251
Afro-Asian Countries, 52, 53, 55, 61, 76n, 107, 122, 137, 177
Aidit, D. N., 134
Alaska, 176
Ali Sastroamidjojo, 50, 51, 53, 53, 54, 105
Allison, John M., 118, 119, 119n
Ambarpura, 14
Ambon, 82
A.N.Z.U.S. Council, 208
Arafura Sea, 9
Aru Islands, 78
Asia, 9, 11, 38, 50, 51, 62, 64, 115, 128, 132, 136, 208, 251
Asian-African Conference at Bandung, 54, 55
Atjeh, 76
Australasia, 9
Australia, 8, 9, 11n, 12n, 19n, 36, 37, 38n, 58, 64, 65, 65n, 66, 67, 68, 69, 94, 95, 114, 121, 205, 206, 207, 208, 209, 230, 236
    East New Guinea, 8, 11, 11n, 14, 27n, 64, 65, 65n, 94, 99n, 237
    House of Representatives, 209, 228
Azores, 141

B

Bali, 12, 18, 21n
Banda, 13n, 137
Bandung, 20, 54, 55
Barwick, Garfield, 208
Batavia, 49
Batjan, 13
Bay of Pigs, 124
Belgium, 19n, 37n, 58, 114, 239
Belgrade Conference of Non-Aligned Countries, 62, 132
Berg, C. C., 12
Berlin, 124, 140, 141
Biak, 11, 16n, 92, 110n, 111n, 223, 224
Biak-Numfur Region, 89
Bingham, Jonathan B., 125, 127
Bogor, 54, 55
Bomberai Peninsula, 10n
Borneo, 17, 44, 44n
Bot, T. B., 80, 94, 95, 122
Brackman, Arnold C., 124, 136, 176, 177
Brazil, 213
Brezhnev, Leonid, 77n
British Commonwealth of Nations, 23n
Brunei, 27n
Bukittinggi, 59
Bunker, Ellsworth, 179, 179n, 181, 183, 185, 187, 190, 196, 198, 199, 200, 201, 210, 248

Bunker Plan, 183, 185, 186, 187, 188, 189, 190, 191, 192, 193, 193n, 196, 197, 198, 200, 201, 203, 204, 242, 245
Burma, 54

C

Call to Reflection, 85
Cambodia, 52
Canada, 71, 213
Canberra, 65, 66, 67, 68, 69, 71, 95, 110, 206, 207, 208, 236
Casey, Richard G., 64, 65
Cease-Fire Agreement, 213
Celebes, 59, 76, 110
Ceylon, 54, 213
Charter of Transfer of Sovereignty, 21, 22, 24, 41
Cheribon, 17
Chinese, 136
Christian Trade Union of New Guinea, 90
Cleveland, Harlan, 158
Cochran, H. Merle, 37n, 114
Cold War, 53, 55, 128, 151, 152, 153, 156, 205, 244
Colombo Powers, 54
Communism and Communists, 31, 32, 32n, 38, 54, 56, 61, 75, 76, 84, 95, 117, 118, 125, 128, 130, 131, 132, 133, 134, 136, 137, 140, 142, 157
Communist Countries, 51, 52, 55, 107, 131, 132, 133, 134, 135, 136
Congo, 153, 158
Critchley, T. K., 114

D

Darul Islam Movement, 76
Dayaks, 44n

Declaration on the Granting of Independence to Colonial Countries and Peoples, 87, 104, 106, 126, 251
Democratic People's Party (West New Guinea), 96
Denpasar, 18, 18n
Denpasar Conference, 19, 21n, 42n
De Quay, Jan Eduard, 94, 164, 165, 167, 168, 172, 178, 179, 189, 190, 195, 204
Diah, B. M., 229
Djuanda Kartawidjaja, 53, 55, 62, 70, 120
Drees, Willem, 57
Dulles, John Foster, 117, 118, 119, 119n, 121, 128, 129
Dutch Reformed Church, 84, 85

E

East Indonesia, 10, 13, 17, 18, 19, 21n, 40
Eisenhower, Dwight D., 71, 116, 120, 122, 123, 124, 125, 129
Enarotali, 224, 237, 238
Etna Bay, 78
Eurasians, 16, 16n, 18, 35, 36, 36n, 39, 82, 90, 96, 97
Europe, 10, 11, 14n, 45, 86, 128, 140, 141, 157, 243
European Coal and Steel Company, 86
European Economic Community, 86
Evangelical Christian Church (West New Guinea), 90
Evatt, Herbert V., 64

F

Fakfak, 11, 15, 78, 79, 110n, 183, 189, 220
Far East, 79, 101, 123

Feith, Herbert, 30, 31
Food for Peace Program, 202
Formosa, 9
France, 106, 212n
Free Papuan Movement, 223
Freeth, Gordon, 236

G

Geelvink Bay, 11
General Roman Catholic Association of Officials (West New Guinea), 90
Geneva, 25
Germany, 14, 15
Ghana, 240, 251
Godber, J. B., 205
Goodrich, L. M., 143
Great East, 17, 18, 21n
Greece, 51, 52, 156
Greenland, 8
Guided Democracy, 53, 60

H

Hague Agreement, 20, 21, 22, 49, 115, 116
Hague Round Table Conference, 20, 21, 22, 23, 23n, 24, 25, 25n, 28, 33, 37, 37n, 39, 40n, 41, 42, 43, 43n, 45, 46, 47, 48, 49, 52, 57, 81, 83, 84, 114, 115
Haiti, 212n
Hammarskjold, Dag, 57, 71, 80, 144, 146n, 151, 152, 153, 154, 155, 158, 244, 245, 246, 247
Harahap, Burhanuddin, 51, 52
Harriman, W. Averell, 142, 143, 171, 177
Hasluck, Paul, 206, 228, 229

Hatta, Mohammad, 12n, 15, 29, 31, 55, 120, 121, 177
Hawaii, 176
Het Parool, 100, 188, 204
Hilsman, Roger, 124, 129, 138, 140, 141, 142, 175
Hollandia, 11, 79, 91, 92, 93, 95, 97n, 98, 108, 110n, 123, 214, 220
House of Assembly (East New Guinea), 236
Hungary, 156

I

Iklé, Fred Charles, 186
India, 51, 54, 68, 164, 213
Indonesia,
  Air Force, 202, 223
  Army, 30, 31, 60, 63, 77, 78, 133
  Communist Party (P. K. I.), 31, 32, 84, 113, 131, 133, 134, 135, 136, 137
  "Crush Malaysia" Campaign, 77n
  Declaration of Independence, 126
  Eight-Year Development Plan, 178
  Federalists, 15, 15n, 18, 20, 21, 21n, 22, 27n, 30, 33
  Foreign Ministry, 58
  Government, 17, 23, 24, 31, 43, 50, 52, 53, 54, 56, 57, 58, 59, 60, 61, 62, 63, 66, 68, 69, 70, 72, 76, 77, 77n, 80, 81, 86, 107, 110, 112, 118, 119, 119n, 121, 122, 127, 130, 131, 135, 137, 138, 139, 142, 146, 148, 162, 163, 164, 165, 167, 168, 169, 172, 173, 175, 177, 179, 181, 182, 183, 186, 187, 190,

191, 192, 193, 197, 202, 203, 208, 209, 213, 218, 220, 222, 226, 227, 228, 229, 230, 231, 232, 232n, 233, 234, 235, 237, 238, 247

Independence Day, 15, 16, 22, 23, 35, 38, 43, 49, 74, 223, 226

Investigating Committee for Preparation of Indonesia's Independence, 11n, 27n, 29n

Irian Bureau, 54

Language and Culture, 10, 27

Nahdatul Ulama, 32

National Defense Council, 109

National Front for the Liberation of West Irian, 63, 74, 75

National Planning Council, 134

Nationalist Party (P.N.I.), 31, 32, 95, 97, 221

Navy, 111n

Nationalism, 20, 38, 84, 119, 122, 130, 139

Parliament, 43n, 54, 74, 77, 111, 131

Provisional People's Consultative Chamber, 223

Republicans, 16, 17, 19, 20, 21, 21n, 22, 24, 33, 82

Revolutionary Council of Central Sumatra, 60

Revolutionary Government of the Republic of Indonesia (Padang), 59, 66, 119

Security Council, 55

State Leadership Consultative Body, 134

Supreme Advisory Council, 134

Supreme Command for the Liberation of West Irian, 169

West Irian Liberation Committee, 55, 56

International Court of Justice, 43, 69

Internationalization of West New Guinea Problem, 84, 100, 173, 202, 207

Ireland, 213

Islamic Rebellions, 75

J

Jakarta-Peking Axis, 132

Japan, 11n, 38n, 41, 42n, 84, 208

Japen Island, 11

Java, 12, 13n, 16, 17, 20, 26, 32, 32n, 33, 76, 139, 223

Javanism, 32n

Jayapura, 11, 231, 238

Jones, Howard P., 110, 120, 123, 123n, 131, 137, 138, 142, 146n, 179n, 181

Jordan, 153

Jouwe, Nicolas, 225

K

Kaimana, 110n

Kaisiepo, Frans, 16n

Kaisiepo, Marcus, 225

Karel Doorman, 63, 79, 101

Karendefur, 14

Kennedy, John F., 122, 123, 124, 124n, 125, 127, 128, 129, 136, 137, 139, 140, 142, 143, 147, 148, 164, 169, 171, 177, 178, 179, 180, 182, 185, 195, 196, 201, 202, 205, 220

Kennedy, Robert F., 136, 175, 175n, 176, 177

Khan, Said Uddin, 213
Khrushchev, Nikita, 61, 76n, 77, 220
K.L.M. Royal Dutch Airlines, 176
Kokenau, 110n
Komer, Robert, 143
Korea, 64, 144, 151, 156
Kosasih, Major General, 230
Kotabaru, 219
Kremlin, 132
Krock, Arthur, 195
Kuala Lumpur, 71

L

Laos, 52, 124, 137, 153
Lapian, Emile Jossis, 174
Latin American Countries, 51, 52, 53, 107, 128
League of Nations, 143
Lebanon, 153
Lee Kuan Yew, 62
Lijphart, Arend, 26, 27, 27n, 35, 36n, 39, 82, 85, 86, 204
Linggadjati Agreement, 17, 18, 19, 20, 42, 45, 48, 49
London, 71, 205
Lukman, M. H., 134
Luns, J. M. A. H., 71, 101, 102, 121, 123, 124, 177, 178n, 188, 189, 195, 204, 236
Luns Plan, 103, 105, 108, 186, 187, 204, 207, 220, 251
Luxemburg, 239

M

Macassar, 111
Macmillan, Harold, 205
Madiun Uprising, 133
Madura, 12
Majapahit Empire, 11, 11n, 12, 12n, 27, 41

Malaya, 11n, 12n, 27n, 70, 72
Malaysia, 228, 239
Malik, Adam, 179, 182n, 200, 223, 229, 230, 231, 236, 238
Malino, 16, 18n
Manokwari, 11, 15, 79, 91, 92, 96, 97, 110n, 220, 223, 224, 238
Mansarij, 14
Maramis, Max, 227
Maude, Angus, 28n
McCarthy Era, 141
Melanesian Federation, 65, 206
Melanesians, 10n, 96
Menzies, Robert G., 64, 68, 69, 206, 207, 208, 227
Merauke, 11, 91, 92, 110n, 193, 194, 238
Middleburg (Virginia), 179
Misool Island, 194
Missionaries, 89, 195
Moluccas, 13, 14n, 41, 82
Moscow, 77, 110, 131, 132, 133, 134, 137, 179, 183
Murtono, Lieutenant Colonel, 74

N

Narasimhan, C. V., 219
Nassar, Gamal Abdul, 61
Nasution, General Abdul Haris, 68, 71, 73, 76, 77, 79, 110, 131, 183, 207
National Committee (West New Guinea), 98, 220
Nationalist China, 51, 52
Natsir, Mohammad, 43n, 177
Nebraska, 8
Nehru, Jawaharlal, 61, 164
Netherlands
  Capital Investment in West New Guinea, 34, 57, 74, 82

Colonial Rule, 16, 27n, 29n, 35, 36, 36n, 37, 40, 40n, 44, 45, 46, 50, 64 74, 81, 86, 88, 92, 93, 101, 109

Crown, 23

East India Company, 13, 14

Government, 17, 18, 18n, 20, 21, 22, 23, 24, 25, 36, 36n, 39, 43, 45, 51, 52, 55, 57, 58, 62, 65, 69, 70, 71, 72, 73, 79, 80, 81, 84, 86, 89, 95, 98, 101, 102, 103, 104, 114, 115, 118, 121, 122, 123, 125, 139, 140, 146n, 147, 163, 164, 165, 167, 168, 170, 172, 173, 176, 178, 179, 186, 187, 189, 190, 191, 192, 193, 194, 195, 197, 200, 202, 204, 207, 209, 220, 229, 230, 236, 242, 243

Labor Party, 84

Pacifist Socialist Party, 84, 95

Parliament, 39, 78, 95, 103, 115, 167, 174

"Police Action" in Indonesia, 20, 48, 49

Netherlands-Indonesian Agreement on West New Guinea (New York Agreement), 208, 209, 212n, 214, 217, 218, 219, 221, 225, 226, 229, 231, 235, 239, 251

Netherlands-Indonesian Special Ministerial Conference, 24, 45, 49

Netherland-Indonesian Union, 23, 23n, 24, 25, 25n, 50, 52, 81

New Frontier, 129, 138, 140

New Guinea Council, 24, 81, 94, 95, 96, 97, 108, 123, 218, 220, 221, 222

New York, 8, 167, 170, 189, 199, 201, 229

New Zealand, 238

Nigeria, 106, 213

North Atlantic Treaty Organization (N.A.T.O.), 37, 57, 63, 115, 117, 118, 122, 127, 140, 141, 147, 188, 205, 242

North Borneo, 11n, 27n

North Sea, 38

O

Old Established Forces and Newly Emerging Forces, 132

Ortiz Sanz, Fernando, 222, 223, 224, 231, 232, 234, 235, 237, 238, 239

Overseas Chinese, 132

P

Padang, 59, 119

Pakistan, 54, 68, 216

Palmier, Leslie H., 32, 32n

Pangkalpinang Conference, 16, 36

Paniai, 224

Papare, Silas, 223

Papua,

Autochthonous Population, 9, 10, 11

Elite, 29, 47, 90, 108, 108n, 220, 227

Flag, 98, 108

Front, 98

Militia, 80, 94

Nationalism, 98, 108, 220, 221, 222

Political Development, 93, 94, 97, 108, 225, 232

Self-Determination, 168, 169, 171, 172, 173, 181, 185, 186, 187, 189, 201, 203, 207, 208, 211, 212n, 222, 224, 226, 227, 230, 231, 232, 233, 236, 237, 238, 239, 240, 245, 251

Volunteer Corps, 216
Papuanization, 89, 90, 95, 107
Peking, 131, 135, 137
People's Republic of China, 131, 136, 151
Philippines, 9, 12n, 36, 216
Polderman, Jan, 174
Portugal, 141, 164
Portuguese Timor, 11n, 27n
Preah Vihear, 153, 157

R

Rahman, Tengku Abdul, 70, 71, 72, 73, 102, 120
Rahmat, Basuki, 229
Renville Agreement, 19, 42, 49
Rijkens Group, 85, 85n
Rikhye, Brigadier Indar Jit, 213
Rolz-Bennett, José, 215, 231
Rome, 236
Rotterdam, 123
Royal Dutch Shell, 74
Rusk, Dean, 166, 171, 172, 177, 178n, 201, 208
Rwanda, 212n

S

Sahul Shelf, 9
Sarawak, 27n
Sausapor, 194
Schlesinger, Arthur M., Jr., 128, 134, 136, 141, 143, 177
School of Administration (West New Guinea), 89
Schurmann, C. W. A., 174, 179, 189, 192, 194, 200
Self-Determination, 45, 46, 67, 69, 82, 83, 84, 87, 88, 95, 101, 102, 103, 104, 105, 106, 107, 125, 126 127, 162, 165, 167, 168, 169, 171, 172, 173, 211, 217, 221, 228, 229, 233, 241,

248, 249, 251, 252
Singapore, 62
Somalia, 106
Sorong, 11, 91, 92, 110n, 194
Southeast Asia, 9, 12, 53, 136, 176, 205
Southwest Pacific Commission, 123
Spender, Percy, 37, 64
Spice Islands, 13
Stone Age Culture, 10, 47
Stratenus, R. J., 10, 10n
Subandrio, 53, 54, 60, 61, 66, 67, 72, 77, 78, 80, 105, 108, 111, 122, 133, 146n, 162, 169, 183, 190, 192, 200, 201, 202, 219
Sudarso, Jos, 109
Sudjarwo Tjondronegoro, 179, 235, 236
Suez Canal, 153
Suharto, General, 229, 230, 232, 233
Sukardjo Wirjopranoto, 174, 183
Sukarno, 11, 11n, 12n, 15, 23, 27, 30, 30n, 31, 32, 32n, 43n, 53, 54, 56, 57, 59, 60, 61, 68, 70, 75, 77, 78, 83, 83n, 84, 99n, 109, 110, 111, 112, 116, 117, 118, 120, 122, 124, 124n, 125, 127, 130, 133, 134, 135, 136, 137, 138, 139, 146, 146n, 164, 165, 168, 169, 175, 178, 179, 179n, 183, 187, 190, 191, 192, 193, 200, 201, 202, 210, 211, 220, 227, 228, 229
    Independence Day Speeches, 23, 35, 38, 43, 49, 74, 226
Sumatra, 16, 17, 20, 26, 30n, 59, 139
Supiori Island, 224
Sweden, 213

T

Taiwan, 121, 132
Ternate, 13
Thailand, 238, 239
Thaim, Doudou, 105
Thant, U, 152, 254, 155, 155n,
    158, 159, 160, 161, 165, 170,
    171, 172, 173, 174, 175, 179,
    189, 190, 191, 192, 194, 197,
    199, 200, 201, 202, 203, 209,
    210, 211, 215, 218, 219, 227,
    231, 244, 245, 246, 248
Third World Countries, 128, 145,
    154, 157, 241, 244, 246
Third World Crisis, 147, 148, 152,
    153, 241, 243, 244, 246
Tidore, 13, 14, 20, 41, 54
Times of Indonesia, 121
Trikora (Triple Command), 109,
    164, 204
Troika, 158
Truman, Harry S., 129

U

Ukrainian S.S.R., 48
Umbarpun, 14
Unilever, 85
Union of Soviet Socialist Republics,
    10, 48, 49, 62, 76, 77, 113,
    114, 128, 131, 132, 133, 136,
    140, 150, 151, 157, 158, 220,
    242, 245
United Arab Republic 63
United Kingdom, 14, 15, 48, 63,
    204, 205, 206, 207
United Nations, 20, 46, 47, 48,
    48n, 49, 50, 51, 53, 54, 55,
    56, 57, 59, 65, 66, 69, 70,
    72, 73, 80, 86, 87, 88, 98,
    100, 101, 108, 112, 112n,

    116, 120, 125, 126, 141, 150,
    151, 152, 153, 157, 158, 159,
    160, 161, 162, 163, 170, 179,
    183, 185, 186, 192, 193, 194,
    199, 201, 202, 204, 206, 209,
    210, 211, 216, 219, 221, 226,
    227, 229, 230, 232, 235, 237,
    241, 244, 246, 247, 248, 250,
    251

Administration of West New
    Guinea, 124, 126, 127, 185,
    186, 187, 201, 203, 213, 214,
    215, 216, 217, 222
Administrator, 203, 210, 218
Charter, 45, 46, 51, 102, 106,
    126, 150, 151, 152, 170, 194,
    210, 248
Commission for Indonesia, 19n,
    20, 21, 21n, 37n, 42n, 49, 57,
    58, 71, 114
Committee of Good Offices on
    the Indonesian Question, 19,
    19n, 20, 48, 49
Consular Commission at Batavia,
    48, 50
Flag, 211, 215, 220
General Assembly, 45, 50, 51,
    52, 53, 61, 65, 66, 72, 81, 86,
    100, 101, 102, 103, 104, 106,
    116, 117, 118, 120, 125, 139,
    140, 150, 151, 153, 177, 204,
    210, 211, 213, 235, 239, 244,
    251
Peacekeeping, 150, 156, 157,
    158, 171, 173, 174, 241, 244,
    245, 246
Secretary-General, 51, 53, 57,
    58, 80, 101, 102, 106, 125,
    144, 149, 153, 154, 155, 158,
    159, 160, 211, 231, 235, 239,
    244, 246

Security Council, 48, 49, 112n, 150, 151, 153, 194, 209, 228, 244

Security Force (U.N.S.F.), 210, 214, 216, 219, 248

Temporary Executive Authority (U.N.T.E.A.), 210, 211, 213, 215, 216, 217, 218, 219, 221, 227

Trusteeship, 70, 94, 100, 101, 102, 103, 125, 173, 207

United States,

and the U.N., 155, 156, 158, 159, 163, 166, 167, 168, 180, 202, 207, 208, 245, 246

Air Force, 213

Central Intelligence Agency, 119, 141

Embassy in Jakarta, 110, 176

Government, 71, 76, 78, 116, 118, 119, 120, 121, 122, 123, 125, 126, 127, 129, 130, 131, 136, 140, 141, 143, 146, 146n, 147, 148, 149, 151, 155, 157, 160, 162, 164, 165, 166, 167, 175, 178, 179, 180, 182, 185, 188, 189, 193, 195, 196, 197, 198, 199, 201, 202, 203, 205, 243, 247

National Security Council, 143

Pentagon, 141, 142

State Department,

Far Eastern Bureau, 141, 152, 143

"Orthodox" Views of, 127, 141

United States of Indonesia, 17, 18, 19, 20, 21, 21n, 22

Uniting for Peace, 150, 151, 152

Universal Declaration of Human Rights, 250

V

Van der Kroef, Justus M., 12, 18n, 30n, 32n, 40n, 79, 93, 97, 222

Van der Veur, Paul W., 88, 98n, 216

Van Mook, Hubertus J., 18n, 42n

Van Roijen, J. H., 165, 179, 194, 200, 210

Vietnam, 130

Visser, S. H., 78, 122

Vogelkop Oilfields, 91

Vogelkop Peninsula, 10n, 11, 34, 223

W

Waghete, 224, 237, 238

Wake Island, 176

Warner, Denis, 28n

Was Island, 194

Watt, Alan, 206

West Germany, 238

Western Countries, 48, 51, 52, 107, 130, 151, 177, 209

White House, 120, 123

Wilopo, 50

World War II, 11n, 14, 16n, 26, 35, 36, 36n, 38, 81, 89, 143, 146n

Y

Yamin, Mohammad, 11n

Young, Oran R., 144, 145, 146, 147, 148, 149, 150, 151, 154, 155, 155n, 157, 160, 163, 166, 168, 180, 186, 242, 245, 246

Z

Zain, Zairin, 164, 166, 171